Production Workflow
Concepts and Techniques

Frank Leymann
Dieter Roller

ISBN 0-13-021753-0

9 780130 217530

90000

Production Workflow
Concepts and Techniques

Frank Leymann

IBM Germany Development Inc., Böblingen

Dieter Roller

IBM Germany Development Inc., Böblingen

Prentice Hall PTR
Upper Saddle River, New Jersey 07458
http://www.phptr.com

Library of Congress Cataloging-in-Publication Data

Leymann, Frank.
　Production workflow : concepts and techniques / Frank Leymann.
Dieter Roller.
　　p. cm.
　ISBN 0–13–021753–0
　　1. Management information systems　2. Workflow–Management.
　　3. Production management–Data processing.　I. Roller, D. (Dieter).
　1951–　　.　II. Title.
　T58.6.L495　2000
　658.5—dc21　　　　　　　　　　　　　　　　　　　　　　　CIP

Editorial/Production Supervision: *Craig Little*
Acquisitions Editor: *Mike Meehan*
Manufacturing Manager: *Pat Brown*
Marketing Manager: *Bryan Gambrel*
Cover Design Director: *Jayne Conte*
Cover Design: *Anthony Gemmellaro*
Composition: *PreTEX, Inc.*

Prentice Hall books are widely used by corporations
and government agencies for training, marketing, and resale.

The publisher offers discounts on this book when ordered
in bulk quantities. For more information, contact
Corporate Sales Department at 800-382-3419,
fax 201-236-7141, email: corpsales@prenhall.com, or write
　Corporate Sales Department

　Prentice Hall PTR
　One Lake Street
　Upper Saddle River, NJ 07458

Printed in the United States of America

10　9　8　7　6　5　4　3　2　1

ISBN　0-13-021753-0

Prentice-Hall International (UK) Limited, *London*
Prentice-Hall of Australia Pty. Limited, *Sydney*
Prentice-Hall Canada Inc., *Toronto*
Prentice-Hall Hispanoamericana, S.A., *Mexico City*
Prentice-Hall of India Private Limited, *New Delhi*
Prentice-Hall of Japan, Inc., *Tokyo*
Prentice-Hall (Singapore) Pte. Ltd., *Singapore*
Editora Prentice-Hall do Brasil, Ltda., *Rio de Janeiro*

For our wives and kids

Lukas and Susanne

Ines, Andrea, and Sieglinde

Trademarks

Companies use trademarks to help identify their products. We have tried to identify all trademarks mentioned in this book; however, we may have missed some. Thus all other names mentioned in this book may be trademarks or registered trademarks of other companies. We acknowledge all of these that we have not included in the following list.

The following trademarks or registered trademarks are the property of the following organizations:

AIX, CICS, DB2, IBM, IMS, MQSeries, MVS, OS/2, Parallel Sysplex, System/390, S/390, VisualAge are trademarks or registered trademarks of International Business Machines Corporation.

CORBA, OMG, and OTS are trademarks or registered trademarks of the Object Management Group.

ChangEngine and Hewlett-Packard are trademarks or registered trademarks of Hewlett-Packard Computer Company.

Excel, Exchange, Visual Basic, Windows, and Windows NT are trademarks or registered trademarks of Microsoft Corporation.

Java, and JavaScript are trademarks or registered trademarks of Sun Microsystems Inc.

Netscape is trademark of Netscape Corporation

Oracle is a registered trademark of Oracle Corporation

R/3 and SAP are trademarks or registered trademark of SAP Corporation

PeopleSoft is a trademark of PeopleSoft Inc.

UNIX is registered trademark of The Open Group

1-2-3 is a registered trademark of Lotus Development Corporation

Companies also protect their intellectual property by copyrighting it. We thank the following people and organizations for their permission to reproduce their work in this book.

Workflow Management Coalition for the Figures 3.1, 3.8, 3.9, 3.15, and 3.23

Object Management Group for the Figures 6.11 and 6.12

GIGA Information Group for Figure 1.4

Prof. Dr. Stefanie Teufel for Figure 1.9

International Business Machines Corporation for Figures 1.3 and 9.15

Contents

Foreword

Andreas Reuter
International University in Germany

It was observed over two thousand years ago that all things are in constant flux—by Plato or by Heraclitus, depending on which source you want to draw on. This observation, no matter who the originator, is so fundamental that it is all too easy to dismiss it as trivial and move on to more important subjects. Nevertheless, the principle manifests itself again and again in different settings and with different consequences. The challenge in successfully managing organizations of any kind is not to maintain some desirable state—each state is but a transient phase in a complex process, and a process is a much more appropriate representation of what business is about than a set of states. Business has to constantly change in order to remain successful—only the paranoid survive.

Interestingly, computer-based tools meant to support business have, until very recently, focused on states rather than processes. Consider a database: the contents of a database at any given point in time represent the state of an application. When the state of the application changes, the database changes accordingly (if all goes well), but nowhere in the database is a representation of what caused the change or what the change is aimed at—in other words: databases have no idea about processes (and so-called active databases are a different story altogether).

Traditionally, state changes have been brought about by the application programs that implement the functions of the business: account debit, item checkout, customer inquiry, etc. But those programs again work in isolation from each other, typically without any information about which application ran before, which one will run next—and what this decision depends on. The way the business functions, the order in which certain things have to be executed, everything that typically is summarized under the name of "business rules," is nowhere made explicit in the electronic image of the business: the database does not store it, and the various application programs are not embedded into anything like a process schema. Rather, those business rules are maintained in conventional check lists, operations guidelines, manuals, and their contents is implemented by a large set of organizational means that operate above the level of the application programs.

That is not a satisfactory state of affairs, given the high degree of automation in many businesses. Orders are always processed in the same fashion, so is payment tracking, production scheduling, etc. So what needs to be solved is the problem of how to define a global schema (in analogy to the database schema) that formally represents all the processes and operational constraints in a business, such that the applications can be run more or less automatically, depending on the current state, which is kept, as we said, in the database. And this cannot be done in a proprietary, application-specific way, because in the network, applications from different domains on different platforms need to be integrated seamlessly—think of the recent mergers in various industries. One problem industries have to face is how to consolidate and automate their (new) business processes.

The technology that comes to the rescue is workflow management, and consequently it has drawn a lot of attention both from the research community and from industry in the recent years. But as is usually the case with rapidly evolving new technologies, there are many different approaches and there is terminological confusion. People in academia often use the opportunity to apply their favorite results from graph theory, while vendors often use what they already have and relabel it as workflow management systems.

This book is different. It presents all the issues of workflow management from a business perspective, i.e., it never forgets the problems that workflow is supposed to solve. It clearly defines the key concepts, explains the fundamental differences between predefined workflow and ad hoc workflow, discusses the interactions between the application layer on one hand and the database layer on the other, etc. But it also introduces just the right amount of theory to make the discussion rigorous from a scientific point of view. And—most importantly—it presents all the complex system issues that have to be solved when integrating workflow management into a large distributed system. Thus, it makes clear that workflow is not just another application, but that it fundamentally changes the way large-scale applications are developed, handled, and controlled.

All these technical issues are set against the backdrop of an example that is just complex enough to highlight all the important issues.

The authors of this book are arguably the best-qualified for that job: both are seasoned software developers with many years of experience in all aspects of that field. At the same time, they have always maintained close contact with the research community and have made a number of important contributions there. And finally, they routinely go out and try to understand what customers (users) need and what that means for the evolution of system architectures.

I have highly enjoyed reading this book, and I look forward to teaching from it. It fills a gap in our technical literature in that it really provides the full picture on workflow management for application developers, managers, and systems people as well. I wish that the book may have the impact it deserves.

Bruchsal – Heidelberg, June 1999

Andreas Reuter

Preface

Why Read This Book ?

Workflow is a new information processing technology that helps implement business processes that can be easily adapted to the changing needs of a dynamic environment. These processes are no longer just intra-enterprise business processes, such as claims processing in an insurance company or loan processing in a bank, but also inter-enterprise business processes, where multiple enterprises' business processes are connected to efficiently manage a business process. An example of an inter-enterprise business process is the order activity involved in a manufacturing process that starts the appropriate order entry process at a parts supplier. While the production planning process and the entry order process of the part supplier are different processes controlled by their own enterprise, they are combined to efficiently meet their common needs.

Workflow management systems help to define and carry out these business processes in a heterogeneous and distributed environment. They make sure that within a business process the right activity is performed at the right time, at the right place, by the right people, with the right data, using the right tools. Applications that are built using workflow management systems are called workflow-based applications.

Standard application software vendors are beginning to provide their applications as workflow-based applications. These applications consist of a set of business processes that invoke functions of business objects. Tools supplied by standard application software vendors allow for the easy modification of the business processes so that they can be tailored to the specific needs of customers.

Since those workflows are mission critical for a company, they must be managed in the same way as any other critical resource within a company. This management requires functions and capabilities that go beyond the simple administrative type of workflows, such as managing processes with an office mail system. These workflows are called *production workflows*, and systems that manage production workflows are called *production workflow management systems*.

Production workflow management systems thus must provide the scalability, availability, and performance characteristics that are expected from other components that are used to build those mission-critical applications. Typical components are database management systems, message queuing systems, and transaction processing (TP) monitors. This set of components is collectively referred to as middleware.

The authors expect that middleware providers follow IBM and make workflow management systems an integral part of their middleware offerings, building on components that may already be available in their portfolio.

The mission-critical nature of workflow-based applications mandates that the customer's investment is protected. The Workflow Management Coalition (WfMC), a consortium of workflow management system vendors and users, had set itself the goal to establish standards for workflow management systems. Those standards define a set of interfaces for clients to interact with the workflow management system, for applications that are carried out by the workflow management system, and for workflow management systems to communicate with each other.

What You Will Find in This Book

This book focuses, as its title indicates, on the following aspects of workflow and workflow management systems:

- The concepts underlying workflow, and in particular, production workflow, the relationship between workflow and other technologies, and the applicability of workflow to other less traditional areas.

- The techniques that are applied in the implementation of a production workflow management system, highlighting the architecture and system structure with emphasis on availability, reliability, and scalability.

We have chosen two business processes that we use throughout the book: a very simple loan process when we talk about basic concepts; and a more elaborate process, a travel reservation process, when we talk about the constructs that the workflow management system offers for modeling business processes or when we describe some of the more complex features such as compensation of actions within a business process.

What You Will Not Find in This Book

This book does not present:

- How to use a particular workflow management system, whether it is end-user functions, system management tools, or programming interfaces. You can find this information in the appropriate workflow management systems' documentation. The samples in the book are for illustration only.

- Detailed information about workflow system standards. We outline their intended goals and structure; however, for detailed information, we refer you to publications of the appropriate standards bodies, such as the Workflow Management Coalition or the Object Management Group.

- Comparison of functions and implementations of different production workflow systems. The intent of the book is to present and discuss the concepts behind production workflow and how these concepts can be delivered by a workflow management system to allow you a judicious judgement of the capabilities of individual workflow systems.

- Information about ad hoc workflow management systems, for example, as delivered by Lotus Notes or Microsoft Exchange. We discuss the differences between ad hoc and production workflow systems in the book; you should obtain, however, detailed information from the appropriate workflow management systems' documentation.

- Information about systems that have workflow built in, such as document or image processing systems. We will briefly discuss their functions when positioning them to workflow management systems; however, for details, consult other books.

Who Should Read This Book

This book addresses a broad audience, including:

- Application programmers with an interest or need in building workflow-based applications

- Application analysts who design workflow-based applications

- Consultants in business reengineering and application restructuring

- Product developers in related areas, such as developers of business objects

- Marketing people who need to understand the benefits of workflow-based applications and the characteristics of production workflow systems

- IT managers who want to understand the system structure of production workflow systems and how those systems provide for availability, scalability, and performance

- Computer science undergraduates and graduates looking for an in-depth discussion of workflow and workflow management systems

Why We Wrote This Book

We, the authors, have been involved in the development of the IBM production workflow management system MQSeries Workflow and its predecessor IBM Flow-Mark for years. This book reflects our understanding of workflow and production workflow in particular. As we have yet to see a product version of a workflow system that incorporates all of the presented concepts and techniques, we have elected to neutrally talk about *the* workflow management system instead of discussing individual concepts using, for example, IBM's MQSeries Workflow. In particular, we want to present the concepts and techniques of production workflow and not discuss specific implementations of these. A number of the concepts and techniques presented in this book have been implemented in a production workflow management system such as MQSeries Workflow; some may never find their way into a product despite the fact that they are worth implementing. You should also note that a number of these concepts and techniques are patented, anyone planning to build a workflow management system using them must obtain the appropriate rights before incorporating them.

What You Will Find in Each Chapter

Here is a summary of each chapter:

1. **Chapter1 Introduction.** Gives an overview of workflow management and provides a basis for the more in-depth discussions in the other chapters of the book. Discusses the types of workflows, sketches how workflow relates to objects, outlines its role in the middleware stack, compares it to computer-supported cooperative work, shows the value of business processes as an enterprise resource, introduces the concepts of transactional workflow, and outlines the association to other technologies, such as security administration and software distribution. Focuses on specifying the goals and requirements that an implementation of a production workflow management system must meet.

2. **Chapter 2 Business Engineering.** Describes business modeling as a means to significantly improve the efficiency and performance of the operation of a company. Shows that the result of business modeling is a set of documents that describe the goals of the company and the business processes that help to achieve these goals. Defines business processes as a combination of business logic, organizational information, and information technology information. Discusses how simulation of the business processes can determine the human resources needed to perform the business processes, and derives organizational changes that lead to a lean and efficient organization that is

competitive and therefore successful in the market. Presents how the technology of data mining can discover the structure of business processes by analyzing audit trail information written either by the workflow management system or by instrumenting the existing applications.

3. **Chapter 3 Workflow Management System Basics.** Describes the basic structure of workflow management systems as consisting of a buildtime component, which provides the capabilities to define all workflow and workflow management system relevant information, and a runtime component, which executes workflows and interacts with the user. Provides an in-depth discussion of the functions that each of the components provides and shows how the components interact with each other. Discusses the basic structure of workflows and the working together of different workflows in a parent-child or peer-to-peer relationship. Outlines the functions that the workflow management system provides to monitor, analyze, and correct workflows during their execution. Shows which of the functions typically offered by a workflow system have been standardized by the Workflow Management Coalition (WfMC) and indicates how this work helps to protect user investment.

4. **Chapter 4 Metamodel.** Provides a rigorous mathematical formalization of the metamodel of a workflow management system. Follows the approach taken in the development of relational databases, where each of the constructs can be described textually or through a language (SQL, in this case), but also mathematically.

5. **Chapter 5 Advanced Functions.** Describes advanced functions, including the support of events to allow business processes to wait for some external action to take place, the dynamic materialization of objects that are processed by the activities of the business process, the staging of objects to the proper locations to reduce the effects of network latency when users are working with the object, and functions that specify the performance characteristics of parts of a business process.

6. **Chapter 6 Workflow and Objects.** Discusses the construction of component-based software via scripting. Contrasts the lightweight scripting delivered by scripting languages such as JavaScript to combine software components into desktop applications and the heavyweight scripting delivered by workflow systems to combine software components into heterogenous, distributed applications. Shows how object-oriented analysis and design present a base for building workflow-based applications. Discusses the role of workflow in object request broker environments, in particular, the common object request broker architecture (CORBA) of the Object Management Group (OMG).

7. **Chapter 7 Workflow and Transactions.** Discusses various transaction models (sagas, nested transactions) that have been developed over time to allow applications to have a more complex transactional behavior and describes how these models can be accommodated in a workflow management system. Sketches distributed transactions and their atomic commitment. Describes how compensation spheres and atomic spheres take the concept of transactions even further and how they help to implement complex business transactions. Shows how stratification of distributed transactions allows forward recoverability of workflow-based applications in practical situations.

8. **Chapter 8 Advanced Usage.** Describes the applicability of workflow technology in areas where workflow has yet to play a significant role. Shows how workflow can be used efficiently for tasks, such as providing the support for enforcing dynamic semantic integrity rules in a relational database, controlling the distribution of exactly those code pieces that are required by each user involved in the execution of a business process, or deriving security privileges needed by users in a business process to perform the appropriate tasks. Presents a new way to perform systems management by looking at the processing of business processes instead of just monitoring individual programs or computer systems.

9. **Chapter 9 Application Topologies.** Presents the structure of workflow-based applications and shows how in this new structure the data and flow dependencies hidden in the applications are externalized and managed by database management systems and workflow management systems allowing the easy change of the applications. Reviews client/server topologies, underlying communication protocols, the purpose of TP monitors, and the structure of message monitors and message brokers, to provide a basis for understanding the architecture and system structure of a production workflow management system.

10. **Chapter 10 Architecture and System Structure.** Describes the architecture and system structure of a production workflow system. Shows how portability is achieved by means of a message queuing system and a relational database management system. Discusses how such a system provides the characteristics, such as scalability, availability, and reliability, that are relevant for a production workflow management system.

11. **Chapter 11 Development of Workflow-based Applications.** Discusses process-based CASE, a development environment for developing, testing, and maintaining workflow-based applications. Describes how a combination of animation, simulation, and monitoring can verify the correct execution of workflow-based applications. Shows how this approach also helps in

designing and tuning the various components of the applications as well as the network that hosts the application.

How To Use This Book

We recommend you read the book as you would reading a novel, starting at the beginning and continuing until the end. In this way, you start with more general information, then dig deeper into each of the various aspects of production workflow. However, different sections of the book are relatively independent of other sections, to allow you to focus on different themes. The only required reading is Chapter 1, Introduction, since it provides the basic foundation for all of the subsequent chapters.

For example, if you are interested in application development, you would read Chapter 2, Business Engineering, to understand the motivation for process management and the starting point for developing workflow-based applications; Chapter 6, Workflow and Objects, to understand the relationship between object technology and workflow technology; Chapter 9, Application Topologies, to understand the benefits of workflow-based applications; and Chapter 11, Developing Workflow-based Applications, to understand how workflow-based applications are constructed and optimized.

If you are interested in modeling workflows, you would want to read Chapter 2, Business Engineering, to understand the basic principles of business processes; Chapter 3, Workflow Management System Basics, to understand the basic structure of a workflow management system and its fundamental functions; Chapter 4, Metamodel, to understand the various constructs that are available to model workflows; and Chapter 7, Workflow and Transactions, to discuss the transactional properties of workflows.

If you are interested in transactions, you would want to read Chapter 6, Workflow and Objects; Chapter 7, Workflow and Transactions; and Chapter 9, Application Topologies.

Or, if you are interested in the system structure of a production workflow management system, you would want to read Chapter 10, System Structure and Architecture.

Disclaimer

The authors have made a reasonable effort to ensure that the information in this book is accurate. The authors do not offer any warranties or reprensations nor accept any liabilities related to the information contained in the book.

The information contained in this book is distributed on an "as is" basis without any warranty of any kind, either expressed or implied and including, but not limited to, the implied warranties of function of the technologies and concepts or merchantability or fitness for a particular purpose. The use of this information or the implementation of any of these techniques is a reader responsibility and depends on the reader's ability to evaluate, to implement, and to integrate the techniques into the reader's operational environment. Readers attempting to adapt these techniques do so at their own risk.

Opinions expressed in this book, as well as any errors and ommissions, are strictly those of the authors. The contents of this book in no way reflect the official opinions or positions of the International Business Machines Corporation.

Acknowledgments

This book started as a presentation about workflow that we have given over and over again to audiences with all levels of computer literacy. Their comments helped to shape our understanding of workflow and the depth and breadth of this technology. In particular, we acknowledge the discussions we had with Edwin Vogt about the three dimensions of workflow; with C. Mohan, about the aspects of workflow and transactions; Marc-Thomas Schmidt, about workflow standards; and Matthias Kloppmann, about implementation aspects of a production workflow management system.

We were lucky to have two colleagues, Thomas Bernhardt and Frank Gilchrist, take the time to review the complete manuscript. Their huge number of corrections and suggestions helped enormously. We are very grateful to them for investing so much time to help us.

Many other people helped us by reviewing selected chapters. We really appreciate the help of Juan Roldan Guepner, Dieter König, Elke Painke, and Claudia Zentner.

Thanks go to the MQSeries Workflow development team that demonstrated that the basic concepts we show in this book can actually be implemented with the expected results.

We also would like to thank Mike Meehan, our acquisitions editor, for his encouragement and flexibility. We tried hard to meet him in person but always failed. One day we will. Thanks go also to Craig Little, our production editor, who patiently answered all our questions about the art of typesetting.

Finally, we thank our friends in accepting that producing a book, in particular in the final weeks, consumes all spare time. It's over, at least for now.

Chapter 1

Introduction

In this chapter, we discuss the basics of workflow technology and show the applicability of this technology. It provides a basic understanding of the various aspects of workflow and provides the basis we will build on in the rest of the book.

We have divided the chapter into four parts: in the first part, we define what a business process is, its relationship to workflow, and the different aspects and types of workflows; in the second part, we show the characteristics of applications built on workflows; in the third part, we show some more advanced applications of workflow; and in the fourth part, we state the requirements for a production workflow management system. We finish off by sketching the relationships between workflow and other information processing technologies.

1.1 Business Processes

Most people associate business processes with the typical operations in a bank or an insurance company: the loan process in a bank or claims processing in an insurance company. Such operations have led us to understand business processes as a sequence of activities performed by various persons, the visible result being various pieces of paper.

These activities are typically repeated over and over, following the same well defined pattern, the *process model*. This is the type of processing well established in manufacturing: assembly-line production of cars in the automobile industry, or customer-specific assembly of a personal computer in the factories of PC makers are well known examples. This similarity in processes has led to the metaphor of insurance companies and banks being nothing but paper factories, with paper as the final product.

What about the area of software development? It also is guided by a set of rules that determine the sequence of steps to be followed. In the waterfall model, the steps are Architecture, High-Level Design, Low-Level Design, Coding, Unit

Test, and System Test.

Or, let's look a the work of a database administrator. A database administrator performs a set of precisely prescribed processes consisting of a number of steps that may be executed sequentially or in parallel. User interaction in this type of process is minimal, and this user interaction is limited to one person, the database administrator.

This type of a business process allows us to conclude that all batch jobs being run can also be considered some kind of business process. The only difference from the database administrator example is that there is no user interaction. The steps in these batch jobs are described by some kind of scripting language that provides the flexibility to take appropriate actions if one of the steps in the batch job fails to complete correctly. The job control language (JCL) of the OS/390 operating system, one of the most successful operating systems for mainframes, supports such batch jobs, which in turn implement a business process. Code Example 1.1 shows a sample specification of a business process, using OS/390 JCL.

Code Example 1.1 Using the Operating System Job Control Language

```
//OVERDUE JOB
//*-----------------------------------------------------------
//* STEP 1 : DETERMINE CUSTOMERS WITH OPEN BILL
//*-----------------------------------------------------------
//EXTRACT   EXEC PGM=OVERDUE
//IUSERS    DD   DSN=CUSTOMER.DATA,DISP=OLD
//OUSERS    DD   DSN=OVERDUE.USERS,DISP=(NEW,PASS)
//*-----------------------------------------------------------
//* STEP 2 : WRITE LETTER TO CUSTOMER
//*-----------------------------------------------------------
//WRITE     EXEC PGM=PRINT,COND=(4,LT,EXTRACT)
//OUSERS    DD   DSN=OVERDUE.USERS,DISP=OLD
//*-----------------------------------------------------------
//* STEP 3 : DELETE FILE
//*-----------------------------------------------------------
//DELETE    EXEC PGM=DELETE,COND=EVEN
//OUSERS    DD   DSN=(OLD,DELETE)
//
```

The process is used for a credit card company to write a letter to all of the customers that have not paid their open bill. In the first step, all customers that have not paid their bill are selected. This information is saved in a file, identified by OUSER. The second step uses the data obtained in the first step and writes a letter to each customer. If all customers have paid their bill on time, the second step is skipped (COND=(4,LT,EXTRACT)). In the third step, the file is deleted, regardless of whether the second step has been carried out (COND=EVEN). This process shows all of the characteristics of a process. It consists of a set of activities (we called them steps) that are carried out in a particular sequence. Some of the activities may be skipped as the result of a previous activity indicating so. Data is passed from activity to activity. We later call these characteristics control flow and data flow.

The examples above illustrate that the notion of business processes covers a wide spectrum; there is no such thing as a typical business process. The business of a user determines what a business process is: for the database administrator, it is the reorganization of a database; for the controller, it is the creation of the monthly balance sheet; for the CEO of a bank, it is the granting of a loan.

It is this variety of business processes that needs to be addressed by a production workflow management system and that we cover in the book.

1.2 Business Processes as Enterprise Resource

Enterprises are considering information more and more as an important resource [LA94]. They consider it now to be a major asset that is as important as the more traditional ones such as land, labor, and capital. The information includes all data about all resources that are needed to achieve the goals of the enterprise. It is generally agreed that this information should be structured and presented as formally as possible. The set of actions needed to come up with this formal specification is called "enterprise modeling."

The conceptual base for enterprise modeling is sometimes called a *hypersemantic data model* [PTE89]. The result of modeling a particular enterprise is an *enterprise model*. An enterprise model consists of two parts: the *data model* and the *knowledge model*.

The data model describes the structure of all resources of the enterprise. It is thus somewhat like the syntactical component of the enterprise model, that is, it specifies the static aspects of an enterprise. In this sense, the data model describes *what* is available in the enterprise to reach the specified goals. Most enterprises build their data model via *semantic data models*. Some of the more prominent semantic data models are the entity/relationship model [Che76], EXPRESS [ISO], and the unified modeling language (UML) [Rat97].

The knowledge model describes the use of the resources and their connections. It is thus the semantic component of the enterprise model; it specifies the dynamic aspects of an enterprise. In this sense, the knowledge model describes *how* the enterprise uses its resource to achieve its goals. The knowledge model contains constraints, heuristics, and procedures. Constraints define the local and global consistency of resources; for data resources stored in databases, constraints define the valid states in the database. Heuristics describe how to derive data. Procedures define events and correlated actions, set sequences of actions, and describe business processes.

1.3   Virtual Enterprises

Traditionally, business processes are carried out completely within the boundaries of a company. The processes start within the company and finish within the company. External requests come in as phone calls, faxes, postal mail, or, to a limited extend as electronic messages, for example, in electronic data interchange (EDI) or extended markup language (XML) format. These requests are handled by appropriate personnel who start the appropriate business process for each request. As these business processes move to completion, actions, such as shipping goods to the originator, take place. Once the process is complete, the appropriate results are returned to the originator again in the form of phone calls, faxes, postal mail, or electronic messages.

Inquiries about the status of a business process were usually received as phone calls, with the customer waiting for the result. The call center operator would immediately perform the appropriate query against the proper application system to determine the status and give the corresponding answers to the customer. This dialog would go on for some time until the customer was happy with the answer. As a result of all the involved manual interactions, the service to customers and suppliers was limited to certain operation hours.

In a fast-paced global market, companies can no longer operate in this traditional way of doing business. Consumers select those companies where they can do business any time they want. To support the cycle time needed by customers and suppliers, the business processes of customers and suppliers must interact with a company's business processes without any human intervention. Figure 1.1 depicts the interactions between a company and its customers and suppliers, as well as the interactions between the different parts of a company, such as the sales head office and the manufacturing plant. These interactions range from simple inquiries to complex interactions between companies to the situation where organizational units of different companies are tied together by sharing data and business processes and operate like an independent enterprise (*virtual enterprise*).

Customers no longer make phone calls or mail order forms when they want to do business with a particular company. They no longer have to deal with an operator at a call center when they want to know the status of the order they had placed a few days ago. They enter the company's URL on their Web browser and are then connected to the company's home page, from which they can select the appropriate application system. The Web browser runs on such diverse devices as a personal computer, a mobile phone with a built-in monitor, or even a microwave oven.

Business processes of different companies honor each other's requests without any manual intervention. No interaction is required to have a company's business processes talk to the appropriate business processes of customers, suppliers, distributors, or even government agencies, such as the tax department.

Figure 1.1 Connected Business Processes

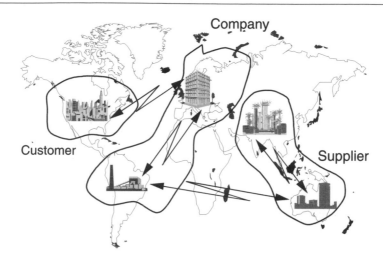

The levels of interaction between the different business processes covers a wide spectrum:

- An activity in a business process invokes another business process. That new business process executes totally independently of the original business process.

- An activity in a business process invokes another business process and waits until that new business process has completed.

- An activity in a business process invokes another business process, and an activity later in the business process waits until that new business process has completed.

Very complex scenarios can be built with these basic structures. We discuss these structures in detail in section 3.4.3 on page 87. Typical business processes that are made up of these basic structures are the business processes that define the interactions between the manufacturing company and its suppliers. A manufacturer of personal computers may have a business process for the assembly of the personal computers. One of the activities is the ordering of motherboards to be delivered by a supplier when the amount of available motherboards falls below a certain level. In this case, a request is sent to the supplier; the request starts the appropriate order entry process. When production of the motherboards has completed and they have been shipped, the final activity in the order entry process sends the appropriate billing request back to the manufacturer. The manufacturer receives the billing request and starts the appropriate accounts payable process.

To make sure that business processes are carried out correctly, each business process has a process administrator assigned to it. If an out-of-line situation occurs, the process administrator is notified so that corrective actions can be taken. A typical out-of-line situation occurs when a time limit is associated with a process and the process takes longer than the time specified. Tools are available to the process administrator to query the state of the business process, assign a higher priority to the business, or shift work from one person to another.

In the case of inter-enterprise business processes, it is also possible that the problem is associated with a process that is running at another company. In this case, it is desirable that a process administrator can also query the state of that other process so that the process administrators of both companies can jointly work on the appropriate corrective actions.

The level of interaction we have discussed so far reflects interaction between independent companies. Each company runs its business in its own way with its own distinct business processes. Each business process is associated with data that is part of the enterprise data. When data is needed by processes of other companies, the data is shipped together with the invocation of the other process.

Within an enterprise, the difference between processes and subprocesses is not visible at all. All programs associated with the different business processes access, in general, the same set of enterprise data. Communication between the applications that make up the business process is not visible to the outside.

Virtual enterprises are enterprises in the sense that they operate as any other enterprise. However, they are not organizationally the same as a typical enterprise. They are made up of parts of different companies, where each company contributes parts to the overall enterprise. In the extreme case, one company contributes by manufacturing the product; another company is responsible for distribution; a third one, for marketing; and a fourth one, for billing.

In this case, the different pieces of the virtual enterprise operate as one enterprise. This collaboration is made possible by the use of common business processes and common data. Each activity within a business process can then be performed by one of the participating companies. The data is accessible to all of the companies. The Internet provides the communication backbone for running the processes and accessing the data.

It is interesting to observe that the same methods for carrying out business processes can be observed if parts of a company are outsourced. For example, a new, independent company is formed to perform a certain task. In this case, existing business processes need to continue to be performed even though there are two independent companies.

Each level of interaction we have discussed requires that the different systems work together without any friction independently of the type of implementation that has been chosen by the involved parties. This requirement mandates that the protocols used to communicate are standardized. Without standardization, bilateral agreements would have to be negotiated and then implemented on both ends for every new set of interactions.

1.4 Processes and Workflows

The *process model* describes the structure of a business process in the real world. It defines all possible paths through the business process, including the rules that define which paths should be taken and all actions that need to be performed. This model is a template from which each *process* is instantiated; that is an instance of the process model is created. Some people use the term *process instance* for the instances that are created from process models. An individual process (process instance) is carried out according to a set of values that determines the actual path through the process. In an insurance company the process model might be called ClaimsProcessing, and from this model a large number of processes are created, one for Joe Smith, one for Laura Miller, and so on.

Processes need not necessarily be run on a computer. A large number of business processes are performed without a single step being performed by a computer. A typical example is that of a manager circulating a document for each employee to read. Whenever an employee receives the document in her mail basket, she reads it, signs it, determines who has not seen it, and then puts it into the mail basket of somebody who has not yet signed it. The employee who signs the document last puts it back into the mail basket of the manager.

Business processes thus may consist of parts that are carried out by a computer and parts that are not supported through computers. As shown in Figure 1.2, the parts that are run on a computer are called a *workflow model*.

Figure 1.2 Processes and Workflows

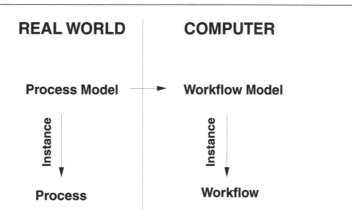

A workflow model may be just a small part of a larger process model, or it may encompass the whole process model. The computer programs that carry out the workflow can be a general-purpose workflow management system or specialized applications that implement the process model. The workflow model is a template for creating workflows in the same sense that the process model is a template for creating processes.

In this book, we follow the convention of using the term *process* when talking about processes and process models, and *workflow* when talking about workflows and workflow models. In fact, we even follow the conventions of even using the terms process and workflow interchangeably. The context will make it obvious which one we are talking about. In cases, where the meaning could be ambiguous, we use the full term.

1.5   Dimensions of Workflow

Business processes, and therefore workflows, have three independent (orthogonal) dimensions. These three dimensions can be graphically depicted as a cube, as shown in Figure 1.3.

Figure 1.3 The Three Dimensions of Workflow

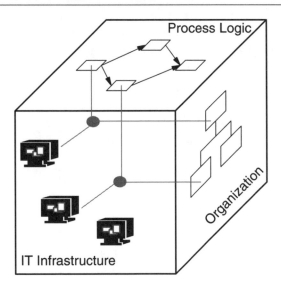

The cube's first dimension represents the *process logic*. It describes *what* in terms of which activities are to be performed and in which sequence they need to be performed. Each box represents either a program that is invoked or another process that is executed either as a local subprocess or as a remote subprocess within the same company or in another company. The arrows show the flow of control from one activity to the next. The flow can be sequential or parallel. If it is sequential, one activity is performed after the other; if it is parallel, two or more activities are executed at the same time, usually reducing the time required to perform a business process.

The cube's second dimension, orthogonal to the process logic, is the *organization* dimension. It describes the organizational structure of the company in terms of departments, roles, and people. This information is used to define *who* should perform each activity. A query can be specified for each activity to identify the set of people in the organization to whom the activity can be assigned. For example, if it has been defined, that an activity can only be performed by someone meeting a particular job function (role), then all persons assigned to the job function are selected and are assigned to perform the activity. If the activity does not interact with a user, the workflow management system carries out the activity on behalf of the selected user.

The cube's third dimension, orthogonal to the process logic and the organization, constitutes the dimension of information technology (IT) infrastructure. It describes *which* IT resources, such as programs that perform a particular activity, are required.

The execution history of a process is thus a sequence of triplets (activity, user, IT resource), or in other words, a series of points (trajectory) in the three-dimensional workflow space W^3 (*w*hat, *w*ho, *w*hich).

1.6   User Support

Several users are involved in running workflows: end users that perform the individual tasks, system administrators that have overall responsibility for the workflow management system and the actions it performs, operation administrators that are responsible that the workflow management system is up and running, and process administrators that monitor the expected processing of the individual business processes.

The individual tasks are typically performed though a graphical user interface (GUI). This user interface could be anything from a Web browser running on a network station, a window on a regular PC, or the tiny monitor of a hand-held device.

End users receive the requests for processing individual activities as *workitems*. These workitems are typically represented as icons. The representation of the icon shows, at least to a certain extent, the type of work that must be performed. These workitems are made available to the user either upon explicit request or upon being pushed by the workflow management system onto the user's desktop. When a user wants to work on a particular activity, she clicks on the appropriate icon, which then starts the associated program. When the work associated with the activity has been completed, the workitem is automatically removed. The user can organize the individual workitems according to specified criteria into *worklists*. Criteria can be priority, age, or type of activity, such as confidential or public.

Operation administrators are provided with a graphical view of the status of each of the different workflow management system components. This interface can be provided either by the workflow management system or by a systems management system. The interface typically supports alerts for out-of-line situations as well as query and change capabilities for all or individual components.

The user interface for process administrators is geared toward managing individual process instances and acting as a focal point for all process-related events. The events are represented as workitems that can be started to perform appropriate process repair actions. The starting point is a graphical representation of the business process. By pointing to individual activities, the process administrator can dig deeper into the structure of the workflow. Corrective actions that could be performed are restarting the process, transferring workitems from one user to another, or repairing a broken process.

1.7   Categories of Workflows

Many schemes have been developed to classify workflows. Figure 1.4 shows one of the more prominent ones. In this scheme, used by GIGA Information Group[Gro], workflows are categorized according to their value to the business and their repetition.

The *business value* defines the importance of a workflow to the company's business. A process of high business value is at the core of a company; it's a core

Figure 1.4 Classifying Workflow According to Business Value and Repetition

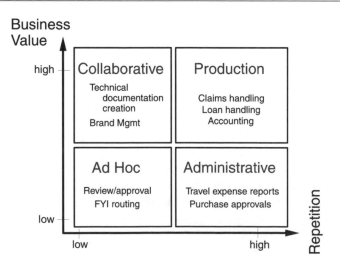

competency of the company. The company has been founded to perform those processes; this means the company is defined as running those business processes. Typical examples of high-business-value processes are the granting of a loan for a bank or the manufacturing of a car by a car manufacturer.

The *repetition* measures how often a particular process is performed in the same manner. It is an indicator of whether the process is worth being modeled. This indicator is important since modeling of a process for the first time is nontrivial and is time consuming, which makes it typically an expensive task. The "for your information routing" business process, for example, is typically performed in large volumes; however the underlying process models are always different.

By using these two characteristics, we can distinguish the four different types of workflows as shown in Figure 1.4.

Collaborative workflows are characterized by a high business value but are executed only a few times. The processes associated with building a ship, creating technical documentation for a software product, or performing brand management for a consumer product fall into this category; all of them are extremely important for the success of the corresponding company. Their underlying process is generally rather complex and is created specifically for the particular task, often by customizing a given project plan. Changes to the underlying plan are fairly common.

Ad hoc workflows show a low business value and low repetition rate. Generally, these workflows either have no predefined structure and the next step in the process is determined by each user involved in the process, or each business process is constructed individually whenever there is a need to perform a series of actions. For-your-information routing is a typical workflow without a defined structure. A manager, for example, sends a note to all his department members with information deemed to be important for them. The receivers of the note can do whatever they want with it, including routing the note to other people who should know about this particular information. Such a process terminates if nobody routes this note to anyone else.

Administrative workflows also show a low business value; however the repetition factor is high. These workflows are the typically administrative processes such as expense account or purchase order processing. In the case of expense account processing, the employee fills out a form, the employee's manager approves it, and the expense account department verifies the correctness and issues the appropriate bank order.

Production workflows are characterized by having a high business value and a high repetition factor. These are the workflows that implement the core business of the company, such as the loan process in a bank or the claims management process in an insurance company. It is their efficient execution that provides a company with a competitive advantage. Often, production workflows are still implemented without a workflow management system because the corresponding processes have

Figure 1.5 Classifying Workflow According to Business Value, Repetition, and Automation

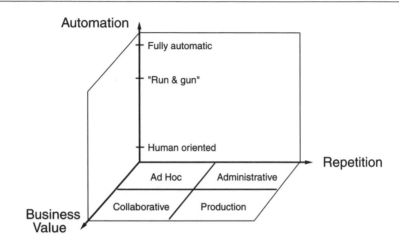

been in place for decades. And because of their importance, the corresponding applications were typically implemented as transaction-processing monitor programs. The scalability, availability, and robustness of these environments are consequently a prerequisite for workflow engines that run production workflows; such a workflow management system is called a *production wfms*.

An additional distinctive dimension to the business value and the repetition factor is the degree of automation of a workflow as shown in Figure 1.5. This measurement shows the independence of a workflow from human intervention, that is, whether the activities of a workflow are mainly performed by humans or by the system. A highly automated process is computation intensive and typically integrates heterogeneous and autonomous application systems.

Fully automatic workflows have many similarities with batch procedures known for decades. They can be found in database administration, such as database reorganization, systems management (e.g. reacting to system events), and data warehousing (e.g. merging and cleansing of different data sources).

A process with a high degree of automation does not necessarily mean the process has no interactions with humans. But typically, a highly automated workflow is fragmented into sequences of activities, each of which is performed by a single user, intermixed with automatically performed sequences. The sequences of activities assigned to a particular user are often worked on in a *stream* environment, meaning the sequence is performed consecutively without any interrupt.

1.8 Application Structure

Applications that are built and executed according to the workflow paradigm are called *workflow-based applications*. They are no longer monolithic or executed on large central computers supporting dumb terminals, nor are they client/server applications where the still-monolithic application has been split into two pieces that are deployed to a large central computer and smaller intelligent workstations or net stations for better exploitation of resources.

These new applications execute on the network where the different pieces of the application are executed on different computers, each of them possibly running a different operating system, database system, or network protocol. Figure 1.6 illustrates this approach schematically.

Figure 1.6 Schema of Workflow-based Application

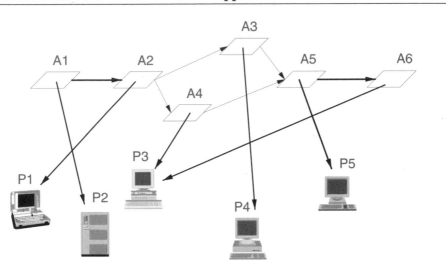

The first activity A1 is processed without any user interaction on workstation P2 running AIX; the second activity A2 is carried out on laptop P1 running Windows 98. Since these applications are not just carried out on a single processor but on different processors connected via a network, they are sometimes also called *networked applications*.

The heart of these applications is the business process that is executed by the workflow management system. Based on the context in which the business process executes, different paths are taken through the process model. Thus, different processes can take completely different routes through the network, are being worked on by different people, and are processed by different programs.

The business process can even be executed by different workflow management systems if a business process invokes a business process outside the domain of the current workflow management system, for example, by sending a request via the Internet to some other company. Agreements between the different vendors and standards established by standards bodies are making this kind of execution happen.

1.9   Workflow and Objects

Enterprises are investing in object technology today to improve the productivity of their programmers and to enable even non-data-processing professionals to build applications by using visual builders. Vendors of standard software split their applications into business objects, allowing programmers to reuse the objects in a different context.

A cornerstone of object technology is the insight that the robustness of systems is normally achieved by encapsulating things that might become subject to change. If, for example, the order in which operations are to be performed can change or if operations can be added or removed, the guidelines of object technology consequently recommend the introduction of a dedicated control object. This control object encapsulates the scheduling of the various operations.

When the functions of the control object are examined, it is obvious that they are just a subset of the functions offered by workflow technology. The control object is represented by a process defined to the workflow management system. This representation enables vendors of standard software to glue together their business objects to form the original, monolithic business application.

Each activity of the process is implemented as a business object that is invoked by the workflow management system. As shown in Figure 1.7 an application thus consists of a business process and a set of business objects, where each activity is

Figure 1.7 Workflow and Objects

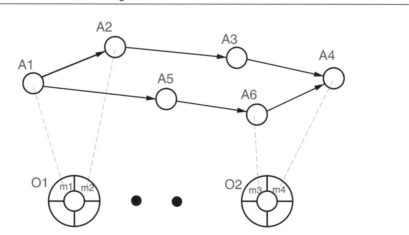

implemented as the invocation of a method of a business object. As illustrated, activity A1 invokes method m1 of business object O1, and activity A2 invokes method m2 on the same business object. This scheme should be compared to the more traditional approach in which a workflow-based application consists of a business process and a set of programs.

Chapter 6 discusses the relationship between workflow technology and object technology in depth.

1.10 Application Operating System

The purpose of an operating system is to provide an environment for the execution of programs. This environment includes the management of resources such as processors, memory, disk storage, and communication lines. The operating system effectively hides these resources by providing appropriate application programming interfaces (APIs) for the programs. A scripting language allows the user of such a system to specify the sequence in which the various executables are to be processed. The operating system will then make sure that the right resources are available to the program at the right time and at the right place.

When an application is made up of different components, the individual components must be called in the correct sequence (flow of control) and data must be passed correctly from one component to other components (flow of data). This knowledge is either built into each of the components or localized in some special components that manage for example the flow of control. If the application is distributed, the various components must exploit the underlying infrastructure to manage this flow of control and data. In addition, they must implement the various recovery mechanisms. The components must therefore not only be built to deal with the local operating system but must also consider the characteristics of the operating systems of other components they are communicating with.

With workflow, the component must only deal with the local operating system characteristics. The workflow management system takes care of the differences in operating systems, network protocols, and communication mechanisms. It just calls the component by using the invocation mechanism of the local operating system. If an operating-system-independent invocation mechanism, such as message queueing, is used, even this dependency can be removed. If the component is written in a portable language and does not perform operating-system-specific input/output operations, the individual component is portable.

Workflow management systems thus provide to applications the same functions that operating systems provide to the individual programs. It relieves the applications from dealing directly with operating systems and communication mechanisms by providing appropriate APIs. Workflow management systems are therefore sometimes referred to as *application operation systems*.

Figure 1.8 Software Stack

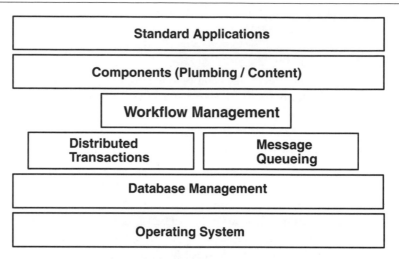

1.11   Software Stack

Figure 1.8 shows the position of workflow technology within a simplified software stack. This software stack shows only those components that are important for the points we want to make.

The base is the operating system, which provides an environment for the execution of programs.

On top of the operating system is a set of programs that are collectively called middleware. They provide the infrastructure necessary for application programs to manage data (database management system), communicate with each other via messages (message queuing system), and implement distributed transactions (transaction managers and TP monitors).

These are the components used by the workflow management system to provide the functions needed for an application operating system. The database management system is used to store the persistent information such as processes or organizational information. The message queuing system provides the infrastructure that is needed for communication between the different components of the workflow management system, either on the same computer or on different ones. The transaction manager helps the workflow management system process messages and make changes to the database under transaction control, providing the robustness required for an application operating system.

The workflow management system is then used by the next layer, which provides the object management infrastructure. This object support, together with workflow support, is then used by standard applications, such as payroll, general ledger, or groupware systems.

1.12 Document/Image Processing

Some business processes are centered around sets of documents that are routed from one person to the next. Document management systems have been developed to support this type of work. Because documents are quite often in the form of scanned images, these systems are also known as image-processing systems.

These systems focus on the management of documents/images, and offer a wealth of functions to manage and manipulate documents/images:

- Functions to scan images and annotate them with text that makes it possible to efficiently locate the images later

- A document store to support not only the simple storage of documents but also to provide functions to group related documents into folders and to search for documents using sophisticated searches

- Archiving functions to remove documents and images from the document library and put them into some slower, but cheaper, storage

- A document editor to create, modify, and annotate documents

- A forms editor to define forms and the rules that should apply to the data entered into the forms by appropriate users

- The capability to define how documents, forms, and folders are routed from person to person within the organization, and the type of action to be performed by each individual

In document/imaging systems, the workflow functions are in general an integral part of the system. A business process is typically represented as a folder. This folder is the entry into all activities associated with the process; it allows the user to perform queries into the document store and to perform actions such as adding a document, filling out a form, or determining the next user to work on the folder. These systems are sometimes also called *folder-management systems*, since the folder is the focal point. Since a folder typically represents a case, such as the loan in a bank or an insurance claim, the term *case processing* is used sometimes for this type of processing.

In contrast to these systems, workflow management systems focus on the underlying business process and the execution of the business as a set of activities. These activities can be anything from mailing a letter via e-mail or making a telephone call to filling out a form, for example, that automatically calculates taxes, or updates a personnel record in a corporate database.

It should be noted that document management systems have their own internal workflow management system. In fact, it is much better to implement them on top of a stand-alone workflow management system since that implementation integrates better with other systems and programs in the enterprise.

1.13   Groupware and Workflow

Workflow addresses only one aspect of groupware, systems that help people to work together on the same piece of work. These systems provide the implementations for computer-supported cooperative work (CSCW). Figure 1.9 [TSMB95] classifies groupware according to the three aspects of CSCW: collaboration, communication, and coordination. Because each of the listed implementations reflects the three aspects more or less strongly, a charge diagram illustrates the strength of each aspect in a particular implementation. The closer an implementation is to an aspect, the more prominent the aspect is in the implementation. Video conferencing, for example, only has the aspect of communication; it does not have any coordination or collaboration aspects.

Figure 1.9 Classifying Groupware According to Communication, Coordination, and Collaboration

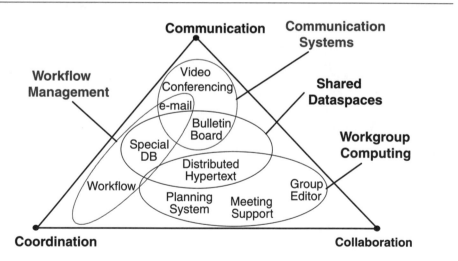

This classification schema suggests four major groupings:

- Communication systems help people exchange information, quite often as a one-way communication. This exchange includes video conferencing, e-mail, and bulletin boards on which people post their opinions.

- Shared data spaces provide people with the facilities to share data. Bulletin boards are used as a means of sharing data as in the case of Question & Answer forums on the Internet. Distributed hypertext links documents, making it possible for a group to connect their individual data to a larger web of information. Special databases are typically used to allow people work together by sharing information.

- Workgroup computing helps small projects work together by focusing on the collaboration aspects. The most prominent example is a group editor that helps people jointly write one document, for example, the specification of a computer system. Meeting support helps people organize their collaboration; planning systems to coordinate this working together.

- Workflow management systems focus on the coordination of people performing different tasks to create the final work product. Special databases are typically used as part of the workflow-based application; this means the activity implementations work with these databases. A lightweight version of a workflow management system can also be built on top of an e-mail system by using scripting capabilities within the e-mail system.

1.14 Different Views of Applications

Different people within an organization view the company's applications differently. Figure 1.10 illustrates two major views.

Business administration and management typically view applications as some kind of business process that is performed by different parts of the organization and that results in the delivery of the required item. From their perspective the mechanics of achieving this result is immaterial; their major concern is the efficiency of the business process to achieve the goals specified in the business strategy. This concern causes them to mainly focus on business goals, such as how long it takes to process a customer order, how satisfied the customers are with the company's service, or how quickly a customer complaint can be processed. A second set of business goals deals with the efficiency of business processes, such as how efficient the business process is in terms of costs and people.

Figure 1.10 How Different People View Applications

In contrast to business administration and management, information technology (IT) personnel view applications as a combination of a vast amount of data stored in files and databases that are processed by a large amount of programs operating on the data and interacting with the users. These programs are so important for the enterprise that they are implemented as transactions. The IT people are mainly concerned with the availability and efficiency of the programs and the data those programs access. Consequently, they are concerned with the availability and efficiency of the underlying systems, such as database management systems, operating systems, transaction managers, or communication systems, on which those programs depend.

Workflow helps to bridge this gap because it connects these views into a set of workflow-based applications. These workflow-based applications consist of the process models that the business administration looks at and the activity implementations that are the transactions the information processing people see. Workflow thus helps to achieve a consistent and coherent view of applications.

1.15   Transactional Workflow

Applications that implement the core functions of the company's business are implemented as transactions. The ACID paradigm, the fundamental concept of transactions, when implemented makes these applications robust and safe. The ACID paradigm defines that a collection of operations within a transaction has the following properties:

- Atomicity—Either all of them are applied to the system or none of them are,

- Consistency—They lead to a new valid state of the system,

- Isolation—They do not affect (until explicitly made visible) operations outside the collection,

- Durability—They are not undone because of any later system failure.

The transfer of money from one bank account to another bank account is the prototype of a transaction. The transaction consists of two operations; the withdrawal of money from one account and the deposit of money into the other account. In this case, both operations must succeed or none of them may succeed (atomicity). As the amount of money remains the same, the new state is a valid state of the system (consistency). The new state of the two accounts is not available to any other operation, until the transaction has completed (isolation). The changes must not be lost under any circumstances (durability).

Workflows or parts thereof must also have transactional properties. Depending on the time required to execute this transaction, different techniques need to be applied.

In highly automated workflows, that is workflows with little or no user interaction, the individual activities are often carried out with programs that have transactional behavior. Because of the streamlike behavior (short-lived, no user interaction) of these workflows, collections of such activities can be grouped together to build a new transaction. Such a transaction is called a *global transaction*. Global transactions allow automated recovery in such workflows; whenever an error occurs, all effects of the different activity implementations are automatically undone. The definition of the transaction boundaries is part of modeling the workflow. We call such a set of activities that are part of the transaction an *atomic sphere*. A typical example of an atomic sphere is the funds transfer we discussed earlier. Enforcement of the global transaction, that is atomic sphere, can be achieved by the workflow management system using traditional techniques.

The typical execution time for an atomic sphere is in the range of tenths of seconds to seconds at the most. If the execution of a transaction takes longer, the standard techniques that are applied in atomic spheres can no longer be used efficiently. A number of advanced transaction models have been developed to cope with long execution times by weakening some of the ACID properties. Typically, those new transaction models require special programming by the application developer. This type of long-running transaction is called a *business transaction*.

A typical example of a business transaction is our trip reservation example shown in Appendix A. After the client's itinerary is accepted, corresponding reservations for flights, hotel rooms, and rentals cars need to be made. To shorten the processing time, the three reservations are made in parallel. These three operations must be performed as a transaction. Either all reservations are successful or none of them should be successful.

The processing time of the transaction is measured in minutes or hours; however, none of the advanced transaction models can be directly applied here. The implementers of the different reservation systems had no knowledge of each other at the time they built the system, nor did they want to take this fact into consideration. Each of the systems performs its own transactions and exposes its results independently of each other. This behavior requires that the individual transactions need to be undone by compensation transactions that compensate the effects of the original transactions. The compensation of a flight reservation is the cancellation of the reservation. The definition of the business transaction boundaries and the compensation activities is, as for global transactions, part of modeling the workflow. We call the set of activities that are part of the transaction a *compensation sphere*.

Figure 1.11 shows the space that global transactions and business transactions occupy in the classification scheme shown in Figure 1.5 on page 12.

We extensively discuss the usage and properties of atomic and compensation spheres in Chapter 7.

Figure 1.11 Classifying Business Transactions and Global Transactions

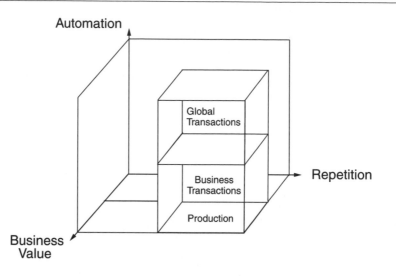

1.16   Advanced Usage

Workflow technology not only applies to the traditional applications we have discussed so far, such as loan processing, it can also be used beneficially for other applications, such as for project management.

A project management system helps managers and team leaders plan and control the execution of projects. To support these tasks, it keeps a database in which all project-related data is stored.

At the beginning of the project, the user specifies all project-related information, such as the individual tasks, the sequence in which the tasks need to be performed, how much of the tasks can be performed in parallel, and the resources, such as people, to perform these tasks. With this information, the project management system generates the appropriate charts, in particular, the GANTT charts (project plan), that show which resource must be available at which time. In addition, the user can specify which resources are actually available at which time. This specification enables the project management system to generate an adjusted GANTT chart that reflects the actual allocation of resources. This chart is refined, by different resource allocations, until the project plan fits the desired time frame.

During the lifetime of a project, actual data, such as the actual time or resource it took to perform a particular task, is collected and entered by the project manager. This information makes it possible to control the project progress and take appropriate actions, such as allocating more resources, if required. The quality of the project plan depends on the actual data being accurate, complete, collected, and entered into the project management system as early as possible.

Figure 1.12 Project Management

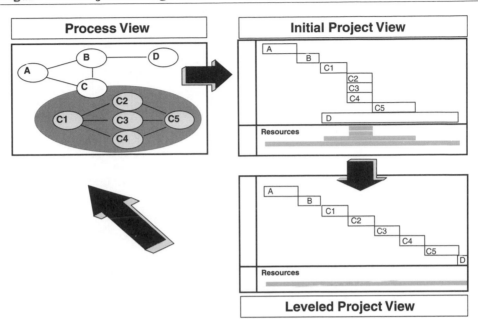

Figure 1.12 illustrates how workflow technology can significantly add to the capabilities of a project management system.

One models a project in the workflow management system as a business process either by modeling it directly in the workflow management system or by reverse-engineering it from an existing project plan in the project management system. We call this representation of a project the *process view*. When a new project is started, the process view is translated into the GANTT chart, which represents the *project view* of the project. This transformation is done under the assumption of unlimited resource and results in an initial project plan. The GANTT chart is then reworked using the available level of resources, until a satisfactory project plan has been found. We call the project to be leveled and the appropriate GANTT chart the *leveled project view*. When this stage has been reached, information in the GANTT chart that is process relevant, such as the amount and type of resources that are needed or the time scale of the project, is extracted and imported into the workflow management system. The workflow management system updates the process model with this information, for example, the assignment of roles to activities.

When the project is started, an appropriate process is created from the process model. This process now helps to control the execution of the process by proactively tracking the project progress. It collects the appropriate actual data from the project members and, if this data is not provided in a timely fashion, sends out reminders or even notifications to the project manager.

This is just one example of the advanced use of workflow technology. Chapter 9 provides an in-depth discussion of some additional examples.

1.17   System Requirements

In section 1.2 on page 3 we discussed process models as an enterprise resource. They therefore must be treated in the same way as data that the company owns. They must be protected against any accidental or intentional damage. Tight access control must be exercised to make sure that the structure of the business processes is not revealed to unauthorized users and that the structure of business processes cannot be altered with malicious intent. It is imperative that the business processes be executed exactly as defined.

Similar functionality has traditionally been delivered by transaction processing (TP) monitors. The structure of the business processes was an integral part of the application that was executed by the TP monitors. A production workflow management system therefore must provide the same level of operational and enterprise characteristics as that delivered by TP monitors. Actually, a production workflow management system must exceed these levels as workflow-based applications typically operate in a heterogeneous and distributed environment.

1.17.1   Operational Requirements

The following list highlights some of the more prominent operational requirements that a production workflow management system must fulfill.

- It must support *business transactions* and *global transactions*.

- It must be *reliable*. All internal operations must be performed as transactions. For example the invocation of an activity implementation, must be performed once and only once. The workflow management system must ensure that in the case of a failure, no completed action is undone and all actions that have not yet been completed are undone and started anew.

- It must show high *availability*. Actually, the workflow management system should support continuous operation; that means that the management of the underlying data and the communication software should not require the system to be quiesced even when changes, such as upgrading the different components of the workflow management system, are made to the workflow management system. High availability means that the workflow management system implements a system structure that allows the workflow management system to be up and running 24 hours a day 7 days a week.

- It must be designed for high *capacity*. Ideally, this would mean the support of an unlimited number of users working with the system and an unlimited number of processes maintained by the workflow management system.

- It must be *scalable*. This requires that the workflow management system be structured in such a way that additional resources either make the system perform faster or provide for higher throughput.

- It must provide the capability to record *process traces*. The trace information should include all relevant actions, such as the start of a process or the execution of an activity implementation. All trace information must be written to persistent storage. This trace information is usually called the *audit trail*. It allows for the monitoring of the system characteristics, such as the current number of actions being performed or the average duration of a process. It also helps check if the corresponding goals are met. And, it provides the data for statistical analysis, such as calculating the costs associated with carrying out a process.

1.17.2 Enterprise Requirements

Since workflow-based applications are typically executed in a heterogeneous and distributed environment, even within the same corporation, the workflow management system must also address issues that are important from an enterprise perspective.

- It must support *multiple platforms*. Platform refers to the operating system and network protocol the workflow management system operates on. In addition, it is required that the workflow management systems on the different platforms can communicate with each other. Platform also means that the workflow management system must be able to invoke applications that implement activities on different platforms using different invocation mechanisms.

  This flexibility is required to support the integration of a wide variety of existing programs, such as legacy applications running on a mainframe using IBM's Customer Information Control System (CICS) or IBM's Information Management System (IMS) as transaction monitor, or standard software such as SAP R/3.

- It must participate in *systems management*. This requirement has multiple facets. First, the workflow management system must be enabled to assist the systems management system in the distribution of workflow management system code to the various servers and clients. Second, it should assist the systems management system in the automatic distribution of the software each user needs to perform the assigned activities. Third, it must provide the systems management system with information about its status. This information allows the systems management system to monitor the workflow management system and take proper actions if the workflow management system becomes unavailable for whatever reason.

- It must provide *central administration*. Each one of the individual workflow management systems offers administration functions. These administrative functions fall into two categories: the administration of processes and the administration of the workflow management system. It is important that both types of functions are available centrally.

- *Standards compliance* is an important requirement for a number of reasons.

  1. In a large enterprise, it is likely that workflow management systems of different vendors are involved in the execution of workflow. This variety requires that the different workflow management systems implement some standard that defines the exchange format between different workflow management systems.

  2. Uncontrollable events, such as the disappearance of a workflow management system vendor, may require the installation of a new vendor's workflow management system. It is important that (ideally) the activity implementations and process models need not be adapted or even rewritten. This desired flexibility requires that the workflow management system honors the standard that regulates the invocation of activity implementations and complies with a common metamodel.

  3. Central administration requires that the workflow management system implements the standard that defines the information to be returned and the actions to be taken as the result of an administration request.

  4. Statistical analysis of process traces requires that the audit trail written by the different workflow management systems follow the appropriate standard. Otherwise, significant pieces of information are lost.

  5. Users typically interact with the workflow management system by using a graphical user interface (GUI). This GUI is very identical throughout the company. This standardization is particularly important in cases where different workflow management systems are installed within a company. User should not need to learn to use a new GUI every time they change jobs. This need for continuity requires that the workflow management system implements the standard that defines the functions that a client performs. Without this standard, the customer would need to invest in various differing GUIs.

- A sophisticated *security* system is a definitive must for a workflow management system. We subsume under this requirement all aspects of security and authentication. These aspects include the protection of the workflow management system's data against any access coming outside the workflow management system, the encryption of messages that flow between different workflow management systems, the authentication of users when they access the workflow management system, and an elaborate access control scheme that allows the granular assignment of access rights to workflow management system entities such as process models, processes, and audit trail information.

1.18 Relation to Other Technologies

So far, we have sketched how workflow is related to object technology, transaction management, and project management. There are many additional software technologies that are more or less closely related to workflow. Figure 1.13 lists some of the more prominent ones. We start our discussion with business engineering and then continue clockwise around the circle.

Business Engineering is a collection of activities and techniques that helps define the optimal business processes for a company to make the company competitive. Those pieces of the collected information that can be managed by a computer are moved over to the workflow management system. We discuss business engineering and its relationship to workflow in Chapter 2.

Figure 1.13 Relations to Technologies

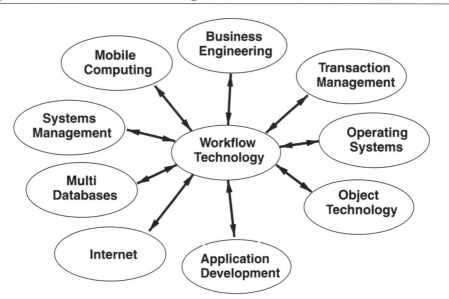

We described the support of global and business transactions in section 1.15 on page 20. Several later chapters address the relationship of workflow technology and transaction management. Chapter 9 elaborates on the use of transaction managers in applications, Chapter 7 provides an in-depth discussion of the transaction support needed in production workflow management systems, and Chapter 10 shows how the transactional support is realized in the workflow management system.

In section 1.10 on page 15, we described how a workflow management system is conceptually an application operating system and how the workflow management system is built on top of message queuing, database management, transaction management, and operating systems. In chapter 10, we show how such a workflow management system is implemented on top of those components and how it exploits each of these underlying systems.

The relationship between workflow and object technology has many facets. We discussed one of them, the use of objects as activity implementations, in section 1.9 on page 14. This application view is workflow-centric; we present an object-centric view of applications that use workflow in Chapter 6. We show how the structure of workflow-based applications can be derived from object-oriented analysis and design.

Development of applications is typically performed with the aid of an application development methodology particularly suited for the type of application that needs to be implemented. We devoted Chapter 11 to an in-depth discussion of a development methodology for workflow-based applications. We call this approach *process-based CASE* (computer-assisted software engineering). This approach starts with the global definition of business processes, using one of the many business process modeling tools, and derives from the collected information the workflow specifications and the structures of the databases that are used by the activity implementation. Another approach is to start with object-oriented analysis and design (OOA/D) and derive from this information the workflow specifications and database structures. We discuss this in detail in Chapters 6 and 11.

The Internet is the backbone of electronic commerce. It provides the mechanism that enables workflows to easily span companies all over the world. Users have access to workflow management system functions, such as starting a business process or querying the state of a particular business process, using their familiar browser, such as Netscape browser or Internet Explorer. For example, users can order a customized car and track its delivery. We elaborate on the relationship between workflow technology and the Internet in Chapter 2 in the context of business engineering and in Chapter 9 in the context of Web applications.

Applications often operate on multiple databases, where each database is managed by a different database management system. The involved database management systems must provide a particular behavior if the application needs to be executed as a transaction. The database management systems must operate as resource managers in a two-phase commit protocol. Not all database management systems support this protocol, nor are all applications structured for the exploitation of these features: transaction integrity must be achieved differently. Workflow technology can provide the required transactional behavior by means of compensations spheres as discussed in section 1.15 on page 20.

Systems management systems help to manage the complete information technology infrastructure, including distributing code to the proper computers, observing the correct operation of applications, communication lines, processors, informing operations people about out-of-line situations, and taking predefined corrective actions. Applications must be instrumented to provide the proper information to the systems management system and to accept requests from the systems management system. Workflow-based applications are no exception. However, no particular instrumentation is required from the activity implementations; the workflow management system provides the appropriate hooks into the systems management, for example, to allow the systems management system to perform workload balancing. We discuss these aspects in detail in Chapter 10. In addition, the workflow management system's knowledge about IT structures and organizational information can be easily used to assist the systems management system in its tasks. The workflow management system, for example, knows which user needs which piece of code. This information is required by the systems management system to perform code distribution. We discuss those aspects in Chapter 8.

Not all participants in a business process use office workstations; sales or marketing people need to have access to information when they are on the road. Thus, workflow management systems must support the mobile user by providing access to the workflow management system at any time. In Chapter 6 we discuss the appropriate support in the context of standardization work of the OMG.

Chapter 2

Business Engineering

Business reengineering is one of the most important topics on the agenda of a large number of companies. It has been triggered by a changing business environment that requires companies to be more flexible and to react faster to change [HC94]. New processes are defined; existing ones are changed or even abandoned.

These processes are no longer only intra-enterprise processes, such as claims processing in an insurance company or loan processing in a bank. Multiple enterprises are connecting their tasks in inter-enterprise processes to more efficiently manage their own processes. The order activity in a manufacturing process of a car company, for example, starts the appropriate order entry process at a parts supplier. Companies may even use common processes to tie together parts of the various companies to form virtual companies.

Those business processes are not only processes that deal with customers; internal administrative processes are also business processes. A typical example of such an administrative process is the handling of an expense account form. The employee fills in the proper information; the form is routed to the employee's manager for approval and further to the accounting department for writing the appropriate check and mailing it to the employee. Another administrative process is the backup and restore process for databases as performed by database administrators.

One of the key objectives of the reengineered business processes is to minimize the time required for execution. In a well-defined business process, all unnecessary tasks have been eliminated, all tasks that can be performed in parallel are performed in this manner, and tasks that are performed in parallel use different resources when possible. Resources in this context refer to the people performing activities and the equipment and the software that the activity uses. The environment in which those business processes run is thus typically a distributed and heterogeneous environment.

This chapter is devoted to the discussion of business engineering. Business engineering is the analysis, specification, and modeling of business processes with their associated resources. The resources referred to here are the organizations that carry out these business processes and the information technology resources that are used by the involved personnel to perform individual tasks within the business process.

The purpose of the chapter, however, is not to discuss business engineering in-depth; we just provide enough information to show how these concepts influence some of the concepts of workflow and how the concepts can be folded into the appropriate workflow constructs.

In business engineering, different methods and their supporting products abound. We therefore limit ourselves to describing the fundamental concepts and leave the details to the appropriate books. To show the type of interface exploited by business engineering tools, we show some screen shots from two business engineering tools, ARIS Easy Design from IDS Prof. Scheer [Gmb] and Workflow BPR from Holosofx [Inca].

2.1 Business Modeling

The objective of business modeling is to come up with a set of documents that describe the current operation of the company and the intended operation of the company. Numerous methods are available to obtain the information, ranging from simple paper and pencil style to sophisticated computer-assisted modeling.

Figure 2.1 shows the typical deliverables of business modeling:

Figure 2.1 Business Modeling Output

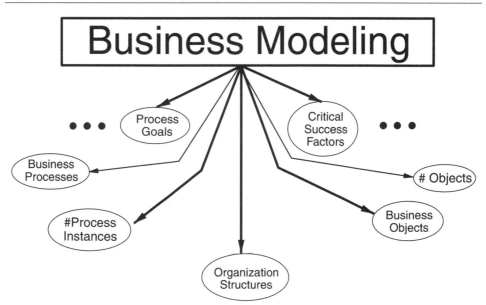

- *Process goals* is one of the most important deliverables and includes strategic items, such as the growth of the company over a specified period of time, the level of customer satisfaction, or the profit level to be maintained. It forms the basis for all subsequent activities. Without a thorough understanding of these goals and without agreement on them by all involved parties, all future activities are doomed to failure.

- *Business processes* are initially constructed on a very high level. They show just the major activities, the organizations that are involved in performing these activities, the goods associated with each activity, the computer systems that are used, and the data that is processed. On this level, most activities are, in fact, blocks of activities. The data could be just the definition of a database, such as the customer database, or a field in the customer database, such as the risk associated with the customer. Over time, the individual activities are refined either into subprocess, either by using an appropriate subprocess that exists already in a business process library or by creating a new subprocess.

- The *number of process instances* is just one of the pieces of statistical information that is collected during business modeling. This information is used, as we show later, in simulation, for example, to determine the number of people that are needed to perform the tasks in the business and to derive from this number the costs associated with the business process.

- An important aspect of business modeling is the creation of efficient *organizational structures* which includes areas of responsibilities, span of control, and reporting structures. Organizations are traditionally structured hierarchically with well-defined levels of responsibility. These structures therefore do not match well with the structure of business processes. To make business processes as efficient as possible, it is imperative to make organizational changes to allow business processes to freely flow across organizational barriers. We discuss the aspect of organization optimization in section 2.8.2 on page 48.

- The activities of a business process work with *business objects*. A business object in business modeling is not necessarily a business object in the strict sense of object technology, where it means something that provides that provides services via well-established interfaces. It could just be a piece of information that activities work with, such as a customer address, or that determines the flow of control through a business process, such as amount of a loan. For example, this information can also be used, for example, to determine access rights that people need to perform the required tasks. It is also used if the activity implementations need to be created, in which case the information is used to derive the structure of the application database. We discuss this subject in detail in Chapter 11.

- The *number of business objects* is another piece of statistical information. It can be used to determine the amount of required storage. Size information together with the access frequencies derived from the number of processes allow optimization of the physical structure of data store. We discuss this subject in Chapter 11.

- A business process can only be deployed and executed successfully if a certain set of criteria is met. We call the members of this set *critical success factors*, as they are crucial to the achievement of the goals that have been set for the business process. Critical success factors could be properties of the involved people, such as skills, or properties of the IT infrastructure, such as the power of the workstations that the people work with, or the servers that handle the requests of the people.

2.2   Business Logic

An important portion of a process model is the definition of the process logic. It involves two major facets: the flow of control and the associated flow of data.

The *control flow* defines the execution sequence of various *activities*, which are defined as the tasks that need to be carried out as part of a business process. Figure 2.2 illustrates the control flow as exemplified by the activities of a loan process in a bank. business tasks that need to be carried out as part of a business process. Figure 2.2 shows a sample loan process in a bank.

In the figure, the nodes represent the activities. The arrows of the graph that connect different activities are the *control connectors* that define the flow of control from one activity to the next activity.

Figure 2.2 Control Flow

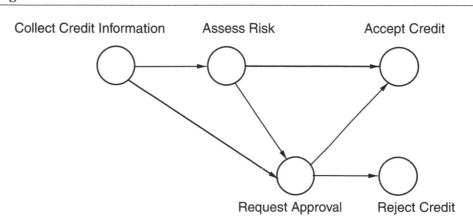

An activity can be the source of multiple control connectors. If more than one control connector path is taken, the activities at the end of the control connector are performed in parallel. Performing activities in parallel helps to realize one of the objectives of workflow: to reduce the overall process execution time. An activity that is the source of parallel work to be performed is called a *fork* activity. An activity that is the target of parallel work is called a *join* activity.

All activities are associated with conditions that define whether the activity can be carried out (*join condition*), when the activity can be carried out (*activation condition*), and when the activity has completed successfully (*exit condition*).

The join condition is checked after all incoming control connectors have entered the activity. When a control connector enters an activity, it has assigned a value of either true or false. The join condition is then expressed in terms of these truth values, such as, all must be true or at least one of the control connectors must be true. If the join condition evaluates to false, processing of the activity is skipped and all outgoing control connectors of the skipped activity are set to false. If the join condition evaluates to true, processing of the activity continues with checking of the activation condition. Since the join condition is not evaluated until all control connectors have entered the activity, the workflow management system needs to wait at a join activity until all control connectors have entered the activity. A join condition is therefore a synchronization point.

The activation condition is checked after the start condition has evaluated to true. If the activation condition is not met, the workflow management system waits until the condition is true. For example, if the activation condition states that the activity should be carried out after five o'clock, then the workflow management system waits until five o'clock.

The exit condition is checked after the activity has been carried out to ensure that the activity has completed.

Typically each activity is also associated with two types of data: data that the activity needs for operation and data that the activity generates and that is required by activities performed later in the business process. The data and the flow of the data from one activity to another is modeled by data connectors.

Figure 2.3 shows the flow of data in our loan process example.

The `Collect Credit Information` activity obtains the information that is associated with a credit, such as the name of the customer and the credit amount. This information is then passed to the `Assess Risk` activity. In this activity, the risk associated with the loan is determined.

The data that flows within the business process also determines which paths should be taken. A control connector is only followed if the attached condition, the *transition condition*, evaluates to true. In the example, the credit request is accepted immediately if the credit amount is less than or equal to $ 10.000 and the risk has been determined to be low. These *transition conditions* implement the business rules that are associated with a business process.

Figure 2.3 Data Flow

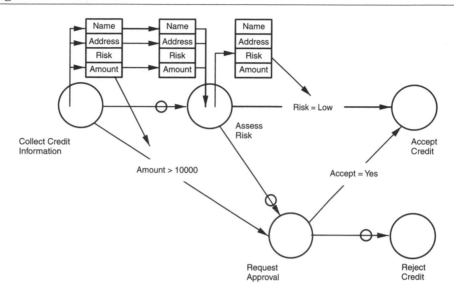

After the business logic has been defined, the business process modeler specifies, as discussed briefly in section 1.5, for each of the activities who is responsible for carrying out the activity (organizational information) and which information technology resource, such as programs, is used to carry out the activity.

2.3 Enterprise Structure

The determination of which person performs a particular activity is called *staff assignment*. However, the assignment is typically not expressed by a person's name but by organizational information such as role, department, or position. Using the name of the person makes the process very inflexible. Whenever the person moves to some other part of the company, the process model needs to be updated with the person replacing the current employee. Actually, it could even mean replacing the person's name in all running processes. Therefore, the staff assignment is given as a query in terms of roles, departments, or positions. When the appropriate activity is processed, organizational information is contacted and the appropriate person is selected (*staff resolution*). This approach requires that organizational information is managed by the workflow management system or at least made available to the workflow management system. *Available* means that the workflow management system has access to the information. Typical systems that manage organizational information are personnel systems, quite often supplied as a human resource (HR) module by application software vendors. In this case, the workflow management system may access the HR system directly or the customer may provide appropriate exit routines. If not already done, modeling the organizational structure is part of the business engineering process.

Depending on the sophistication of the business modeling tool, other relationships can be specified between activities and organizational information. An example is *controls* to specify that the activity is controlled by a particular department and *is responsible* to indicate that the specified organization has overall responsibility. Note, however, that not all workflow management systems support relationships in the same manner if at all. Some of the relationships are for documentation only.

Organizational information is collected and created in two steps. First, the organizational constructs or structures are defined; second, these constructs are populated. The approach is similar to the creation of a database, where first the database schema is defined and then the database is loaded with the appropriate data. In fact, defining the enterprise structure is the same process as defining and populating the personnel or organizational database.

The structure of the enterprise is typically described by an entity/relationship approach—an approach widely used in the design of relational databases [Teo94].

Each of the organizational constructs, such as departments, roles, positions, teams, and persons, is represented by a particular entity. Each entity is uniquely identified by its name, such as DEPARTMENT, ROLE, or PERSON and is associated with a set of attributes. Attributes are identified by their name and have certain characteristics, such as the type and length of data they hold and the valid values they can assume. Typically, one attribute is the key attribute that identifies a particular instance of the entity. The NAME attribute in the DEPARTMENT entity identifies a particular department. Other attributes help to specify other criteria in the staff assignment. The LOCATION and TYPE attributes in DEPARTMENT could, for example, be used to specify that a particular task must be performed by the sales department in New York (TYPE = SALES AND LOCATION = NEW YORK).

Affiliated entities are connected via relationships. These relationships identify dependencies between entities, such as the reporting path from department to department, or associations, such as the members of a department. Relationships are identified by the involved entities and the role they play for each of the involved entities. The cardinality of the relationship identifies how many instances of the different entities can be connected. Other specifications define whether the relationship between two entities is optional or mandatory. The relationships may have attributes associated with them. A typical example is a VALID FROM attribute in the REPORTING TO relationship between two different departments. This attribute allows, for example, the entry of organizational information that will not become effective until a specified date. The workflow management system needs to honor this information when performing staff resolution.

Figure 2.4 An Organization Metamodel

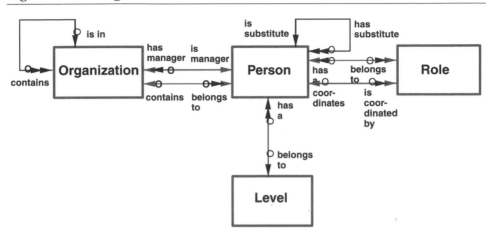

Figure 2.4 shows a simple organizational model, the one implemented by MQSeries Workflow. Entities are represented by rectangles; relationships, by arrows. A single arrowhead indicates that the cardinality of the relationship on this side is one; that is at most one instance can be created. A double arrowhead indicates that the cardinality of the relationship is many; an unlimited number of instances can be created. The "0" indicates that the relationship on the appropriate side is optional. The roles a relationship plays are attached as labels.

The entity `Organization` models organizational units, such as departments, main departments, divisions, and so on. The relationship between organizations with the roles `is in` and `contains` reflects the hierarchical enterprise structure. When following the relationship with role `contains` for a given organization, one obtains all organizations that report to the organization; following the relationship with the role `is in` returns the organization to which the organization reports. The `Person` entity represents the individual employees of the company. The relationship with the roles `is manager` and `has manager` identifies the manager of an organization; the relationship with roles `contains` and `belongs to` identifies the members of the organizational unit.

The organizational structure is now populated with the appropriate data. Figure 2.5 shows a simple organization that uses the organizational elements shown in Figure 2.4. It shows the organization chart of a bank and represents the branch located in Annapolis. The branch is headed by F. Doolittle. The branch has the four departments: Marketing, Revision, Contracts, and Loans. Each of the departments has a number of people assigned to perform a particular role. The contracts department, for example, has three people that perform the role of financial officer.

Figure 2.5 Organization

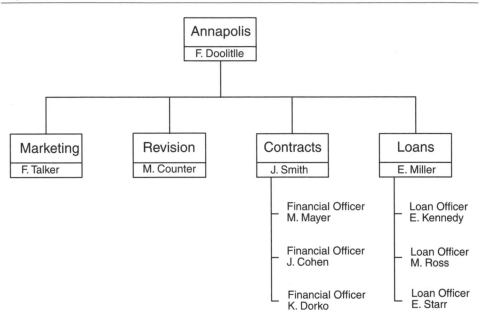

2.4   Information Technology Infrastructure

The third dimension that needs to be modeled is the information technology infrastructure. It presents, as we showed in section 1.5 on page 8, the *which* aspect of workflows; that is which tools and programs are used to perform the requested tasks. From a business engineering standpoint, the IT infrastructure includes the following pieces of information:

- The programs that are used by individual end users for processing activities. Also included are additional tools, called support tools by some workflow management systems, that a user can call on when carrying out a particular activity.

- Legacy systems, such as programs that reside on host systems, which are invoked either directly by the workflow management system without user interaction or by the end user.

- Databases with important data that can be accessed by the tools or legacy systems.

Other information that is important from a workflow management system perspective are the hardware and software structures that are used by the workflow management systems to carry out the processes, in particular:

- The distribution of the workflow management system to different processors

- The underlying network used by the workflow management system

This information is not essential for the basic modeling of business processes; however, it should be specified if the more advanced features of business engineering, such as simulation, are used.

2.5 Business Modeling Example

A large number of business engineering tools are available addressing the different needs and levels of sophistication of the users. Starting on the low end are tools that are no more than specialized drawing tools; they just help to document business processes and are used by specialists in departments or by consultants to sketch the basic structure of a business process. On the high end are business engineering tools that offer sophisticated modeling including simulation of business processes, interfaces to workflow management systems, and monitoring of business processes using the results produced by the workflow management systems.

In this section, we present screen shots of the business engineering tools ARIS Easy Design of Prof. Scheer GmbH and Workflow BPR from Holosofx Inc. The screen shots show how one would model the sample loan process.

2.5.1 ARIS Easy Design

ARIS Easy Design of IDS Prof. Scheer GmbH, a German-based company, is one of the company's products for business engineering. It offers simple modeling and model exploration through a Microsoft Explorer-style interface.

Figure 2.6 shows the sample loan process modeled in the tool. The star-like icon represents an event, in this case, the request for a loan. The desktop-with-a-person icon represents an office task; in the example, the Assess Risk or the Reject Credit activity. The associated person icons identify the role of the person that performs the appropriate task. Arrows between the individual tasks specify the flow of control and the business rules associated with each of the connectors. For example, the request approval task follows the collect credit information task immediately when the credit exceeds $10,000. The letter icon represents the output of the two final activities, that is a letter to the customer.

Figure 2.6 Loan Process Modeled with ARIS Easy Design

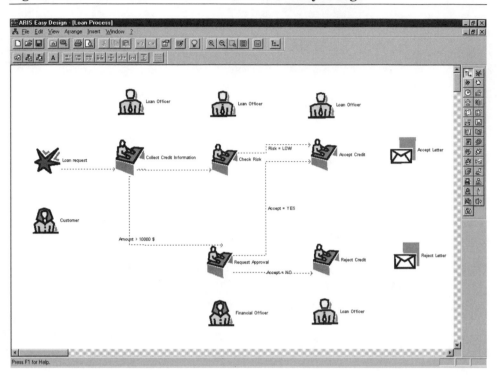

2.5.2   Workflow BPR

Workflow BPR is a business modeling tool developed and distributed by Holosofx, a California-based company. Figure 2.7 shows the loan process represented as an activity-decision diagram.

The individual activities are presented as squares with the edges cut off. Arrows indicate the flow of control from one activity to another. The possibility that the control flow can take two different paths is identified by the diamond-shaped decision icon. For each decision, the probability that a certain path is taken is collected and displayed. For example, the probability that the loan is approved at the Request Approval activity is 50% as reflected in the appropriate *Approved* decision with 50% for the Yes path. The probabilities are used later in simulating the behavior of the process. In fact, it is even later compared with the actual probabilities taken from the audit trail written by the workflow management system. The data connectors show the flow of data through the process; the data is identified by the diskette symbol.

Figure 2.7 Workflow BPR Example

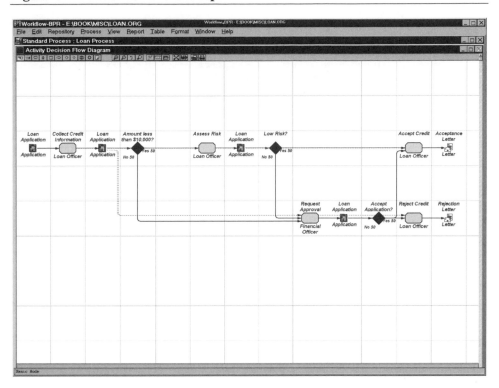

2.6 Business Process Reengineering

Companies that are getting involved in business engineering and moving to work-flow-based applications typically do not start from scratch. They have applications in place; these applications may be inflexible, but they work. The term *business process reengineering* refers to all actions that are performed to discover these business processes and to all actions performed in business engineering.

Customers are moving to workflow-based applications because of the typical problems with their existing applications:

- The applications were not static. They had to be changed time over time to accommodate new business or legal requirements. The rationale for the changes are very often not documented; it was or still is in the heads of the people responsible for the changes. Thus, it is extremely hard to make the appropriate changes in these applications.

- The control and the data flow of the underlying business process is deeply buried in the applications. Whenever a change needs to be made to the business process, the appropriate changes need to be made in those application programs.

The first task that needs to be performed in a business reengineering effort is to document the current business processes. Discovering existing business processes is a time-consuming and error-prone task. In the next section, we discuss the problems associated with this exercise and how workflow management systems can help in the discovery of current business processes.

The second task is to identify the problems associated with the business processes and to define a set of changes that should be made to these business processes. Changes to business processes could range from minor adjustments to a complete reimplementation of the business process.

M. Hammer and J. Champy had the latter change level in mind when they defined the notion of business reengineering in their famous book "Reengineering the Corporation" [HC94]:

> Reengineering is the fundamental rethinking and radical redesign of business processes to achieve dramatic improvements in critical, contemporary measures of performance, such as cost, quality, service, and speed.

They state that the typical simplistic approach of reimplementing the business processes with the aid of a workflow management system does not provide the desired improvements. If a business process was inefficient in the first place, it will continue to be inefficient even when moved to a more flexible environment.

To make sure that the specified goals of cost, quality, service, and speed are achieved, the business processes must be analyzed according to the proposed measurements before and after the processes have been deployed across the business. Naturally this is not only true for reengineered business processes but also for newly developed business processes.

The advanced functions in business engineering tools are geared to help solve exactly these problems. They provide analysis capabilities that can be used on business processes before they are deployed, and they provide monitoring capabilities that can be used after the business processes have been deployed. The number of ways of performing these tasks is manyfold. We limit ourselves to discussing a few of them, such as organization optimization, simulation, and monitoring.

2.7   Process Discovery

Modeling business processes, large business processes particularly, is an error-prone process, time consuming, and therefore costly. Whether the modeling is done as part of a business reengineering effort to understand the current structure of the business process or as an effort to define brand new business processes does not make a difference. As a result, enterprises are sometimes reluctant to spend a rather large amount of money for this effort without being sure that workflow technology will provide the benefits they are looking for. The reduction of the modeling costs and the ability to get results early in the project is thus desirable.

An inherent problem of reengineering business processes and, to a lesser extent, creating new business processes is the need to define a complete model of a business process before it can be transferred to a workflow management system for performing the business processes.

Users involved with the carrying-out of a business process usually have an in-depth knowledge about the tasks they have to perform themselves. They understand the tool or tools to be used, the data they are expected to enter, the output to be produced by the tool, and the assumptions for task completion. A business process modeler, can in general, easily obtain sufficient information about each task that is part of a business process by interviewing the appropriate people.

Most people involved in a business process however have little or no knowledge about the overall structure of the business process they are involved in. They typically know at most the activity or activities preceding their own activity and the activity or activities following their activity; that is they have only local information about the business process.

Determining the sequence of activities of an existing business process thus is a challenging and time-consuming task. Techniques such as interviewing the participants in a business process have to be used to collect local information. This local information is then transformed into the global information that then contains the overall structure of the business process, which is the global sequencing of the tasks within the business process.

Discovering the sequence of activities within a business process thus becomes an iterative process. The combined information needs to be discussed and verified with the involved people over and over again—one of the main reasons why this task is so time consuming. Even if agreement has been reached about the correct sequence of activities, it is still likely that the business rules associated with the flow of control from one activity to the next activity, the transition conditions, are in error. We have often observed, that it is difficult for business professionals to specify these transition conditions as correct Boolean expressions without any help—the second reason why process discovery is a time consuming and particularly error-prone task.

2.7.1 Discovery of Activity Sequences

The efforts associated with determining the correct sequence of the tasks within a business process can be greatly reduced by having the workflow management system help in determining the sequence. When the various tasks are carried out under the control of the workflow management system, those sequences can be automatically discovered, after an initial deployment phase, by applying mining technology to the data of the audit trail written by the workflow management system. Figure 2.8 illustrates the process described below.

Figure 2.8 Evolutionary Process Modeling via Process Mining

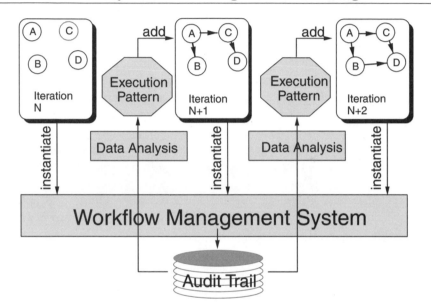

Obtaining sufficient data about the individual activities is not a problem. We start with this information and make those activities available to the workflow management system. For each activity, we define the programs that support the individual activities an define as the people who perform these activities. This set of unrelated activities is the first iteration of the particular business process. The initial process model just consists of a set of isolated activities ("discrete process model"). No information about sequencing of the activities is to be provided.

Next, this process model is made available to users, who can now start appropriate processes. When a process is started, the workflow management system schedules all activities having no predecessor. Since no activity has a predecessor in the first iteration of the model, all activities are scheduled. Scheduling refers to the action whereby all of the people who qualify to perform the associated task get a corresponding work request. A work request is called a *workitem*. Because users have local process knowledge, they will work on the activities applicable in the current situation. Based on this knowledge, users selectively perform activities by assuming responsibility for them and starting them. Triggered by the user, the workflow management system then launches the program that implements the activity. When an activity is completed, the workflow management system removes it from the list of work still to be performed for the subject process.

The workflow management system stores an entry into the audit trail for all relevant actions such as the start and completion of an activity. This entry contains all important information about the event, such as the type of event, the activity associated with the event, the input passed to the activity, the output produced by the activity, and the time the event occurred. As a consequence, the sequence in which the activities are performed is reflected in the audit trail. The audit trail also includes the context data that caused the business process to be carried out in a particular sequence.

After a certain period of time, the audit trail contains the sequences of activities and the corresponding context information for many business processes. The data can now be analyzed to find repeating patterns in the sequences of how the activities have been performed together. Patterns that occur rather frequently are very likely a reflection of a fraction of the underlying business process. These discovered fractions are then added to the current process model as a further step toward the final process model. This new process model forms the base for the next iteration step in discovering the underlying business process and replaces the current process model.

As Figure 2.8 suggests, this sequence of analyzing the audit trail and making appropriate changes to the process model is repeated until no further changes occur, at which point the full business process has been discovered.

2.7.2 Example

Figure 2.8 contains a simple example of how to derive a process model from the audit trail written by the workflow management system. We assume that there is a business process that contains four discrete activities.

As a next step, we put the process model into production and run it four times. The appropriate processes are named P1, P2, P3, and P4. For each of the processes, the workflow management system writes into the audit trail, the information about when each of the activities started and when it ended. From the audit trail, the complete information about each of the activities can be extracted. Table 2.1 shows the sample results that were derived. The time interval in which an activity is processed is determined for all activities. The time intervals are used to simplify the processing. The individual timestamps in the audit trail are simply translated into time markers, starting with 1 and increasing for each new timestamp.

We can now perform a simple analysis of the activities in the collected data. It is obvious that activities whose time interval overlaps must have been processed in parallel. If, for example, as shown for process P1, activity B is processed in the time interval (3,7) and activity C is processed in the time interval (4,5), then activity B and activity C have been processed in parallel. We collect those activities into a set of activities that we know are executed in parallel. The start time of the set is set equal to the earliest start time of an activity in the set; the end time of the set, to the latest end time of an activity in the set. Those sets are shown in Table 2.2 by curly brackets around the activities that are executed in parallel. For example {B,C} indicates that B and C are carried out in parallel. The activities in a particular process that do not overlap are sorted according to the start time of their time interval, which results in the sort order shown in Table 2.2.

Table 2.1 Activity Information Derived from Audit Trail

Process Model	Process	Activity	Interval
P	P1	A	1,2
P	P1	B	3,7
P	P1	C	4,5
P	P1	D	8,9
P	P2	A	1,3
P	P2	B	5,6
P	P2	C	4,6
P	P2	D	7,8
P	P3	A	1,3
P	P3	B	4,5
P	P3	C	5,6
P	P3	D	7,8
P	P4	A	2,3
P	P4	B	4,6
P	P4	C	5,6
P	P4	D	7,9

Table 2.2 Processing Order of Activities

Process Name	Instance	Precedence Relations
P	P1	A→{B,C} {B,C}→D
P	P2	A→{B,C} {B,C}→D
P	P3	A→B B→C C→D
P	P4	A→{B,C} {B,C}→D

Data mining technologies can now be applied to determine the patterns within the precedence relations. These patterns are then transformed in a straightforward manner into the process model that is shown in Figure 2.8 on page 44 as the result of carrying out process discovery.

2.7.3 Outlook

The previous example only indicates the basic type of analysis that can be performed. Much more detail could be derived through more advanced data mining functions. For example, using the context information could derive the transition conditions that are associated with the control flow, producing more details on the underlying business logic. Further information about the data mining algorithms that are used to discover process models can be found in [AGL98].

Data mining is not the only technology that can be used for analyzing the audit trail. When the audit trail is stored in a relational database, which is the case for many workflow management systems, other techniques, such as the online analytical processing (OLAP) functions offered by relational database management systems [Cha98], can also derive the appropriate process model structure.

2.8 Process Optimization

Optimal processes are characterized by minimal crossing of organization boundaries and a high level of parallelism. These properties allows the processes to be carried out as quickly as possible. A simple analysis that reveals the characteristics of a process can be done by drawing a process graph as seen from an organizational view. Based on this analysis, the number of steps can be reduced, as discussed below or the organization needs to be changed, as discussed in section 2.8.2.

2.8.1 Step Optimization

Staff assignment is typically expressed in organizational units, such as roles, departments, or levels. Business processes that often cross organizational boundaries tend to be inefficient because of changing responsibilities, long delay times, and so on. Diagrams that show which organizational unit performs which activity in which sequence allow the derivation of corresponding indicators. Figure 2.9 shows a graphical representation of such an activity sequencing.

It is quite obvious that the ping-pong type of control flow between role 2 and role 3 needs some further investigation. Unless there is a good reason for this kind of process logic, the process could be easily streamlined: combine A2, A4, and A6 into one activity or sequence of activities that is then carried out by role 2; combine A3 and A5 into one activity or a sequence of activities that is then carried out by

Figure 2.9 Unnecessary Steps in Process Model

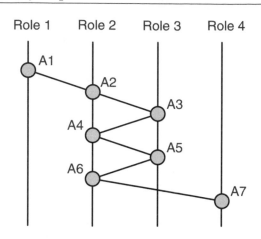

role 3. Note, that these actions often result in "streams" as discussed in section 7.3 on page 246.

2.8.2   Organization Optimization

If the structure of the organization is optimized for the process flow, then the flow of a business process is also optimal. Performing staff resolution to derive the selected persons in the appropriate organizational unit yields the flow of a process through an organization, as depicted in Figure 2.10.

Figure 2.10 Modifying Organizations for Optimal Processing

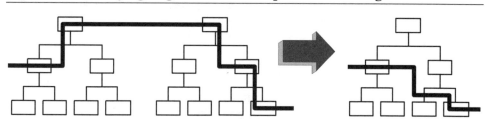

It is obvious that the process reflects the hierarchical structures of the organization. The two pieces of the organizations seem to be so disjoint and tightly controlled that any interorganizational request is channeled through the complete hierarchy before any action can be taken. By elimination of unnecessary organizational elements, as shown in the desired organization, the organizational structure is made much leaner. Thus the process can be executed much faster and with greater productivity.

2.9 Process Analysis

The analysis in the previous section—to determine how to optimize processes—was a simple static analysis of raw information gathered from the simple analysis of the process. This analysis does not take into account the quantitative aspects, such as the number of processes or the probabilities that certain paths are taken. It also does not generate any quantitative aspects, such as the amount of resources needed to carry out the modeled business processes. Nor does it consider the impacts of one process on another process when processes compete for human resources or computing resources.

This failure is rectified through simulation. An example of simulation in the context of business engineering is the determination of human resources needed to perform the business process, the skills needed to be able to handle the business process, and the costs associated with performing the process. This derived information allows the comparison of different ways of implementing a business process and determines by various metrics, the most effective one. Simulation in the context of business engineering does not look at whether the hardware or software is able to handle the expected load; we discuss this aspect in Chapter 11. From an overall perspective, this load-handling also needs to be taken into account when calculating the total costs for running the processes.

2.9.1 Instrumentation

Simulation requires the instrumentation of the process models. Instrumentation of a process means assigning values and probabilities to those pieces of the process model that cannot be deduced from the available information. The different types of simulation may sometimes require additional data, but the following information generally needs to be provided:

- The number of process that are created in a certain time frame must be assigned. For very accurate simulation, the distribution pattern, that is the probability distribution, for the creation of the processes must be specified. Typical distribution patterns are constant, exponential, or uniform. For a constant distribution pattern, the processes are created at a constant rate; for an exponential distribution pattern, values smaller than the specified mean value occur more often than greater values; uniform distribution produces a random value between a lower boundary and an upper boundary. For a formal discussion of various distributions, see [LK82]. In addition, it should be possible to specify customer-specific distribution patterns. For example, it could be that a business process is typically started in the periods from 9 a.m. to 11 a.m. and 2 pm. to 4 pm..

Figure 2.11 Instrumenting a Process

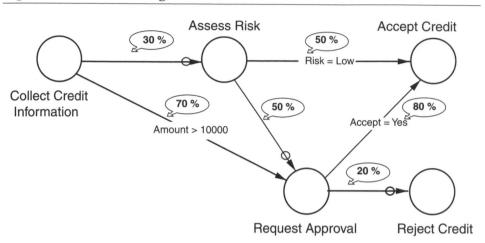

- Each control connector must be assigned a probability that it evaluates to true. The case that multiple control connectors may evaluate to true indicates parallel work, and therefore the sum of the probabilities exceeds 100 percent. The probabilities are specified as relative frequency or percentage of the activity from which the control connector starts.

- Each activity's exit and start condition must be assigned a probability that it evaluates to true. The exit condition is assigned a failure rate, that means how often the exit condition associated with an activity fails, so that the activity must be repeated. The start condition is also assigned a failure rate. If the start condition fails, the activity will not be executed and outgoing control connectors evaluate to false.

- Activities are performed through execution of the associated programs. The time to execute the program and the time it takes the user to enter the input data must be collected. The distribution pattern of the time needed to perform the activity needs to be specified as well.

Figure 2.11 shows only a subset of the instrumentation of our simple loan process; only the control connectors are instrumented. The percentages attached to the control connectors indicate the probability that the control connector path is being taken. It is assumed that the process is performed 1,000 times a week.

2.9.2 Simulation

Analytical and discrete event simulation are the types of simulation that determine the appropriate process statistics. These statistics are derived from the instrumentation information.

Analytical simulation uses mathematical methods to derive statistical information. It uses the basic probabilities assigned to the activities and control connectors to derive the number of times a particular activity is executed. This information allows one to calculate the probability that a process is carried out in a particular manner and to estimate the minimum length of time that it would take for the process to complete. Analytical simulation does not account for limitations in resources, such as other processes competing for the same person. It also does not address any variations that occur over time, such as the creation of processes. Thus, analytical simulation provides only an initial picture about the process statistics. The advantage of analytical simulation is twofold: it only needs limited instrumentation and can be performed very quickly without the need of massive compute power. Actually, there is no need to perform the more sophisticated discrete event simulation if the analytical simulation shows that the work load cannot be handled either by the human or by the computing resources.

Discrete event simulation simulates the behavior of a workflow management system that implements the metamodel used in the business engineering tool. This simulation includes navigation through the process as well as performance of staff resolution. It maintains all actions that need to be performed as events in a queue. These events include requests such as start a process, navigate to the next activity, or finish a process. Events are created as the result of processing an event or by daemons that, for example, create processes based on the specified distribution pattern. In addition, state information is kept for all resources, such as people, so simulation can account for business processes that compete for resources. Discrete event simulation thus supports all dynamic aspects of business processes. The downside of discrete event simulation is the amount of computing resources needed to perform the simulation.

2.9.3 Processing Statistics

In this section, we show in a simple example how the resources needed to perform a process and the associated costs can be calculated by analytical simulation.

From the probabilities shown in Figure 2.11 and the number of process instances, it is easy to calculate how often a particular activity is executed. Table 2.3 shows this information. Each activity is represented by a row. Each column entry indicates how often the activity is executed after the activity that the column represents.

Table 2.3 Activity Execution Frequency

	Collect Credit Info	Assess Risk	Request Approval	Total
`Collect Credit Information`				1000
`Assess Risk`	300			300
`Request Approval`	700	150		850
`Reject Credit`			170	170
`Accept Credit`		150	680	830

The table also shows that of the 1,000 started loan process, 83 percent are accepted as they reach the `Accept Credit` activity and 17 percent are declined as they reach the `Reject Credit` activity. Existing statistics could be used to determine whether this number is correct. If it is too far off, the probabilities assigned to the various flows must be wrong. The exact probabilities can later be derived from statistical analysis of the audit trail produced by the workflow management system.

Similarly, the table allows one to derive the probability of the different execution paths of a process model—in this simple example by multiplying the probabilities along the corresponding paths. This derivation provides a good estimation of how the process is typically performed. Table 2.4 shows the probability of the different types of process instances sorted by their probability.

Table 2.4 Process Path Probability

Rank	%	Number	Process Instance
1	56	560	`Collect Credit Information    -  Request Approval – Accept Credit`
2	15	150	`Collect Credit Information – Assess Risk – Accept Credit`
3	14	140	`Collect Credit Information    -  Request Approval – Reject Credit`
4	12	120	`Collect Credit Information – Assess Risk  -  Request Approval  -  Accept Credit`
5	3	30	`Collect Credit Information – Assess Risk  -  Request Approval  -  Reject Credit`

The next step is to determine the number of people that are required to perform the work associated with the processes. This task requires that for each activity the amount of time that is needed to perform it must be defined. Table 2.5 shows this value for each of the activities in the process, together with the roles that will be assigned to the activity. The role assignments have been previously specified for each of the activities.

Table 2.5 Activity Duration

Activity	Amount of Time	Performing Role
`Collect Credit Information`	10	Loan Officer
`Assess Risk`	5	Loan Officer
`Request Approval`	20	Financial Officer
`Accept Credit`	5	Loan Officer
`Reject Credit`	5	Loan Officer

2.9.4 Time Determination

The first thing that Table 2.5 allows us to do is to calculate the minimum processing time for each of the different ways that the process can be executed. Table 2.6 shows the processes ranked by elapsed time.

Table 2.6 Processing Time of Different Paths

Rank	Time	Process Instance
1	20	`Collect Credit Information  -  Request Approval - Accept Credit`
2	35	`Collect Credit Information - Assess Risk - Accept Credit`
3	35	`Collect Credit Information  -  Request Approval - Reject Credit`
4	40	`Collect Credit Information - Assess Risk - Request Approval - Accept Credit`
5	40	`Collect Credit Information - Assess Risk - Request Approval - Reject Credit`

2.9.5 Resource Determination

Again using Table 2.5, we now can determine the amount of total time that is needed for each of the activities. Table 2.7 summarizes the results.

Table 2.7 Activity Processing Time per Role

Activity	Number of Executions	Loan Officer Time (min)	Financial Officer Time (min)
`Collect Credit Information`	1000	10000	
`Assess Risk`	300	1500	
`Request Approval`	850		17000
`Accept Credit`	830	4150	
`Reject Credit`	170	850	
Total Process	1000	16500	17000
Average Process	1	16.5	17

From this information, we can determine how many loan and financial officers are required to perform the thousand weekly processes. Using a 40-hour week, we need seven full-time loan and seven full-time financial officers to the processes.

2.9.6   Cost Determination

We can further deduce from this information the people costs associated with running this process. These costs contain not only the salary being paid but also overhead costs such as rent for buildings or computers, the salary for employees not directly involved in the operation, and contributions to the health care and social security payments of the employees. Using the total hourly costs of $36 per hour for a loan officer and $54 for a financial officer, the costs for processing the individual activities and the total process can be calculated, as shown in Table 2.8.

Table 2.8 Activity Processing Costs

Activity	Individual Cost	Total Cost
`Collect Credit Information`	6	6000
`Assess Risk`	3	900
`Request Approval`	18	15300
`Accept Credit`	3	2490
`Reject Credit`	3	510
Total		25200

Thus, the execution of a single process costs $25.20 for personnel.

2.9.7 Graphical Representation

The previous examples presented information gathering as well as the analysis and the results in tabular form. We used this presentation to illustrate how the analysis is performed. In practice, all business engineering tools that perform any kind of analysis present their results in graphical form, such as pie charts or bar charts. Some of the business engineering tools are using some form of animation to illustrate the results. For example, they show graphically how money flows through the process graph or show how the size of the worklists of the users is growing or shrinking.

2.9.8 User Support

No business engineering tool can provide all reports or graphical representations that users want to see or produce. Most business engineering tools solve this problem by generating output files either in some proprietary format or in the format that is understood by standard data analysis tools, such as Microsoft Excel or Lotus 1-2-3.

2.9.9 Process Optimization

The determined information can now be used in the discussion of process alternatives for optimizing costs. As can be seen from Table 2.8, more than half of the costs are associated with approval that needs to be done by the financial officer. If we want to reduce process costs, the approval activity is the obvious starting point for redesigning the process.

This activity becomes a prime candidate to reduce the costs associated with running the process. It is obvious that reducing the number of business processes for which the approval activity is carried makes an impact. This reduction could be done by increasing the amount in the transition condition of the control connector that flows from the `Collect Credit Information` activity to the `Request Approval` activity, for example, by changing the amount from $10,000 to $20,000. Assume that 30 percent of all processes are for loans in the range of $10,000 and $20,000, the probability that the path between the `Collect Credit Information` activity and the `Assess Risk` activity is taken increases to 60 percent, and the corresponding probability that the path between the `Collect Credit Information` activity and the `Request Approval` activity is taken decreases to 40 percent. Further we give the loan officer more responsibilities to approve loans. This increases by 60 percent the probability that the path from the `Assess Risk` activity to the `Accept Credit` activity is taken, which in turn decreases by 10 percent the probability that the path from the `Assess Risk` activity to the `Request Approval` activity is taken. Using these new probabilities, we recalculate the costs and number of executions with the results shown in Table 2.9

Table 2.9 Optimized Activity Processing Costs

Activity	Number of Executions	Individual Cost	Total Cost
Collect Credit Information	1000	6	6000
Assess Risk	600	3	1800
Request Approval	640	18	11520
Accept Credit	872	3	2616
Reject Credit	128	3	384
Total			22320

Thus, the execution of a single process now costs $22.32 for personnel.

2.10   Business Engineering and Workflow

When business engineering for a business process has been completed, the next step is to actually implement the business process. This step can be done more traditionally by implementing everything, including the control and data flow in the programming language of choice. The more natural way of doing this, however, is to implement the business process as a workflow-based application using a workflow management system. This approach has, as we have discussed, so many advantages that the traditional approach should only be used under exceptional circumstances.

The information collected during business engineering is generally not sufficient for producing a workflow implementation of the business process. Additional information must be added so that the workflow management system can perform its tasks, such as carrying out activity implementations. The workflow management system also needs information such as setup parameters.

The boundaries between business engineering and workflow modeling are not clear-cut. Business engineering tools are pushing down into the original workflow space by adding functions such as simulation. Workflow management systems are pushing up into the business engineering space by extending their simulation capabilities with business related information such as cash flow. Sometimes, both the business engineering tool and the workflow management system offer the same function, just presented differently, for example, organization modeling.

Similarly, the boundary between workflow modeling and programming is also not clear-cut. Here workflow goes into the programming space. The constructs available for building process models are the typical ones found in a parallel programming or scripting language: sequential execution, parallel execution, subroutine calls, macros, and looping constructs. These constructs allow to continue the specification of a process model to a level of granularity that is equivalent to the instruction level in a program. Production workflow management systems are not designed and implemented to carry out large numbers of small activities efficiently. On the other hand, implementation should not be a major consideration when workflows are designed. Thus, workflow management systems may provide the capability to translate sets of small activities, including the invocation of the associated activity implementations, into a programming language and then compile the generated piece of code. When the business process is carried out, the workflow management system calls this piece of code instead of navigating through the individual activities. We discuss this approach in section 5.8 on page 206.

The workflow management system stores in its database all necessary information: the buildtime information, such as process logic, the organizational structure, or the information needed to execute activity implementations; and the runtime information, such as all information about business processes that are currently executed or users that are logged on to the workflow management system. This functionality makes the workflow management system's database a natural place to store the information that needs to be exchanged between the workflow management system and the business engineering tool. Figure 2.12 shows this information exchange.

Figure 2.12 Exchange of Information

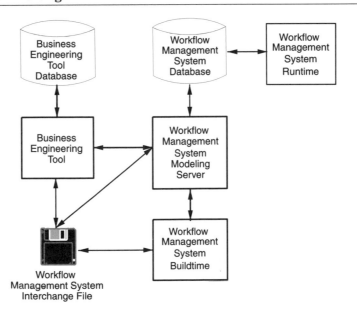

The buildtime information in the workflow management system's database is managed by a component of the workflow management system; we call this component the *modeling server*. It provides an API, which is used not only by business engineering tools but also the workflow management system components, that provides a GUI to model business process and other buildtime information. This API typically supports two types of operation: (1) direct access to the objects in the database, and (2) importing and exporting information as a file with the appropriate definitions in the workflow management system's proprietary process definition language. We discuss this API and the process definition language in detail in the next chapter.

After the engineering work on the process has completed, the workflow-relevant information is moved into the workflow management system's database. Typically this transfer is done by generating a file in process definition language and importing it into the workflow management system's database. The workflow management system's buildtime is now used to increment this information with required additional information. In the final step, the information is checked for completeness and then translated into some internal format for efficient use by the workflow management system's runtime facility. Now it is possible to start business processes.

When the information is exchanged between the business engineering tool and the workflow management system, information is typically lost for a simple reason: the metamodels of the business engineering tool and the workflow management system are different. The main reason that the metamodels are different lies in the very nature of the business engineering tool and the workflow management system. The metamodel of the workflow management system must be very precise. It must allow for the exact description of how the business process should be executed. The metamodel of the business engineering tool must be simple and easy to understand. Thus, mapping the constructs of the two different metamodels typically requires special treatment for each of the constructs. Some of the constructs map easily, whereas others cannot be mapped at all since they have different behaviors or they do not exist in the other metamodel.

2.11   Monitoring

During design of the business processes, certain assumptions were made, such as the number of processes that are created or the amount of activities that are carried out by each person involved in the business processes. These assumptions determined process characteristics such as the amount of time it takes to complete a business process.

It is important that the business processes are actually carried out according to these assumptions. To ensure that this is the case, the business processes must be monitored. It is the purpose of a process performance monitor to provide information about the status of the system either on demand or automatically, to issue alerts if out-of-line situations occur, and to provide facilities for a process administrator to perform the necessary corrective actions.

This information can then be presented in various formats. An interesting approach is to display the information in the form that is used in power plants or factories. All important factors, such as the number of processes carried out per hour, are presented on scales with green and red: green indicates that everything is running as expected; red indicates that problems are encountered. In such a case, the process administrator can dig deeper into the problems by looking at the structure of the process that caused the problems to be reported. Ideally, such a process presentation is provided in the format used when the business process was engineered with the business engineering tool or the buildtime component of the workflow management system.

All of the data that tools need for displaying or printing in the desired form is managed and provided by the workflow management system. We discuss this set of information in Chapter 3 in more detail.

Figure 2.13 shows how the workflow management system provides the required information so that the business engineering tool can display or print it in the desired form.

In the simplest form, the business engineering tool obtains the information from the audit trail that the workflow management system writes for all important events. The audit trail can be examined either by periodic queries via a workflow management system supplied API or, if the audit trail is managed in a relational database, by issuing SQL calls. When the audit trail is managed in a relational database that supports database triggers, an elegant method can be used: placing database triggers on the audit trail. Whenever a particular tuple is inserted into the audit trail, the trigger is invoked. The trigger analyzes the appropriate tuple that has been inserted and, based on its contents, in general selectively, sends an appropriate message to the business engineering tool.

Another form for the business engineering tool to obtain the information is via an API provided by the workflow management system. This interface can typically be used in two different ways: (1) the tool calls the workflow management system whenever it needs some information, either on demand or periodically or (2) it registers itself with the workflow management system via the standard callback mechanism and is invoked whenever the workflow management system encounters an event that is deemed to be significant.

Figure 2.13 Monitoring

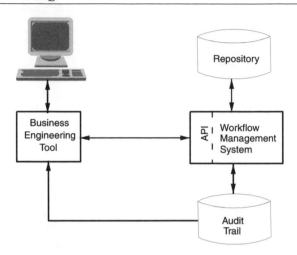

Chapter 3

Workflow Management System Basics

Chapter 2 discussed the basic structure of business processes as a combination of business logic, organizational structures, and information technology resources. It showed how business processes are designed and then handed over to a workflow management system for further refinement and deployment.

This chapter extends that information and discusses the structure, functions, and metamodel of a workflow management system in detail. To that end, we have divided the chapter into four parts.

The first part presents the buildtime component of a workflow management system. This component provides the functions that are available to define process logic, organizational structures, and information technology resources to the workflow management system. It also discusses the various ways this information can be gathered and entered into the system.

The second part provides a precise, yet informal, description of a metamodel. A formal description of the metamodel can be found in Chapter 4. The metamodel defines the constructs that are available to model process logic, organizational structures, and information technology resources.

The third part presents the structure and functions of the runtime component of the workflow management system, that is the component that runs the actual business processes.

The fourth part presents the standards published by the Workflow Management Coalition and shows how these standards protect user investment in process models and programs that interface with the workflow management system.

Figure 3.1 Major Components of a Workflow Management System

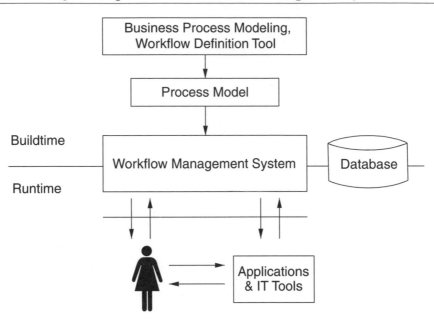

3.1   Main Components

We pointed out in the introductory chapter that workflow management systems are considered middleware. They follow a standard structure for middleware products such as relational database management systems. They consist of a set of components, shown in Figure 3.1. For ease of understanding, we relate them to the appropriate parts in a relational database management system.

- *Metamodel* defines the constructs and the associated functions that are supported by the workflow management system, such as the structure of a process model and the operations that can be performed on an instance of the process model. The equivalent in a relational database management system is the model of a table that consists of columns and rows and the SQL operations that can be used to operate on a table.

- *Buildtime* provides the functions to define user-specific constructs in terms of the metamodel. The constructs that can be defined are process models, organizational structures, and the information technology (IT) aspects, such as the programs that implement the activities of the process and the distribution of the workflow management system components across servers and networks. The relational database management system equivalents are the functions provided in the data definition language (DDL), such as `CREATE TABLE` for creating a table.

- *Runtime* performs operations on the user-defined constructs based on the operational semantics defined by the metamodel, such as creating processes, navigating through the process, or controlling the processes. The relational database management system equivalent are the functions provided by the data manipulation language (DML), such as `INSERT` for inserting a tuple into a table.

- *Database* holds all of the information that is managed by the buildtime and runtime components. It therefore contains not only the user defined constructs, such as process models, but also the instances of those constructs, such as the actual processes. The relational database management system equivalents are the database catalog and the user-defined tables that keep the appropriate instance data.

Another important component, which is not directly a part of the workflow management system but an integral part of the overall solution, are the applications and IT tools that are invoked and controlled by the workflow management system. The most important component in the overall solution, however, is the user who works with those applications and IT tools as well as communicates directly with the workflow management system.

3.2 Types of Users

A workflow management system is used by many different users performing different tasks. This diversity of users is typical for middleware and operating systems.

Most users carry out individual activities within a business process. We call those users *end users*. Their main work is to carry out the work assigned to them, such as collecting customer information or processing the request for approval in our simple loan process. Other tasks those users can perform are to transfer work from other users to them, to specify that they would like to receive work for somebody who is not in the office, or that they are not in the office so that no work is assigned to them.

The definition of process models, the organizational structure, and the information technology structure is carried out by *process modelers* or a *business analysts*. They are interested in whether the assumptions they have made when creating the processes are valid when the process is deployed and put into production. They are also interested in whether the processes are carried out as expected.

Process administrators are responsible for managing processes. Several methods can designate a person as process administrator: (1) explicitly specification when the process model is defined; (2) designation as process administrator for processes that fall into the same category; or (3) dynamic assignment as process administrator, based on values associated with a particular process. The process administrator is informed whenever something goes wrong with a process for which he is responsible, for example, when nobody is available to carry out a particular task or an activity implementation fails to execute. Appropriate functions allow the process administrator to take appropriate actions. Section 3.7 on page 106 discusses these functions.

Operation administrators are responsible for the correct operation of the workflow management system itself. They assist the system in adapting to changing needs, for example, by switching resources to adjust the number of user that work with the system.

System administrators have the overall responsibility for the correct functioning of the system. Privileges allow them to perform any needed functions. They serve as a backup when process or operations administrators cannot deal with a problem for any reason.

Customer support people help customers in their business with the company. They use information provided by the customer on a phone line, for example, to query the state of the customer's process, such as a claim, or to start a new process, such as an order.

External users, in general, customers, typically communicate with the workflow management system via a Web browser to perform the functions that are usually provided by the customer support people.

3.3   Buildtime

The buildtime component of the workflow management system provides the functions and capabilities to define, test, and manage all workflow-related information. The set of information includes all three dimensions of workflow: the process models, the organizational information, and the programs that are used to carry out the processes. All information is stored in the workflow management system's database.

In general, the buildtime component also provides functions to define and manage administrative and system-management-related information. Typical examples of this type of information are session-related information, such as the maximum amount of time a user can work with the workflow management system, or operational characteristics, such as the actions the workflow management system should take if the response time exceeds a defined limit.

The buildtime of a workflow management system usually manifests itself in two different ways. One way is the definition of the workflow information by means of a graphical end user interface, the other is by a proprietary or standardized (work)flow definition language.

3.3.1 Graphical User Interface

With the graphical user interface (GUI), process models are typically defined by placing the various activities as icons on the empty drawing area of the process model editor and then connecting the activities with arrows that represent the flow of control from one activity to the next. Staff is defined in the usual way of defining organizational data—with organization charts. Organization charts represent the reporting structure of the individual organizational units of a company. Typically, they also identify the manager of each organizational unit and the people assigned to each organizational unit.

Figure 3.2 shows the loan process as it would be presented in the modeling screen of the buildtime of MQSeries Workflow. The icons represent the individual activities, with the activity name written directly above the icon. The solid-line arrows represent the control connectors; the appropriate transition condition is shown attached to the control connectors. The data connectors are shown as dashed lines.

Figure 3.2 Building Processes Graphically

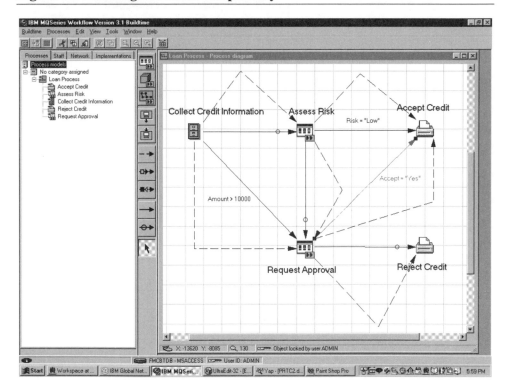

The graphical interface is the first thing that most users see of a workflow management system; thus, users erroneously associate this interface with the buildtime component of a workflow management system. Actually, most workflow management system vendors sell the GUI as the buildtime component. The buildtime is actually the application programming interface and import/export functions.

3.3.2   Flow Definition Language

A scripting language can also be used to provide information to a workflow management system. The language allows the easy exchange of workflow definitions, such as process models or organizational structures, between business engineering tools and workflow management systems, between the same workflow management system on different processors, or even between different workflow management system implementations.

MQSeries Workflow calls this language *flow definition language* (FDL); we adopt this name when talking about a workflow management system's scripting language. The Workflow Management Coalition uses the term *workflow process definition language* (WPDL). The language reflects the underlying structure of the metamodel. Each of the constructs, such as process model or persons, is identified by means of a keyword and must be given a name that uniquely identifies it. The different properties of the constructs are then further identified by a set of parameters and, optionally, a set of keywords. Constructs, parameters, and values are all identified by strings of characters. These definitions can therefore be manipulated with simple character editors that are available on all platforms.

It should be noted that this scripting language represents the underlying metamodel and not the GUI. This is simply because only a language can provide the necessary precision for nontrivial metamodels. Actually, the most precise way to describe the metamodel is by specifying it in mathematical terms. That is way we devote Chapter 4 to providing a rigorous treatment of the metamodel of a workflow management system.

Code Example 3.1 shows parts of the loan process in the proprietary flow definition language of MQSeries Workflow.

As can be seen, each of the major constructs (they start in the first column for easier reading) is identified by a keyword: PROCESS defines a process model, PROGRAM identifies a program that is being invoked by the workflow management system, ROLE identifies a role within the organization, and PERSON identifies a person that is involved in carrying out workflows. Each of the constructs has an associated name by which the individual constructs are later identified. The same name is used again, specified in the END statement that closes the construct. The process is called Loan Process, the two programs are Collect Credit Information Program and Assess Risk Program, the two roles are the Financial Officer and the Loan Officer, and the persons are MMayer and MRoss.

Code Example 3.1 Flow Definition Language

```
PROCESS  'Loan Process'

   PROGRAM_ACTIVITY 'Collect Credit Information'
     PROGRAM 'Collect Credit Information Program'
     DONE_BY 'Loan Officer'
   END 'Collect Credit Information'

   PROGRAM_ACTIVITY 'Assess Risk'
     PROGRAM 'Assess Risk Program'
     DONE_BY 'Financial Officer'
   END 'Assess Risk'

   CONTROL FROM 'Collect Credit Information'
     TO 'Assess Risk'

END 'Loan Process'

PROGRAM 'Collect Credit Information Program'
   WINNT
      EXE
         PATH_AND_FILENAME 'CCI.EXE'
END 'Collect Credit Information Program'

PROGRAM 'Assess Risk Program'
   AIX
      EXE
         PATH_AND_FILENAME 'AR.EXE'
END 'Assess Risk Program'


ROLE 'Financial Officer'
   RELATED_PERSON MMayer
END 'Financial Officer'

ROLE 'Loan Officer'
   RELATED_PERSON MRoss
END 'Loan Officer

PERSON MMayer
   FIRST_NAME Mike
   LAST_NAME  Mayer
END MMayer

PERSON MRoss
   FIRST_NAME Mary
   LAST_NAME  Ross
END MRoss
```

Constructs typically reference other constructs. The RELATED_PERSON in the role definition specifies which person holds which role(s). In our example, it shows that the role of Financial Officer is held by Mike Mayer and the role of Loan Officer is held by Mary Ross.

Constructs can be built from other constructs. This is obvious in the definition of the process. The process consists of a set of activities. As these are implemented by programs, they are defined by the PROGRAM_ACTIVITY keyword. These two activities are then implemented by the programs referenced from the PROGRAM keyword and are carried out by the roles specified by the DONE_BY keyword followed by the ROLE keyword. The flow of control between the different activities is then defined by the CONTROL FROM/TO keyword; in this case, control flows from the Collect Information activity to the Assess Risk activity.

3.3.3   Support of Modeling Tools

As we have pointed out, workflow modeling is typically performed with a graphical user interface. This tool can be a business engineering tool or the workflow modeling tool delivered by the workflow management system. As all information is managed in the workflow management system's database, those tools operate either in connected or in disconnected mode.

In connected mode, the tool does not have its own tool store but uses the database of the workflow management system. It retrieves data from the workflow management system, manipulates the information, and then stores it back into the workflow management system's database. For this mode of operation, it is therefore mandatory that the tool is always connected to the workflow management system. Another drawback of this operation mode is the fact that the tool operates directly on the workflow management system's database. Some of the tool's operations can be quite expensive in terms of operations against the database. For example, determining the staff during simulation of a process model may require extensive queries against the organizational structures. Because the runtime uses the same data when carrying out process models, the activities of the tool will have a negative impact on the performance of the runtime component: a situation that is not necessarily desirable. An partial solution is to establish a test and a production environment.

The intended interaction of a buildtime tool with the workflow management system, the disconnected mode, is shown in Figure 3.3. The modeling tool obtains the necessary information from the workflow management system and stores it in it's own tool store. The data in the workflow management system's database can be locked when the tool is obtaining it (*checkout*), so that no other user can modify this data in the database. The tool then operates on its own tool store without a need to be connected to the workflow management system. When the user is finished, the data is moved from the tool store to the workflow management system, releasing any locks that have been held (*checkin*).

Figure 3.3 Support of Modeling Tools

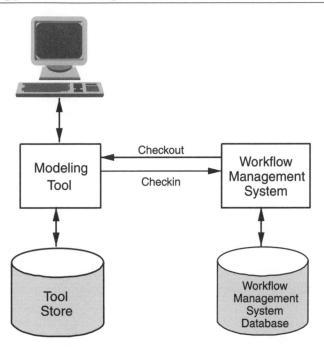

The disconnected mode solves all disadvantages that are associated with the connected mode: (1) it allows the tool to work completely independently of the workflow management system, something that consultants desire, and (2) manipulation of the information is much faster since the information is locally available. This mode of operation is the standard mode of operation in CAD systems, where engineers check out a particular part, such as a motor, make the appropriate design changes, and after days or even weeks, check in the new design.

3.3.4 Support by Line-of-Business Applications

A significant amount of information, such as organizational information, that is needed by the workflow management system is typically not provided by business engineering or workflow modeling tools. It is maintained by standard applications; personnel systems, for example, maintain all information about employees and the associated organizational information. Typically, all relevant changes to this information are made in this system. Since those systems generally have not been designed to support workflow management systems, periodic runs need to be made to extract the changed information and import it into the workflow management system's database. The extraction of data is usually done by a batch-oriented program because of the amount of data. As the data is extracted, it is usually converted into a flow definition language format and stored into a file. This technique makes the information easy to import into the workflow management system's database.

3.3.5   Putting Processes into Production

When a process model is put into production, the process model must be frozen. In this frozen state, a process model is called a *process template*. In the object-oriented world, it would be called a factory that creates processes. The *translate* function freezes a process model into a process template. Typically, the storage structures for efficiency of process execution, that is for the processing through the runtime of the workflow management system, are optimized. The process model storage structures are optimized for the buildtime, that is for easy modifications during modeling.

3.3.6   Application Programming Interface

Regardless of the mode of operation and the type of tool that interacts with the workflow management system, no application program has direct access to the workflow management system's database. The risk of damaging information with the inherent potential of rendering the database totally unusable is just too great. Even the buildtime tools delivered by the workflow management systems are normally not allowed to work directly against the database.

The buildtime component manages the workflow management system's database for all definitional data, such as process models or organizational information. It provides an API that can be used by any type of program to enter, modify, and extract information from the workflow management system's database. The API typically supports two different modes, *batch* mode and *interactive* mode. They are different in the way programs interact with them and in the way they are intended to be used.

In batch mode, the information is exchanged in the form of flow definition language. This mode is particularly useful when large amounts of data need to be imported into the workflow management system database or exported from it. When the interface is invoked for entering information, the flow definition language can either be supplied in a file or as a reference to some memory. When the data interface is invoked for exporting information, the flow definition language statements can be received in a file or in memory.

In interactive mode, the information in the database can be directly managed by the typical database functions—create, retrieve, update, and delete—against each of the different constructs. Because the operations are performed directly against the workflow management system database, the functions are intended to be used only on a limited number of objects. Typical examples would be the change of the properties of an activity within a process model or the addition of a new person.

3.3.7 Interactive Mode

In interactive mode, the application programming interface typically provides an object-oriented interface. Each construct is represented by an object; for example, a person would be represented by a `Person` object. Operations on these objects are to create the object, retrieve the object, update the object, delete the object, and relate the object to other objects.

Code Example 3.2 shows how an application uses the C++ form of the API to create a person in the database. First, an instance of the service that manages the objects is created, then an instance of the person object. The first action is to log on to the modeling service provided by the workflow management system. Then the attributes `FirstName` and `LastName` are set. Then, the service is asked to create the person. For simplicity, no return code checking is shown.

Code Example 3.2 Interactive API

```
APIRET rc ;
FmcjModelingService service ;
FmcjPerson person ;
rc = service.Logon ("userid","password") ;
person.FirstName ("Dieter") ;
person.Lastname ("Roller") ;
rc = service.CreatePerson(person) ;
```

Because there is often more than one person modeling information in the workflow management system database, such as other people working on process models, the buildtime must provide a mechanism to support the concurrent processing of the information in the database. This means that the buildtime must provide the capability to ensure that a user does not modify the information that another user relies upon when performing some modifications to the data in the database. An extreme case is the situation where a user performs some changes to a process model and another user deletes the process model in the meantime. To avoid this situation, the buildtime supports the notion of locks. Those locks can be placed on each of the major constructs, such as process models or persons. They are acquired or released by a user using the *lock* and *release* functions that are provided as methods for the objects that represent the constructs. If a user has put a lock onto a construct, only the holder of the lock can manipulate the construct or release the lock. Different lock modes provide flexibility for what other users can do with the construct; one such lock type makes the construct visible only to the lock holder.

For ease of modeling, constraints of process models are not immediately enforced by the buildtime. The *verify* function checks process models for correctness and completeness. The requester identifies the process model to be verified and is returned a list of all inconsistencies, such as incorrect mapping of data. These inconsistencies must be removed before the process model can be put into production, that is translated into a process template.

3.3.8 Batch Mode

Batch mode offers two functions: *export* to extract information from the workflow management system's database and *import* for entering information into the workflow management system's database.

Export

The export function extracts selected information from the workflow management system's database and makes it available as set of flow definition language statements. Which information should be selected is specified in a query passed to the export function as a parameter or as a set of queries specified as flow definition language. The queries are expressed similar to the SQL queries in a relational database management system. For example, the query `SELECT PROCESS WHERE CATEGORY = CONFIDENTIAL` extracts all process models that have been defined as confidential.

As an option, all constructs that are exported can be locked so that no other user can work with them in the meantime. Exporting with locking is provided by the *checkout* function. The checkout function is complemented by the *checkin* function.

Import

We described in the previous section how the flow definition language describes user-specific information such as process models or persons. This description is not sufficient for maintaining the workflow management system's database. As there is no interaction during importing of flow definition language statements, extra functions are needed to specify what should be done with a particular construct. Typically, the following functions needed which are specified as special keywords preceding the construct are needed. Figure 3.3 illustrates the use of the keywords.

- `CREATE`—Creates the construct in the database. A construct with the same identifier must not exist in the database.

- `INSERT`—Creates the construct in the database if a construct with the same identifier does not exist in the database; otherwise, updates the existing construct.

- `REPLACE`—Replaces an existing construct in the database and returns an error if the specified construct cannot be located.

- DELETE—Deletes the specified construct.

In addition, similar functions must be provided for the creation and deletion of relationships between different constructs, such as the relationship between a person and a role.

The flow definition language must also provide the functions to lock and unlock constructs.

When a file is imported, the complete set of flow definition language statements is processed in one database transaction. For large files in particular, this situation is undesirable. If the import is carried out when the runtime is active, then the database operations of the import function can impact the runtime, if the data (such as organizational data) is shared between the buildtime component and the runtime component. This situation occurs because as the import function puts data into the database, it obtains database locks on the data it is working with. As more and more database locks need to be held by the import function, the runtime will have problems accessing the database. The database locks are not released until the database transaction has completed. Another disadvantage is that the complete flow definition language file must be reprocessed if an error causes the import processing to terminate. Therefore, the import function must provide options to split the flow definition language stream into multiple pieces that are committed independently in the database. One option is the specification of a counter that indicates that after processing of a specified number of constructs, the database should be committed. Another option is to have a special keyword in the flow definition language that indicates when the processed constructs should be committed. Code Example 3.3 shows the contents of a file that is imported; the code example also illustrates the use of functions to modify constructs. Note the similarity to mini batches, a technique used for a long time to checkpoint large batch jobs.

Code Example 3.3 Import Transactions

```
LOCK    PERSON MRoss
SELECT  PERSON MRoss
UPDATE  PERSON MRoss
UNLOCK  PERSON MRoss
DELETE  PERSON MMayer
COMMIT
CREATE  PROCESS 'Loan Process'
```

The figure shows that the person MRoss is locked before it is retrieved from the database. No other user can now obtain or modify this person record. After the person record is updated, the lock is released. Note there is no need to lock a construct before an operation can be carried out. It is therefore not necessary to lock the person MMayer before it is deleted. The keyword COMMIT commits the changes to the database.

For ease of use, the combination of import and unlock is provided as a separate function *checkin*. This function complements the *checkout* function.

3.4   Metamodel Overview

The metamodel is made up of constructs that are available to users to model their environment, such as process models, organizational structures, or the topology of the workflow management system. See Chapter 4 for a more detailed and more rigid discussion of the process model aspects of the metamodel.

3.4.1   Organization

The activities of a workflow can be categorized by the way they are carried out. Manual activities are assigned to people and are activated upon an explicit request from a person. Automatic activities are typically performed by the system without any user interaction. However, regardless of how the activity is carried out, it is usually performed on behalf of a user. This is carrying out on behalf of a user is often required for security or accounting purposes.

This behavior requires that the name of the users that should carry out a particular activity must be specified in the business process. This name must also be defined in the workflow management system so that the system can work to the user.

The big disadvantage of specifying users explicitly in the business process is that it requires a change of the business process whenever the responsible person or the duties of the responsible person change. Thus, it is better to express the assignment of people to activities in organizational terms, such as roles, departments, or positions. Instead of specifying that Mary Mayer should perform the job, one would specify that a financial officer must do it. When an activity is carried out, the workflow management system determines who holds the job of a financial officer and assigns the work to the selected person. If Mary Mayer is in this position today, she gets the work. If Mary moves out and is replaced by Joe Smith, at that very moment, Joe gets the work assigned.

It is not just the organizational units that the workflow management system needs to know about. It also needs to know about the relationships between the different organizational units and the persons within these organizational units. For example, if a business process has an activity being carried by a person and the next activity being carried out by the person's manager, then the appropriate organizational information must be maintained in the workflow management system. This information is needed to allow the workflow management system to deduce the manager of a person. In the organizational structure we presented in Figure 2.4 on page 37 the organizational unit a person belongs to is determined by following the member relationship, then from the organizational unit, following the is_managed_by relationship to the appropriate person who is the manager.

The structure of the organization is described by instantiating the organization model. This model is usually described as a set of entities and relationships, as shown in Figure 2.4 on page 37, which illustrates the organization metamodel built into MQSeries Workflow. Different workflow management systems implement different organization metamodels with different levels of sophistication.

A workflow management system can support a fixed organization model or a variable organization model. In a fixed organization model, the different entities and relationships between the entities are fixed and cannot be changed. If the workflow management system supports a variable organization model, one can change the organization model (the metamodel) or even create a complete new model. The underlying datamodel used to model the organization metamodel could be an entity/relationship model, an object oriented model, or any other type of metamodel typically used to describe databases. It would allow process modelers to build any type of organization model they need to. In general, the underlying metamodel could provide specializations for constructs that are typical in modeling organizational structures. An example is the reports_to relationship that helps to establish reporting paths in organizational structures.

Another distinguishing feature is whether the workflow management system itself manages the organizational data. Three cases can be differentiated:

1. The workflow management system manages all organizational data in its own database.

2. The workflow management system shares the data with other systems, and each of the systems can modify the shared data.

3. The workflow management system only accesses organizational data that is managed by some other system.

Each of the approaches has its advantages and disadvantages, where in general the advantage of one approach is the disadvantage of the other approach.

In previous discussions of buildtime, we have assumed that the workflow management system manages the organizational data in its own database. In this case, the workflow management system uses the first approach. The disadvantages of the approach are a possible duplication of data that already reside in other systems (see section 3.3.4 on page 69) and if so, the possibility that the data gets out of sync. However, the first approach offers also a set of advantages:

- The data in the workflow management system's database can be optimized for the workflow management system so that only the data that is needed by the workflow management system is maintained in the database. This data then can be maintained in storage structures that are optimized for the workflow management system.

- There is no impact on other systems that own or share the data.

- The workflow management system itself is, for efficiency, installed on various processors in the distributed environment. One instance of the workflow management system might be installed in Tokyo; another instance of the workflow management system might be installed in New York; and a third instance in Berlin. However, all three instances together however form a single workflow management system, so it is beneficial if all three instances have their own identical copy of the organizational data. The access to the organizational data is through local accesses and very efficient.

- The buildtime tools either supplied by the workflow management system itself or furnished by independent vendors have easy access to the organizational data when performing simulation.

The use of a directory is prototypical for the second approach. All data, such as users and departments, are maintained in the directory. Information is accessed by means of via the standard directory protocols, such as the lightweight directory access protocol (LDAP). The advantage of this approach is that all systems share the same data. For example, information about a user is maintained only in one location and that data does not need to be copied over to the workflow management system.

The advantage of the third approach is also, as with the second approach, that the data must not be copied over to the workflow management system.

The typical disadvantage of approaches 2 and 3 is performance. It takes longer for the workflow management system to access data in a distributed environment when the accessed system does not provide for distribution.

Another problem arises for approaches 2 and 3 if the metamodel of the workflow management system is different from the metamodel of the system that holds the organizational data. This will unfortunately be true in most cases unless the workflow management system has been designed to be tightly integrated with the system that manages the organizational data. Thus, in the approaches where the organizational data is held by another system, the workflow management system in general must know how to dynamically map its own organizational metamodel to the metamodel of the system that holds the organizational data. Note that if the workflow management system holds the organizational data, this mapping must is done only when the data is moved from a system into the workflow management system.

The main use of the organizational data in the workflow management system is to perform staff resolution, that is to determine for the individual activities which user(s) the task should be assigned to. This is typically expressed as a query against the organizational data. If the workflow management system manages the organizational data, the query can be directly carried out by the workflow management system. If the workflow management system does not maintain the organizational data, then the workflow management system has to map the "staff query" to the query language of the system that maintains the organizational information.

There are at least three ways of mapping this query to the metamodel of the system that holds the organizational data.

The first method is to provide a staff resolution exit. Whenever the workflow management system needs to determine the staff that should perform a particular activity, it invokes the staff resolution exit. The staff resolution exit then invokes customer-supplied code that performs the appropriate staff resolution. Upon completion, the customer code must return to the workflow management system a set of users that qualify. The customer code can perform any type of operation. Actually, this would require that the workflow management system's metamodel just knows about users and nothing else. Code Example 3.4 shows how staff resolution for the `Assess Risk` activity is carried out by a staff resolution exit. The staff resolution exit is named `User Resolution` and is defined to the workflow management system as any other program. When called, the workflow management system passes the staff query `Role = 'Loan Officer'`. Upon completion, the staff resolution exit returns a set of users. The workflow management system then generates workitems for these user.

Code Example 3.4 Performing Staff Resolution via Staff Resolution Exit

```
PROGRAM_ACTIVITY 'Assess Risk'
    DONE BY EXIT 'User Resolution'
        USING 'Role = '''Loan Officer'''
END 'Assess Risk'
```

The second mapping method is to have some mechanism that maps the workflow management system's metamodel to the other metamodel. This approach only works if the metamodel can be mapped at all, so the applicability of this approach is limited. In addition, even if the metamodels can be mapped, the method requires tool support, either delivered with the workflow management system or generally available, to create the mapping of the workflow management system's requests to requests against the system that holds the organizational data.

A third method can be applied if the metamodel can be expressed as a subset of the metamodel of the system that holds the organizational data, and the workflow management system can directly access the organizational data. For example, the organizational data is stored in a relational database management system, and the workflow management system's metamodel can be defined to the relational database management system as views on the organizational data.

Workflow management systems may actually choose to support all three approaches to provide the greatest level of flexibility to customers. In particular, a interesting combination includes the usage of a directory to maintain user data.

3.4.2   Process Model

Over the years, several methods have been developed to allow the description of process models. The most common one now is that of a process graph. It underlies the workflow management system products of IBM's MQSeries Workflow and the built-in workflow management systems in SAP R/3, for example. The reason for making process graphs the premier method lies in its simplicity on one hand and its expressive power on the other hand. For this reason, we used process graphs in the preceding chapter when we talked about business engineering.

In the preceding chapters we outlined the basic constructs in defining process models. The structure of a process model is a set of activities, control connectors, transition conditions, input containers, output containers, and data connectors. In this section, we not only refine the constructs that we have discussed so far but also add new ones that are important for workflow-based applications. For a detailed discussion of the constructs, see Chapter 4.

Containers

All processes and all activities are associated with context. Context is defined as the data that is passed to the process or activity when invoked. A process or an activity can also return data. The data that is passed to the process or activity is called the *input container*; the data that is returned by a process or activity is called the *output container*.

The process input container typically provides the overall context of a business process. It determines how a specific business process should be executed by defining which paths should be taken through the business process. For a loan process, for example, the process input container contains the number of the customer who requests a loan. The activity input container provides the appropriate context for the execution of the activity; for example, let's say that the input container provides a customer number. The customer number could be used by the program that implements the activity to access the customer database and retrieve all information associated with this customer number. The activity would then return the appropriate information in the output container. The output container can then be used by later activities or to further define which paths should be taken by the business process.

Each container is associated with a data structure. These data structures are defined separately from the container so that they can be used in different containers. A data structure represents a semicomplex object. The basic building blocks are fields that represent the basic types, such as String, Binary, Float, or that reference another data structure. These basic blocks can then be further aggregated, such as in an array of the same field or a set of different fields. Aggregations can be further aggregated, building structures like sets of arrays. Section 4.2 on page 122 provides an extended discussion of containers and their structure.

Sequencing Activities

The major constructs in drawing processes are activities and control connectors. The activities describe the tasks to be performed, and the control connectors describe the potential sequence in which the activities are to be carried out. Figure 3.4 shows schematically the structure of such a process graph.

Figure 3.4 Defining the Sequence of Activities

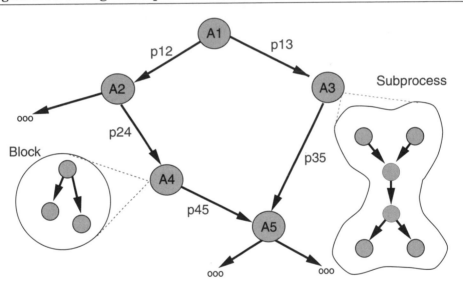

Activities are represented as named circles; the name typically describes the purpose of the activity. Activities come in various flavors to address the different tasks that may need to be performed. They may have different activity implementations to meet these diverse needs. *Program activities* are performed by an assigned program, *process activities* are performed by another process, and *blocks* implement a macro with a built-in do-until loop. We discuss the different activity types shortly in more detail.

Control connectors are represented as arrows; the head of the arrow describes the direction in which the flow of control is moving through the process. The activity where the control connector starts is called the *source* activity; where it ends is called the *target* activity. When more than one control connector leaves an activity, this indicates potentially parallel work. Control connectors must not point backward; that is they must not form loops. Depending on how that backward loop is drawn, there may be associated situations whose side effects are difficult to understand (so-called race conditions). Mathematicians call a graph whose arrows just point in one direction a *directed* graph, and a graph that does not allow cycles is called an *acyclic* graph. Thus, we are dealing with a *directed acyclic graph* or *DAG* for short.

An activity from which multiple connectors leave is called a *fork* activity; an activity that is the target of multiple control connectors is called a *join* activity. Activities that have no incoming control connector are called *start* activities. Activities that have no outgoing control connectors are called *end* activities.

Processing of the process graph is generally called *navigation*. It starts with the processing of the start activities. After an activity has been processed, navigation continues by following the outgoing control connectors.

As shown in Figure 3.4, each of the control connectors is associated with a Boolean predicate; p12, for example, is such a predicate associated with the control connector between A1 and A2. This Boolean predicate is called *transition condition*. The condition is stated as a boolean expression where the variables within the expression are fields in the process input container and the containers of activities. Figure 2.3 shows some typical transition conditions; for example control passes from the `Collect Credit Information` activity to the `Request Approval` activity if the amount of the loan is greater than $10,000.

When the transition condition of a control connector evaluates to true, the flow of control follows this control connector to the target activity. When the transition condition of a control connector evaluates to false, the flow of control does not follow this control connector. In this case, if the target activity is not a join activity, it is not carried out and all outgoing control connectors of the target activity evaluate to false.

If the target activity is a join activity, navigation stops at the activity until all incoming control connectors have been evaluated; that means they have an assigned value of true or false. Thus, a join activity is, by definition, a synchronization point. When all control connectors have entered the join activity, the *join condition* of the activity is evaluated. This join condition determines whether the activity should be carried out or not. It is expressed in terms of the truth value of the incoming control connectors. A simple form is to specify whether all incoming control connectors must be true or whether it is sufficient that at least one of the incoming control connectors evaluates to true. If the join condition evaluates to true, the activity is carried out. If the start condition evaluates to false, the activity is not carried out and all outgoing control connectors evaluate to false.

The process of skipping an activity and flagging the outgoing control connectors as false is repeated until navigation halts or control has reached an end activity. This process is called *dead path elimination*. It ensures that the process will eventually terminate. A process has finished when all end activities have been reached. An end activity is considered to be reached if it has either been carried out or skipped. A formal treatment of navigation and the aspects of dead path elimination can be found in section 4.7 on page 162.

Mathematicians call a graph that has properties (weights) associated with the arrows a *weighted* graph. The graph that we are using to describe process models is therefore a *weighted directed acyclic* graph.

Making Data Available

Processes and activities have containers associated with them. These containers are only locally available and not available globally. Thus, the input container of an activity is only available to the appropriate activity. If another activity needs data from a previous activity's output container or from the process input container, this data must be made available to the activity by copying the information from the other containers. Specifying which data needs to be copied from where is the purpose of *data connectors*. Figure 3.5 shows how data is copied from the output container of one activity to the input container of the next activity.

Figure 3.5 Copying Fields Between Activities

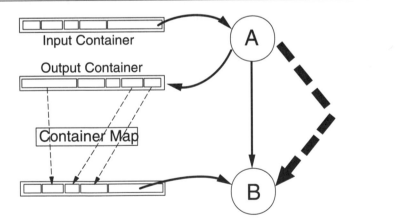

The dashed arrow is the data connector. It indicates that the output container of activity A should be copied to the input container of activity B. The output container of an activity is typically different in structure as are the contained fields from the input container of another activity. Fields may have different names and different types. Thus, the simple specification of a data connector is not sufficient; it is also necessary to specify the appropriate container map. This map specifies which field from the output container is used to fill a field in the input container. The map also specifies what data transformation is to be performed, if any, before the data is stored in the input container.

Data connectors can not only be drawn between the output container of one activity and the input container of another activity but can also be drawn between the input container and the output container of the same activity. This makes it unnecessary for the activity implementation to copy values from the input container to the output container even if the activity implementation has no need for the fields.

Another method of making data available is by specifying default values for fields in the input and output container. This method addresses the problem that arises when the source field has no value.

Enabling Queries

Customers often want to inquire about the status of a particular business process, such as the order they had placed a while ago. In the past, companies have established call centers where the customer would talk to a customer representative to find out the status of the order. The customer would then supply a set of properties that were associated with the business process, such as the order number or the customer name. The customer representative used this information to make the appropriate query against the system and find the appropriate status. This functionality is now more and more delivered by the Web.

To support this function, appropriate data must be associated with each business process. The inquiry may be on data that is supplied when the process is started or collected during the carrying-out of the process. This support is provided by allowing the specification of *key data container* and supporting the appropriate queries against it. The key data container is filled by mapping fields in input and output containers to the appropriate fields in the key data container.

The Inner Details of Activities

Activities describe the actual work that needs to be performed. Figure 3.6 shows the inner details of an activity and indicates what is being done in the individual parts of an activity.

The *query on organization database* and *proper implementation* form the core of the activity.

The query against the organization database specifies in organizational terms who should carry out the activity. Since people in the organization are typically called staff, this query against the organizational database is also called a *staff query*. When the activity is ready for processing, this query is carried out and returns a set of users that are assigned to the activity. The process of finding the appropriate people is called *staff resolution*.

The proper implementation specifies what is used to carry out the activity and how it is to be carried out. The implementation could be a program that is executed or another process that is invoked.

Figure 3.6 Fine Structure of Activities

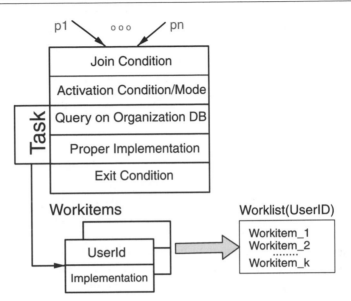

The combination of the proper implementation and the query against the organization database is called a *task*. When the activity needs to be carried out, staff resolution returns the list of users that need to be assigned to the activity. Multiple users are selected for an activity, on the theory, that the more people know that a work request requires their action, the more likely it is that the work request is performed soon. The workflow management system ensures that only one user performs the requested work. The workflow management system then builds for each user a *workitem* consisting of the user identification and the proper implementation. As user then uses the workitem to launch the appropriate implementation. Facilities provided by the runtime allow the user to organize workitems with the same characteristics into *worklists*.

The other three properties of an activity are conditions. These conditions specify when the activity is to be carried out, how the activity and thus the implementation are carried out, and how often the activity is invoked.

We already discussed the join condition as a means of specifying when a join activity can be started. The approach we have taken so far is to treat the join activity as a synchronization point and have only a simple start condition. A more powerful form of join conditions that eliminates these limitations is discussed in section 5.3 on page 191.

The *activation condition* specifies when the activity actually should be activated. It is a Boolean expression. When it evaluates to true, staff resolution takes place and workitems are generated. An example of using activation conditions is to make sure that an activity is not started before 6 p.m. to avoid a possible heavy impact on more critical work. The *activation mode* defines whether the start of the activity should *manual* or *automatic*. When defined as manual, the activity must be started manually by the assigned user, usually by double-clicking an appropriate icon on the worklist. When an activity is defined to be started automatically, the activity is started immediately, causing the activity implementation to be launched right away. Typically, automatic activities have no user interaction. Processes that consist solely of activities that are started automatically and have no user interaction are similar to batch jobs.

The *exit condition* is used to control when an activity really has completed. The exit condition is a Boolean expression that can reference fields in the output container plus a special return code field. The return code field can be used by the activity implementation to set an appropriate return code. This return code would indicate whether the activity implementation has executed successfully or whether it needs further processing. When the exit condition evaluates to true, navigation continues; when it evaluates to false, the workitem is put back onto the user's worklist so that it can be started again. A typical example where an exit condition is quite helpful is the writing of a letter. For example, if a user wanted to go to lunch before finishing the letter, the user would exit the editor in such a way that the editor sets the return code so that the exit condition fails. This failure causes the workitem to appear on the worklist again, allowing the user to continue to work on it later. This behavior is possible since the workflow management system remembers the state of all workitems. The exit condition can therefore control when the work is finished. It controls the *semantic* success of the work. See section 4.3.4 on page 134 for an in-depth, formal treatment of exit conditions.

Mathematicians call a graph that has properties (colors) associated with the nodes a *colored* graph. The start, activation, and exit condition are properties of the activities, the nodes of the graph. Thus, the conditions color the graph. The graph that we are using to describe process models is therefore a *colored weighted directed acyclic* graph. Chapter 4 describes in precise mathematical terms exactly what this means.

Running Activities

When an activity is carried out, the proper implementation is invoked. Figure 3.7 shows the typical execution of a program activity. It is assumed that the activity is a manual activity, that is it must be started by a user.

When the user clicks on a workitem on one of his worklists (**1**), the workflow management system builds the input container for the activity (**2**): in a first step, the default values are inserted into the container; in a second step, all incoming data connectors are processed and the appropriate mappings are performed. Then, the workflow management system invokes the program (**3**). The program obtains the

Figure 3.7 Running an Activity

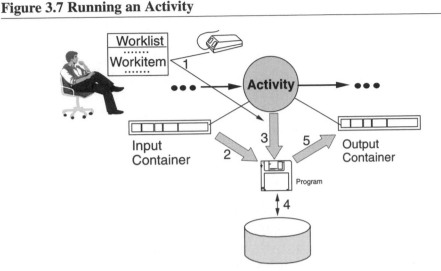

necessary information from the input container (**2**), performs the necessary actions such as interacting with the user or accessing a database (**4**), puts any new values into the output container (**5**), and then returns to the workflow management system. The workflow management system evaluates the exit condition; if the exit condition evaluates to true, navigation continues. If the exit condition fails, the workitem reappears again on the worklist so that the user can continue the activity later.

If the activity is an automatic activity, the same actions are performed by the workflow management system. However, the activity implementation is started automatically. If the exit condition fails, the workflow management system generates a workitem for the user on whose behalf the activity was carried out, allowing the user to take the appropriate actions.

Different Types of Activities

Activities come in different flavors. Each of the flavors serves a different purpose.

The simplest activity type is one that has no implementation at all. Its main purpose is to inform users that they should take certain actions such as to call a customer. We call this type of activity, for obvious reasons, an *information activity*.

An activity type that is implemented by a program is called a *program activity*. To provide for flexibility, the program itself is defined separately; thus the process modeler does not need to deal with the characteristics of the program that implements the activity. We discuss this later in section 3.4.4.

An activity type that is implemented by a process is called a *process activity*. The process is then called a *subprocess*. In general, the subprocess is invoked and the process waits until the subprocess completes; however, there are other ways that processes are connected to each other. We discuss this later in section 3.4.3.

Sometimes an activity needs to be executed multiple times. A typical example of this type of activity occurs in processes associated with the development of software. The driver build process, that is the process to build a software executable, typically contains an activity `Compile`. The intent of this activity is to compile all modules that need to be recompiled because they have been changed. In this case, the activity `Compile` needs to be performed as many times as there are modules that require recompilation. Thus, the implementation of the activity, the compiler, should be invoked multiple times where each invocation is for one of the modules. Preferably, these different invocations (compilations) should be handled in parallel. This special handling is the purpose of the *bundle activity*. The bundle activity conceptually consists of two phases: the planning phase and the processing phase. The planning phase determines, based on data supplied in the input container, how many instances of the activity implementation need to be scheduled and prepares the appropriate input container for each of the invocations. The processing phase then schedules the invocation of the implementation, which can be a program or even a process. When the implementations have completed, the processing phase combines the individual output containers into the output container of the bundle activity.

Since the process model is a directed graph a loop can not be drawn. The *block activity* provides this functionality. The block activity contains a single activity or a process graph. When the activities in the block have completed, the exit condition of the block activity is evaluated. If it evaluates to false, the block activity is restarted with the start activities within the block. Thus, the block activity conceptually implements a DO-UNTIL loop. This construct makes a backward control connector superfluous, which is the programming equivalent of the GOTO statement. We know from structured programming that there is no need for a GOTO statement as long as there are the IF-THEN-ELSE and the DO-UNTIL constructs.

Meeting Deadlines

For most business processes, it is important that they be carried out in a certain time, either for legal reasons or to meet some company-specified, quality-of-service goals. The workflow management system provides a facility that makes sure that the processing of a process does not stop without being noticed. The workflow management system allows the modeler to specify time limits at the process or activity level. Actions can be specified that should be taken when the specified time limit is exceeded. The typical action is to notify somebody so that appropriate corrective actions are taken; some workflow management systems therefore call this facility *notification*. Code Example 3.5 shows the specification of such a notification facility for the `Request Approval` activity in the loan process.

Code Example 3.5 Informing the Manager

```
PROGRAM_ACTIVITY RequestApproval
   DURATION 2 DAYS
      WHEN EXCEEDED NOTIFICATION TO MANAGER
      SECOND_NOTIFICATION 2 DAYS
END RequestApproval
```

Two days after the work has been scheduled for one or more users and has not been completed, the manager is informed. If the manager has not made sure that the work completes within the next two days, a second notification is sent to the process administrator.

Another option is to just ignore the activity and treat it as expired.

Managing Errors

A large number of errors can occur when a process is executed: an activity implementation can return wrong data in the output container, the implementation of an activity cannot be located, or a user is not authorized for an activity implementation. The workflow management system uses a set of default actions to cope with these situations, such as flagging the activity as *inError* and informing the process administrator so that appropriate corrective actions can be taken. However, it may be sometimes desirable in a specific situation, or even in general, for a whole process model to override the workflow management system's default behavior. Code Example 3.6 shows such a specification on the activity level: if the activity implementation is not found, a message is sent to the operator of the workflow management system.

Code Example 3.6 Overwriting the Default Error Actions

```
PROGRAM_ACTIVITY RequestApproval
   ON_ERROR
      WHEN PROGRAM_NOT_FOUND
         NOTIFICATION TO OPERATOR
END RequestApproval
```

3.4.3 Subprocess

A subprocess can be carried out by the workflow management system that controls the process from which the subprocess is spawned. Such a subprocess is called a *local* subprocess. If the subprocess is processed by another workflow management system, regardless whether it is from the same vendor or from a different vendor, the same operating system platform or a different one, it is called a *remote* subprocess.

Several models define how a subprocess behaves with respect to its parent process. In general, these are the same models we find in regular programming. The Workflow Management Coalition has coined particular names for them, which we use when describing their properties.

Autonomy

A subprocess is a process in its own rights. It is derived from a process model that has been defined independently; that means it can be carried out as process in its own right. Even when executed as a subprocess, it executes independently of the parent process that created it.

Typically, autonomy rules define the rights the parent process has for the subprocess. It spans the whole spectrum from the subprocess being absolutely autonomous to the subprocess being totally controlled by the parent process. For example, if the subprocess is completely autonomous, actions such as terminating the parent process do not affect the subprocess.

Connected Discrete

In this model, the connected discrete, an activity within a process A connects to an activity in another process B. The execution of the appropriate activity in process A causes the creation and start of process B. Both processes operate independently of each other with no synchronization between the two processes. For obvious reasons, this model is also called a *chained* services model.

Figure 3.8 shows that end activity A5 causes the creation of process B. Whereas this may be a typical case, it is not required that the process is started from an end activity; any one of the activities of process A can start the subprocess.

Figure 3.8 Connected Discrete Model

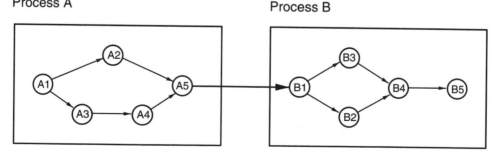

Hierarchical

In this model, the hierarchical, an activity within a process A represents the execution of another process B. The execution of the activity causes the creation and start of process B. Processing of the activating activity is suspended until process B terminates. After control has returned, navigation through the process graph continues.

Figure 3.9 shows such a model. Activity A4 represents the execution of process B. When A4 is executed, an instance of process B is created and started. When activity B5, the end activity of process B, completes, control is returned to activity A4. Now, navigation continues to activity A5.

Figure 3.9 Hierarchical Model

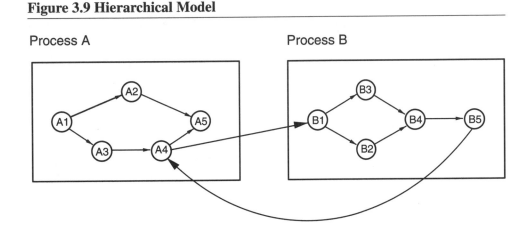

As can be seen from the figure, there exists a hierarchial relationship between the calling process, the parent process, and the child process, the subprocess. People usually have this model in mind when talking about subprocesses. In programming, this structure would be called a nested structure and this model is also called a *nested* model.

3.4.4 Programs

We pointed out earlier that the implementation of program activities are executables that are defined separately. The reasons for defining these programs are simple:

- There should be a clear separation between the conceptual construct of an activity and the actual implementation associated with the activity. This separation allows the modeler to first focus on the business process with its activities and then on the actual implementation of the individual activity. We have more to say about this approach in Chapters 6 and 11,

- The actual implementation is generally different for each of the different operating systems. When defining the activity, it is unknown on which operating system the activity will be executing and thus definitions may not be provided for each of the different operating systems on which the program will eventually run on,

- It should be possible to change the implementation without impact on the activity in the business process. Thus, the workflow management system should resolve the actual program to invoke when actually running the activity. In object-oriented programming, this is called *late binding*.

Figure 3.10 illustrates the relationship between activity and program. The double arrow on the relationship indicates that a particular program can be the activity implementation of many activities. Each program is associated with a set of operating-system-specific definitions. When the activity is carried out, the workflow management system locates the associated program, then, depending on the operating system on which it needs to be carried out, selects the appropriate definition. Code Example 3.7 shows a flow definition language fragment that illustrates how programs are defined and how the relationship between an activity and its implementation is expressed.

The PROGRAM keyword in the activity definition relates the activity to a program. This program is defined by a PROGRAM section, which has appropriate definitions for Windows NT and AIX. When the activity is carried out on Windows NT, the COLLINF.DLL in the directory D:\PROGRAMS is invoked. When the activity is carried out on AIX, the INFCOLL.EXE is executed.

The operating system is only one of the properties that the workflow management system must know about an activity implementation. Another property the workflow management system must know is the mechanism that the workflow man-

Figure 3.10 Relationship Between Program and Activity

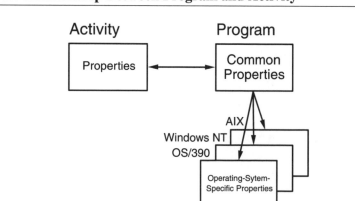

Code Example 3.7 Defining Programs

```
PROGRAM_ACTIVITY 'Collect Credit Information'
    PROGRAM 'Collect Information'
END 'Collect Credit Information'

PROGRAM 'Collect Information'
    WINNT
        DLL
            PATH_AND_FILENAME D:\PROGRAMS\COLLINF.DLL
    AIX
        EXE
            PATH_AND_FILENAME INFCOLL.EXE

END 'Collect Information'
```

agement system should use to launch the activity implementation. This is shown schematically in figure 3.11. Sometimes the invocation mechanism can be deduced from the implementation type directly. For example, the launching of an EXE on Windows NT is done by the operating system's mechanism to launch an executable. However, there are may other invocation mechanisms.

Figure 3.11 Invoking Programs

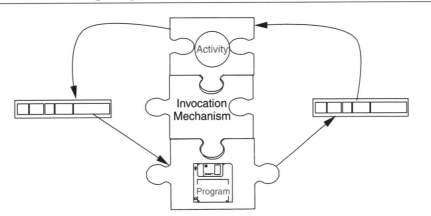

As shown in Figure 3.11, the input and output containers are made available to the activity implementation. The way they are made available to the activity implementation depends on the invocation mechanism. New applications could use the supplied API to access containers. For older applications that cannot be changed, a particular data stream may need to be created from the fields in the containers.

Figure 3.12 shows some typical invocation mechanisms that are used. It also shows that besides the invocation mechanism, the workflow management system must also know the identifier of the activity implementation. For an executable, the identifier is the name of the program. For other invocation mechanisms the identifier could be something different, such as the identifier of a business object.

Figure 3.12 Implementations and Their Invocation Mechanism

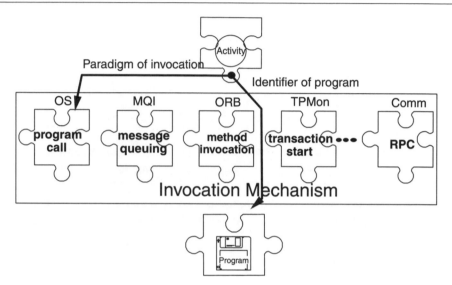

Starting from the left in Figure 3.12, the first puzzle piece represents the invocation mechanism that is supplied by the operating system (OS). This is the mechanism to invoke programs, such as EXEs, DLLs, or CMD files. It is the main mechanism for running programs on a workstation. By definition, this is a synchronous protocol. The workflow management system invokes the program and then waits until the invoked program has completed.

The next puzzle piece represents the message queueing invocation mechanism (MQI). See section 9.4.2 on page 319 for details on message queuing. In this invocation mechanism, the appropriate component is invoked by sending a message to the component. The target component reads the message, performs the appropriate actions, and sends back a message that contains the output container and other appropriate information, such as a return code. It should be noted that this is the only one of the listed invocation paradigms that works asynchronously. For this invocation mechanism, the workflow management system sends the message and then forgets about the message. When the invoked program sends back a message, the workflow management system picks it up and continues.

Method invocation is the standard method in object-oriented systems. The acronym ORB stands for object request broker, a facility that has been standardized by the Object Management Group (OMG). See section 6.3 on page 224 for details on the object request broker. The ORB manages objects and mediates method calls to objects in a distributed environment. The invoker of a message does not need to know the location.

Legacy applications, in particular those running on mainframes, are typically managed by a transaction processing (TP) monitor, such as IBM's Customer Information Control System (CICS) [IBM94a] or IBM's Information Management System (IMS) [IBM94b]. An application that is carried out by entry of a transaction identifier with appropriate data such as a customer number, on a dumb terminal is an example of a legacy application. After the request is processed, the output is sent back to the user. The workflow management system needs to support the invocation of these transactions by interacting with the TP monitor. It must provide the TP monitor with the correct input and must manage the output from the TP monitor.

The last puzzle piece shows a method that allows the remote invocation of a program by a remote procedure call. A remote procedure call is the remote equivalent of the local operating system invocation which is shown in the leftmost puzzle piece. See section 9.4.1 on page 317 for details on remote procedure calls.

As can be inferred from this list, the workflow management system will never be in a position to provide all available invocation mechanisms, including all the necessary mapping of the input and output containers, to the invocation-mechanism-dependent storage structures. Thus, a workflow management system must provide a mechanism to allow a user to realize all kinds of invocation mechanisms. Figure 3.13 shows how this goal can be achieved.

Figure 3.13 Invoking Any Type of Application

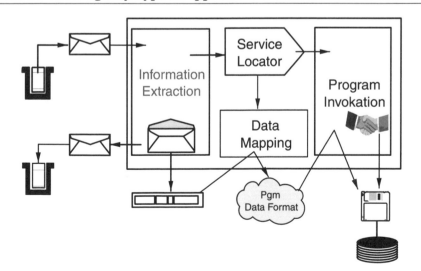

The figure shows the program execution component of the workflow management system that is responsible for invoking and controlling the appropriate activity implementations. The component receives a request as a message, for the execution of such an activity implementation. The program execution component waits on the queue, and when a message arrives, it performs the following set of actions: (1) it maps the input container to the structure needed by the invocation mechanisms (2) calls the identified object via the invocation mechanisms; (3) maps the data returned by the invoked implementation to a message; and (4) sends the message back to the workflow management system.

The structure of the program execution component can be opened in such a way that users can replace the individual components with their own routines. That means the user must provide routines for (1) mapping the data in the input container to a particular data structure, and mapping the data in the data structure to the output container, (2) the invocation mechanism to invoke the activity implementation, (3) checking for security, if applicable and (4) accessing a directory for determining the characteristics of the service that provides the activity implementation.

Code Example 3.8 shows how such a definition could look like when global routines are used. It defines that the program `QueryAccount` is implemented in the OS/390 environment as an external service. The service is provided by `IMS17`, a particular instance of the Information Management System, as indicated by the service type `IMS`. The name of the transaction is `QUERY_ACC` and the transaction is of the `MPP` type. It is invoked by the `MQ` invocation paradigm. These parameters are then passed to the routines to make the appropriate decisions.

Code Example 3.8 Defining an IMS Transaction as Implementation

```
PROGRAM QueryAccount
    OS390
        EXTERNAL
            SERVICE             IMS17
            SERVICE_TYPE        IMS
            INVOCATION_TYPE     MQ
            EXECUTABLE          QUERY_ACC
            EXECUTABLE_TYPE     MPP
            MAPPING_TYPE        3270
END QueryAccount
```

3.4.5 Lists

As shown in Figure 3.7 on page 85, users can manage their workitems in worklists. A worklist contains all workitems that have the same common characteristics. For example, a user can have a worklist for all loan process workitems and another worklist for all high-priority workitems. Obviously, a workitem can be part of multiple worklists.

Code Example 3.9 shows the definition of a worklist that contains all workitems for loan processes sorted by the priority assigned to each processes. The type PUBLIC indicates that the worklist can be used by everyone; the specification of PRIVATE would restrict the usage to a particular user. The VIEW keyword allows the modeler to specify exactly which fields of a workitem the user wants to see.

Code Example 3.9 Definition of a Worklist

```
WORKLIST LoanProcesses
  TYPE PUBLIC
  VIEW
    WHERE PROCESS_NAME = LoanProcess
  ORDER
    BY PRIORITY
END LoanProcess
```

Worklists can be defined not only for persons but also for all types of organizational constructs. Such a worklist is called a *group worklist*. A typical example of a group list is a role worklist. In this case, all users assigned to that role would work from that worklist.

The list concept can be used also for process models, processes, notification items, and activities. This generalization helps users to organize their work exactly the way they would like to have it.

3.4.6 Settings

The operation of the workflow management system needs a number of settings. These settings fall into the two categories:

- Operational settings that define the operational characteristics of the workflow management system. An example is the length of time the system should keep messages that have been sent to a user as the result of a query but that have not been processed by the user.

- Session settings that define the characteristics of the session that a user establishes with the workflow management system. Typical examples are the time after which a session expires and the user needs to connect to the workflow management system again, and the time that must elapse before a user can connect to the system after a number of connection attempts have failed because the user could not provide a valid password.

We provide a detailed description of these settings in various sections in Chapters 10 and 11.

3.4.7   Topology

The topology that is the easiest to maintain and therefore the most desired is that of a single workflow management system residing on a single processor to which all users connect. This approach, however, is only achievable in very limited situations, such as small companies or departmentwide setups. Therefore a workflow management system must be able to deliver its services via a set of servers that can be placed everywhere. A user gains access to the workflow management system by connecting to one of these servers. The information about the individual servers and their placement, including the assignment of users to servers, is stored in the workflow management system's database. We discuss this in detail in Chapter 10.

3.4.8   Graphical Representation

Processes, activities, lists, programs, and all other constructs are typically exposed to the end user via a graphical user interface. The workflow management system provides default icons for the individual constructs. However, process modelers can supply their own icons. In that way process modelers can provide visual clues to the end user, such as a telephone icon to indicate that an inquiry by phone must be made or a document icon to indicate that a document must be written.

3.4.9   Versioning

Workflow-based applications are quite often mission-critical applications that need to be available 24 hours a day, 7 days a week. For these applications the workflow management system cannot be quiesced to make changes to process models, organizational structures, or information technology resources. It must be possible to enter changed data well in advance and have it made valid automatically.

This requirement can be met by versioning each of the major constructs of the workflow management system, using a *valid from* date. A typical entity that is versioned this way is the process model. When a process is created from the process model, the workflow management system always picks up the current process by comparing the valid from date specified in the process model with the current system date. For example, we have two versions of the loan process, one with a valid from date of January 1, 1998 and one with a valid from date of January 1, 1999. When a process is created during the year of 1998, the first version is used to create the process. Starting January 1, 1999, processes are created from the second version. The process modeler could have entered the second version in October 1998; it would not be used until the current date is a 1999 date.

Figure 3.14 illustrates that not only entities but also the relationships between the different entities need to be versioned. It shows the assignment of people to the role of financial officer. The date assigned to the relationship is an effective date, the date by when the role assignment should become effective.

Figure 3.14 Versioning With Timed Relationships

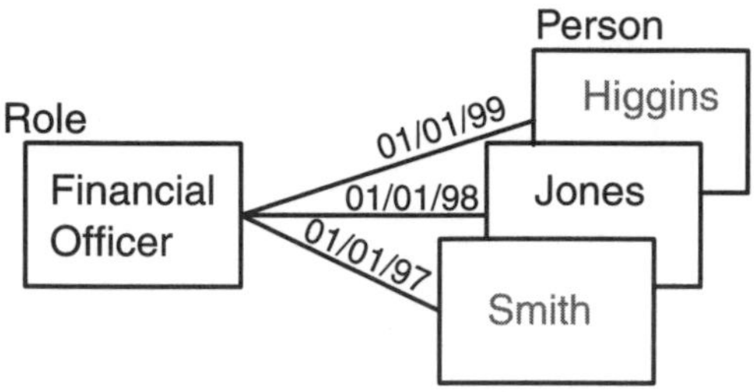

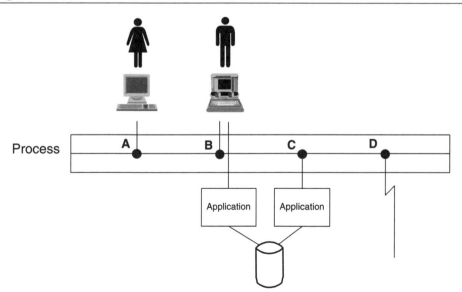

3.5 Runtime

The main purpose of the runtime component of the workflow management system is to proactively drive processes. The runtime component navigates through a process model and interacts with users and applications, as illustrated in Figure 3.15. This figure is based on a similar one used by the Workflow Management Coalition to illustrate the basic processing of a process.

Figure 3.15 Process Execution

The type of action that the workflow management system performs for each of the activities depends on the setting of activity properties and associated activity implementations. Activities can be defined as automatic without the user explicitly starting the activity implementation, the can be defined as manual in which case the activity implementation must be started by a user. The activity implementation itself can run on the user's workstation, on the processor where the workflow management system runs, on a different processor, or on a mixture of these representing a client/server application. It can run unattended, in which case it does not interact with the user; or attended, where it interacts with the user. It can perform database operations, that is retrieving, storing, or updating data, possibly to be used by other activity implementations, or it can just display or collect information that is passed by the workflow management system from activity to activity.

Figure 3.15 illustrates the different ways activities and their respective implementations can be executed. Activity A is a manual activity that is executed on the user's workstation. Activity B is also a manual activity but is implemented as a client/server application that accesses a database. Activity C is an automatic activity that runs an activity implementation that does not interact with a user and that accesses the database. Activity D is also an automatic activity; however, the activity implementation executes on a different processor, which is indicated by a remote request being executed.

3.5.1   The Life of a Process

A process typically goes through many states and state transitions during its lifetime. Figure 3.16 shows the most important states a process goes through in its life. The transition from one state to another state is performed either by the workflow management system or by some explicit request from an authorized user.

Figure 3.16 Process Life Cycle

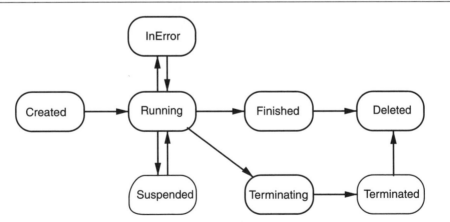

The initial state of a process is *created*. The process is put into this state by an explicit create request for a specific process model. It is possible to specify a start date. When the date comes, the process is automatically started. This feature allows one to enter a large number of processes, for example at the beginning of the month, and then start processes over the month at the specified times. No activities are carried out for those processes. However, they are shown in appropriate queries. For example, a process administrator could issue a query to find out all processes that have been created by Joe Smith but that have not yet been started.

The main state of a process is the *running* state. The process is put into this state either by an explicit start request from a user or by an implicit request when the process is started as a subprocess. It can also be put into this state implicitly by the system if a particular start date was specified when the process was created. In the running state, the process is carried out, the navigation through the process takes place, workitems are created for participants, and activities are carried out. A process stays in this state until the process finishes, and then it goes into the *finished* state. The process stays in this state until explicitly deleted by a user or after a user-specified time has expired, which results in the process being automatically deleted by the workflow management system.

A process goes into *suspended* state when a user requests this state explicitly. In this state, navigation has stopped, no more workitems are generated, and no more activities are carried out. The process stays in that state until it is explicitly put back into the running state by a resume request from a user or after a specified time has been exceeded.

There are situations where further processing of a process would not be meaningful. In this case, the process can be terminated by an authorized user. This termination causes all activities associated with the process, such as navigating through the process, to be stopped. Immediately after the request has been received, the process is put into the *terminating* state. After all activities have stopped, the process is put into the *terminated* state.

In certain situations, carrying out a process cannot be continued. In this case, the process is put into the *inError* state. In this state, navigation through the process is stopped; an authorized user can perform appropriate recovery actions. This situation is discussed in detail in section 3.7.3 on page 109. After appropriate action, the process can be put back into the running state for continuation.

Note, that the figure just reflects the major states and state transitions of a process. Many more states are available to cope with subtleties.

3.5.2 The Life of an Activity

Activities also assume many different states and go through many state transitions. Figure 3.17 shows the main states that the activity can assume and the major transitions from state to state.

When a process is created, all activities are put into the *inactive* state. No actions are performed for activities that are in this state. However, they are shown in appropriate queries. For example, a process administrator could query, in a process monitor, which person will be assigned to the activity.

Figure 3.17 Activity Life Cycle

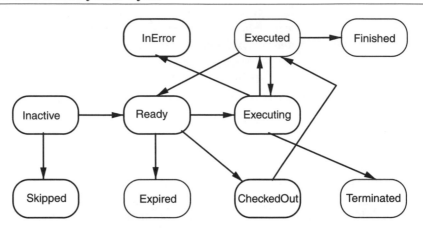

When staff resolution has been performed for an activity and appropriate work-items have been generated, the activity goes into the *ready* state.

When a user selects a workitem associated with an activity, the activity goes into the *executing* state. The workflow management system now launches the appropriate activity implementation, such as a subprocess or a program. The activity stays in this state until the activity implementation completes. The activity then goes into the *executed* state. If the activity was defined with an automatic exit condition, and the exit condition is met, the activity goes immediately into the *finished* state. If the activity was defined with a manual exit condition, the transition from the executed to the finished state must be requested by the user who carried out the activity. After the activity has reached the finished state, navigation of the process continues by following the outgoing control connectors.

If an activity is not carried out because the appropriate path is not being taken or the join condition failed, the activity is skipped and goes into the *skipped*, sometimes called *dead*, state.

Sometimes, activities no longer need to be carried out. In this case, the activity goes into the *expired* state and navigation continues.

Instead of the workflow management system carrying out a program activity by launching the associated activity implementation, the user can carry out the activity implementation outside of the control of the workflow management system, through the support of a checkout facility. The user *checks out* the activity, which is put into the *checkedOut* state. The user can start the activity implementation at any time. The activity implementation uses the appropriate API to read the activity input container and to write to the activity output container. When the user has completed the task, the activity is *checked in* and the activity goes into the executed state as if the workflow management system was responsible for carrying out the activity implementation.

In certain situations, the activity implementation cannot be carried out correctly. Typical examples are that the program can not be found or that the program terminates abnormally. In this case, the activity is put into the *inError* state. Functions are then available to correct the error an rerun the activity, or to just rerun the activity.

In the same way that processes can be terminated, activities can be terminated. In fact, activities are typically terminated as the result of the termination of the process.

3.5.3 How Users Work with the System

Before a user can perform any work, he must establish a session with the workflow management system. The session is initiated by the user starting the appropriate workflow management system client component and providing his user identification and password. If both entries are correct, the workflow management system establishes a *session*. Within a session, the workflow management system assumes that all requests are coming from the user that who established the session. The session is ended when the user explicitly terminates the session. The session can also be terminated automatically by the workflow management system if the user has not been active for a specified period of time. This measure prohibits unauthorized use of the system if a user forgets to terminate a session.

Interaction with the workflow management system is usually via a graphical user interface (GUI). Three variants of a GUI can be distinguished:

First, all workflow management systems offer their own GUI for manipulating processes, workitems, and so on. Figure 3.18 shows the GUI of MQSeries Workflow [IBM98a].

The GUI uses the typical operating system metaphors to represent the individual constructs and the way that users work with these constructs. The figure shows the typical Explorer style that users are accustomed to on workstations that run the Windows NT operating system. The left pane contains a tree view of the objects the user can work with, for example, folders for process lists and worklists. The user can select the way he would like to see the contents of the folders. In the figure, the process list that contains all active processes is presented in report format; the worklist in icon format. The user can also select which properties of the objects, such as processes or workitems, should be presented. Actions on the objects are then carried out by either a double-click on the object or from a pull-down menu for selecting an appropriate action. For example, the user starts a workitem just double-clicking on it. This action launches the appropriate activity implementation. This approach frees the user from the need to know details, such as the parameter that need to be provided, about the activity implementation.

Figure 3.18 Graphical Runtime

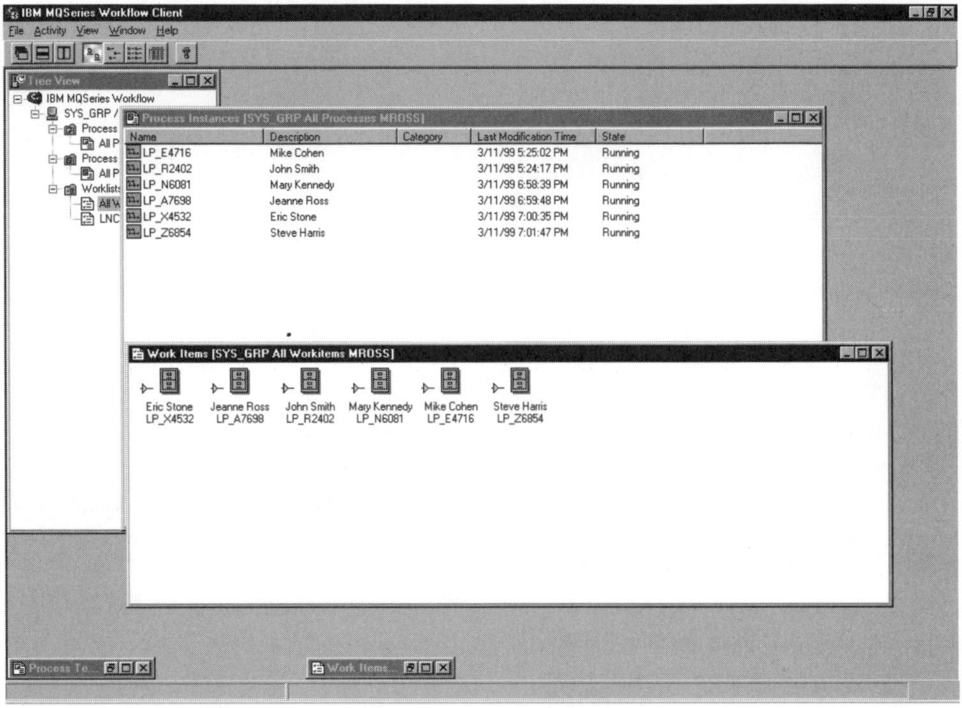

In the second variant of a GUI, the workflow management system functions are delivered via the graphical metaphor of the desktop of another system. Figure 3.19 shows how these functions are presented on the Lotus Notes desktop. Workitems are represented as documents, worklists are shown as folders.

The third variant of a GUI is one that companies write for themselves so that the workflow management system functionality is presented in a way the company's people are familiar with.

3.5.4   Working with Workitems

End users interact with the workflow management system via worklists that contain workitems.

There are three different modes of obtaining workitems:

- *Pull* mode—In this mode the user must explicitly request that new workitems are made available in the appropriate worklists. The advantages of this approach are that the user is in full control and that the structure and contents of the lists do not change without an explicit user request.

Figure 3.19 Lotus Notes Interface

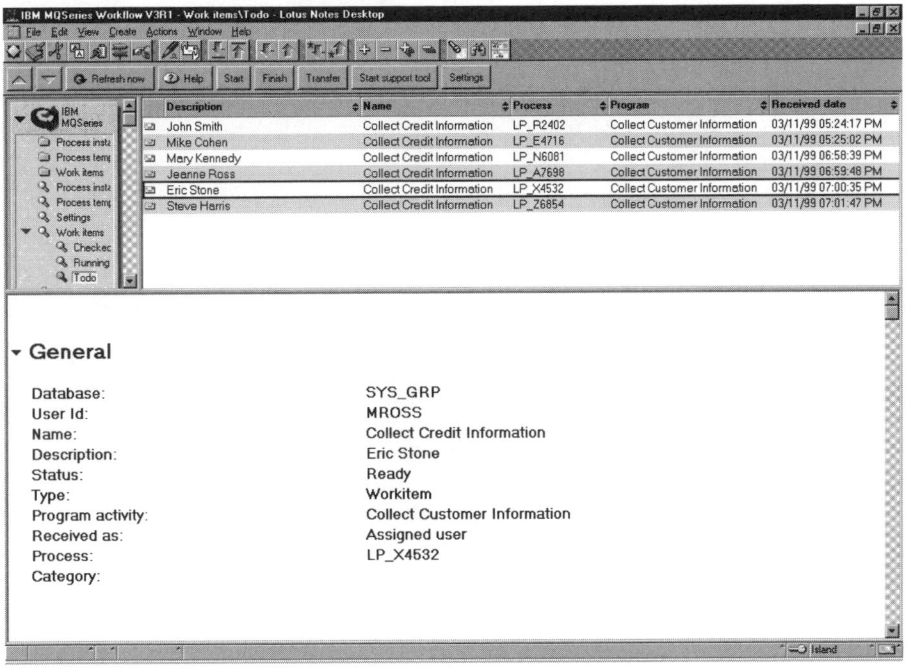

- *Push* mode—Any new workitem that is created by the workflow management system is immediately pushed onto the appropriate worklist. The advantage of this approach is that urgent workitems are immediately pushed onto the worklist for immediate action. The disadvantage of this mode is that the worklists constantly change.

- *Grab* mode—The workflow management system delivers ready wis to a user when needed. Whenever the user has completed processing of a particular workitem, a new workitem is made available. In fact, there is no need to have the workitem displayed; the workflow management system can immediately start the activity implementation. Whenever an activity implementation completes, the next activity implementation is started. This is particularly interesting if group worklists are used. Typically, group worklists have the problem that when a user wants to work with a workitem, quite often another user has already started working on it. This situation often happens in the pull mode, less frequently in the push mode. This problem does not exist at all in grab mode.

The functions that a user can perform with a workitem are either direct workitem functions or activity functions.

A typical workitem function is the capability to delete a workitem. This is a valid function as long as other users are holding a workitem for the same activity. If a user is unable to process the workitem, it can be *transferred* to another user to carry out the appropriate task. A user can also put a workitem on hold either indefinitely or for a limited period of time. In this case the workitem does not show up in the appropriate worklists until the specified time has been exceeded or the user explicitly releases it.

Typical activity functions are to perform the following actions:

- *Start* the implementation associated with the activity.

- *Restart* the activity, which put the activity back into the ready state so that it can be started again.

- *Reexecute* the activity implementation immediately.

- *Finish* the activity that has been defined with exit mode set to manual.

- *Suspend* the subprocess that is associated with the activity.

- *Resume* the subprocess.

- *Terminate* the activity implementation.

As soon as one of the above activity functions has been carried out, the workitems held by other users are put into a special *disabled* state. That means whenever a user selects a workitem, no other users that hold a workitem for the same activity, can select the workitem and work on it. The disabled state indicates this prohibition to users.

When an activity has completed, the workitem is removed from the worklist unless the user specified that no automatic removal should take place. In this case, the user must explicitly delete the workitem.

3.5.5   Working with Processes

We discussed in section 3.5.1 the different states a process can assume. Most of these state changes are carried out as the result of user operations that are typically initiated through the GUI.

To carry out a process, the user selects one of the process models that are shown in a list of process models for which the user is authorized. The actions that can be specified by the user are then (1) to create a process, or (2) to run a process. Running a process is a combination of creating and immediately starting a process. Part of creating a process is supplying data for the input container of the process.

As soon as a process has been created, it is made part of process lists. These process lists show the process as an icon with an indicator for the appropriate state. Actions that can be performed for selected process icons are the following:

- *Start* the process if not yet running.

- *Suspend* the process indefinitely or for a specified time.

- *Resume* a suspended process.

- *Query* the process data, such as the description of the process and name of the process.

- *Update* process data, such as the description of the process.

Depending on settings, the process is immediately deleted when it completes. In this case, the process is also removed from the process list.

Process lists can contain not only processes that the user has started but also processes for which the user has registered interest. As with workitems there are options how the process list should be treated. In pull mode, the process list is refreshed upon an explicit user request. In the push mode, any new process, and even every new state of a process, is immediately reflected in the process list.

3.5.6 Working with Activities

Typically, a user works with activities only indirectly via the appropriate workitem functions. However, a small set of functions can be carried out directly on the activity. Activities are represented as icons in an activity list. The set of functions includes the following actions:

- *Create a workitem* for a particular user.

- *Reschedule* to generate a new set of workitems.

- *Query* to obtain the details about an activity, including the state.

- *Repair container* to update the containers of an activity.

- *Force finish* to complete a repaired activity.

We discuss the last two functions in more detail in section 3.7.3 on page 109.

3.6 Audit Trail

All important events in the life of a process or an activity can be recorded as an entry in the audit trail. Each entry in the audit trail contains a number of the pieces of information including, but not limited to, the following items:

- Date and time when the event takes place.

- Identifier of the event that uniquely characterizes the event, such as activity started or process finished.

- Identifier of the process for which the event is written. If the process is carried out as a subprocess, the appropriate parent process identification is also written so that the proper correlations can be made.

- Requestor of the action, which could be either a user or the workflow management system itself.

- Identifier of the activity for which the event is written.

- Identifier of related objects, such as the identifier of a subprocess if the event is the start of an activity that is implemented as a subprocess.

Identifiers of processes, activities, and users can identify the appropriate objects in other requests to the workflow management system. For example, the identifier of a process could be used in appropriate process functions.

The audit trail can be used for a number of different purposes; two of the more prominent ones are:

- To satisfy legal requirements requiring that the complete life cycle of a process is kept for a significant number of years. In the airline industry, for example, this information must be kept for 30 years.

- To obtain statistical information, such as how many processes of a particular process model have been processed and which of the different paths have been taken and how often. This information can be used to verify assumptions that were made during simulation.

As the amount of data that is written into the audit trail increases, the size of the audit trail can grow very fast. Workflow management systems must provide an option to allow process modelers to specify for each process model the amount of data that is to be written into the audit trail. That means a process modeler can select the events for which information is written into the audit trail. If one is only interested in the average duration of processes, it is sufficient if only start and completion of a process are recorded as events in the audit trail.

3.7   Process Management

In section 3.5.5 we covered the functions that are typically available to end users to start and manipulate individual processes. There is, however, another set of functions that are not carried out by the typical end user. These functions are performed by specifically authorized people such as process or system administrators, by call center people answering customer requests, or by applications that provide support to customers, such as applications deployed on the Web. We subsume this set of functions under the notion of *process management*. They fall into six categories: process queries, process monitoring, process repair, process history maintenance, process analysis, and resource management.

3.7.1 Process Queries

The category *process queries* includes all functions that are provided to locate particular processes and query their current state and processing history.

Locating a particular process or a set of processes that have the same property is a common task in workflow management systems. For each request, the user specifies selection criteria which are then used to filter out the appropriate processes. There are two types of properties which the user can use as selection criteria: operational properties, such as the state or start date of a process, and business properties, such as the name of the customer.

Queries that deal with the operational properties are typically used by process or system administrators to monitor the workflow management system or repair processes that have not been carried out correctly.

Queries that deal with the business properties are typically used by call center people or customers using a Web browser for example. Those properties are managed by the workflow management system in modeler-specified key data containers that are associated with the individual process models. These types of queries must be honored regardless where the actual process is carried out in a distributed environment.

Both types of queries return the appropriate process identifiers, which allow the user to query the details about the process. Appropriate functions return the current state of each of the control connectors and activities. Because the returned data also contains the graphical representation of the process, a GUI can present the process in the same format as was defined in the buildtime with an appropriate color coding of the individual icons to show the state of the individual activities. This tool to display the status of a process is generally called the *process instance monitor*. This function is also made available to typical end users to help them better understand the context in which they are carrying out an activity.

A detailed execution history of a process can be obtained by performing appropriate queries against the audit trail. Depending on the settings for auditing, even minor events, such as transferring a workitem from one user to another, can be located.

A query that is of particular importance in call centers is to predict how long it will take to complete a process and to identify the people that will be involved in completing it. How accurate the appropriate prediction will be depends on the amount of information that has been collected in the past. It is the same set of information that is collected during process analysis, as described in section 3.7.5. The people that will be involved in completing the process can be determined by performing staff resolution for the remaining activities.

3.7.2   Process Monitoring

The correct and timely execution of individual business processes can be ensured by using the notification mechanism, discussed in section 3.4.2 on page 86. Whenever a particular process is out-of-line, this is not meeting the specified deadlines, appropriate actions are taken. Notification is a powerful mechanism when out-of-line situations occur rather infrequently. It is a rather inappropriate mechanism if these situations occur often. In this case, the process administrator could be swamped with notifications.

Process monitoring takes the notification mechanism to a higher level. Instead of looking at individual processes, it looks at the processing of groups of processes. Process monitoring does is not just recognize out-of-line situations but also records and displays the current state of the workflow management system. It includes functions to take snapshots of the workflow management system's throughput: to trace the change in throughput of the workflow management system, to track the amount of work that is generated and processed by an individual or group of users, and to define actions if certain thresholds are exceeded. Depending on the focus, at least three different flavors of monitors can be differentiated: the process monitor, the workload monitor, and the system monitor.

The *process monitor* presents the current or accumulated states of processes of a particular process model. For each process instance, the states and other related information of each activity are counted, such as the average amount of time it took to process an activity, the number of processes currently active, the minimum and maximum amount of workitems per activity. This information can be presented graphically in the representation that was used when the process was modeled. Using the thresholds defined for each activity during process engineering, the process monitor can flag out-of-line situations of serious trouble well in advance. For example, if an activity has been defined to complete on the average in one day and it is determined that it takes on average two days then this result reflects an out-of-line situation. The severity of the out-of-line situation could then be reflected by different color coding for the individual activity: green could reflect normal processing; yellow, slightly out-of-line processing; and red, a severe problem. This could then be coupled with a notification mechanism. If such an out-of-line situation occurs, the administrator can then use appropriate functions to dig deeper into the process structure to analyze each activity individually.

The *workload monitor* supports the monitoring of the amount of work that is carried out by the users and organizations. This monitor helps to identify place where work piles up and other places where not enough work is available for the assigned people so the workload can be balanced by reassignment of work. The appropriate functions are presented in section 3.7.6.

The *system monitor* provides an overall picture of the workflow management system's operation. It is the most comprehensive view of the total system. In its most advanced form, it is reduced to a GUI that resembles the monitoring being done in manufacturing or power plants, where analog or digital meters display the current state of the plant. Out-of-line situations cause alerts to be signaled and are indicated by a gauge in the red area of the display.

3.7.3 Process Repair

Errors occur even in the best-tested business processes either as the result of an error in the process itself, an error in an activity implementation, or even an error in the operation of the workflow management system. Some of the errors are detected by the associated activity (see section 3.5.2 on page 99). In this case, the activity goes into an *inError*, state and an appropriate alert is sent to the responsible process administrator. The alert contains appropriate information that identifies the type of error that occurred. From this information, the process administrator can initiate appropriate actions to repair the process, allowing the process to reach its designed completion. To support this procedure, workflow management systems provide a set of functions for manipulating activities and processes.

Manipulation of activities includes functions that change the containers of the activity and the state of the activity. Typically, those functions are used together; that is activity containers are updated and then the state of the activity is changed.

If it is known, for example, that an activity implementation has completed successfully but the workflow management system could not complete its own processing, the process administrator can update the output container and force finish the activity. This action causes the activity to be treated as if it has finished, and navigation continues, using the values supplied in the output container.

Another example is when the activity implementation terminates abnormally as the result of incorrect data in the input container. The data in the input container could be incorrect because of mapping data. In this case, the process administrator would need to update the input container and restart the activity.

Some of the repair functions are not limited to a specific process but can be applied to a set of processes. For example, if an activity implementation could not be located, then probably a whole set of processes will experience this problem. Therefore, the process administrator must be able to correct this error with a single function invocation.

3.7.4   Process History Maintenance

The lifetime of processes and workitems depends on settings that are defined for the appropriate process models. Depending on legal or business rules, they are either deleted immediately as soon as the process or workitem is completed, after a predefined period of time, or never. Thus, depending on the settings, the database of the workflow management system grows larger and larger.

This growth is also the case for the audit trail, as the following example illustrates. The example assumes that a full audit trail is written; other options produce significantly less output. The typical size of an entry in the audit trail is 1 kilobyte with an average of 5 entries per activity. If 10,000 processes with 10 activities are carried out every day, then the audit trail grows by 500 megabytes every day, or 15 gigabytes every month.

This situation mandates, for performance and usability, that processes and workitems be removed from the database and that their appropriate entries are removed from the audit trail. All related information must be removed when a process is removed, to keep the database in a consistent state. This means that all of the process information, including the associated workitems and entries in the audit trail, must be removed in a single step. The removal of the information can be based on different criteria, such as all processes that are older than a six months, or all processes that are loan processes for small businesses and that are older than three months.

Sometimes legal reasons mandate that the process history be kept for a considerable amount of time. So, the processes, workitems, and the entries in the audit trail cannot just be deleted but must be archived to some other media. Functions, such as condensing the audit trail, deleting entries from the archive, and querying the archives, are provided to manage the archives. Advanced functions may allow a user to not only query the database but also to query the database and the archive together.

3.7.5   Process Analysis

We have seen that the audit trail is a valuable source of information. In particular, it can be used to determine whether the assumptions that were made when the process was built are correct. Typical assumptions that have been used in process simulation are the number of processes, the average processing time for activities, and the probabilities that certain paths are taken. Based on these assumptions, organizational and computing resources have been allocated. *Process analysis* compares these estimates with the actuals, and thereby helping process administrators to take appropriate actions, or even automatically applies appropriate changes.

3.7.6 Resource Management

Most out-of-line situations are caused by a shortage in resources to perform a particular task. Resources in this context can be people or IT resources. *Resource management* is a set of functions that help to move or reassign resources from places with surplus resources to places with insufficient resources. The process monitor can help to identify these places.

The workflow management system offers two functions to manage human resources. The *transfer workitem* function allows the transfer of a single workitem, or even sets of workitems, from one user to another user or from one organizational construct, such as role or department, to another organizational construct. Query workitem functions help to determine the actual number of workitems that are assigned to a user or an organizational construct. The *change organizational structure* functions allow temporary reassignment of people to different organizational structures or units. For example, if there is a shortage in financial officers, one could reassign people working as loan officers to the role of financial officers.

The set of functions to control the information technology resources has a wide range. If a processor gets overloaded, one could shut down other work running on that processor—a function typically provided by the operating system. A more workflow-oriented function is to move users that interact with a particular workflow management system to another instance of the workflow management system.

3.8 Authorization

Each user is allowed to carry out certain functions, for example, a process administrator can terminate a running process. Each user is assigned one or more roles that carry with it a set of authorizations. The authorizations represent a set of privileges which allow the user to carry out a set of functions. Table 3.1 illustrates typical user types in a workflow management system, with a sample of their appropriate privileges.

Table 3.1 User Types and Privileges

User Type	Privileges
Process Administrator	Terminate process. Suspend process. Repair process.
Operation Administrator	Stop workflow management system. Change settings of workflow management system.
General User	Start workitem Change password. Transfer workitem.

These individual authorizations/roles are not granular enough to cope with the diversity of objects with which authorizations deal. A process administrator, for example, should not be able to perform all authorized functions on all processes but only on processes of a particular process model. This objective requires that the overall authorization scheme allows grouping of objects so that a person can have a particular authorization for a group of objects. Figure 3.20 shows the grouping of processes.

Figure 3.20 Grouping of Processes for Authorization

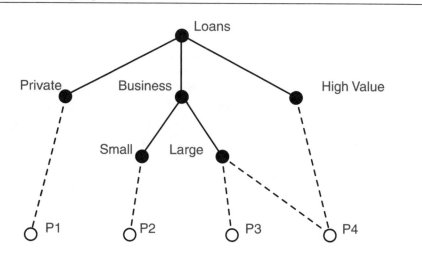

It shows that loan processes are categorized into private, business, and high-value loan processes. The business loan processes are then further grouped into small and large business loan processes. Each process is then assigned to one or more of the categories. For example,P1, is a private loan process, and P4 is a loan process for large businesses with a high value.

Each of the authorizations, such as process administrator, is then assigned a set of categories. If Joe Smith is assigned the authorization of a process administrator for high-value, large business processes, then he would be able to exercise the appropriate rights for all processes that are of the type P4.

3.9   Application Programming Interface

The workflow management system provides access to all data and functions via an application programming interface(API). The interactions
with the users, as described in section 3.5.3 on page 101 are performed by clients that exploit these APIs. The APIs are grouped according to the functions they deliver:

- *Worklist API*—Manage worklists and workitems

- *Operation API*—Control the overall operation of the workflow management system

- *Administration API*—Perform administrative functions, such as repairing broken workflows or controlling access to the workflow management system

- *Process API*—Start, stop, suspend, resume, query, or subscribe to workflows

- *Audit trail API*—Query the contents of the audit trail

- *Buildtime API*—Model processes, the organization, and the information technology infrastructure

- *Container API*—Allow activity implementations to obtain and set container data

The workflow management system delivers the APIs in two different flavors: as programming language constructs for the various programming languages, such as C, C++, or Java, and as a messaging interface.

The programming language interface is the traditional way of providing the API. It is well suited for writing graphical

user interfaces, particularly when the API is delivered as software components. Depending on the component model, these components are made available as well known entities: for example, ActiveX controls, that can be used in visual builders to script together client applications; Java Beans, which allow the application to run in a Web browser; or VisualAge parts, which can be used for visual composition of activity implementations.

The programming language interface also provides integration into existing desktop applications, such as Lotus Notes or Microsoft Exchange (see section 3.5.3 on page 101).

The messaging interface allows applications to interact with the workflow management system by sending requests as messages to a defined message queue, obtaining the results of the request as messages, or receiving the results of subscriptions as messages (see section 9.6.3 on page 333 for details). This interface style is the preferred format of interfacing for message-based applications. The data format to be used can be any type, from a proprietary message format to a standardized one, such as XML. Code Example 3.10 on the following page shows the request for starting a process in an XML format.

Code Example 3.10 Start Process Request in XML Format

```
<?xml version='1.0' standalone='yes'>
<!DOCTYPE WorkflowMessage SYSTEM 'WFMSXMLIF.dtd'>
<WorkflowMessage type='request'>
   <CorrelId>MyCorrelId</CorrelId>
   <ProcessStart>
      <ProcessTemplate>LoanProcess</ProcessTemplate>
      <InputData>
         <Name>Joe Smith</Name>
         <Amount>10000</Amount>
      </InputData>
   </ProcessStart>
</WorkflowMessage>
```

3.10   System Structure

The system structure of a workflow management system is the typical structure that
many application systems exhibit: a three-tier structure as shown in Figure 3.21.

Figure 3.21 Three Tier System Structure

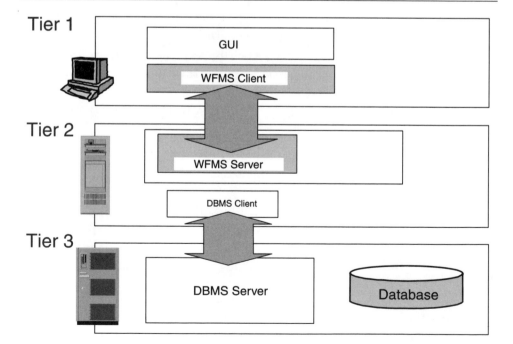

Tier one, typically the machine on which end users work, runs the end-user application that uses the API supplied by the workflow management system to interact with the workflow management system server that runs on the second tier. It also runs the program executor component that launches the programs that a user works with. Communication between client and server is provided by the workflow management system.

The database management system that holds the database runs on the third tier. The greatest benefits are normally realized if the three tiers are deployed onto three different machines; however, this is not a necessity—the tier can placed on any combination of machines. Another typical setup would be to combine tier two and three on one machine.

A user can use a Web browser to access the workflow management system. Since according to Figure 3.21, the workflow management system client runs on tier 1, the Web browser is normally referred to as tier 0.

The workflow management system server itself is not a monolithic piece of code, but consists of a set of different, independent components. The more prominent ones are the workflow execution server and the program execution server. The workflow execution server carries out all actions associated with the execution of a process, such as starting the process, navigating to the next activities, performing staff resolution, and dispatching workitems. The program execution server controls the execution of those activity implementations that do not need to interact with the user. The program execution server receives appropriate requests from the workflow execution server via some communication mechanism, so one could setup the workflow management system server again as a client/server structure by moving the program execution server to a different processor.

We discuss the system structure and all related availability and scalability aspects in detail in Chapter 10.

3.10.1   Interactions Between Workflow Management Systems

So far, we have assumed that a business process is carried out a by a single workflow management system. This assumption is usually true for intracompany business processes. However even in smaller companies, multiple workflow management systems might need to work together to carry out a particular business process. And of course, for business processes that span multiple companies where the processing of a business process by multiple workflow management systems is natural.

Different workflow management systems could mean multiple instances of the same workflow management system implementation running on different operating systems. Such a setup is typical for companies that are not centralized. For example, a company has three main offices, one in Tokyo, one in Berlin, and one in New York. Most of the business processes are confined to one of the main offices; only a small number of the processes touch more than one office. In this case, it is beneficial to have three workflow management systems installed, one in each main office, since it minimizes the network traffic between the users and the workflow management system.

Regardless of whether the involved workflow management systems are from the same vendor or from different vendors, the workflow management systems must work together to carry out the distributed business process.

In the simpler case, the workflow management systems interact on a subprocess level. The granule of dividing a business process for the combined execution is the subprocess. This means a workflow management system requests the execution of a subprocess only from another workflow management system. The only knowledge the calling workflow management system must have is the name of the workflow management system that carries out the subprocess. Otherwise, the subprocess is carried out the same way as the calling workflow management system would carry it out. Such a subprocess is called a *remote* subprocess, indicating that it is carried out by a remote workflow management system. If the invoking workflow management system carries out the subprocess, the subprocess is called a *local* subprocess.

This interaction allows the implementation of all types of subprocess handling, such as the chained and the hierarchical subprocess model. In this mode of operation, the different workflow management systems exchange information when a subprocess is initiated, a subprocess terminates (not in the chained model), and when a parent process queries the subprocess. Each workflow management system writes its own audit trail. Existing options define whether the audit trail should be shipped back to the requestor. If not, appropriate consolidation runs must be carried out if the complete audit trail of those business must be kept in one place.

Figure 3.22 shows a more tight coupling between the different business processes.

Different activities are carried out by different workflow management systems. Activities A1 and A4 are carried out by workflow management system A; activities A2, A3, and A5, by workflow management system B. This requires that the involved workflow management systems have knowledge about each other. When a workflow management system performs staff resolution for an activity, it must know whether the selected users are registered with itself or another workflow management system. The workflow management systems must exchange information about users or must use some common repository that holds all users. The workflow management system that started the process owns the process and performs all staff resolutions. The other workflow management system just dispatches the workitem and carries out the activity implementation. When finished, it returns control to the calling workflow management system together with the audit trail information. The owning workflow management system inserts the audit trail information into its audit trail. This approach has the advantage that the owning workflow management system maintains an audit trail with all events and can answer all queries about the status of the process.

Figure 3.22 Joint Execution of a Process by Two Workflow Management Systems

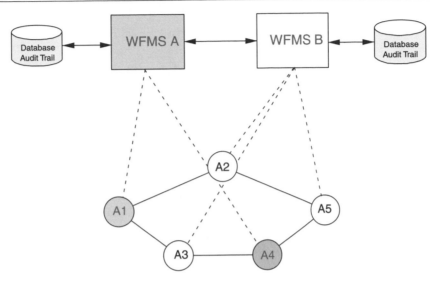

3.11 Workflow Standards

The Workflow Management Coalition is a nonprofit organization that has been founded in 1993 by a number of vendors and users of workflow management systems. The organization defines standards for workflow management systems so that different workflow management systems' implementations can interoperate; customers can thereby have their investment protected when moving from one implementation to another.

To achieve this goal, the Workflow Management Coalition standardizes two major aspects of workflow management systems: the metamodel underlying a workflow management system, that is the constructs to model processes; and a set of interfaces that defines the functions supported by the workflow management system.

This section outlines the specified high-level architecture and the set of interfaces. We do not go into any detail; interested readers should visit the Workflow Management Coalition's home page[Wor].

Some of the work done by the Workflow Management Coalition is being carried forward into the appropriate standard committees in the Object Management Group. The first standard that has been accepted by the OMG is the workflow management facility. Section 6.4 on page 226 discusses this standard in detail.

Figure 3.23 shows the Workflow Management Coalition's architecture model for a workflow management system, called the *workflow reference model*. A particular implementation or instance of a workflow management system is called a *workflow enactment service*. This service enacts, or runs, the workflows. The work-

Figure 3.23 Workflow Reference Model

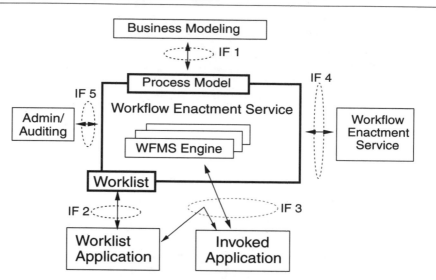

flow enactment service may consist of a single workflow engine, a set of identical workflow engines, or even set of specialized workflow engines. Having specialized engines can be beneficial if the processes that need to be carried out have quite different characteristics: some processes may need a production workflow engine; others, a workflow engine geared toward image handling; and others, workflow engines to accommodate frequent changes. The different workflow management system engines can be supplied by one vendor or even a set of vendors.

The reference model does not define the system structure nor the underlying architecture of a compliant workflow enactment service or workflow management system. The implementers of a workflow management system have complete freedom in structuring their system, as long as the interfaces, shown as IF1 to IF5, conform to the specified standard.

Five sets of interfaces are defined, as shown in Figure 3.23, and named Interface 1 through Interface 5.

Interface 1 standardizes how different systems can exchange process model and organizational information. It allows business modeling tools to provide the appropriate input to the workflow management system. The interface is specified as a tag language similar to the flow definition language we are using in the book. This tag language is called the *workflow process definition language (WPDL)*.

Interface 2 defines the functions that are available for users to interact with the workflow management system. It includes functions to manage workitems and processes. We showed them as separate application programming interface sets in section 3.9 on page 112. This interface is defined by a set of C programming language functions and allows exploiters of workflow management systems to develop their own user interfaces independently of the workflow management system that delivers its services to the end user. This interface allows applications to combine workitems created by different workflow management systems into one presentation and is valuable because the use of multiple workflow management systems is not uncommon in large enterprises.

Interface 3 standardizes the invocation of activity implementations. This interface allows companies to build executables that can be plugged in as activity implementations into every workflow management system; that means the executables can be reused. A standard for this interface has not been released yet, probably because is the most complex interface, particularly in light of the many invocation mechanisms that exist.

Interface 4 defines the handling of subprocesses between different workflow management systems. Functions are defined for starting subprocesses, querying the state of subprocesses, and subscribing to changes to process data associated with the subprocesses. The type of subprocesses that are supported are the chained services and hierarchical model, as described in section 3.4.3 on page 87. A much more granular level of interaction between the different workflow management systems, such as sharing the execution of the same process with the different activities transparently carried out by the different workflow management system has not yet been specified. Interface 4 distinguishes between the actual interface specification and appropriate bindings. The interface specifications are provided as a set of C programming language functions. Since such an interface does not define how the actual interaction between the different workflow management systems is carried out, appropriate bindings are necessary. The only binding that has been proposed so far is a MIME binding.

Interface 5 defines the structure of the audit trail and the different entries that a workflow management system must be able to provide to be compliant.

Chapter 4

Metamodel

In this chapter, we describe a metamodel for workflows. This metamodel is close to the one implemented by MQSeries Workflow, and less close to the one defined by Workflow Management Coalition. Depending on the richness of functions, the metamodel of a workflow management system contains more or less concepts and constructs. We limit ourselves to the most fundamental concepts to allow an in-depth discussion of these basic concepts. We present some of the more elaborate ones in Chapters 5 and 7.

We present for each construct or concept the following information:

1. A textual description of the construct that includes the purpose of the construct and how it is interpreted by the workflow management system.

2. A mathematical formulation of the construct, under the heading **Definition**. This formulation includes a definition of the concept and its appropriate interpretation. The end of the actual formal definition is indicated by a small black square. We provide this formal definition to be as precise as possible. Precision is needed for discussion business processes and their behavior. We assume that the reader has some basic knowledge of set theory. Readers that are not familiar with this level of mathematics or are not interested in it can skip this part.

3. An example that shows the usage of the construct, under the heading **Example**.

4. The example in the *flow definition language* under the heading **Language Representation**.

4.1 The Notion of a Metamodel

When a business process is modeled, all of its possible forms of execution are described by a process model. Each running process corresponds to an instance of the process model.

This notion is similar to what we know from data modeling. All data of interest to a particular subject area is defined by the data model, that is as an entity/relationship structure or a set of table schemes. The data items that correspond to a real world object are represented by instances of this data model, that is as entities and relationships or as rows in tables.

The constructs and associated language used to formulate a data model as well as the precise prescription of the properties and behavior of instances of an associated data model are referred to as a *metamodel*. For example, the relational model of data provides constructs, like tables, columns, and keys, to model data. The metamodel also describes the properties of instances; for example no two rows in a table are allowed to have the same key values. The metamodel further describes how instances behave, for example, what is returned as the result of a query.

The notion "metamodel" is used because a particular data model may be perceived as an instance of the constructs provided by the metamodel. For example, based on the relational model the table `Person` is an instance of the construct `Table`, and the column `Name` of the `Person` table is an instance of the construct `Column`. For short, a model whose instances can themselves be instantiated—they are a model as well—is referred to as a "metamodel." For more background on this subject see [Ley94] and the literature given there.

The constructs and language provided by a metamodel are called its *syntax*, and the description of the properties and behavior of instances built according to this syntax is called its *semantics*. The syntax and semantics of our workflow metamodel are based on graph theory: Let $\mathcal{P}$ denote the set of all process models. A particular process model $P \in \mathcal{P}$ is represented as a special kind of directed graph G, called "PM-Graph" (see section 4.6 on page 160).

The node set N of G consists of the set of all activities of the associated process model P (see section 4.3 on page 128). The edge set E of G prescribes all possible sequences of activities within P (see section 4.4.1 on page 136). A set of conditions $\mathcal{C}$ (business rules or predicates) determines the actual activity sequencing of a particular instance of P (see section 4.4.1 on page 136). These conditions are formulated in terms of the context of a process model P, that is by the data its activities manipulate (see section 4.2 on the following page).

Very often G and P are not distinguished. G is the mathematical representation of the model P of a given business process. When an actual business process is performed according to the model P, different terms with different connotations are used:

- The term *instance* of a process model P is used if the enactment of the rules represented by the model P should be emphasized. An instance is realized by navigation through the corresponding graph G.

- The term *process* is used if the performance of a concrete business process by an organization is in the foreground. A possible support from information technology is ignored.

- The term *workflow* is used if the support of a business process in a computing environment is the relevant aspect.

Since we are mainly dealing with workflows, we will take the liberty of using all three terms interchangeably. Consequently, a workflow management system runs a workflow by enacting a process model P, resulting in an instance of P by navigating through the graph corresponding this model.

The instance of G is reflected by the time-dependent state of its encompassed activities and conditions and by the data actually associated with the workflow (see section 4.7 on page 162). Performing an activity of a workflow will modify this data, in general. The conditions, C, therefore determine the next activities to be performed, based on the actual data. In general, each activity performed influences the actual path taken through the graph, which is the sequencing of activities.

Depending on the actual data produced by the activities or passed to the process, different paths are taken by the workflow (see Figure 4.1 on the facing page). Thus, a process model can be perceived as a road map, the conditions are road blocks that block roads, based on the current traffic situation, that is the process context, and a process instance is the actual traffic in the area depicted by the map.

4.2 Process Data

A process model and its contained activities and conditions have data associated with them that describes all of the information required by the corresponding business process for appropriate execution. This data includes information needed as input by the various activities, data required by conditions to determine the actual sequencing of activities, and the data to be exchanged between activities.

For example, the `Trip Reservation` process (see Appendix A) has as input the name and the address of the customer reserving a trip and requests all necessary information about the customer's credit card. The `Debit Credit Card` activity uses this information for billing the customer for the bookings. A condition enforcing that credit cards from certain companies are not accepted requires the name of the credit card company as input.

We call the set of all data required by a particular process model for its correct execution its *process data*. Process data represents the actual context in which an instance of a process model is operating.

Figure 4.1 The Relationship of Process Models and Workflows

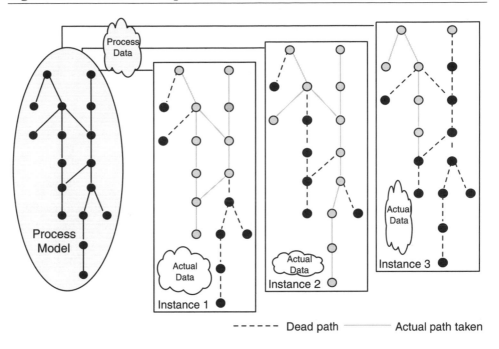

- - - - - Dead path ——————— Actual path taken

4.2.1 Data Elements

The workflow management system passes process data between the various activities and it provides selective access to it for both, activity parameterization and its own processing, such as condition evaluation and container mapping. The type of all process data must therefore be known to the workflow management system.

For this reason, the metamodel provides for the definition of process data. Process data is collected in a set V, which is associated with a process model P. A member $v \in V$ is called a *data element*. Each data element has an associated name and structure. The name of a data element allows selective access to it; its structure prescribes its composition from already defined data elements. If a data element has no internal structure or there is no need to know the internal structure, then the data element can be associated with an atomic structure. We capture the specification of data elements in the following iterative definition.

Definition (Data Elements)   Let M be a set of names and S be a set of structures. Then

1. $m \in M \wedge s \in S \Rightarrow < m; s > \in V$
   that means each pair consisting of a name and an already defined structure as a valid data element.

2. $\zeta_1, \ldots, \zeta_k \in S(k \in \mathbb{N})$
   where $\zeta_1, \ldots, \zeta_k$ represents the *atomic* structures that exist from the very beginning, such as INTEGER, FLOAT, or STRING.

3. $d \in V \Rightarrow d(k) \in S(k \in \mathbb{N})$
   where $d(k)$ denotes an *array* of k elements over d; that means an array of an already defined data element is a new valid structure.

4. $\overline{V} \subseteq V \Rightarrow \times\overline{V} \in S$
   where $\times\overline{V}$ denotes a *tuple* over $\overline{V}$: that means a tuple over an already defined data elements is a new valid structure, and card $\overline{V} < \infty$.

   ∎

The definition works as follows. Based on the atomic structures data elements can be defined by assigning a name to an atomic structure. These data elements can then be used to build tuple structures or array structures. These structures are referred to as constructors because of their constructive nature. The tuple constructor is represented by ... . The array constructor is represented as $\times$. By assigning a name to these newly defined structures, on creates new data elements that can be the basis for building new data elements with the available constructors. As an extension of our definition, other *constructors* are possible here, such as a list constructor or a set constructor.

Remark   The tuple constructor is the only constructor available to define table schemes in the relational data model. The associated atomic structures are the column data types provided by the implementing database management system. The use of constructors to recursively build new structures is well known from the field of data models. Our data elements are called *complex objects* or *compound objects* in this area (see [Ull88] and the references there for more details).

4.2.2   Domains

Next, we must define how to build valid instances based on the definition of a data element. This building rule is again iterative and corresponds to the iterative way for defining data elements.

Definition (Domain)   Each data element $v \in V$ has an associated *domain* $\mathrm{DOM}(v)$ that represents all of its corresponding well-formed values:

1. $\mathrm{DOM}(< m, \zeta_i >) := \mathrm{domain}(\zeta_i)$
   (i.e., the domain of an atomic element is the set of all valid values of the associated atomic structure, e.g., domain(FLOAT) are all floating point numbers.)

2. $DOM(< m'; < m; s > (k) >) := DOM(< m; s >)(k)$
   (i.e., the domain of a data element structured as a k-element array is the set of all arrays with at most k values from the domain of the data element being the base for the array.)

3. $DOM(< m'; \times \{< m_1; s_1 >, \ldots, < m_r; s_r >\} >) := \underset{1 \le i \le r}{\times} DOM(< m_i; s_i >),$
   (i.e., the domain of a tuple-structured data element is the Cartesian product of the domain of the components of the tuple constructor.)

A value from a domain $DOM(v)$ of a data element $v \in V$ is called an *instance* of v.

◼

If other constructors are available for defining structures of data elements, iterative definitions of the domains of these constructors must be added to the definition above.

In the relational data model, a valid instance of a table scheme (as defined by a tuple constructor based on given column data types) is a row in the table. The domain of the table scheme is the set of all possible valid rows.

Example (Data Elements and Instances)   The `Person` data element is a tuple with the components `Name`, `Salary`, `Address`, and `Hobbies`. `Name` and `Salary` have an atomic structure, namely, `STRING` and `FLOAT`. `Address` has a tuple structure with two atomic string components called `City` and `Country`. `Hobbies` has an array structure consisting of at most 15 elements named `Hobby` of atomic type `STRING`.

Figure 4.2 shows two instances of `Person`. Frank has a salary of 4000, lives in Berlin, Germany, and has jogging and reading as hobbies. Dieter has a salary of 5000, lives in Munich, Germany and has biking, cooking, and wine as hobbies.

Language Representation (Data Elements)   In FDL, the keyword `STRUCTURE` starts the definition of a data element. The name of the data element follows immediately after this keyword. The description of the data element is terminated by the keyword `END` followed by the name of its corresponding `STRUCTURE` statement. The following defines the data elements `Address` and `Hobby`.

```
STRUCTURE   'Address'
   'City':      STRING;
   'Country':   STRING;
END 'Address'

STRUCTURE   'Hobby'
   'Hobby':     STRING;
END 'Hobby'
```

Figure 4.2 A Sample Data Element and Sample Instances

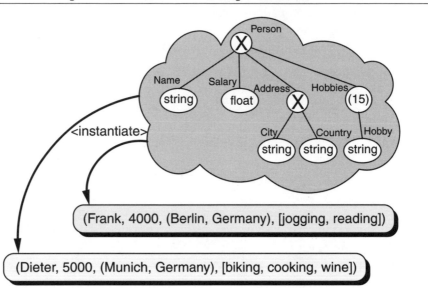

These two data elements are used to build the `Person` data element defined above.

```
STRUCTURE 'Person'
    'Name':     STRING;
    'Salary':   FLOAT;
    'Address':  'Address';
    'Hobbies':  'Hobby'(15);
END 'Person'
```

4.2.3   Containers

Activities as well as processes have both input data and output data. The output of a condition is always simply a truth value (an instance of `Boolean`), so only the input data of conditions must be specified. Input and output data are represented as collections of data elements. Such a collection is called a *container*.

Activities and process models represent something that happens, so we collectively refer to them as $\mathcal{H}$; that means $\mathcal{H} = N \cup \mathcal{P}$ is the set of all activities and process models. V denotes the set of process data associated with all process models (usually we only need the process data of a particular process model, but for the following definition we need a broader scope), and $\mathcal{C}$ denotes the set of all conditions. Let $\wp(M)$ denote the power set of a given set M; that means the set of all subsets of M.

Definition (Container) The map ι assigns to each activity, process model, and condition its *input container*:

$$\iota : \mathcal{H} \cup \mathcal{C} \rightarrow \wp(V)$$

This means,

$$\forall X \in \mathcal{H} \cup \mathcal{C} : \iota(X) \subseteq V \text{ with card } \iota(X) < \infty$$

The map o assigns to each activity and process model its *output container*:

$$o : \mathcal{H} \rightarrow \wp(V)$$

This means,

$$\forall X \in \mathcal{H} \cup \mathcal{C} : o(X) \subseteq V \text{ with card } o(X) < \infty$$

■

A collection of instances corresponding to the data elements $\iota(X)$ or $o(X)$ is called a *container instance* or an instance of the container.

Thus, containers are explicit groupings of input and output data. An input container $\iota(X)$ and an output container $o(X)$ are a distinguished set of data elements associated with X as X's possible input data and possible output data, respectively.

We represent containers as sets. Thus, the data elements within a container are not ordered. This is similar to the representation of table schemes in the relational data model and has the same advantages as the relational data model. Containers can be empty.

Many implementations, such as MQSeries Workflow, prescribe that containers have a tuple structure and that this tuple structure always includes system-defined components as data elements. These components define information that describes the workflow to which the container belongs to. For example, a system-defined data element holds the name of the activity. As a consequence, containers are never empty in such implementations. Furthermore, at most a single component within this tuple structure is foreseen for the data element (which of course can be an arbitrary complex object) describing the proper application data.

Example (Containers) In our running example, the activity `Flight Reservation` has an input container with a single data element called `Itinerary` and an output container with a single data element called `Flights`.

Language Representation (Containers)   In FDL, each activity is associated with a pair consisting of the name of the application-specific data element of the activity's input container as the first component and the name of the application-specific data element of its output container as the second component. This name pair must follow the name of the activity, as shown in the following FDL snippet encoding the activity from the running example.

```
PROGRAM_ACTIVITY 'Flight Reservation'
   ('Itinerary', 'Flights' )
   ...
END 'Flight Reservation'
```

The keyword PROGRAM_ACTIVITY in the example specifies the type of the implementation of the activity. In case the activity has no application-specific input or output data element, the default data structure is specified as consisting of just the system-provided components.

4.3   Activities

A business process defines how an enterprise achieves a particular goal, such as the granting of a loan or the hiring of a new employee. The business process defines each piece of work that must be performed to achieve this goal.

The metamodel provides the notion of an activity to define the pieces of work encompassed by a business process. This definition includes the specification of an activity's input and output data, the tool to be used to perform the associated piece of work, the person who has the skill and duty to perform it, and the method determine whether the work is complete or not. We discuss these aspects later in detail. Other activity aspects that are not fundamental for the metamodel—for example, escalation information such as the maximal duration of a piece of work and who has to be informed when this time is exceeded—we discussed in the previous chapter.

So, an *activity* is an abstraction of a piece of work that has to be performed within a process. It provides all of the information to determine who has to do what with which data and with what kind of tool. The set of activities of a process defines the node set N of the graph corresponding to the associated process model.

The usual connotation of work is that something happens to produce something. This idea is captured by the data manipulation aspect of an activity. Based on the input provided to an activity in its input container, the activity returns produced data in its output container. Thus, an activity is like a function.

To be more precise, as an abstract specification at the model level, an activity defines the type of its input and its output, and so it is perceived as an operator. The tool that implements the activity and that is later invoked by the workflow management system is passed an instance of the input type and produces an instance of the output type. This distinction is emphasized in the following two definitions. The reader who is familiar with algebraic specifications (see, for example, [EM85]) will note the similarities between activities and activity implementations on one side and signatures and models on the other side.

Definition (Activity) The set of all activities of a process model $P \in \mathcal{P}$ is denoted by N. Each member of N is given by its name A. Usually, an *activity* is written as an operator $A : \iota(A) \rightarrow o(A)$.

■

4.3.1 Activity Implementations

The tool that is used to perform, or at least helps to perform, the piece of work is assigned to the activity. Since we deal with the support of work within a computing environment, we assign to each activity an executable so that it can be supported by a computer. If an activity is supported by a tool that is not attached to the computing environment, we assume that the executable assigned to the activity creates a request to its performing agent to use the particular tool. For example, if an activity consists in making a customer call, the associated executable could display a message with the customer's name, phone number and all required information and should display it with the message that this customer has to be called.

The tool associated with an activity is the representation of the activity within the computing environment. It is this tool that gets the current instance of the activity's input container as input and that produces an instance of the activity's output container as current output of the activity. To emphasize this, the tool associated with the activity is referred to as the activity's *implementation*. An implementation can simply be a program or it can be a process model. In the former case, we call the activity a *program activity*; in the latter case, we call it a *process activity*; a process that implements an activity is called a *subprocess*.

Definition (Activity Implementation) Let $\mathcal{E}$ denote the set of all possible implementations of all activities; that means a member of $\mathcal{E}$ can be a program or again be a process model. The map $\Psi : N \rightarrow \mathcal{E}$ associates with each activity A its *activity implementation* $\Psi(A)$. An activity implementation itself is perceived as a map.

$$\Psi(A) : \underset{v \in \iota(A)}{\times} \mathrm{DOM}(v) \rightarrow \underset{v \in o(A)}{\times} \mathrm{DOM}(v)$$

■

An activity implementation will often have additional input, such as persistent data or user input, that is not defined to the workflow management system. This input has the effect that an activity implementation may produce different results based on the same instance of its input container at different times. For example, an activity that assesses the risk of giving a particular person a credit of a certain amount will once produce the result "low" (if it is the person's first credit) and once the result "high" (if it is the person's tenth credit). So, in a precise sense, $\Psi(A)$ is not a function but a mathematical relation. Since the metamodel does not make any assumptions about the deterministic behavior of activity implementations, we have chosen the simpler definition of a map instead of a relation.

Example (Program Activity Implementation)   The Flight Reservation activity from our running example is implemented by a program called Flight Application. The program runs on OS/2 and has a file name of FlgtRsv.exe.

Language Representation (Program Activity Implementation)   The fact that an activity is a program activity is made explicit by preceding the name of the activity with the keyword PROGRAM_ACTIVITY. Then, the specification of the activity follows and is ended by an END keyword followed by the name of the activity whose specification now ends. The name of the program that implements the activity is supplied by the keyword PROGRAM. See the following snippet.

```
PROGRAM_ACTIVITY 'Flight Reservation'
    PROGRAM 'Flight Application'
END 'Flight Reservation'
```

Instead of giving all the necessary details about the program implementing an activity in the PROGRAM_ACTIVITY clause, a new separate clause beginning with the PROGRAM keyword is used. This approach allows the reuse of details about a program within definitions of implementations of other activities.

The following FDL snippet shows some of the keywords available for defining programs. The OS2 keyword indicates that the subject program runs on OS/2. The keyword EXE defines the program as an EXE file. The file name of the program, FlgtRsv.exe, and the path in which it is to be found are defined by the PATH_AND_FILENAME keyword. The START FOREGROUND causes the program to be started in the foreground, so that the user can immediately enter data. Other keywords define more details of the program (see Appendix A for more information).

```
PROGRAM 'Flight Application'
    OS2
        EXE
            PATH_AND_FILENAME 'FlgtRsv.exe'
            START FOREGROUND
END 'Flight Application'
```

Language Example (Process Activity Implementation)   Our running example includes a process activity, which is an activity implemented by another process model. The Contact Customer activity is another business process with its own model. Within the FDL, this situation is indicated by preceding the name of the activity by the keyword PROCESS_ACTIVITY instead of using the PROGRAM_ACTIVITY keyword. The associated process that implements the process activity is identified by the PROCESS clause.

```
PROCESS_ACTIVITY 'Contact Customer'
   PROCESS 'Contact Customer Process'
END 'Contact Customer'
```

So, at the FDL level, the map Ψ assigns to each activity a PROGRAM or PROCESS clause, depending on its type of implementation.

The map Ψ links an activity with the computing environment. Ψ is the definition of the executable used to perform the piece of work represented by the activity A. If $\Psi(A)$ is a program, this definition includes all details, such as the program's path name, location, or mode of execution, required to invoke the executable appropriately.

4.3.2   Performing an Activity

We discussed in Chapter 3 what it means to execute an activity. Figure 4.3 illustrates what happens in terms of the metamodel.

Figure 4.3 Executing an Activity

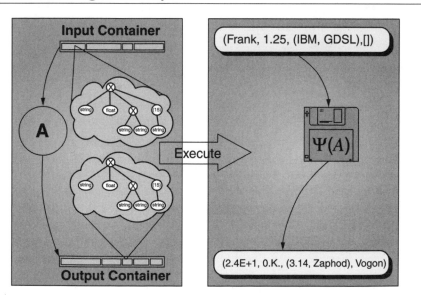

When a workitem is started, the workflow management system knows the name A of the underlying activity. Based on this name, it builds an instance of A's input container $\iota(A)$ (*container materialization*—see section 4.7.2 on page 163 for details). Next, the activity implementation $\Psi(A)$ is invoked and receives this instance as input. During its execution, $\Psi(A)$ can pass instances of members of its output container to the workflow management system so that when the activity implementation terminates, an instance of A's output container $o(A)$ is returned to the workflow management system. The workflow management system makes the returned instance persistent (*container dematerialization*).

4.3.3   Staff Assignment

Work is performed by agents. An *agent* is typically a human being, but it could also be a computing entity, such as a daemon running on a particular machine performing a piece of work automatically. The set of agents that actually could perform the work corresponding to a particular activity is dynamically determined. We now describe how the metamodel reflects that fact.

The metamodel assigns a query to each activity to determine the agents who could perform the work corresponding to the activity. Such a query is called a *staff query* because human beings participating in business processes are often called *staff*.

The ability of an agent to perform a piece of work is measured by its membership in particular roles or organizational units. A role of an agent typically reflects skills, in the case of human beings, or computing capabilities, in the case of computing entities. In practice, a staff query computes agents based on an organizational database (see Figure 4.4). Typically, such an organizational database changes in time. Thus, a staff query is time dependent, which means that it may produce different agent sets at different points in time.

Consequently, the metamodel has to consider the notion of time. Since everything in a computing environment is performed stepwise, we reflect time within the metamodel by the set of natural numbers $\mathbb{N}$ (see section 4.7.1 on page 162 for more details). Time-dependent elements of the metamodel will thus be parameterized by natural numbers.

Definition (Staff Assignment)   Denoting a staff query by q, the query will return at any point in time $i \in \mathbb{N}$ a set of agents $q(i) \in \wp(\mathcal{A})$, where $\mathcal{A}$ denotes the set of all agents. Thus, we define as follows: A member of the set $\mathcal{Q} = \{q \mid q : \mathbb{N} \to \wp(\mathcal{A})$ is called a *staff query*. The map $\Omega : \mathbb{N} \to \mathcal{Q}$ is called *staff assignment*, and it associates a staff query with each activity.

■

Figure 4.4 Deriving Eligible Agents from the Organizational Database

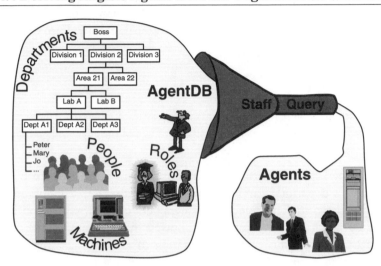

$\Omega(A)$ is a declarative description of the properties an agent must have to be eligible to perform the work associated with the activity A. In practice, $\Omega(A)$ is a query on an organizational database that returns—when executed at time $i \in \mathbb{N}$—as its result the set of all agents that qualify at time i to perform the associated piece of work: $\Omega(A) : \mathbb{N} \to \wp(A)$. The map Ω links each activity with the organizational structure supporting the execution of a business process.

Example   The various reservation activities from our running example are to be performed by specialists in the subject area. For this purpose, corresponding roles are defined, and the staff query assigned to a particular reservation activity determines the members of the role belonging to the activity. For example, the role Flight Specialist represents all people in a company who specialize in reserving flights, and only members of this role are capable of performing the Flight Reservation activity.

Language Representation   In FDL, the staff query assigned to an activity is introduced by the DONE_BY keyword. In the example above, the staff query has to select all members of the role Flight Specialist. As shown in the following FDL snippet, this kind of selection is specified in FDL by the MEMBER OF ROLE clause followed by the name of the role.

```
PROGRAM_ACTIVITY 'Flight Reservation'
   DONE_BY MEMBER OF ROLE  'Flight Specialist'
END 'Flight Reservation'
```

FDL provides the ROLE clause as well as the ORGANIZATION clause with a corresponding END keyword to define roles and organizational units. So, the role Flight Specialist and the Travel department are defined as follows:

```
ROLE 'Flight Specialist'
END 'Flight Specialist'

ORGANIZATION 'Travel'
END 'Travel'
```

The activity Contact Customer can be performed by employees of the Travel department and employees of all other departments reporting directly or indirectly to it. The selection of members of an organization is done in FDL by the ORGANIZATION keyword followed by the name of the organization within the DONE_BY clause; the computation of all members reporting directly or indirectly to a certain organizational unit ("transitive closure") is declared by the INCLUDE_CHILD_ORGANIZATIONS keyword.

```
PROCESS_ACTIVITY 'Contact Customer'
   DONE_BY ORGANIZATION 'Travel'
          INCLUDE_CHILD_ORGANIZATIONS
END 'Contact Customer'
```

So, at the FDL level, the map Ω associates with each activity a DONE_BY clause representing the staff assignment. The staff query $\Omega(A)$ assigned to the activity A is declared within this clause by appropriate keywords like MEMBER OF ROLE or ORGANIZATION.

4.3.4 Exit Conditions

Activities within a business process as well as a business process itself represent long-running actions, in general. Thus, workflow management systems realize that such actions within a computing environment have to deal with long-running pieces of work that must be able to survive even system shutdowns. It must be possible for activities to be interrupted for any duration and then resumed later. For this requirement to be met, the termination of the tool implementing an activity must not be confused with the completion of the piece of work represented by the associated activity. For example, the agent performing the activity with the tool might interrupt his work by terminating the tool with the intention to continue the activity later on.

The workflow management system thus must be able to distinguish the syntactical event consisting of the return of a tool to the workflow system from the semantical event indicating the completion of a piece of work performed with the tool. This capability is added to the metamodel by attaching an *exit condition* to each activity. Like any condition each exit condition has an input container (see section 4.2.3 on page 126) that ties it to the actual process data. Whenever the tool implementing an activity returns to the workflow management system, the associated exit condition is evaluated, based on the current instance of its input container. When the exit condition is met, the associated work is treated as completed; otherwise, it is assumed that the work is only interrupted and will be continued.

Definition The map $\varepsilon : N \to C$ assigns to each activity a predicate called *exit condition*. The exit condition $\varepsilon(A)$ of activity A has its input container $\iota(\varepsilon(A)) \subseteq V$ such that an exit condition is considered as a Boolean function:

$$\varepsilon(A) : \underset{v \in \iota(\varepsilon(A))}{\times} DOM(v) \to \{0, 1\}$$

■

In terms of this definition, when an activity implementation $\Psi(A)$ terminates, A's exit condition $\varepsilon(A)$ is evaluated in the instances of its actual input container $\iota(\varepsilon(A))$. Activity A is considered to be *completed*, that is successfully performed, if and only if $\varepsilon(A)(\iota(\varepsilon(A))) = 1$. If A is not completed, it must be continued at a later time.

Example Reserving flights for a whole itinerary may take quite some time. It may be that some flights can be reserved but they are not immediately confirmed, or some other flights may not be able to be reserved at all because currently there is no connection to the corresponding airline's reservation system. Because of this type of problem, it is desirable to be able to interrupt the work. In the running example, the reservation activities are implemented by applications that allow the performing agent to indicate whether or not the work is finished; this indicator is passed to the workflow management system in the activity's output container from which the exit condition receives the actual value required for its evaluation.

Language Representation In FDL, the exit condition of an activity is introduced by the EXIT keyword. The predicate specifying the exit condition is preceded by the WHEN keyword. In addition, one can specify whether the exit condition should be evaluated immediately when the corresponding activity terminates or whether the user has to request its evaluation at a later time; this specification is done with the keywords AUTOMATIC and MANUAL, respectively. In our example, the Flight

`Reservation` activity is completed if and only if the `Finished` flag is set to "Yes"; the flag is checked by the workflow management system at the time the activity implementation returns.

```
PROGRAM_ACTIVITY 'Flight Reservation'
   EXIT AUTOMATIC
      WHEN '''Finished'' = ''Yes'''
END 'Flight Reservation'
```

So, at FDL level, the map ε associates with each activity an `EXIT` clause representing the proper predicate of the exit condition as well as an instruction to the workflow management system of when to evaluate it.

Figure 4.5 summarizes the fine structure of an activity, as we have described it until now, consisting of a staff query, an activity implementation and an exit condition.

Figure 4.5 Fine Structure of an Activity

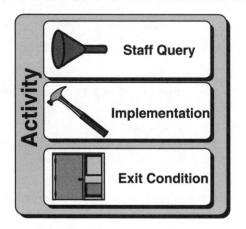

4.4   Control Flow

To define how an enterprise achieves a particular goal, a business process not only prescribes each single piece of work to be performed but also prescribes the appropriate work sequence. We dealt with the description of activities as isolated entities in section 4.3 on page 128; now we show how the metamodel relates activities by defining their valid execution sequences.

4.4.1   Control Connectors

When the model of a process is specified, for each activity A, all of its potential follow-on activities $A_1, \ldots, A_n$ have to be specified. Graphically, this is done by connecting A with $A_1, \ldots, A_n$ by use of directed edges. A directed edge pointing from A to A_i specifies that A_i is a potential successor of A: that means when the activity A completes, the next activities possibly to be performed are A_1 up to A_n. That means the piece of work associated with A leaves the workflow management system's scope of control and some of the pieces of work associated with $A_1, \ldots, A_n$ possibly have to be controlled next; this is why the pairs $(A, A_1), \ldots, (A, A_n)$ are said to define the *potential* control flow within the business process.

Which of A's successors $A_1, \ldots, A_n$ must actually be performed depends on business rules controlling each of the potential transitions $(A, A_1), \ldots, (A, A_n)$. These business rules are called *transition conditions*. To be more precise, the set of business rules affecting the transition of a specific pair (A, A_i) is represented by a predicate called "transition condition".

A transition condition is a predicate in the process data, that is in the data elements of its input container. So, the truth value varies with the instance of the transition condition's input container, that is when the process data changes. Now, whether or not the potential successor A_i of A has to be performed in the actual situation of a particular instance depends on the truth value of the transition condition governing the control flow from A to A_i. Thus, the *actual* control flow taken depends via the transition conditions on the actual process data.

Process data changes when an activity implementation terminates and passes an instance of its associated output container back to the workflow management system, because this container instance becomes a part of the actual process data. So, running an activity implementation will change the actual process data and thus will impact the actual control flow within a business process. And because the output of an activity implementation generally depends on its input, which in turn depends on the output of its predecessors and on the data accessed by the activity implementation itself, the actual flow of control through a given process model P varies from instance to instance.

In the metamodel, the dependency of the potential control flow from A to B on its associated transition condition is made explicitly visible by specifying the control flow as a triple (A, B, p). In other words, the edges of the directed graph G are weighted by predicates in V. The following definition summarizes this weighting:

Definition (Control Connector)   The set $E \subseteq N \times N \times \mathcal{C}$ is called the set of *control connectors* of a process model $P \in \mathcal{P}$. For a control connector $(A, B, p) \in E$, the predicate $p \in \mathcal{C}$ is called a *transition condition*. Each transition condition p is considered as a Boolean function in its input container $\iota(p) \subseteq V$:

$$p : \underset{v \in \iota(p)}{\times} \mathrm{DOM}(v) \rightarrow \{0, 1\}$$

∎

We are now ready to describe in terms of our metamodel a simplified step in interpreting a process model. Let us assume that the activity implementation $\Psi(A)$ of activity A completes, that means it is $\varepsilon(A)(\iota(\varepsilon(A))) = 1$. If control potentially flows from A to B governed by the transition condition p, that means if $(A, B, p) \in E$, then the input container of p is materialized and the transition condition is evaluated according to this container instance. The actual control is passed to B if $p(\iota(p)) = 1$. (See Section 4.7 on page 162 for all of the details.)

Example (Control Connector)   Traveluck, Inc., the company from our running example, does not cooperate with the Shark Ltd. credit card company. A reservation made with a credit card from this company has to be rejected, but reservations with any other credit card will be accepted. This case is modeled as follows:

The activities `Reject Reservation` and `Confirm Reception` are potential follow-on activities of `Get Credit Card`. Thus, there is one control connector from `Get Credit Card` to `Reject Reservation` and another one from `Get Credit Card` to `Confirm Reception`. Attaching the transition condition `Credit Card Company = 'Shark Ltd.'` to the potential control flow definition from `Get Credit Card` to `Reject Reservation` reflects the business rule above; note that `Credit Card Company` is a field in the output container of the `Get Credit Card` activity. If the customer passed any other credit card company, control flows from `Get Credit Card` to `Confirm Reception`.

Language Example (Control Connector)   Control connectors are defined by the CONTROL clause. The FROM keyword specifies the source activity, and the TO keyword the target activity. The transition condition is preceded by the WHEN keyword.

```
CONTROL FROM 'Get Credit Card'
    TO 'Reject Reservation'
    WHEN '''Credit Card Company'' = ''Shark Ltd.'''

CONTROL FROM 'Get Credit Card'
    TO 'Confirm Reception'
    WHEN '''Credit Card Company'' GT ''Shark Ltd.'''
```

If no transition condition is explicitly specified, a transition condition that always evaluates to true is assumed by default, that is control always flows along such a control connector to its target when its source completes. The special predicate OTHERWISE is provided in FDL and evaluates to true if and only if all other transition conditions of control connectors leaving a given activity are evaluated as false. Using this special predicate, the language fragment above is equivalent to the following one.

```
CONTROL FROM 'Get Credit Card'
     TO 'Reject Reservation'
     WHEN '''Credit Card Company'' = ''Shark Ltd.'''

CONTROL FROM 'Get Credit Card'
     TO 'Confirm Reception'
     WHEN OTHERWISE
```

For convenience and brevity, we introduce the following symbols that we will use in some of the more formal parts of this chapter:

- The set of all transition conditions of control connectors pointing to activity A is denoted by $\mathcal{C}^{\leftarrow}(A) := \pi_3(\{e \in E \mid \pi_2(e) = A\})$

- The set of all transition conditions of control connectors leaving activity A is denoted by $\mathcal{C}^{\rightarrow}(A) := \pi_3(\{e \in E \mid \pi_1(e) = A\})$

As usual, π denotes the projection map between Cartesian products, and its indices specify the selected components of the domain onto which to project: For $1 \leq i_1, \ldots, i_k \leq n$, it is $\pi_{i_1,\ldots,i_k} : M \times \cdots \times M_n \rightarrow M_{i_1} \times \ldots \times M_{i_k}$.

4.4.2 Restrictions on Control Connectors

Control connectors cannot bind activities in an arbitrary manner. The following two restrictions are imposed on the set of control connectors of any process model:

1. Between two given activities there is at most one control connector (a property, called *unified*, of the set of control connectors). Two activities are either not linked at all, or they are linked by a single control connector.

2. When moving from a particular activity along one of its outgoing control connectors to one of its successors, and then from the activity reached to one of its successors and so on, one will never come back to the original activity (a property, called *acyclicity*, of the set of control connectors). That means, control connectors must not build loops.

Thus, the set of control connectors of a process model is both unified and acyclic. The following example will clarify what this statement means.

Example (Forbidden Control Flow)   Figure 4.6 depicts a sample invalid process model containing activities A to J. These activities are linked via control connectors as shown in the figure.

- The control connectors (A, B, p) and (A, B, p') build a nonuniform set of control connectors. Substituting for them with the single control connector $(A, B, p \vee p')$ results in an equivalent uniform control flow.

Figure 4.6 Forbidden Control Flows

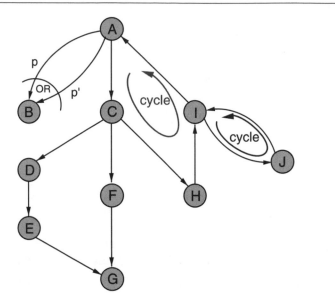

- The control connectors $(A, C), (C, H), (H, I), (I, A)$ build a cycle, that is a loop $A \rightarrow C \rightarrow H \rightarrow I \rightarrow A$.

- The control connectors $(I, J), (J, I)$ build a cycle between the two activities I and J.

- There are two paths between activities C and G, namely, $(C, D), (D, E)$, (E, G) and $(C, F), (F, G)$. These two paths do *not* define a cycle. The direction of the control connectors must always be considered; that is a cycle is defined by a path that is closed when following its encompassed control connectors in their directions.

Both unification and acyclicity are restrictions imposed on the metamodel to improve the comprehension of process models formulated with its constructs. Unification ensures that a single control connector with a single transition condition is specified instead of multiple transition conditions and a join condition. With unification, control flow is much easier to understand, the representation of the underlying business rules is much more compact, and the graph structure of the process model is less complex. Acylicity ensures that work represented by activities is only repeated on the base of simple patterns advocated decades ago in structured programming (see [Fai85] and the references given there), so-called do-until loops. To specify the repetition of a group of activities, these activities can be specified as a process model being the implementation of a new activity; the exit condition of this process activity (see section 4.3.1 on page 129) then represents the proper condition for when to leave the loop.

Arbitrary cycles would introduce ambiguities in a process model and might introduce race conditions. For example, it might happen in an instance of the process model of figure 4.6 that after completion of activity C control flows to D as well as H. Over time, D, E and G are completed, but then the control flow enters C again via the path C → H → I → A → C, and C is reexecuted. Then the question arises whether after C's completion, the transition conditions of (C, D),d (C, F) and (C, H) or whether only (C, H) should be reevaluated. If all transition conditions are reevaluated, D, E and G could be reexecuted, or even F might be executed this time whereas it was not executed the first time. Thus, the problem is: what is the loop that the process modeler wanted to specify? Should the loop affect the complete process model, or just the loop defined by A → C → H → I → A, or another subset (which one?) of the process model? In another instance of the process model, the work along the loop C → H → I → A → C might be performed very quickly, and D is still active while C completes its second time and control is passed again to D. What should happen? Should the current execution of D be interrupted and terminated in favor of a newly started execution of D? This recourse might be desirable because the work along the loop could have generated data that resulted in a new instance of D's input container. The question is, whether the input container instance of the actual performing work represented by D is invalidated by the new container instance and is outdated so that D might even produce incorrect results, or whether the new container instance represents a new piece of work of the same kind within the process instance.

Depending on the concrete process model, the answer to each of these questions can be "yes" or "no" depending on the situation. Consequently, the metamodel would have to provide corresponding parameters to describe the semantics appropriate to a particular process model. Doing so would complicate the metamodel. By its restriction to acyclic graphs, the metamodel avoids these complications without restricting its expressiveness (loops can be modeled as process activities with appropriate exit conditions).

In what follows we provide a more precise definition of the restrictions on control connectors of the metamodel.

Definition (Path)   Let E be the set of control connectors of a process model P, and let $e_1, \ldots, e_n \in E$. The sequence $(e_1, \ldots, e_n)$ is called a *path* from the activity $A \in N$ (the *startpoint* of the path) to activity $B \in N$ (the *endpoint* of the path) if and only if it satisfies the following conditions:

1. $\pi_2(e_{i-1}) = \pi_1(e_i)$ for $2 \le i \le n$
   the target node of each edge is the source of its succeeding edge.

2. $e_i \neq e_j$ for $i \neq j$
   the edges within a path are pairwise distinct.

3. $\pi_1(e_1) = A$ and $\pi_2(e_n) = B$
   the source node of the first edge of the path is the startpoint of the path, and
   the target node of the last edge of the path is the endpoint of the path.

■

Definition (Acyclicity)   A path $(e_1, \ldots, e_n)$ is called a *cycle* iff its startpoint is
also its endpoint; that means $\pi_1(e_1) = \pi_2(e_n)$. The set E of edges of a graph is
called *acyclic* iff the set of all paths in edges of E contains no cycle. A graph is
called *acyclic* if its edge set is acyclic. ■

A cycle is a path having the same node as endpoint as well as startpoint. A
graph whose edge set does not allow any cycle to be built is called acyclic. Note
that cycles are always *directed*; that means two nodes of the graph can be connected
by two different paths such that the *un*directed edges build an *un*directed cycle.

Definition (Unified Edges)   A set of edges E of control connectors is *unified*:

$$\Leftrightarrow \forall e, e' \in E : \pi_{1,2}(e) = \pi_{1,2}(e') \Rightarrow \pi_3(e) = \pi_3(e')$$

■

It is easy to see that each nonunified set of control connectors can be transformed into a unified set. One would substitute a set of control connectors between
two given activities by a single control connector between the activities, with the
target's join condition as transition condition.

4.4.3   Forks and Joins

The main reason for applying workflow technology in practice is to speed up business processes; the three fundamental techniques for achieving speed up are staff
assignment, notification, and parallelism.

Of these three, the primary mechanism provided at the metamodel level to
achieve speedups is the ability to specify parallel control flows. An activity having more than one outgoing control connector represents a *fork*, meaning that the
spawned branches could be worked on in parallel. To be more precise, the only
branches that could be worked on in parallel are those that are spawned by control
connectors whose associated transition conditions have evaluated to true based on
the actual context.

Parallel work must often be synchronized. The metamodel achieves synchronization by joins. A *join* is simply an activity having more than one incoming control connector. Before a join activity can be performed the parallel work along paths reaching the join activity must have *all* traversed the control connectors pointing to the join (see Section 4.4.4). This requirement achieves synchronization of work of parallel branches.

Definition (Forks, Joins)   An activity $A \in N$ is called a *fork* if and only iff it has more than one outgoing control connector; that means

$$A \in N \text{ is a fork } :\Leftrightarrow \exists\, e, f \in E : \pi_1(e) = \pi_1(f) = A \land e \neq f$$

An activity $A \in N$ is called a *join* if and only if it has more than one incoming control connector, that means

$$A \in N \text{ is a join } :\Leftrightarrow \exists\, e, f \in E : \pi_2(e) = \pi_2(f) = A \land e \neq f$$

We denote the set of all join activities by N_* and define $N_\bullet := N - N_*$ to be the set of all *regular nodes*.

■

Note   Specifying control flows has a lot to do with "programming." By supporting forks and joins, the metamodel supports parallel programming, but the usual flow control constructs, which were already discussed, are also supported. The support of *sequences* is obvious, *branches* are specified as complementary transition conditions, *case statements* are formulated as appropriate transition conditions, and do-until *loops* are expressed as exit conditions on subprocesses. Thus, the control flow constructs are complete in the sense that they allow the expression of parallel "programs." In fact, as we discuss in section 5.8 on page 206, they provide for the generation of source code from process model graphs.

4.4.4   Join Conditions

For better control in synchronizing work, a join activity has a join condition assigned. Such a *join condition* is a Boolean expression in the transition conditions of the incoming control connectors of the join activity. To perform a join activity:

1. The transition conditions of *all* of its incoming control connectors must have been evaluated before the truth value of the join condition is computed, and

2. Its associated join condition must be true.

The purpose of (1) is twofold. First, it ensures that parallel work is really synchronized at join nodes: work along paths which could finally reach a join node must be completed before the join node can be started. Second, it ensures that a join condition can be evaluated.

In the metamodel, a map Φ associates with each join activity a join condition $\Phi(A)$ that is a Boolean expression in the transition conditions of *all* control connectors pointing to the join activity. Without loss of generality, we assume that this expression is in disjunctive normal form.

Definition (Join Condition)   Denote by φ_A the set of all Boolean conditions in disjunctive normal form of transition conditions of control connectors pointing to the activity $A \in N$; that means

$$\varphi_A := \{ \bigvee_{1 \leq j \leq k} \bigwedge_{1 \leq i \leq l_j} p_i' \mid p_i' \in \{p, \neg p \mid p \in \{\mathcal{C}^{\leftarrow}(A)\}\}$$

Then, $\Phi : N \to \bigcup_{A \in N} \varphi_A$ assigns *join conditions* with

- $\forall A \in N : \Phi(A) \in \varphi_A$, and

- $\forall A \in N_{\bullet} : \Phi(A) = 1$ (that means a regular node has a trivial join condition)

Thus, a join condition $\Phi(A)$ can be perceived as a Boolean function

$$\Phi(A) : \underset{p \in C^{\leftarrow}(A)}{\times} \underset{\nu \in \iota(p)}{\times} DOM(v) \to \{0, 1\}$$

■

Note   As long as a transition condition in a join condition is not evaluated, the join condition has the truth value *unknown* (see section 4.7.4 on page 167). Thus, we are dealing with three-valued logic in the case of join conditions. If a transition condition p is not relevant for a join condition, it is assumed to be represented as $(p \wedge \neg p)$; because the join condition is a disjunction, it is then dependent on the truth value of the other transition conditions.

Roughly, a join activity A can be performed iff its join condition evaluates to true in the actual input containers of the transition conditions of its incoming control connectors; that means iff $\Phi(A)(\iota(p_1), \ldots, \iota(p_{n_A})) = 1$ for $C^{\leftarrow}(A) = \{p_1, \ldots, p_{n_A}\}$. Section 4.7 on page 162 provides a precise definition of how join conditions are evaluated and when activities can be performed.

Example To speed up its trip reservation services, Traveluck, Inc. performs the reservation of flights, hotels, and cars for a trip in parallel. If all reservations are confirmed, the trip schedule is built. Otherwise, if any of the necessary reservations cannot be confirmed, the customer is contacted to discuss an alternate itinerary.

The corresponding activities `Build Trip Schedule` and `Contact Customer` are thus join activities which wait until all parallel reservation activities for a trip have been completed. The join condition of `Build Trip Schedule` is the conjunction, that is an AND combination, of its incoming transition conditions because all reservations must be confirmed before the schedule can be built.

Language Representation A join condition is defined by the `START` clause, the proper condition is preceded by the `WHEN` keyword, and `ALL CONNECTORS TRUE` specifies that the transition conditions of all incoming control connectors must be "true" before the activity can be scheduled—which is exactly the intended conjunction:

```
PROGRAM_ACTIVITY 'Build Trip Schedule'
    START AUTOMATIC
        WHEN ALL CONNECTORS TRUE
END 'Build Trip Schedule'
```

The join condition of `Contact Customer` is simply the disjunction (i.e., an OR combination) of the incoming transition conditions. When at least one of the reservations completed without being able to get all of the confirmations, a new itinerary has to be discussed with the customer.

```
PROCESS_ACTIVITY 'Contact Customer'
    START AUTOMATIC
        WHEN AT_LEAST_ONE CONNECTOR TRUE
END 'Contact Customer'
```

Here, `AT_LEAST_ONE CONNECTOR TRUE` specifies the intended disjunction. At the flow definition language level, the map associates with each activity a `START` clause representing the activity's join condition. The FDL presented in [IBM98b] currently does not support arbitrary Boolean expressions as join conditions but only the ANDing and ORing of the incoming transition conditions. ∎

The metamodel prescribes that join conditions be evaluated if and only if the transition condition of each incoming control connector has been evaluated. As a result parallel work is synchronized. The other effect is that workflow executions are easier to understand. If the metamodel would allow a join activity to be started as soon as the value of its associated join condition is known to be true, race conditions could occur, as shown in Figure 4.7.

For example, assume in the process model depicted in Figure 4.7 that A completes before B and that p evaluates to true. If joins did not enforce waiting, $\Phi(C) = p \vee q$ would be known to be true independently of q's truth value,

Figure 4.7 Racing in Early-Firing Join Conditions

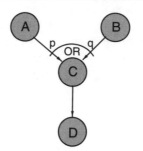

and C could be started. When C completes before B, D can be started. When B completes and q is true, C could be scheduled again and, after that D too. In which situations should this be done? In another instance of the same model, C may still be active when B completes; if q is true should C be terminated immediately or is C allowed to complete regularly? Does the decision depend on whether or not B produced output that results in a modified input container of C ? To avoid dealing with these problems (addressing them would make the metamodel more difficult to comprehend, the metamodel prescribes waiting at joins until all incoming transition conditions have been evaluated.

4.4.5   Dead Path Elimination

Waiting at joins until all incoming transition conditions have been evaluated increases the level of complexity for implementations of workflow management systems. A workflow management system must automatically resolve situations where it becomes clear that the work along a path finally reaching a join activity at the model level will not reach the join activity within the current instance of the process model. Not resolving these situations will result in "eternal waits" at the corresponding join activities.

For example, Figure 4.8 shows a simple process model with the join activity D. Assume that in a particular instance of this model A and B completed, p has been evaluated to true and r has been evaluated to false. C will never be scheduled because the transition condition r of its sole incoming control connector is false.

Consequently, the path from B to D is "dead"; it stopped at C, and q will never be evaluated. Thus, the join condition of D will never be evaluated, and the instance of the model will "wait forever" at D. But in practice, D could be started because its join condition is known to be true, independent of q's truth value, and the parallel branches of work joining at D are already finished; thus, there is nothing more to synchronize by waiting.

To solve this problem, we observe that each situation in which an instance waits forever at a join activity encompasses a path to the join that includes an

Figure 4.8 Dead Paths and Avoiding Waiting Forever at Joins

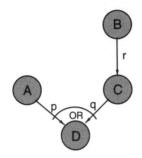

activity known to be never executed. The following is a complete list of such so-called *dead activities*:

- A regular node with an incoming control connector whose transition condition evaluated to false, and

- a join activity whose join condition evaluated to "false".

To avoid waiting forever, the metamodel prescribes that dead activities must be detected. Furthermore, whenever a dead activity A is detected, then:

- all paths $(A, A_{i_1}), p_{i_1}, (A_{i_1}, A_{i_2}, p_{i_2}), \ldots, (A_{i_{n_i}-1}, \ldots, A_{i_{n_i}}, p_{i_{n_i}})$ originating in A are computed, where

    { A_{i_j} is a regular activity $(1 \leq j \leq n_i - 1)$, and

    { $A_{i_{n_i}}$ is either a join node or a node with no outgoing control connectors

- p_{i_j} is treated as evaluated and set to false, for $1 \leq j \leq n_i$.

This processing is called *dead path elimination*. Basically, dead path elimination computes transitive closures until joins or end nodes and treats all transition conditions along the computed paths as evaluated with truth value false. Note that this is by definition recursive; that is when the join node reached in one of the paths above is again a dead activity, dead path elimination continues.

We will now describe dead path elimination more formally. The following notations allow us to be more concise.

Definition (Successor)   Let $A \in N$ be an activity; we define

- $A^{\rightarrow} := \{B \in N | \exists\, e \in E : \pi_1(e) = A \land \pi_2(e) = B\}$
  as the set of all successors to A.

- $A_*^{\rightarrow} := \{B \in A^{\rightarrow} \mid \exists\, C \in N : C \neq A \wedge B \in C^{\rightarrow}\}$
  as the set of all join nodes succeeding A, that means $A_*^{\rightarrow} = A^{\rightarrow} \bigcap N_*$

- $A_\bullet^{\rightarrow} = A^{\rightarrow} - A_*^{\rightarrow}$
  as the set of all regular nodes succeeding A, that means $A_\bullet^{\rightarrow} = A^{\rightarrow} \bigcap N_\bullet$)

■

Definition (Dead Node)   We denote by $\mathcal{D}(P)$ the set of all *dead nodes* of the process model P. It is $A \in D(P) :\Leftrightarrow$

- $A \in N_\bullet$ and $p(\iota(p)) = 0$ for $\mathcal{C}^{\leftarrow}(A) = \{p\}$
  that means A is a regular node with an incoming control connector whose transition condition evaluates to false, or

- $A \in N_*$ and $\Phi(A)(\iota(p_1), \ldots, \iota(p_{n_A})) = 0$, for $\mathcal{C}^{\leftarrow}(A) = \{p_1, \ldots, p_{n_A}\}$
  that means A is a join node whose join condition evaluates to false.

■

Since we are using the terms "node" and "activity" interchangeably, an activity is "dead" if and only if it is "dead" when considered as a node. Dead path elimination then requires to determine all successors $A^{\rightarrow}$ of A and to determine which of these successors are dead themselves. During this processing, the transition conditions $\mathcal{C}^{\rightarrow}(A)$ of all outgoing control connectors leaving A are set to false. As a consequence, all regular successors $A_\bullet^{\rightarrow}$ of A are dead again because they have incoming transition conditions that are evaluated to false. All join successors $A_*^{\rightarrow}$ of A having a join condition that evaluates to false are dead too. So, the activities that "survive" under dead path elimination are join activities whose join conditions did not compute as false (which means true or unknown). Because this processing again applies to all successors that are determined to be dead, the following algorithm performs dead path elimination whenever a dead activity is detected.

Algorithms and Definitions (Dead Successors)   Define the following sets:

- $X_0 := \{A\}$,

- $X_i := X_{i-1} \cup \bigcup_{B \in X_{i-1}} (B^{\rightarrow} - \{C \in B_*^{\rightarrow} \mid \Phi(C) \neq 0\})$, for $i \geq 1$

The set sequence $(X_i)_{i \in \mathbb{N}}$ is monotone increasing.   Since $X_i \subseteq N$ and $\mathrm{card}(N) < \infty$, $(X_i)_{i \in \mathbb{N}}$ becomes stationary, which means

$$\exists n \in \mathbb{N} : X_0 \subsetneqq X_1 \subsetneqq \ldots \subsetneqq X_n = X_{n+1} = \ldots$$

For each $A \in N$ we call the associated set X_n the set of all *dead successors* of A, and denote it by $\mathcal{D}^{\rightarrow}(A)$.

■

When dead paths originating from an activity A detected to be dead are eliminated, $\mathcal{D}^{\rightarrow}(A)$ is the set of all dead activities reachable from A. The immediate successors of an activity in $\mathcal{D}^{\rightarrow}(A)$ are known to be not dead in the current context of the process. These are activities that might be performed immediately or that might be detected to be dead in the future. Thus, this set is important for navigating through process models.

Definition (Dead Successor Boundary)   The set

$$\delta \mathcal{D}^{\rightarrow}(A) := \{\pi_2(e) | e \in E \wedge \pi_1(e) \in \mathcal{D}^{\rightarrow}(A)\} - \mathcal{D}^{\rightarrow}(A)$$

is called a *dead successor boundary* of A.

■

The dead successor boundary of A consists of all nodes which are not dead but which have an incoming control connector that originates in a dead successor of A. A node B in $\delta \mathcal{D}^{\rightarrow}(A)$ is reachable from A via a path which traverses dead nodes only, but B itself is not dead in the current process context. The concept of a dead successor boundary is an important concept in navigation, as we will see in section 4.7.11 on page 176.
Based on the definitions above, the following can be proven :

Note   For each dead node A the dead successor boundary consists of join nodes only, that means $\delta \mathcal{D}^{\rightarrow}(A) \cap N_{\bullet} = 0$. For $X \in \delta \mathcal{D}^{\rightarrow}(A) \cap N_*$, the truth value of its join condition $\Phi(X)$ is either true or unknown. ■

Example   Figure 4.9 shows an instance of a process model where A is a dead activity. A is dead because the transition condition of (X,A) has been evaluated in our example with truth value false.
Computing the dead successors of A results in $\mathcal{D}^{\rightarrow}(A) = \{A, B, C, D, F\}$. According to our algorithm, A is a member of $\mathcal{D}^{\rightarrow}(A)$ because the dead activity itself builds the first set X_0 of the set sequence to be computed. The next iteration computes X_1 by determining all successors of A which are not join nodes having a

Figure 4.9 Sample Dead Path Elimination

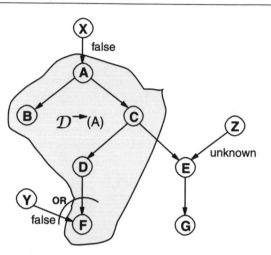

join condition known to be true or unknown; since A has no successors that are join nodes, all successors qualify in this iteration: $X_1 = \{A, B, C\}$. B has no successor at all, and D is a successor of C which is not a join node; thus, D is automatically a member of X_2. E is a successor of C and it is a join node; but the truth value of the transition condition of (Z,E) is not yet evaluated (otherwise, its truth value would not be unknown), which means it is $\Phi(E) \neq 0$, so E is not a member of X_2 (E may become dead in the future or may be performed later on). Thus, it is $X_2 = \{A, B, C, D\}$. To compute X_3, we have to determine the dead successors of the nodes added in the preceding step; the only node added is D, and D has a single successor F, which is a join node. The join condition $\Phi(F)$ of F is computed to be false because the transition condition of (D,F) is set to truth value false by the dead path elimination processing itself and the transition condition of (Y,F) is "false" in the example; ORing both values results in the truth value false for $\Phi(F)$. Thus, F is added in this iteration; that is $X_3 = \{A, B, C, D, F\}$. Since F is the only node added and has no successor, the iteration stops, that means $\mathcal{D}^{\rightarrow}(A) = X_3$.

The only node of the process model outside of $\mathcal{D}^{\rightarrow}(A)$ having an incoming control connector that originates in $\mathcal{D}^{\rightarrow}(A)$ is E. Thus, the dead successor boundary of A $\delta\mathcal{D}^{\rightarrow}(A) = \{E\}$.

4.5   Data Flow

Beside specifying each single activity and the appropriate sequencing of work, the model of a business process also specifies the flow of data within a process. Section 4.2.3 introduced containers to define the data required as input by an activity or predicate and the data passed back to the process as output. In this section, we show how the metamodel describes the flow of data between containers.

4.5.1 Data Connectors

The model of a business process encompasses the definition of the process data of its instances. This definition is given in two parts. The first part is the collection of input and output containers of all activities and conditions of the process model. The second part is the specification of how data is exchanged between the activities in the process model. Especially, the definition prescribes

1. which activities or predicates expect input data from which other activities (these are the *data dependencies* within the business process), and

2. how the data elements of an input container are composed from data elements of the output containers of these other activities (the *data mapping* between containers).

Assume A is an activity and B is either another activity or a predicate. If B requires data as input that is expected to be produced by A, then B is obviously data dependent on A. In this case, data has to flow from A to B when activity B is performed, and its input container thus has to be materialized (see section 4.3.2 on page 131).

The data dependency of B on A is expressed by a *data connector*, a directed edge from A to B. The metamodel allows the definition which data elements of B's input container expect values from which data elements of A's output container. This definition is done by simply specifying the corresponding pairs of data elements (v_1, v_2) with $v_1 \in o(A)$ and $v_2 \in \iota(A)$. The set of all such pairs specified for A and B is denoted as $\Delta(A, B)$. The result of adding the pair (v_1, v_2) to $\Delta(A, B)$ is that when the input container of B is materialized at runtime, the data element v_2 of the input container $\iota(B)$ will receive a copy of the actual instance of the data element v_1 of the output container $o(A)$. This behavior justifies the name *data map* for an element of $\Delta(A, B)$.

The metamodel defines a map Δ that associates with each pair (A, B) a set $\Delta(A, B)$; the map is called *data connector map*. Whenever an activity B is data dependent from another activity A there must be at least one data map specified having a data element from A's output container as source of the data map and a data element from B's input container as target. Thus, the existence of a data connector between A and B is equivalent to the fact that the set $\Delta(A, B)$ is not empty.

Because of this observation, the metamodel focuses on the map Δ instead of data connectors, and the metamodel expresses data dependencies by nonempty sets of data maps instead of explicitly specifying data connectors. The benefit of this approach is that control connectors remain the only kind of explicitly defined connectors making it much easier to talk about things such as "paths from A to B" which otherwise must be qualified as "path of control connectors" or "path of data connectors."

Certain restrictions apply to data connector maps or data connectors. An activity A can only produce data that is expected as input by another activity B if A runs before B. Thus, the control flow must first enable A to complete before B can be scheduled. For this purpose, the metamodel requires that there must be a path from A to B (in which case B is called *reachable* from A) if a data connector is specified from A to B. In particular, an activity cannot expect input from an activity that can run in parallel.

Often, an instance of an input container must be composed of instances of data elements of different output containers. Because of this, the metamodel allows each activity or predicate to be the target of any number of different data connectors.

Example   Figure 4.10 shows a sample data flow depicting data connectors as dashed arrows and data maps as arrows drawn with dashes and dots.

Figure 4.10 Specifying Data Flows

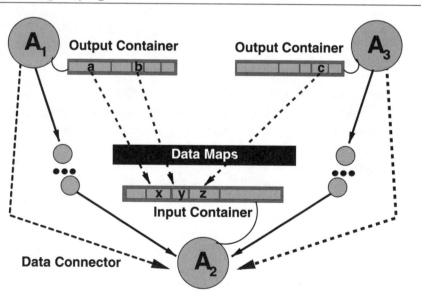

The input container $\iota(A_2)$ of activity A_2 receives data from the output container $o(A_1)$ and $o(A_3)$ of activities A_1 and A_3. Data member x of $\iota(A_2)$ receives a copy of data member a of $o(A_1)$, data member $y \in \iota(A_2)$ receives a copy of $b \in o(A_1)$, and $z \in \iota(A_2)$ receives a copy of $c \in o(A_3)$. Thus, it is $(a, x), (b, y) \in \Delta(A_1, A_2)$ and $(c, z) \in \Delta(A_3, A_2)$. The example shows that there might be any number of intermediate activities along the path between the source and the target of a data connector: An activity producing data for another activity is not necessarily an immediate predecessor of the latter activity. ■

The following definition summarizes the metamodel aspects of data flow within a process model.

Definition (Data Connector Map)   Let $A \in N$ be an activity, and let $B \in N \cup \mathcal{C}$ be an activity or a predicate. The map

$$\Delta : N \times (N \cup \mathcal{C}) \rightarrow \bigcup_{A \in N, B \in N \cup \mathcal{C}} \wp(o(A) \times \iota(B))$$

satisfying the conditions

1. $\Delta(A_1, A_2) \in \wp(o(A_1) \times \iota(A_2))$,

2. $\Delta(A_1, A_2) \neq \emptyset \Rightarrow A_2$ is reachable from A_1,

3. $\forall A_2 \in N : (x, z), (y, z) \in \bigcup_{A_1 \in N} \Delta(A_1, A_2) \Rightarrow x = y$,

is called a *data connector map*. An element (v_1, v_2) is called a *data map*. The set of all *data connectors E* is defined as

$$E := \{(A, B, \Delta(A, B)) \in N \times N \times \wp(V \times V) \mid \Delta(A, B) \neq \emptyset\}$$

■

Condition (1) enforces the rule that a data connector specifies only data maps from the output container of the activity it originates from to the input container of the activity or predicate it points to.

Condition (2) allows a data connector to exist between two nodes only if the control flow connects the source of the data connector with the target of the data connector. Note that values from output containers of activities skipped by dead path elimination are provided by a special function, as discussed in section 4.7.2 on page 163.

Again, any number of "intermediate" activities can be between source and target of a data connector. As a consequence, the amount of time passing between the production of data and its consumption might be arbitrarily large and might even encompass system shutdowns. Because of this, an implementation has to store at least all data needed by a succeeding activity or predicate. In practice, all input containers and all output containers are made persistent (see Chapter 3).

Condition (3) prohibits two different data maps from having the same data element as target. This constraint avoids conflicts when container instance is composed during materialization and multiple data maps could provide instances of their source data members that could be copied to the target. Randomly choosing one of the source data members as the one providing the instance that would be copied would destroy the determinism of the metamodel.

Example   Traveluck, Inc. sends a document describing the final itinerary to the customer. To build this document, the details of all reservations made for this trip must be provided. This detailed data is produced by the activities performing the reservations for flights, hotels, and rental cars. It must therefore be passed to the activity that creates and prints the document. For this purpose, data flow connectors are defined from Flight Reservation, Hotel Reservation, and Car Reservation to Build Trip Schedule.

Language Representation   In FDL, data connectors are defined by the DATA clause. The source activity of the data connector is preceded by the FROM keyword; its target activity by the TO keyword. The data map that is associated with the data connector follows this definition. The map is identified by the MAP keyword, which is followed by the source data member. The source data member is followed by the TO keyword, which is followed by the target data member. Note that a "dot notation" is used to qualify the correct data member in complex data structures. Appendix A provides the definitions of the data structures referred to in the following FDL snippet.

```
DATA FROM 'Car Reservation'
     TO 'Build Trip Schedule'
     MAP 'Rental Cars' TO 'Cars.Rental Cars'

DATA FROM 'Hotel Reservation'
     TO 'Build Trip Schedule'
     MAP 'Hotels' TO 'Hotels.Hotels'

DATA FROM 'Flight Reservation'
     TO 'Build Trip Schedule'
     MAP 'Flight' TO 'Flights.Flight'
```

Thus, at the FDL level, a data connector $(A, B, \Delta(A, B))$ is represented by a DATA clause and the associated data connector map $\Delta(A, B)$ is given by a list of correlated MAP clauses.

4.5.2   Data Maps with the Same Target

In practice, condition (3) is relaxed in case two different data connectors point to the same target. Data maps with the same target data member but having source data members in different output containers are allowed in many implementations to ease the specification of data flows in process models with alternative branches.

The fragment of a process model shown in Figure 4.11 can be specified in such a way that either A_1 or A_2 will be performed in a given instance of the process model; that means in any given instance either the output container of A_1 will be produced or that of A_2. The data flow is defined in such a way that data member c of the input container of A_3 is the target of two different data maps, one having data member a from the output container of A_1 as source, the other b from the output container of A_2. While this is in conflict with condition (3), there is no conflict in any given instance since either the output container of A_1 is available or that of A_2, so there is no situation in which a choice must be made whether c should get a copy of a or a copy of b. If only one of the data maps, for example (a,c), would be allowed, there would be instances in which A_2 would be performed but not A_1; so, no automatic materialization of the input container of A_2 would be possible because c requests a copy from a container that was not built. Note that similar situations would occur in more complicated scenarios encompassing dead path elimination.

Figure 4.11 Data Maps with the Same Target

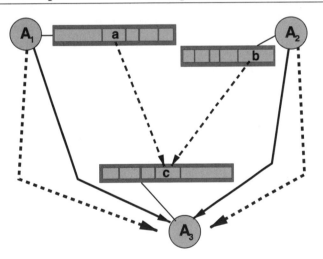

Allowing multiple data maps with the same target introduces certain situations in which instances of containers are randomly built, if no special care is taken even if the sources of the data maps stem from different output containers. Based on the data flow specified in Figure 4.11, data element $c \in \iota(A_3)$ will receive a copy of the instances of data elements $a \in o(A_1)$ and $b \in o(A_2)$ in case the control flow allows the branches from A_1 to A_3 and from A_2 to A_3 to be performed in parallel and both succeed. Whether the instance of c will finally hold a copy of a or of b is determined by the implementation of the workflow engine instantiating the process model and is thus "random" as seen from the outside.

The metamodel assumes that the result of applying data maps is deterministic. We do not discuss the details of how to achieve this determinism, but one possible solution could be the implementation of a *copy policy*. The copy policy would specify how input containers are materialized in case of conflicting maps. Many different copy policies are possible, for example:

- "Last Writer Wins" — This policy assumes that the last value written is the actual value. Thus, the youngest output container referenced by a set of data maps with the same target is used for performing the copy operation.

- "Last Starter Wins" — The activity producing the youngest container might be the activity starting earliest. Activities starting later might nonetheless terminate earlier but might have received more actual data as input, thereby producing more actual output. So, this with the "Last Starter Wins" policy, the output container of the activity that started last—that is, after all other activities that have output containers referenced by a set of data maps with the same target—is used for performing the copy.

- "Explicit Sequencing" — Conflicting data maps are ordered explicitly by the modeler. From the set of applicable data maps the high-order map is taken at runtime for determining the source for the copy operation.

4.5.3 Process Model Input and Output

A process model $P \in \mathcal{P}$ may have both an input container $\iota(P) \subseteq V$ and an output container $o(P) \subseteq V$ (see section 4.2.3 on page 126). The reason for having process containers is twofold. First, data can be passed as input to an instance of a process model as a whole at the time of its instantiation, and the instance can pass back results at the time of its termination. As a consequence, a process can be treated as a computing abstraction which gets data as input, performs some computation, and returns data as output (so-called long computation or complex request—See Chapter 7). Second, from this perspective, a process model looks like an activity and can be used as an activity implementation. As a side effect, the latter establishes process models as reusable entities because they can be modeled once and exploited as activity implementations in many different process models.

To pass data as input to a process instance, the metamodel allows for the specification of how data elements of the input container of the corresponding process model are copied to data elements of input containers of its encompassed activities and predicates. The metamodel also allows for the specification of how data elements of activities included in the corresponding process model are copied to data elements of the output container of the process model.

As before, such copy prescriptions are defined by data maps. The meaning of the data map (v_1, v_2) is that data element v_2 will be instantiated by copying the actual instance of data element v_1 and assigning it to v_2. Either

- v_1 is a data element of the input container $\iota(P)$ of the process model P and v_2 is a data element of the input container $\iota(A)$ of an activity A, or

- v_1 is a data element of the output container $o(A)$ of an activity A and v_2 is a data element of the output container $o(P)$ of the process model P.

The set of all data maps between data elements of one of the process containers and data elements of one of the containers of activity A is denoted by $\overrightarrow{\Delta}(A)$. The corresponding map $\overrightarrow{\Delta}$ is called a *process data connector map*.

Example   The process model sketched in Figure 4.12 contains activity B, which is implemented by another process model. B has a data dependency on activity A, so a data connector from A to B is drawn with $(a, b) \in \Delta(A, B)$. Similarly, activity C has a data dependency on B with $(f, g) \in \Delta(B, C)$. Also, data is flowing from the input container of B to the activities encompassed by B. For example, data element $c \in \iota(B)$ of the input container of B is copied to data element $x \in \iota(D)$ of the input container of activity D; thus, it is $(c, x) \in \overrightarrow{\Delta}(D)$. Process B returns data when it has terminated. The data elements $d, e \in o(B)$ of the output container of B receive copies from the data elements $y, z \in o(E)$, respectively, from E's output container; thus, it is $(y, d), (z, e) \in \overrightarrow{\Delta}(E)$. ∎

Figure 4.12 Data Flowing Through a Process

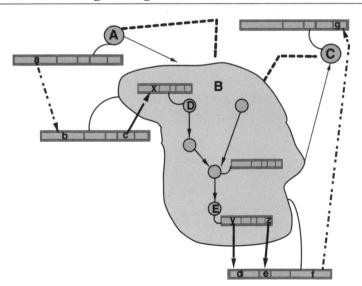

The following definition reflects how data is exchanged between the containers of a process model and its encompassed activities.

Definition   (Process Data Connector Map) Let $P \in \mathcal{P}$ be a process model and let N be the set of all activities of P. The map

$$\overrightarrow{\Delta} : N \rightarrow \bigcup_{A \in N} (\wp(\iota(P) \times \iota(A)) \cup \wp(o(A) \times o(P)))$$

is called a *process data connector map* if it satisfies the following conditions:

1. $\forall A \in N : \overrightarrow{\Delta}(A) \in \wp(\iota(P) \times \iota(A)) \cup \wp(o(A) \times o(P))$

2. $\forall B \in N : (x, z), (y, z) \in \wp(\iota(P) \times \iota(B)) \cup \bigcup_{A \in N} \Delta(A, B) \Rightarrow x = y$

3. $(x, z), (y, z) \in \bigcup_{B \in N} \wp(o(B) \times o(P)) \Rightarrow x = y$

An element $(v_1, v_2) \in \overrightarrow{\Delta}(A)$ is called a *data map*.

■

Condition (1) enforces the rule that the process data connector map targeting or originating in activity A specifies only data maps with A as target or origin, respectively.

To avoid conflicting copy operations at runtime, conditions (2) and (3) prohibit more than one data map with the same target data element. Condition (2) combines data maps originating in a data element of the process model's input container with data maps between activity containers, and it enforces unique source data elements for all data maps with the same target; it is thus an extension of condition (3) from section 4.5.1 on page 151. Condition (3) enforces unique source data elements for all data maps with the same target data element from the process model's output container.

Similar to the case we discussed in section 4.5.2 on page 154, conditions (2) and (3) are relaxed in practice to allow for

- data maps with different origins pointing to the same data element of the process output container, and

- data maps with the process input container as origin pointing to the same data element of the process output container that other data maps point to.

The same conflicts resulting in a random behavior may occur. Again, copy policies can be used to ensure the determinism required by the metamodel.

Example   When a client reserves a trip from Traveluck's home page by starting a corresponding business process he provides some information as input. This information is used for activities, for example, billing the client's credit card. When an itinerary cannot be confirmed, a new one is negotiated and returned as output.

Language Representation   The input container of a process model is referred to in FDL as SOURCE; its output container, as SINK. The specification of data flowing from the process input container to an input container of an activity is performed by a DATA clause specifying SOURCE as origin of the flow and the name of the activity as its target. Thus, the FROM keyword of this DATA clause is succeeded by the SOURCE keyword, and its TO keyword is followed by the activity's name. Each data map is defined by a separate MAP keyword, as introduced earlier for usual data connectors. The next FDL snippet specifies that the Name and Address data elements of the process input container are mapped to the corresponding fields of the Customer data element of the input container of the activity Bill Credit Card; for the definitions of the related data structures see Appendix A.

```
DATA FROM SOURCE
     TO 'Bill Credit Card'
     MAP 'Name' TO 'Customer.Name'
     MAP 'Address' TO 'Customer.Address'
```

When data flows from an activity's output container to the process output container, the activity's name as origin of this flow is preceded by the FROM keyword in the corresponding DATA clause. The SINK as the target of the flow is preceded by the TO keyword. Again, a separate MAP construct is to be used for each associated data map. Within the Contact Customer activity, negotiations with the customer can be performed when there are problems making the required reservations for the itinerary. The resulting new Itinerary as well as the information about the Traveler is passed from the output container of Contact Customer to the process output container.

```
DATA FROM 'Contact Customer'
     TO SINK
     MAP 'Traveler'  TO 'Traveler'
     MAP 'Itinerary'  TO 'Itinerary'
```

The process data connector map $\overrightarrow{\Delta}$ is represented in FDL by a set of DATA clauses. If applicable, two separate DATA clauses are specified for each activity A to represent $\overrightarrow{\Delta}(A)$: one DATA clause for input received from the process input container, and one DATA clause for output produced for the process output container.

4.6 Summary: PM-Graphs

In this section, we combine all of the definitions given earlier, producing a definition that summarizes the syntax of the metamodel:

Definition (PM-Graph)   A tuple $G = (V, \iota, o, N, \Psi, \mathcal{C}, \Omega, \varepsilon, E, \Phi, \Delta, \vec{\Delta})$ is called a *process model graph* (or *PM-Graph* for short):$\Leftrightarrow$

1. V is a finite set of *data elements*. Each data element $v \in V$ has a finite set DOM(v) assigned.

2. $\iota : N \cup \mathcal{C} \cup \{G\} \rightarrow \wp(V)$ is called an *input container* map.

3. $o : N \cup \{G\} \rightarrow \wp(V)$ is called an *output container* map.

4. N is a finite set of *activities*.

5. $\Psi : N \rightarrow \mathcal{E}$ is called an *activity implementation* map with
    $$\Psi(A) : \underset{v \in \iota(A)}{\times} DOM(v) \rightarrow \underset{v \in o(A)}{\times} DOM(v)$$

6. $\mathcal{C}$ is a finite set of *conditions*. Each condition p is a map
    $$p. \underset{v \in \iota(p)}{\times} DOM(v) \rightarrow \{0, 1\}$$

7. $\Omega : N \rightarrow \mathcal{Q}$ is the *staff assignment* map with
    $\Omega(A) : N \rightarrow \wp(\mathcal{A})$; $\mathcal{A}$ is a finite set of *agents*.

8. $\varepsilon : N \rightarrow \mathcal{C}$ assigns to each activity an *exit condition*.

9. $E \subseteq N \times N \times \mathcal{C}$ is a set of *control connectors* that has the following properties:

    (a) E is *unified*; that means
         $$\forall e, e' \in E : \pi_{1,2}(e) = \pi_{1,2}(e') \Rightarrow \pi_3(e) = \pi_3(e')$$

    (b) (N,E) is acyclic.

10. $\Phi : N \rightarrow \underset{A \in N}{\bigcup} \varphi_A$ assigns join conditions.

    $$\Phi(A) \in \varphi_A := \{ \underset{1 \leq j \leq k}{\bigvee} \underset{1 \leq i \leq l_j}{\bigwedge} p'_i \mid p'_i \in \{p, \neg p \mid p \in \mathcal{C}^{\leftarrow}(A)\}\} \text{ with}$$

    (a) $\forall A \in N : \Phi(A) \in \varphi_A$,

    (b) $\forall A \in N_\bullet : \Phi(A) \equiv 1$

11. $\Delta : N \times (N \cup \mathcal{C}) \to \bigcup_{A \in N, B \in N \cup \mathcal{C}} \wp(o(A) \times \iota(B))$ is the *data connector* map
   with

   (a) $\Delta(A, B) \in \wp(o(A) \times \iota(B))$
   (b) $\Delta(A, B) \neq \emptyset \Rightarrow B$ is reachable from A
   (c) $\forall B \in N : (x, z), (y, z) \in \bigcup_{A_1 \in N} \Delta(A, B) \Rightarrow x = y$

12. $\overrightarrow{\Delta} : N \to \bigcup_{A \in N} (\wp(\iota(P) \times \iota(A)) \cup \wp(o(A) \times o(P)))$ is the *process data connector map* with

   (a) $\forall A \in N : \overrightarrow{\Delta}(A) \in \wp(\iota(P) \times \iota(A)) \cup \wp(o(A) \times o(P))$
   (b) $\forall B \in N : (x, z), (y, z) \in \wp(\iota(P) \times \iota(B)) \cup \bigcup_{A \in N} \Delta(A, B) \Rightarrow x = y$
   (c) $(x, z), (y, z) \in \bigcup_{B \in N} \wp(o(B \times o(P)) \Rightarrow x = y$

■

A process model graph $G = (V, \iota, o, N, \Psi, \mathcal{C}, \Omega, E, \Phi, \Delta, \overrightarrow{\Delta})$ encompasses two graphs.

1. The control flow graph $G_{control} = (N, E, V, \iota, o, \mathcal{C}, \varepsilon, \Phi)$

2. The data flow graph $G_{data} = (N, E, V, \Delta, \overrightarrow{\Delta})$, where the edge set E represents data connectors:

$$E \subseteq N \times N \times \wp(V \times V) \quad \text{with} \quad (A, B, \Delta(A, B)) \in E :\Leftrightarrow \Delta(A, B) \neq \emptyset$$

The control flow $G_{control}$ and the data flow G_{data} specify the logic of a business process in terms of the sequencing and data provision of activities; that means it describes *what* has to be done (see section 1.5 on page 8). $G_{control}$ is a weighted, colored, directed, acyclic graph.

The link to the organizational structure of an enterprise running the business process is achieved with the staff assignment map Ω, which describes *who* has to do something (see section 1.5 on page 8).

The tools supporting the execution of activities is determined by the activity implementation map Ψ, which describes *which* tools have to be used (see section 1.5 on page 8). Note that Ψ and G_{data} are interrelated. G_{data} has an abstract view in terms of data exchanged between activities, and Φ has a more concrete view in terms of data processed by tools.

When discussing transactional properties of workflows in Chapter 7, we will extend the metamodel defined so far. A PM-Graph G will be overlaid by two hypergraphs $\mathcal{R}$ and $\mathcal{G}$. $\mathcal{R}$ will represent the units of work that are long running or include activities, which are not implemented as usual transactions ("compensation spheres"), and $\mathcal{G}$ corresponds to units of work that have a traditional "all-or-nothing" semantics ("atomic spheres").

4.7   Navigation

Until now, we have discussed the syntax of the metamodel by incrementally rationalizing and defining all of its elements, finally resulting in the definition of processes model graphs in section 4.6. The corresponding language can be used to specify business processes and to discuss them. But to make this discussion really meaningful, we must ensure that everybody understands a process model graph and all of its constituents in the same manner.

This understanding is especially crucial if a workflow management system has to instantiate a process model graph. The workflow management system assigns work to agents participating and collaborating in the corresponding business process. The workflow management system does these assignment by interpreting of information that the people implementing the workflow management system have defined for it. Thus, the people modeling the business process and the workflow management system instantiating the process model must have the same understanding of what is meant by the model.

For this purpose, we define precisely how to interpret a process model graph by specifying the possible states of each element of the metamodel and the operations that transform these states. In other words, we describe the *operational semantics* of the metamodel.

4.7.1   Reflecting Time

Interpretation of a process model happens at discrete points in time, for example, when an activity implementation terminates. Thus, we can represent the aspect of time in the metamodel by the set of natural numbers $\mathbb{N}$. The metamodel does not consider process instances which interfere, so we can attach to each process instance its own separate "timeline."

On this timeline, $0 \in \mathbb{N}$ represents the point in time when the associated instance of a process model is created. Whenever a process-relevant event occurs, such as the termination of an activity implementation, the current time parameter $i \in \mathbb{N}$ is increased by 1, and the state of all elements of the process model, such as activities, containers, and predicates, of the actual instance for time $i + 1 \in \mathbb{N}$ is computed. This is referred to as *navigation*. Navigation is captured in our metamodel by a set of maps parameterized by time.

The computation of new states during navigation depends not only on the current state of process model elements but also on the process data representing the actual context of the business process. Exactly one process-relevant event is processed at any given time. For example, if multiple activities terminate concurrently, they are processed sequentially.

At any point in time, $i \in \mathbb{N}$, the elements of a process model associated with an instance have a well-defined state. These states are assigned by special maps, which we introduce later on. The computation of instances of containers associated with a process instance is described next.

4.7.2 Computing Container Instances

Let X be an activity, a process model, or a predicate. At any given time, the metamodel assigns an instance to the input container and output container of X. When an instance of a process model is created, all of its associated containers are assigned a default instance. After that, container instances are computed by running activity implementations, processing data connector maps, and performing dead path elimination. The following definitions make this more precise.

Definition (Actual Instances)   Let $P \in \mathcal{P}$ be a process model; N its set of activities; and $\mathcal{C}$, its set of conditions. For $X \in \mathbb{N} \cup \mathcal{P} \cup \mathcal{C}$ and a data element $v \in \iota(X) \cup o(X)$, we denote by ${}^i v \in \mathrm{DOM}(v)$ the instance assigned to v at time $i \in \mathbb{N}$. Similarly, we denote by ${}^i \iota(X)$ and ${}^i o(X)$ the instance of the input container and output container of X, respectively, at time $i \in \mathbb{N}$.

■

When a process model is instantiated, i=0, all of its associated containers are assigned default instances by instantiation of their data elements with default values. Note that this is only a conceptual perception. To save storage space, an implementation of a workflow management system typically creates container instances on demand and not in advance. Default values might then be used by the implementation for missing information.

Definition (Default Instances)   Let $P \in \mathcal{P}$ be a process model; N its set of activities; and $\mathcal{C}$, its set of conditions. Then:

$$\forall X \in N \cup \mathcal{C} \cup \{P\} \forall v \in \iota(X) \cup o(X) \exists w_{X,v} \in \mathrm{DOM}(v) : {}^0 v = w_{X,v}$$

■

Specifying these default values is part of process modeling and may have been done long before the actual instance of the process model is created. Thus, data that is more current or meaningful than these defaults can often be provided by agents participating in the actual instance. This is especially relevant for output containers of activities that are dead in the actual process instance but that are sources of data connectors. To reflect instances of output containers of these dead activities, the metamodel provides the following map.

Definition (Dead Data Map)   The partial map

$$\Lambda : \mathbb{N} \times \mathbb{N} \times V \to \bigcup_{w \in V} \text{DOM}(w)$$

is called a *dead data map*. It is $\Lambda(i, A, w) \in \text{DOM}(w) :\Leftrightarrow w \in o(A)$; otherwise, Λ is not defined.

■

Assume an activity A is activated at time $j \in \mathbb{N}$, $j > 0$. This means that the activity implementation $\Psi(A)$ is invoked, and the actual instance of the input container ${}^j\iota(A) = ({}^jv_1, \dots, {}^j v_k)$ of the input container $\iota(A) = \{v_1, \dots, v_k\}$ of A is passed to $\Psi(A)$. Let $\Psi(A)$ return at time $i > j$; since the container instance ${}^j\iota(A)$ has not been changed in the meantime, the instance of A's output container $o(A) = \{w_1, \dots, w_r\}$ returned by $\Psi(A)$ can be defined as $\Psi(A({}^{i-1}v_1, \dots, {}^{i-1} v_k)$.

Definition (Output Container Instance)   Let $A \in \mathbb{N}$ be an activity; $\iota(A) = \{v_1, \dots, v_k\}$ its input container; $o(A) = \{w_1, \dots, w_r\}$ its output container; and $\Psi(A)$ its activity implementation. Then:

- $\omega(i, A) \in \{\text{terminated,completed}\} \Rightarrow \dot{o}(A) = \Psi(A)({}^{i-1}v_1, \dots, {}^{i-1} v_k)$

- $\omega(i, A) = \text{dead} \Rightarrow \dot{o}(A) = \{\Lambda(i, A, w_1), \dots, \Lambda(i, A, w_r)\}$

- $\omega(i, A) \notin \{\text{terminated,completed,dead}\} \Rightarrow^i o(A) = \{{}^0w_1, \dots, {}^0 w_r\}$

■

Note: The output container of a terminated activity might change in a later step because the associated activity implementation will be started again. Once an activity is completed, its associated output container does not change (with a grain of salt: see what happens during rollback of back a sphere).

The output container of a dead activity is determined by the dead data map. It is explicitly allowed that the dead data map returns different instances at different times. In practice, values are requested for only those elements that are sources of data maps, and this request happens at the time the target of a data map is computed.

Thus, when an activity becomes activated, its input container is computed, based on data connectors, dead path processing, output container instances of preceding activities, and process input data. The same is true for input containers of conditions. The data elements of the materialized container are assigned the actual instances of the sources of their data maps, and data elements that are not target of a data map keep their default value.

Definition (Mapping Data Elements)

- $\forall X \in N \cup C \forall v \in \iota(X) : (w, v) \in \Delta(A, X) \cup \overrightarrow{\Delta}(X) \Rightarrow^i v =^{i-1} w$

- $\forall P \in \mathcal{P} \forall v \in o(P) : (w, v) \in \overrightarrow{\Delta}(X) \Rightarrow^i v =^{i-1} w$

- $\forall X \in N \cup C \cup \{P\} \forall v \in \iota(X) \cup o(P) :$
  $\{(w, v) \mid A \in N \wedge (w, v) \in \Delta(A, X) \cup \overrightarrow{\Delta}(X)\} = \emptyset \Rightarrow^i v =^0 v$

∎

Note: Container materialization is well defined because of the policies followed when multiple data maps have the same target (see section 4.5.2 on page 154). The output container of a process is materialized when the process "returns" (see section 4.7.7 on page 171).

4.7.3 Activity States

At any point in time, each activity within a process instance has a well-defined state. The set of all states relevant to navigation is denoted by S. Navigating through a process model includes the assignment of a state to activities (and predicates—see section 4.7.4) in compliance with the operational semantics of the metamodel.

Section 4.7.13 on page 179 presents a state-transition diagram for activities, that is a graphical description of activity states and their valid changes. The following states of activities are relevant for navigation and are included in S. Later sections give precise definitions of these states.

- *Initial*—This is the state to which an activity is assigned to when its encompassing process model is instantiated.

- *Executable*—An activity enters this state when it first detects that the corresponding piece of work has to be performed.

- *Activated*—The state that an activity enters when an agent invokes the implementation associated with the activity.

- *Terminated*—An activity enters this state when the agent performing the underlying work of the activity stops and the associated exit condition has not yet been met.

- *Completed*—An activity enters this state after its exit condition is met.

- *Dead*—An activity that is touched by the dead path elimination process enters this state.

At any given point in time the state of an activity is given by a map.

Definition (Activity State Map)   The *activity state map*

$$\omega : \mathbb{N} \times N \to S$$

associates at any point in time $i \in \mathbb{N}$ each activity $A \in N$ with its actual state $\omega(i, A)$. For each $i \in \mathbb{N}$, $\omega_i(A) := \omega(i, A)$ defines a map $\omega_i : N \to S$.

■.

Completed activities as well as dead activities are crucial for navigation. So, it is convenient when describing navigation to define special maps that provide exactly these activities.

Definition (Completed Map and Dead Map)   The *completed map*

$$\lambda : \mathbb{N} \to \wp(N), i \mapsto \omega_i^{-1}(\text{completed})$$

derives at any point in time $i \in \mathbb{N}$ the set of all activities $\lambda(i) \subseteq N$ that have completed until that time. The *dead map*

$$\delta : \mathbb{N} \to \wp(N), i \mapsto \omega_i^{-1}(\text{dead})$$

presents at any point in time $i \in \mathbb{N}$ the set of all dead activities $\delta(i) \subseteq N$. For short, we use $\lambda_i := \lambda(i)$ and $\delta_i := \delta(i)$.

■

Note   Usually, once an activity is completed, it stays in this state forever. This is true for workflows that do not make use of recovery features of our metamodel (see chapter 7 for what happens during rollback of a sphere).

4.7.4 Predicate States

At any point in time, each predicate within a process instance has a well-defined state. The relevant states of a predicate are *evaluated* and *not-evaluated*, indicating whether or not the truth value of a predicate has already been determined. These states are also included in S. As before, a map is used to determine the state of a predicate.

Definition (Predicate State Map)   The predicate state map

$$\xi : \mathbb{N} \times \mathcal{C} \to S$$

associates at any point in time $i \in \mathbb{N}$ each predicate $p \in \mathcal{C}$ with its actual state $\xi(i, p)$.

■

The predicate state map satisfies the following conditions, which represent the rules for valid state changes of predicates.

1. $\forall p \in \mathcal{C} : \xi(0, p) = \text{not-evaluated}$
   i.e, when a process is instantiated, all predicates are in the not-evaluated state.

2. $\forall A \in \lambda_i \forall p \in \mathcal{C}^{\to}(A) : \xi(i, p) = \text{evaluated}$
   i.e., a transition condition of a control connector leaving a completed activity is in the evaluated state.

3. $\forall A \in \delta_i \forall p \in \mathcal{C}^{\to}(A) : \xi(i, p) = \text{evaluated}$
   i.e. the transition condition of a control connector traversed by dead path elimination is in the evaluated state (and the transition condition is set to false—see section 4.4.5 on page 146).

4. $\forall p \in \mathcal{C} : \xi(i, p) = \text{evaluated} \wedge j > i \Rightarrow \xi(j, p) = \text{evaluated}$
   i.e., once a predicate is in the evaluated state it stays in that state basically forever unless it is in a sphere. See Chapter 7 for information on the rollback of spheres.

5. $\forall A \in N : \omega_i(A) \in \{\text{terminated, completed}\} \Leftrightarrow \xi(i, \varepsilon(A)) = \text{evaluated}$
   i.e., exit conditions of terminated or completed activities are in the evaluated state.

6. $\xi(i, \Phi(A)) = \text{evaluated} \Leftrightarrow (\forall p \in \mathcal{C}^{\leftarrow}(A) : \xi(i, p) = \text{evaluated})$
   (.e., a join condition is evaluated if and only if all of its constituting predicates are in the evaluated state.

7. In all other situations, $p \in C$ has the not-evaluated state.

Evaluating a predicate means to compute its truth value based on its actual input container instance. As long as a predicate is in the state "not-evaluated", this computation has not been performed; that means its truth value is simply not known. We introduce a third truth value called unknown (denoted by ?) to reflect this situation. The truth value of a predicate that is in not-evaluated state is defined to be unknown, that means

$$\forall p \in C \forall w \in \underset{v \in \iota(p)}{\times} \mathrm{DOM}(v) \forall i \in \mathbb{N} :$$

$$\xi(i, p) = \text{not-evaluated} \Rightarrow p(w) :=?$$

According to item (6) above, as long as at least one predicate $p \in C^{\leftarrow}(A)$ is not evaluated, the join condition $\Phi(A)$ is not evaluated. Thus, the join condition has the truth value unknown.

$$(\exists p \in C^{\leftarrow}(A) : \xi(i, p) = \text{not-evaluated})$$

$$\Rightarrow \forall w \in \underset{q \in C^{\leftarrow}(A)}{\times} \underset{v \in \iota(q)}{\times} \mathrm{DOM}(v) : \Phi(A)(w) =?$$

If a predicate is in the evaluated state, it has a truth value assigned. This truth value is computed at the time its state changes from not-evaluated to evaluated, and the computation is based on the predicate's input container instance at this time. Since the input container of the predicate does not change once it is materialized, the truth value of a predicate is fixed from that time on.

4.7.5   Dead Activities

We introduced the concept of a dead activity in section 4.4.5 on page 146. In this section, we will use what we have learned in earlier sections, such as section 4.7.2 on page 163, to produce a precise mathematical definition of a dead activity.

Definition (Activities in State "Dead") $A \in \delta_i :\Leftrightarrow$

- $A \in N_\bullet \wedge p(^i\iota(p)) = 0$, for $C^{\leftarrow}(A) = \{p\}$, or

- $A \in N_* \wedge \Phi(A)(^i\iota(p_1), \ldots, ^i\iota(p_{n_A})) = 0$, for $C^{\leftarrow}(A) = \{p_1, \ldots, p_{n_A}\}$, or

- $A \in \mathcal{D}^{\rightarrow}(B)$ for $B \in \delta_i$.

■

Note   The dead path elimination procedure described in section 4.4.5 on page 146 ensures that this map is well defined. Furthermore, the set sequence $(\delta_i)_{i \in \mathbb{N}}$ is monotone increasing. Thus, an activity that enters the dead state stays in this state forever unless it is within a sphere, as discussed later in Chapter 7. Also, the set of dead activities can only grow but never shrink.

Basically, dead path elimination is performed whenever it is detected that a particular activity can principally never reach the executable state within the current process instance. The activity is said to be dead.

For what follows we need a convenient way to indicate whether or not a control connector has been traversed by the dead path elimination procedure. The next definition provides that way.

Definition (Dead Edge Traversal Map)   The map

$$\Xi : \mathbb{N} \times E \rightarrow \{0, 1\}$$

with $\Xi(i, e) = 1 :\Leftrightarrow \pi_1(e) \in \delta_i$, and $\Xi(i, e) = 0$ otherwise, is called a *dead edge traversal* map.

■

When a control connector is traversed by dead path elimination at time i, the transition condition of this control connector enters the evaluated state, and its truth value is defined to be false:

- $\Xi(i, e) = 1 \Rightarrow \xi(i, \pi_3(e)) = $ evaluated

- $\Xi(i, e) \Rightarrow \forall w \in \underset{v \in \iota(\pi_3(e))}{\times} \mathrm{DOM}(v) : \pi_3(e)(w) = $ false

4.7.6   Executable Activities

An activity with no incoming control connectors is called a *start activity*. We denote the set of all start activities by N'.

$$A \in N' :\Leftrightarrow \{e \in E \mid \pi_2(e) = A\} = \emptyset$$

Note that each process model P has at least one start activity but can have more than one. The existence of a start activity is a consequence of the acyclicity of the control flow graph $G_{control}$ of the PM-graph representing P.

Work within a process always begins with the start activities of its associated process model P. That means when P is instantiated, all of its start activities enter the executable state.

Definition (Activities Becoming "Executable" at Process Instantiation Time)   An
activity A *becomes executable* at time $0 :\Leftrightarrow A \in N'$.

■

For times i>0, activities become executable as a result of a *navigation step* that
takes place when another activity enters the completed state. The navigation step
determines all control connectors leaving the completing activity and computes the
truth value of each associated transition condition. If the endpoint of such a control
connector is a regular node (see section 4.4.3 on page 142), the corresponding
activity enters the executable state if and only if the associated transition condition
is true; otherwise the join condition of the endpoint must be true. This is captured
in the next definition.

Definition (Nonstart Activities in State "Executable")   Let $A \in N - N'$ be an
activity that is not a start activity. For i>0, A becomes *executable* at time i :$\Leftrightarrow$

1. $\exists (X, A, p) \in E : \xi(i, p) = \text{evaluated} \land \xi(i - 1, p) = \text{not-evaluated}$,

2. One of the following applies:

    (a) $A \in N_{\bullet} \land p(^{i}\iota(p)) = 1$
    (b) $A \in N_{*} \land \Phi(A)(\{^{i}\iota(q) \mid C^{\leftarrow}(A)\}) = 1$

■

The only events that trigger a state change of a transition condition from not-
evaluated to evaluated is the completion of an activity and dead path elimination.
Since dead path elimination is triggered by activity completion too, state changes of
transition conditions are all triggered by activity completion. Consequently, process
instantiation and activity completion are the only two origins of activities becoming
executable.

The previous two definitions result in the following property the activity state
map ω must satisfy for each $i \in \mathbb{N}$.

$$A \in N \text{ becomes executable at time } i \Rightarrow \omega(i, A) = \text{executable}$$

Note, that the reverse is not true. An activity might be in the executable state
at time i without having become executable at that time. It might have entered
the executable state some time before but nothing triggered a state change for the
activity in the meantime.

4.7.7 Returning Process Instances

An activity enters the completed state when its associated activity implementation returns and its exit condition is met. If the exit condition is not met, the activity enters the terminated state. See sections 4.7.8 and 4.3 for precise definitions. While the concept of "returning" has the obvious semantics for programs as activity implementations, the corresponding concept requires a definition in case the activity implementation is a process model:

For this purpose, let A be an activity that is implemented by a process model, which means $\Psi(A) = \hat{P} \in \mathcal{P}$. We assume that the state of metamodel constructs, such as activities and conditions, is used to specify $\hat{P}$ and can be determined via the corresponding state maps of P. This means there is no need to consider separate state maps like $\hat{\omega}, \hat{\xi}, \dots$. Thus, for $\hat{P} = (\hat{N}, \hat{E})$ and $P = (N, E)$, it is $\hat{N} \subseteq N$ and $\hat{E} \subseteq E$. Also, the state maps of $\hat{P}$ are restrictions of the corresponding state maps of $P : \hat{\omega} = \omega \mid_{\mathbb{N} \times \hat{N}}$ and so forth.

When activity A becomes executable, $\hat{P}$ is instantiated and the semantics discussed for instantiating process models apply. Especially, the start activities $\hat{N}'$ of $\hat{P}$ become executable; that means

$$\omega(i, A) = \text{executable} \Rightarrow \forall B \in \hat{N}' : \omega(i, B) = \text{executable}$$

When the first start activity of $\hat{P}$ is activated, activity A enters the activated state. At this time the input container of A, that means the input container of $\hat{P}$ is materialized. The data maps of the specified process data connector map (see section 4.5.3 on page 156) of $\hat{P}$ are applied to materialize the input container of the activated start activity.

Once the process activity $\hat{P}$ is instantiated, navigation takes place as for any other process model. Over time each, activity will either enter the completed or dead state. Thus, navigation stops since there will be no more state changes. The process instance is finished and returns to its "starter," conceptually. This is the subject of the next definition.

Definition (Process Instance Return) Let P be a process model and N its activities. An *instance* of P *returned* at time $T \in \mathbb{N} :\Leftrightarrow$

1. $\forall A \in N : \omega(T, A) \in \{\text{completed}, \text{dead}\}$,

2. $\forall t < T \, \exists A \in N : \omega(t, A) \notin \{\text{completed}, \text{dead}\}$.

■

Note that when A completes, its output container is materialized according to the process container map of $\hat{P}$. Obviously, the definition applies not only to process activities but to process instances in general. The first point in time when all activities of a process instance are in the completed or dead state is the time when the process instance is finished and returns. At this time, its output container is materialized.

4.7.8   Terminated Activities

The semantics encompassed by the terminated or completed states are that the corresponding activity had a chance to produce results. Therefore we require that the activity must have been in the activated state before it can enter either the terminated or completed state. Having been activated ensures that the corresponding activity implementation has been invoked and was thus able to produce its results.

An activity that does not satisfy its exit condition when its activity implementation returns enters the terminated state. It did not finish successfully and it must be continued at a later time, that is navigation cannot proceed to another activity. All of this is captured in the next definition.

Definition   (Activities in State "Terminated")   Let $A \in N$ be an activity with activity implementation $\Psi(A)$. Then, $\omega(i, A) = $ terminated $:\Leftrightarrow$

1. $\exists j \in \mathbb{N} : j < i \wedge \omega(j, A) = $ activated,

2. $\exists k \in \mathbb{N} : j < k \le i \wedge \Psi(A)$ returned at time k,

3. $\forall k \le r \le i : \varepsilon(A)(^r\iota(\varepsilon(A))) \ne 1.$

■

Note that condition (3) not only requires that the exit condition is not met at the time the activity implementation returns but that the exit condition is not met at any time between the time that the activity returned and to the current time. Since a terminated activity has to be activated at a later time, it might very well be that this activation happens at a time $t_1 > k$ and that when the activity implementation returns at time $t_2 < i$, the exit condition is met (in which case the activity is completed—see below). Thus, condition (3) cannot be relaxed to $\varepsilon(A)(^k\iota(\varepsilon(A))) \ne 1$.

In practice, some workflow management systems provide the capability to force a terminated activity into the "completed" state through external intervention. This resolves situations in which the exit condition could never be met and waiting forever would be the consequence. For example, an activity might request that a customer call be made. If the customer had moved to an unknown location then the calls could not take place. The exit condition could therefore never be satisfied. To resolve this situation, the performing agent, assuming that he had the appropriate authorizations, would force this activity to complete as soon as he realized that the call could not be made.

4.7.9 Completed Activities

As required before for terminated activities, the activity implementation of a completed activity must have returned after having been activated earlier. The completed state is different from the terminated state in that to get to the completed state, the activity's exit condition must be met. But, condition (3) of the following definition does not require that the exit condition be met *immediately* after the return of the activity implementation. It is sufficient that it is met some time after the return of the activity implementation.

Definition (Activities in State "Completed") Let $A \in N$ be an activity with activity implementation $\Psi(A)$. Then, $A \in \lambda_i :\Leftrightarrow$

1. $\exists j \in \mathbb{N} : j < i \wedge \omega(j, A) = \text{activated}$,

2. $\exists k \in \mathbb{N} : j < k \leq i \wedge \Psi(A)$ returned at time k,

3. $\exists r \in \mathbb{N} : k \leq r \leq i \wedge \varepsilon(A)(^r\iota(\varepsilon(A))) = 1$

■

The navigation algorithm makes sure that an activity that has been completed remains in this state forever. The navigation algorithm proceeds, interpreting the process model. It leaves the activity without ever returning to it. Thus there cannot be any event triggering a state change for the activity unless it is part of a sphere, as discussed in Chapter 7.

Condition (3) allows for the exit condition to be evaluated at some time after the return from the associated activity implementation without having to invoke the activity implementation again. As a consequence, the metamodel supports a mechanism, sometimes found in workflow management systems, that put pieces of work already performed by an agent on the agent's worklists. This mechanism enables the agent to track the amount of work being performed. By explicitly requesting the evaluation of the exit condition, navigation is performed on the basis activities identified to be completed at that time. Note that when an activity implementation returns but the exit condition of the associated activity is not evaluated, the truth value of the exit condition is unknown (see section 4.7.4 on page 167). Thus, the activity is in the terminated state because the exit condition has not been met.

4.7.10   Selecting Activities for Execution

In section 4.7.6, we defined the exact point in time when an activity enters the executable state, the time when it is first detected that the piece of work corresponding to an activity has to be performed. The following definition allows us to conveniently refer to this set of activities.

Definition   (Executable Map): The map

$$\eta : \mathbb{N} \times \mathbb{N} \to \{0, 1\}$$

with

$$\eta(i, A) = 1 :\Leftrightarrow A \text{ becomes executable at time i}$$

and is called a *executable map*. The set

$$\eta_i := \{A \in N \mid \eta(i, A) = 1\}$$

is called the set of *recent executable activities*. The map $\tau : N \to \mathbb{N}$ assigns to each activity the time it becomes executable; that means

$$\tau(A) = i :\Leftrightarrow A \in \eta_i$$

∎

Based on this definition, the activity state map ω is required to have the following property for i>0.

$$A \in \eta_i \Rightarrow \omega_i(A) = \text{ executable } \wedge \omega_{i-1}(A) \neq \text{ executable}$$

"Becoming executable" is something that happens at a single, precise point in time. Thus, each activity can only be executed once. This is the content of the following note.

Note $A \in \eta_i \Rightarrow \forall j \neq i : A \notin \eta_j$.∎.

As soon as an activity enters the executable state, particular agents may decide to perform the corresponding piece of work. The activity becomes selectable for execution, which means that it can be performed at any time. Consequently, the metamodel has to provide a construct for deriving the set of all activities selectable for execution at any given time. Simply determining the set of all activities in the executable state is not enough because activities in other states, for example, the terminated state are allowed to be executed too. Thus, a more complicated construct is needed.

Definition (Selection Family)   The following set sequence $(\sigma_i)_{i \in \mathbb{N}}$ is called *selection family*:

1. $\sigma_0 := \eta_0$

2. $\sigma_i := (\sigma_{i-1} \cup \eta_i) - \{A \in N \mid A \in \lambda_i - \lambda_{i-1}\}, i > 0$

An activity $A \in N$ is called *selectable* for execution at time $i :\Leftrightarrow A \in \sigma_i$.

■

Thus, at instantiation time, only the start activities are selectable. At any later point in time $i>0$,

- only those activities are selectable that have been selectable before; that means the set σ_{i-1},

- all activities that become executable at time i, thus the set η_i, are also selectable at that time, but

- all activities that complete at time i (i.e, the set $\{A \in N \mid A \in \lambda_i - \lambda_{i-1}\}$) are no longer selectable.

Only activities that are selectable for execution can be chosen to be performed. Performing an activity means to start its associated activity implementation. Starting an activity implementation means to invoke a program in the case of a program activity, or to instantiate a process, in the case of a process activity. The activity enters the activated state at this time. Thus, an activity that enters the activated state must be selectable; this is another property the activity state map must satisfy.

$$\forall A \in N : \omega(A) = \text{ activated } \Rightarrow A \in \sigma_i$$

Note that the reverse is not true since activities in the terminated state are selectable for execution too. An activity in the terminated state has not met its exit condition yet, so its associated piece of work has to be continued at a later time. Because of this requirement, terminated activities are always selectable for execution as proved by the following.

Note $\forall A \in N; \omega_i(A) = \text{ terminated } \Rightarrow A \in \sigma_i.$ ■

4.7.11   Performing Navigation: Computing Actual Successors

We are now ready to define precisely how a navigation step is performed in the metamodel. For this purpose, for each activity that completes at a particular time, we define its successors. These successors, referred to as the actual successors of the activity, become executable at some point in time. The definition is constructive in the sense that we prescribe the sets of activities to be computed in a stepwise manner resulting in the actual successors of a given activity.

Definition (Actual Successors)   Let $A \in N$ be an activity that enters the "completed" state at time $i \in \mathbb{N}$; that means $A \in \lambda_i - \lambda_{i-1}$. Let

1. $M(A) := \bigcup_{X \in A^{\rightarrow} \cap \delta_i} \delta\mathcal{D}^{\rightarrow}(X)$,
   i.e. $M(A)$ is the union of all dead successor boundaries of dead successors of A,

2. $M_1(A) := \{X \in M(A) \mid \Phi(X)(\{^i\iota(q) \mid q \in \mathcal{C}^{\leftarrow}(X)\}) = 1\}$,
   i.e. $M_1(A)$ is the set of all activities of $M(A)$ having a join condition that evaluates to "true".

3. $M_2(A) := \{X \in A_{\bullet}^{\rightarrow} \mid (A, X, p) \in E \wedge p(^i\iota(p)) = 1\}$,
   i.e., $M_2(A)$ is the set of all regular successors of A having an incoming transition condition that evaluates to "true".

4. $M_3(A) := \{X \in A_{*}^{\rightarrow} \mid \Phi(X)\{^i\iota(q) \mid q \in \mathcal{C}^{\leftarrow}(X)\}) = 1\}$,
   i.e., $M_3(A)$ is the set of all join successors of A having a join condition that evaluates to "true".

The set $\Sigma_i(A)$ of i-*actual successors* of A is defined as follows:

1. $\Sigma_i(A) := M_1(A) \cup M_2(A) \cup M_3(A)$, for $A \in \lambda_j - \lambda_{i-1}$.

2. $\Sigma_i(A) := \emptyset$, else.

$\blacksquare$

Note that $M(A)$ (item (1) in the preceding definition) cannot simply be defined to be $\delta\mathcal{D}^{\rightarrow}(A)$. This is because dead successor boundaries are only meaningful for dead nodes (see section 4.4.5 on page 146) but A itself is not dead.

The following note proves that the collection of all i-actual successors in a given process instance is exactly the set of all activities that become executable at time i. Consequently, the concept of actual successors represents a precise computational manner that determines activities that can be performed next. In practice, the i-actual successors of a given activity are computed exactly at the time when this activity completes.

Note It is $\eta_i = \bigcup_{A \in \lambda_i - \lambda_{i-1}} \Sigma_i(A)$; that means for each activity X, it is $\tau(X) = i \Leftrightarrow$ $\exists A \in \lambda_i - \lambda_{i-1} : X \in \Sigma_i(A)$, for i>0. ∎

4.7.12 Performing Navigation: Managing Workitems

As soon as an activity becomes executable, it is *scheduled*; this means all agents are assigned to it who actually qualify under its associated staff query. Each of these agents is allowed to perform the corresponding piece of work. The pair, consisting of an activity and an agent who is allowed to perform the activity, is referred to as a *workitem*. Thus, at any given time "scheduling" means to derive workitems based on activities that become executable at that time (see Figure 4.13).

As discussed in section 4.3.3 on page 132, the staff query associated with an activity A is denoted by $\Omega(A)$. When evaluated at time i, a staff query returns the set of agents $\Omega(A)(i) \subseteq \mathcal{A}$. We define the scheduled workitems as follows.

Definition (Scheduled Workitem) The set

$$\gamma_i := \{(A, a) \mid A \in \eta_i \wedge a \in \Omega(A)(i)\}$$

is called the set of i-*scheduled workitems*. It consists of all workitems derived from all activities that become executable at time i.

∎

Figure 4.13 Performing Scheduling for Actual Successors

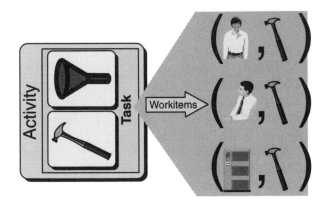

Recall from section 4.7.10 on page 174 that agents can perform work at any time after a workitem has been scheduled for them. Furthermore, when a particular agent starts performing the work represented by a workitem, all other workitems created for the same activity but for different agents must be discarded. Otherwise, more than one agent might perform the same work, which would be a waste of time and resources. To reflect this operational behavior, the metamodel requires additional constructs.

Definition (Activating Agent Map)   The partial map

$$\alpha : \mathbb{N} \times \mathbb{N} \to \mathcal{A}$$

satisfying the constraints

1. α is not defined for $i < \tau(A)$,

2. $i \geq \tau(A) \Rightarrow \alpha(i, A) \in \Omega(A)(\tau(A))$,

is called an *activating agent map*. It associates the agent which activated A at time i with each activity $A \in N$.

■

The activity state map ω is required to have the following property.

$$\forall A \in N : \omega(i, A) = \text{ activated } \Rightarrow \alpha(i, A) \text{ is defined}$$

The following note is an immediate consequence of this property.

Note $\forall A \in N \; \forall i \in \mathbb{N} \; \exists j < i : \omega(i, A) = \text{activated} \Rightarrow \omega(j, A) = \text{executable}.$ ■
We can now formally define how workitems are managed correctly.

Definition (Workitem Family)   The set of all workitems builds a set sequence $(\Gamma_i)_{i \in \mathbb{N}}$ called a *workitem family*:

1. $\Gamma_0 := \gamma_0$

2. $\Gamma_i := (\Gamma_{i-1} \cup \gamma_i) - \{(A, a) \mid a \neq \alpha(i, A)\} - \{(A, a) \mid A \in \lambda_i - \lambda_{i-1}\}$, for i>0

■

Thus, at any given time the set of all workitems consists of

- all workitems that have been scheduled exactly at this time (i.e., means the set γ_i),

- all former workitems (i.e. the set Γ_{i-1}), but

  { when an activity is activated, all workitems are discarded if they resulted from the assignment of the same activity to other agents during scheduling (i.e. the set $\{(A, a) \mid a \neq \alpha(i, A)\}$)

  { when an activity completes, the corresponding workitem is discarded (i.e., the set $\{(A, a) \mid A \in \lambda_i - \lambda_{i-1}\}$). Note that, according to the first bulleted item, only one workitem corresponding to the activity was left during activation.

4.7.13 Performing Navigation: Informal Description

Sections 4.7.11 and 4.7.12 provide the complete algorithm for how to perform navigation within the metamodel. Navigation takes place whenever an activity completes. For a completing activity, its actual successors are computed; for each of the actual successors the corresponding workitems are scheduled; the workitem family is maintained accordingly. The following is a more detailed but informal description of the steps that constitute navigation.

- Determine all control connectors leaving the completing activity.

- Determine the endpoints of these control connectors by computing the successors of the completing activity.

- Determine the transition conditions of these control connectors.

- Compute the actual instances of the input containers of these transition conditions.

- Compute the truth values of the transition conditions based on these input container instances.

- Determine all regular nodes within the set of computed successors whose incoming transition condition has been evaluated to false; determine all join nodes within the set of computed successors whose join condition evaluate to false (that means the set of dead nodes within the computed successors is determined).

  { Perform dead path elimination for each of these nodes.

{ Compute the dead successor boundary for each of these nodes. (This computation results in the set M(A).)

{ An activity from any of these sets with a join condition that evaluates to true enters the executable state. (This results in the set $M_1(A)$.)

- Determine all regular nodes within the set of computed successors whose incoming transition condition has been evaluated to true. (This results in the set $M_2(A)$.)

- All activities from this computed set enter the executable state.

- Determine all join nodes within the set of computed successors whose join condition evaluates to true. (This results in the set $M_3(A)$.)

- All activities from this computed set enter the executable state.

- All other successors remain in their current state and must wait for a future navigation step for a possible state change.

- Perform staff resolution for all activities that entered the executable state based on the previous steps. For each of these activities the following are carried out.

    { Determine its associated staff query.

    { Evaluate the staff query.

    { For each agent returned create, the corresponding workitem.

Example (Navigation Step)   Figure 4.14 depicts a sample state of a process instance when activity A enters the completed state. The transition conditions of the outgoing control connectors of A are all evaluated and assume the truth values shown in the figure result.
    Then:

- B is a join activity, and assume that the truth value of the transition condition of (A,B) was the last one required to evaluate the join condition of B. Since the join condition becomes true (based on the assumed truth value of the other incoming transition condition in Figure 4.14), B enters the executable state.

- C is a regular activity, and because its incoming transition condition is true, C enters the executable state.

Figure 4.14 Performing Navigation When A Completes

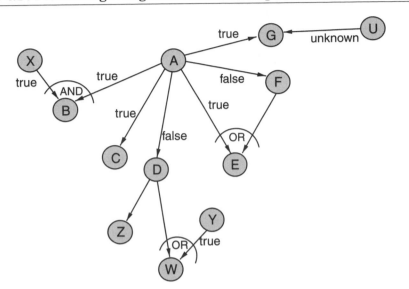

- D becomes dead, and dead path elimination is immediately performed: (D,Z), and (D,W) are flagged as evaluated with the truth value false. As a consequence, Z becomes dead. The join condition of the join node W becomes true because the other incoming transition condition of W is already evaluated as true; as a result, W enters the executable state. (Note that W is not an immediate successor of the completed activity A!)

- E is not immediately detected as executable because it is a join node the join condition of which has not yet been evaluated. The truth value of the transition condition of (F,E) is not available, and thus the truth value of the join condition cannot be computed.

- F becomes dead, and dead path elimination assigns the truth value false to the transition condition of (F,E). As a consequence, the join condition of E now becomes evaluated with truth value true and E enters the executable state.

- G is a join node and must wait until the not-evaluated constituents of its join condition are evaluated before the determination of whether G will finally become dead or executable. ■

Section 4.7.3 on page 165 introduced the activity states relevant for the metamodel. Sections 4.7.5 on page 168 to 4.7.9 on page 173 defined these states precisely and listed properties of these states and their valid transitions. This was continued in sections 4.7.10 on page 174 to 4.7.12 on page 177, where activity states were put into the context of other constructs of the operational semantics of the metamodel.

Figure 4.15 depicts these states and the valid transitions between them. Note, that this is a simplified version of Figure 4.15. This simplification allows us to focus on the essential information.

Figure 4.15 State Transition Diagram for Activities

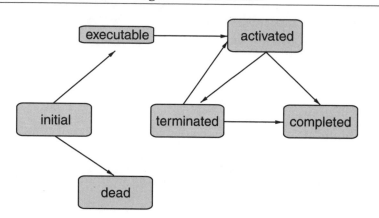

Following is an informal summary of preceding discussion on these subjects.

1. At instantiation time every start activity is in the executable state.

2. At instantiation time each non-start activity is in the initial state.

3. An activity enters the dead state when its incoming transition condition is evaluated to false (for a regular activity) or its join condition is evaluated to false (for a join activity), including dead path elimination.

    Note: Only activities in the initial state can enter the dead state. ■

4. An activity enters the executable state when its incoming transition condition is evaluated to true (for a regular activity) or its join condition is evaluated to true (for a join activity).

    Note: A nonstart activity must be in the initial state to enter the executable state. ■

5. The activity state map may allow only activities in the executable or terminated state to enter the activated state.

6. When an activity implementation of an activated activity returns, the activity enters the completed state if and only if its exit condition is met; otherwise, it enters the terminated state.

7. The activity state map may allow an activity in the terminated state to enter the completed state if and only if its exit condition is met.

4.8   Summary: G-Instances

In this section we summarize the semantics of our metamodel.

Definition (G-Instance)   Let $G = (V, \iota, o, N, \Psi, \mathcal{C}, \Omega, \varepsilon, E, \Phi, \Delta, \overrightarrow{\Delta})$ be a process model graph. A *G-instance* (or *G-process* or *G-workflow* or *G-execution*) is a tuple

$$G^\omega = (\omega, \Lambda, ({}^0\iota(A))_{A\in N}, ({}^0 o(A))_{A\in N}, {}^0\iota(G), {}^0 o(G))$$

consisting of an activity state map $\omega : N \times N \to S$, a dead data map $\Lambda : N \times N \times V \to \bigcup_{w\in V} DOM(v)$, and the families of default instances of the input and output containers of all activities as well as the process model G itself. Furthermore, the activity state map must fulfill all the properties formulated in section 4.7.5 on page 168 to 4.7.10 on page 174.

■

All other aspects of the semantics of our metamodel are derived from the constructs listed in G^ω. Note that the activity state map has some random aspects, which means it is influenced by external factors such as the time when an executable activity is activated. The same is true for the dead data map because, in practice, the corresponding values are obtains from end users or provided by programs.

The transactional enhancements of the metamodel (see Chapter 7) extend the semantics by adding a map initiating the rollback of atomic spheres and compensation spheres.

One of the advantages of representing a metamodel in a formal manner is that one can prove statements formulated in the corresponding language. In our case, properties of process model graphs and their instances can be derived.

We will not go into details here but provide as a sample the following property of instances of process model graphs.

Theorem   If each scheduled activity of a process is guaranteed to complete in finite time, then the process itself is guaranteed to terminate.

$$(\forall A \in N : (\exists i_A \in N : A \in \eta_{i_A}) \Rightarrow (\exists t_A \in N : \omega_{t_A}(A) = \text{completed}))$$
$$\Rightarrow (\exists T \in N : \omega_T(G) = \text{terminated})$$

Proof (Sketch)   G is connected, w.l.o.g. Each node of G is reachable from a start node. When an activity completes, dead path elimination will determine all reachable dead activities and put them into the "dead" state. Activities in dead successor boundaries are either scheduled or must wait for the evaluation of remaining incoming transition conditions. Since such a latter node is reachable from a start node, it is guaranteed that all transition conditions are finally evaluated: either the activity is then scheduled or dead path elimination takes place. ∎

Note   In practice, the above property of the activity state map ensuring termination of a process is guaranteed by notification processing. This means that limits for the completion for each activity can be set and that escalation for activities exceeding these limits resolves these situations.

Chapter 5

Advanced Functions

In Chapter 3 we described the basic functions of a workflow management system. Many of them should be available in commercial products. In this chapter, we discuss some functions that may appear over time. The list is not complete by any means but should provide a flavor of the extensions that can be expected.

5.1 Events

In many business processes it is important that the business process waits at some point until "something happens." We call this "something happens" an *event*. A typical example of an event is a response that should be received from an inquiry that was sent to a customer. The occurrence of the event may be *signaled* from an activity within another process instance of the same process model, an activity of a process instance of another process model, or from any other program such as a Lotus Notes agent.

Figure 5.1 shows a process that needs to wait until some other process has completed a specific activity. It actually represents the situation of waiting for a customer letter. The process on the left is a claims processing process. Activity X requests more information from the customer by sending out a letter. Processing continues until activity Y, which needs to wait until the customer has responded or, until a specified deadline is exceeded. The process on the right is the process that scans in the customer response letter. In the shown activity, a clerk determines the process that is associated with the letter that was received and then causes the waiting event to be signaled.

The structure of the metamodel allows this capability to be seamlessly added to it. Events are modeled as a special type of activity, an *event activity*. An event activity has most of the properties of program and process activities. It is associated with an input and an output container. It can be the source and the target of control connectors as well as the source and target of data connectors. It has a start condition,

Figure 5.1 Events

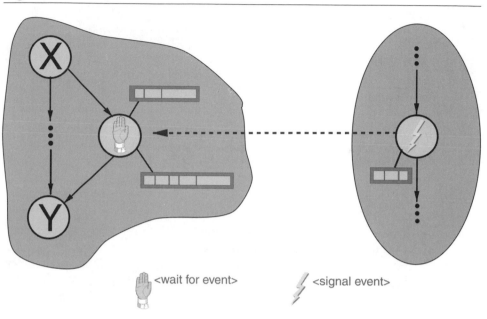

<wait for event>   <signal event>

and a deadline can be specified for it.

To indicate that an activity should wait for the signaling of an event, a control connector is drawn from the event activity to the activity. In Figure 5.1, activity Y waits for the event to happen. Whenever the event occurs, navigation follows this control connector and possibly activates the activity.

Signaling of the event is performed by a program using the supplied event API. The program that signals the event has access to both the input container and the output container of the event activity. The information in the input container can be used by the program to locate the appropriate process that contains the event. After having located the process, the program fills the output container with appropriate values, if any, and signals the event. The event activity is then considered finished and navigation continues as normal.

Control connectors that originate in an event are treated as they usually are. The associated transition conditions are evaluated as soon as the control connectors leave the event. Typically, those transition conditions refer to fields in the output container of the event activity. The derived truth values can be used in start conditions of the target activities. Also, more than one control connector may be originating from the event activity. This allows, for example, control of the process paths depending on values supplied by the program that signaled the event.

An event is *activated* as soon as navigation reaches the event. When an event is activated, appropriate queries show this event is waiting to be signaled. If the event activity is a start activity the event is activated, when the process starts. If the event activity is the target of a control connector, then the event is activated if the start condition of the event activity evaluates to true. Control connectors pointing to events can explicitly activate events within particular process instance contexts (refer to the literature on active databases, for example [Kot89]).

Control connectors can also be drawn between event activities, allowing the modeler to build event chains.

From an architectural standpoint, events are managed in tabular format, as shown in Figure 5.2.

Figure 5.2 Event Tables

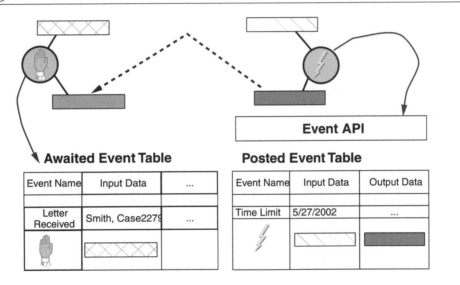

The awaited event table contains an entry for each event that has been activated. For each entry, the table contains the name of the event and the input container associated with the event. Not shown is the identifier of the process the event is part of.

The event is not removed until the event is signaled. If the event is never signaled, the event stays forever. It can be removed by invocation of the delete function supplied by the event API. Another possibility is for the workflow management system's garbage collection facility to automatically remove the events. This choice would cause the event to be removed either when the process finishes or after some specified period of time. A third approach is for the event's expiration processing to remove it.

As pointed out, the event is signaled by a program by identification of the activated event. An event can also be signaled if the event itself has not yet been activated, as is typical for timer events. In this case, the event is signaled well in advance, and no event is waiting in the awaited event table. In this case, the event is put into the *posted event table.*

When an event is activated, the workflow management system first checks if a matching entry can be found in the posted event table. Matching is usually done by comparing the input container of the event, which is stored in the posted event table, with values supplied by the caller. If a match is found, the stored output container is copied to the output container of the event. If no entry is found, the event is stored, as previously described, into the awaited event table.

As shown, events can easily be added to the metamodel as event activities. It is as easy to add the appropriate definitions to the flow definition language. Code Example 5.1 shows the definition of an event that waits for a customer to respond to a previously sent letter. The event activity is identified via the keyword EVENT_ACTIVITY. The name of the event activity within the process model is Wait for Customer Letter. The input container is Customer Identification; it contains information that identifies the customer, such as customer name or the identifier of the request sent to the customer. The output container is Response Information; it contains essential information from the customer's response. The EXPIRATION keyword specifies that the event is canceled if no response has been received from the customer within 14 days.

Code Example 5.1 Event Definition

```
EVENT_ACTIVITY 'Wait for Customer Letter'
    ('Event Identification', 'Response Information')
    EXPIRATION
       AFTER 14 DAYS
END 'Wait for Customer Letter'
```

5.2   Dynamic Modification of Workflows

A major assumption when we discussed the metamodel and the functions of a workflow management system in Chapters 3 and 4 was that all possible paths through a process are described in the process model. This rigid behavior makes sure that the processes are carried out exactly as described and that the user cannot deviate from it. This behavior is desirable in most cases, however, there are situations when a user needs to make changes.

Figure 5.3 shows the typical modifications that users need to make to cope with some of these situations.

Figure 5.3 Modifying a Workflow

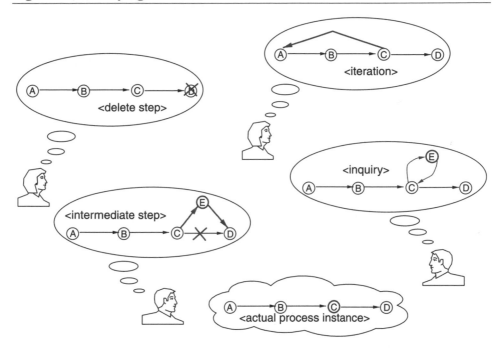

As shown in Figure 5.3, the user is currently working with activity C. The *inquiry* modification allows the user to suspend processing of the activity and transfers control to some other person to get additional information. The typical example is that a user would like to get her manager involved. The *intermediate step* modification adds a new activity to the process. This new activity could be carried out by the user or more likely by somebody else. A doctor in a hospital may decide that the patient's state requires that an additional blood test be carried out. The *iterate* modification causes the process to redo some of the work. The user may have detected that activity C does not produce the correct result and that activities A and B need to be redone. The *delete* modification causes the removal of an activity. For example, a change in government regulations no longer requires a particular report to be created.

The example shows some of the situations where a user needs to modify a running workflow. In some situations, the process was not modeled completely, as in the case when a user needs to contact the manager. This situation could have been modeled into the process from the very beginning.

In other situations, a complete modeling of a business process cannot be done. For hospital processes, such as a chemotherapy process for treatment of cancer, only the normal case is modeled. This case is then modified whenever problems arise, for example, the patient gets the flu. In the hospital environment this information is maintained in a rules database that contains the available medical knowledge what to do in every case. Based on the rules, the modifications are made.

In even other situations, the change is made just to a particular workflow but must be applied to all running instances. In our example of the deletion of a step it would be desirable, to delete the activity from all workflows that have not yet reached the activity.

The workflow management system supports the dynamic modification of workflows via an API that enables the above mentioned operations to be performed. In essence, it offers most of the buildtime functionality, including a check of the modified workflow for correctness. In addition, it enables to have these operations to be carried out for a set of selected processes. An appropriate end-user interface facilitates the task.

However, just offering the functionality is not sufficient. It is not possible for an end user to define an activity and then associate it with a program. This mandates that the workflow management system supports activities the same way it supports process models or programs. Thus, activities can be defined as named entities with all their properties set. Code Example 5.2 shows how an activity would be defined.

Code Example 5.2 Activity for Asking Manager

```
ACTIVITY 'Ask Manager'
  TYPE=PROGRAM
  DONE_BY MANAGER OF PREVIOUS ACTIVITY
  PROGRAM 'E:\wordpro.exe'
END 'Ask Manager'
```

With this capability, the graphical user interface (GUI) can support the end user much better by providing the user with a list of activities that can be added.

Registering activities also helps in the design of processes because predefined activities can be reused. Instead of specifying a new activity for every new process, one could use a registered the same way process activities are defined. Code Example 5.3 shows how the activity defined in Figure 5.2.

Code Example 5.3 Using a Predefined Activity

```
PROGRAM_ACTIVITY 'Request Information'
   ACTIVITY 'Ask Manager'
END 'Request Information'
```

It should be noted that the audit trail will contain entries for the added activities so one could derive a new process structure that includes activities that have been added often.

5.3 Advanced Join Conditions

Join conditions define whether join activities are carried out or not. We have shown in the preceding chapters that join activities are treated as synchronization points, since evaluation of the start condition is not performed until all incoming control connectors have entered the activity. This is a perfect match for most business processes, such as our trip reservation example.

Join conditions are Boolean expressions of the truth values of the incoming control connectors. This expression allows one to specify everything conceivable; however, such specification can be extremely cumbersome. We could simplify the specification through constructs such as 2 OUT OF 3 indicating that two out of the three incoming control connectors must evaluate to true.

However, there are situations where the join activity should not be a synchronization point, to avoid the possibility of a business process being held up unnecessarily. If, for example, in a business process two signatures are required for a document and to speed up the business process appropriate workitems have been generated for five people, then the business process can continue as soon as two of the five people have signed it. There is no need to wait for the other three, since it is immaterial whether they sign or not.

As the join condition is only evaluated when all control connectors have been evaluated (making the join activity a synchronization point), we must be allowed to specify that the start condition should be evaluated at another time. This would allow us to cope with the described situation.

There are conceptually two times when the join condition expression can be evaluated: when all control connectors have entered the activity or when a new control connector enters the activity.

If the join condition is evaluated as soon as a new control connector enters the activity, the join activity is not a synchronization point. If the join condition expression evaluates to true, processing of the activity continues with the evaluation of the activation condition.

As a consequence, the join condition must support evaluation of itself for both situations: when all control connectors have entered the activity and, when a new control connector has entered the activity. In fact, there may be occasions when the join condition shows both situations. For some control connectors, evaluation of the join condition should be deferred until all control connectors have been evaluated, and for other control connectors, the join condition should be evaluated as soon as one of them has been evaluated.

Therefore the join condition is broken up into a part that is evaluated as soon as one of the specified control connectors enters the activity and another part that is evaluated if all specified control connectors have entered the activity.

The flow definition language is extended to allow specification of each part. The keyword IMMEDIATE indicates that the expression should be evaluated immediately; the keyword DEFERRED indicates that the expression should be evaluated after all control connectors have entered the activity.

Code Example 5.4 shows an appropriate specifications.

Code Example 5.4 Execution Time Specification

```
IMMEDIATE (AD OR B) AND DEFERRED (CD)
```

The above specification indicates that the control connector CD must have entered the activity before the appropriate expression part is evaluated. The expression in which AD and B are specified is evaluated as soon as one of them has entered the activity. The join condition evaluates to true if CD evaluates to true and either AD or B evaluates to true.

When the join condition has evaluated to true, processing of the activity continues with the evaluation of the activation condition.

If the join condition contains a DEFERRED specification only, no further actions need to be defined. However, if the join condition contains an IMMEDIATE specification, actions must be defined that are to be taken if one of the control connectors that had not been evaluated enters the activity.

Several options exist of what action could be specified; (1) IGNORE ignores any control connector that comes in later, (2) TERMINATE causes all activities that are in the preceding paths to be terminated, or (3) PROCESS causes the activity to be carried out another time. It is obvious, that for the PROCESS action the join activity can be carried out multiple times. This requires extensions to the appropriate API so that the activity implementation can determine the context in which is invoked. This context includes, among other information, which control connectors have been evaluated to true since the last invocation.

Figure 5.4 illustrates the usage of the IMMEDIATE keyword together with the IGNORE. It shows a portion of a process that handles the processing of conference papers.

When a reviewer has reviewed the paper, she indicates whether the paper should be accepted or not. If yes (Y), the control connector with the transition condition Y evaluates to true and the control connector with the transition condition N evaluates to false; if no (N), the control connector with the transition condition N evaluates to true and the control connector with the transition condition Y evaluates to false. A paper is accepted if two of the three reviewers have voted Yes and is rejected if two of the three reviewers have voted No.

Figure 5.4 IMMEDIATE Evaluation with IGNORE Action

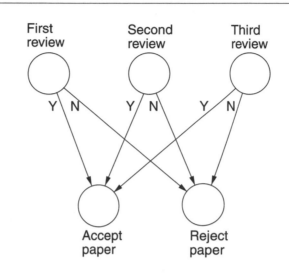

In this case, the join condition is defined as IMMEDIATE 2 OUT_OF 3 IGNORE. Whenever a reviewer completes the review, the appropriate control connectors are evaluated. As soon as two control connectors that enter activity Accept paper or Reject paper evaluate to true, processing of the appropriate activity is carried out. If the third review is completed, the appropriate control connectors are also evaluated. The IGNORE action then defines what should be done if the control connector evaluates to true for an activity that has already been started. If, for example, the first two reviewers voted Y for accepting the paper, then the activity Accept paper has been started; activity Reject paper is still waiting since no incoming control connector has evaluated to true. Regardless of the vote of the third reviewer, activity Accept paper will *ignore* the result. If, for example, the third reviewer votes yes, the control connector coming into the activity Accept paper evaluates to true and the control connector coming into activity Reject paper evaluates to false. Activity Accept paper ignores the control connector; that is it does nothing. For activity Reject paper, all control connectors have now been evaluated. Since no control connector evaluated to true, the start condition fails and the activity is skipped.

There remains one problem with join conditions. Even with the IMMEDIATE option, a new evaluation of the start condition is not carried out until a new control connector enters the join activity. However, there are situations where this is insufficient and where evaluation of the join condition should be performed after a certain period of time.

Figure 5.5 shows a typical business process in the insurance industry. Based on the type of insurance that the customer selects in step `Collect customer information`, one or all of the different paths are processed. When all necessary actions have been carried out for the selected insurances, a contract is printed in the `Print contract` activity. Depending on the selected insurances, the printed contract contains one or more insurance types.

Figure 5.5 Insurance Process

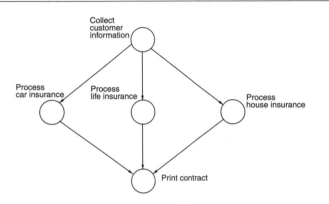

Carrying out the business process this way is ideal: (1) optimal customer satisfaction since the customer receives only one contract that contains everything, and (2) minimal costs for processing the contract. Modeling of the process can be done by use of the available constructs for start conditions; the join activity is a synchronization point. The condition is not evaluated until all control connectors have entered the activity. For the contract to be printed, at least one of the control connectors must evaluate to true. The appropriate specification would then be START WHEN AT LEAST ONE CONNECTOR TRUE.

Unfortunately, this optimal processing of sending out a contract that contains all insurances cannot be achieved in all cases. For example, legislation may mandate that for car insurance, the signed contract must be returned to the customer within 14 days after the customer has applied for car insurance. This time requirement could be different for each type of insurance. For example, for life insurance, the time frame could be 21 days, and for house insurance, 28 days. Thus the contract must be printed at the latest after 14 days if the contract includes car insurance; even if processing of the other insurance types has not yet been completed. Thus evaluation of the join condition cannot wait until all control connectors have been evaluated. Nor can evaluation wait until a new control connector is evaluated. Evaluation of the join condition must be done at the latest 14 days after the customer has sent in the request.

The above scenario requires that it is possible to specify exactly when the join condition should be evaluated. This specification can be achieved by adding a time property to the start condition that indicates when the join condition should be checked. Code Example 5.5 shows how this could be specified with the flow definition language.

Code Example 5.5 Timed Evaluation of Join Condition

```
PROGRAM_ACTIVITY Print Contract
  START
    TIMED FROM ACTIVITY Collect Customer Information
      AFTER 14 DAYS
              FOR ACTIVITY Process Car Insurance
      AFTER 21 DAYS
              FOR ACTIVITY Process Life Insurance
      AFTER 28 DAYS
              FOR ACTIVITY Process House Insurance
  END Print Contract
```

The keyword `TIMED` indicates that evaluation of the join condition should be done after specified time periods. Specification of this keyword is exclusive. If `TIMED` is specified, neither `IMMEDIATE` nor `DEFERRED` can be specified. The `FROM ACTIVITY` identifies the activity that starts the clock. If the `Collect Customer Information` activity has completed, the timer for the `Print Contract` activity starts. The particular times when the start condition should be checked is identified by the `AFTER` keyword. Multiple specifications are possible, as shown in Figure 5.5.

If all control connectors have been evaluated before the first time period has been reached and at least one control connector evaluates to true, the activity is carried out. If, for example, all control connectors have been evaluated within 14 days and at least one insurance type was accepted, a contract with all insurances is printed.

If not all control connectors have been evaluated within the first time period, in the example within 14 days, the join condition is evaluated. As can be seen, each evaluation time is associated with an activity. For example, the first time is associated with the `Process Car Insurance` activity. The specified activity triggers the activation of the activity. If the `Process Car Insurance` activity has been completed, the start condition is set to true regardless of the settings of the other control connectors and processing of the activity is started. If the activity `Process Car Insurance` has not been completed, no action is taken. In this case, the workflow management system waits until the `Process Car Insurance` activity completes or until the next time period is reached, which would be 21 days.

This process of treating the activity as a synchronization point and evaluating it at specified times is repeated until all control connectors have been evaluated.

A sample case may illustrate how these timed join conditions work if not all control connectors have been evaluated in time. It is assumed that a customer has selected all insurance types.

Activity `Process Car Insurance` completes in 5 days, activity `Process Life Insurance` 15 in days, and activity `Process House Insurance` completes 18 days after activity `Collect Customer Information` has started. In this case, evaluation of the join condition for the activity `Print Contract` is performed after 14 days. Since the activity `Process Car Insurance` has been completed, activity `Print Contract` is carried out for the first time. A contract just containing the car insurance is printed. The activity is carried out a second time after all other control connectors have entered the activity. This happens after 18 days, and a contract containing the life insurance and the house insurance is printed.

5.4   Container Materialization

We have shown in the preceding chapters how input containers, output containers, and data connectors pass data between activities and between activities and activity implementations of a business process. We have also shown how this makes the applications flow independent.

A general problem with this approach is that the amount of data passed back from the application to the workflow management system is often not appropriate. Applications generally return to the workflow management system either too much data or no data at all.

No data is returned by existing programs or programs that have been written as general-purpose applications. Consequently, the workflow management system cannot obtain the data that is needed by follow-on applications or for determining the next application to be invoked. This failure has two consequences. First, the workflow cannot be properly used to integrate disparate applications. Second, the control flow logic of the business process using the corresponding program as an activity implementation cannot be properly expressed because it must be based on the "return code" of the program, but this mechanism was not designed to convey business semantics.

A different, but also undesirable, situation arises when the workflow management system is misused as an operational database. In this case, programs written as dedicated activity implementations tend to pass all data possibly needed by other applications in their output container. This behavior also has two drawbacks.

First, containers may be very large either because more data is passed than is needed by the other applications or because some of the data members are very large entities, such as a document or an image.

Second, data in the containers are copies of operational data. As such, they may become outdated between the time an activity implementation puts a data item into a container and another activity implementation reads the data from that container. Other, different, applications may have already modified the data in the operational data store. Thus, the container data and the operational data may frequently mismatch. The frequency with which the operational data is updated defines the chances that the operational data and the container data will not match.

These outlined problems can be solved through container materialization and dematerialization programs. The input containers are constructed by programs called (container) materialization programs. The output containers are stored by programs called (container) dematerialization programs. The actual parameters of workflow-relevant predicates, such as exit conditions or transition conditions, are provided by parameter determination programs.

The workflow management system's standard processing method of materializing the input container and dematerializing the output container of an activity A is carried out transparently by the system-provided materialization and dematerialization programs NM_A and D_A. The materialization program, for example, provides the system provided fields in the input container, such as the activity name.

The container materialization/dematerialization functions allow each activity A to be associated with a series of materialization programs $NM_1,...,M_n(A)$ and dematerialization programs $D_1,...,D_m(A)$. We call $M_1,...,M_n(A)$ the materialization chain of A; and $D_1,...,D_m(A)$, its dematerialization chain (See Figure 5.6). Each member of the chain has access to the container as manipulated by its predecessor. The system-provided materialization and dematerialization programs can be made members of the appropriate chains.

Figure 5.6 Container Materialization and Dematerialization

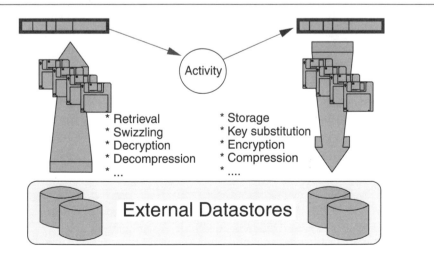

When the workflow management system processes an activity A, it first invokes the activity's materialization chain $M_1,...,M_n(A)$. When $M_n(A)$ finishes, the workflow management system considers the input container of the activity as constructed and invokes the appropriate activity implementation providing the constructed input container.

Thus, each member of the materialization chain is invoked to contribute to the construction of the associated activity implementation's input container. The processing of a materialization program can be manifold. For example, it can access an external database to provide missing values for particular container members, it could overwrite the values of container members, or it could perform the decryption or decompression of container members.

As an example, the first element of the materialization chain of activity A may be the system-provided materialization program M_A. This program provides the values of the predefined members of the container like process information, activity information, and a few other values for some container members. The second materialization program invoked may access a relational database to fetch additional data and an identifier of an image needed by the activity implementation. The third materialization program uses this identifier to fetch the image from a library. Since the image is compressed, a fourth materialization program is required to decompress the image. After that, the materialization of the input container is finished, and the input container passed to the activity implementation.

In another example, the invoked application may be a business object. The container passed by the default materialization program M_A to the second materialization program may provide values of only some object identifications; for example, the target object; and objects that are accessed by the second materialization program to obtain the required values to complete the input container.

When an activity implementation A returns, the workflow management system invokes the dematerialization chain $D_1,...D_m(A)$. When $D_m(A)$ returns, the workflow management system considers the output container of the activity implementation to be constructed and stores it in the workflow management system's database.

Each member of the dematerialization chain will get as input the output container as it was modified by its predecessor. As with materialization chains, the processing of the dematerialization programs in dematerialization chains can be manifold. For example, they could be used to provide encryption facilities and compression facilities, or they could be used to just modify the output container

This function has some quite valuable benefits beside solving the problems that motivate the support for container materialization and dematerialization.

The implementation of business algorithms can be separated from the implementation of accessing and manipulating persistent data. It is possible to write activity implementations that do not deal with accessing persistent data at all. All persistent data is read by via materialized input containers and written by dematerialized output containers based on standardized container manipulations, independently of the concrete datastore used. This enhances the portability and reusability of such an activity implementation.

In practice, different groups of programmers quite often are implementing application logic and data access. Container materialization/dematerialization allows the programmer to ignore this fact when implementing activities for workflows. Thus, an activity programmer can concentrate on providing the proper business algorithm, and a container programmer can concentrate on preparing containers from datastores and for mapping containers to datastores. Materialization/dematerialization of containers make programming of activity implementations even more straightforward, especially when visual builders are used.

The redundancy of data is reduced. Operational data can be separated from remaining container data by substitution of aggregations of container members with a reference stored in the container as a footprint. This substitution is performed by dematerialization programs; corresponding materialization programs will swizzle the references and establish access to the proper data members via container methods. This approach has two advantages. First, the consistency between container data stored in the workflow management system and the corresponding operational data stored in an external datastore is improved. Since in practice, operational data is frequently the target for updates by applications (transactions,etc.) that are not invoked by a workflow management system, storing copies of this data in containers can result in outdated information passed to programs by the workflow management system by means of its container mechanism. Second, the data load of the workflow management system's underlying database is reduced. Removing redundant data from containers reduces the size of the containers stored in the workflow management system's database. This reduction increases the availability of the workflow management system's database by speeding up the related database administration processes, for example, reorganizations.

The number of changes required for existing programs to be integrated with other programs via a workflow management system can be reduced. For example, existing programs may return only references to internal data of the application in the output container; newly provided dematerialization programs can then retrieve all data from datastores and make the data available in the output container. The retrieved data can then be used for navigation purposes or for mapping to the input containers of other activities.

Dematerialization programs can pump aggregations of members of output containers into multiple different datastores, thus performing data replication. This approach contributes to application integration through common datastores that an enterprise might have chosen in addition to integration through a workflow management system. The invoked dematerialization programs can, of course, be the source of data for enrichment and cleansing, or it can produce other data as a side effect.

5.5   Object Staging

We have shown in section 3.5.3 on page 101 that users typically start the implementation associated with an activity by double-clicking on the icon that represents the associated workitem. The appropriate mechanism to carry out the activity implementation is then described in section 3.10 on page 114.

It is important for the productivity of the user that the program completes its access to data as quickly as possible. This speed is necessary to avoid delays in interacting with users. If the method for accessing data from the program is slow, then moving the data to a place where the program can access the data efficiently should be done before the program is invoked. That way the user would not see the appropriate workitem until the appropriate objects had been staged to a place where they could be accessed quickly.

In section 3.10 on page 114, we sketched the basic structure of a workflow management system. To support staging, the system structure needs to be extended to the one shown in Figure 5.7.

Figure 5.7 Staging the Object to the Target

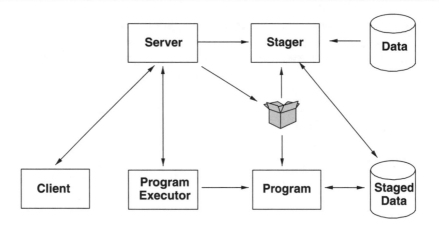

After the workflow management system server has performed staff resolution, it calls the stager to move the object(s) to a predefined location, such as the workstation of the selected user or a LAN server to which the user has access. The stager has access to the input container with the same contents as will be passed to the program. This access provides the staging program with the same amount of information as the program, so the staging program can determine which object(s) should be moved. After the object has been successfully staged, the workflow management system makes the associated workitem available to the workflow management system client. When a workitem is selected by a user, the activity implementation accesses the object(s) from the new location at maximum speed.

When the activity implementation has completed, the workflow management system program executor informs the workflow management system server about the completion so that the workflow management system server can continue navigation. If an object has been staged, the workflow management system server needs to call the stager again so that the modified object is copied back to the original place and so that all copies of the object are deleted.

The program that implements the activity and the staging program(s) that moves the objects close to the program need to be carefully designed and implemented together.

The necessary additions to support staging fit nicely into the metamodel. We outline them using the flow definition language.

Each program that is an implementation of an activity is identified to the workflow management system by the PROGRAM section. We discussed this in section 3.4.4 on page 89. Special keywords define the properties of the program for each of the operating system platforms on which the programs is to be executed. If staging should be performed for a particular program, an appropriate definition must be added to the PROGRAM section. Code Example 5.6 shows the new keyword STAGER which is assigned the value of IMAGE. This usage indicates that a staging program is invoked when an activity is implemented by this program and that the stager program has been defined to the workflow management system under the name IMAGE.

Code Example 5.6 Program Registration

```
PROGRAM
      STAGER IMAGE
```

A staging program must be defined to the workflow management system as would any other program. This definition includes the typical properties such as the operating system on which the program is to be executed, the name of the executable, and the path where the executable can be found.

Code Example 5.7 shows the definition of a staging program through the STAGER section. A special section has been introduced for ease of use; the regular PROGRAM keyword could also have been used. The staging program is registered under the name IMAGE. This name is used when referencing a stager program. The OS2 keyword starts the definitions of the properties of the executable when the staging program is invoked in the OS/2 environment. In this case, the program is found in the directory IMAGE on the E: disk and the program name is IMGCOPY.EXE as identified by the PATH keyword.

The TARGET keyword starts the definition of where the staging program should put the staged objects. In the example, the object is staged to the user's workstation,

Code Example 5.7 Stager Registration

```
STAGER IMAGE
   OS2
      EXE
         PATH 'E:\IMAGE\IMGCOPY.EXE'
      TARGET
         LOCATION USER
         PATH 'E:\IMAGE'
```

as defined by LOCATION USER, into the directory IMAGE on the E: disk as indicated by the PATH keyword.

We have described a rather simple way for the workflow management system to supply the desired staging facility. We just wanted to demonstrate the basic architecture; workflow management systems may devise more-sophisticated mechanisms to achieve the desired functionality.

5.6   Context Management

If the exit condition of a program activity fails, the appropriate workitem is put onto the worklist of a user again. This facility allows the task associated with the activity to be suspended. In this case, the activity implementation must persistently maintain state information so it can continue from where the user left. The activity implementation can achieve this continuity in one of the following methods, each of which is associated with drawbacks.

Option one is for the activity implementation to maintain the information in its own datastore. The identifiers of the process and the activity are passed by the workflow management system as part of the input container and can be used to manage the information in the datastore. This approach has three advantages: (1) the program is responsible for managing the entries in its data store; (2) if the datastore is on the user's workstation, processing on another workstation cannot continue when the workstation is no longer operational unless the program maintains the data store remotely; and (3) a special garbage collection routine must be established to clear any residue. This residue occurs if the process or activity is terminated when the activity implementation has already written the appropriate information to its store.

Option two is for the activity implementation to use fields in the input and output container and to map them from the output container to the input container. When the program wants to suspend itself, it stores the needed information into the fields in the output container and sets the return code appropriately. Those fields are then copied to proper fields in the input container. When the program is restarted, it can obtain these fields again. Despite the fact that containers should contain only process-relevant information, this approach implements the desired behavior much more easily than does the previous one. However, this second approach is associated with a potentially large performance penalty. Fields need to be added to the input and output container in case the activity implementation has to be suspended.

The workflow management system can solve the outlined problem by supporting a scratch pad area. A scratch pad area is a piece of storage that is provided and managed by the workflow management system. The scratch pad area can be used by the activity implementation to keep data from one invocation to the next. The workflow management system has no knowledge about the data in the scratch pad area.

A scratch pad area a used in TP monitors such as IMS [IBM94b] allows programs executing under the control of the transaction manager to maintain data from one conversation step to the next. The size of the scratch pad area is made known to the transaction manager when the program is defined to it.

Access to the scratch pad area is via a set of API calls. GetSPA to obtain the scratch pad area and PutSPA to return the scratch pad area are the important ones.

The workflow management system manages the scratch pad area the same way as manages the containers of the activity. It makes the scratch pad area persistent in the workflow management system's database to provide full recovery.

For efficiency and usability, the workflow management system provides a set of options; some of them are shown in Code Example 5.8.

Code Example 5.8 Scratch Pad Area Definitions

```
SETTINGS
    SPA_SUPPORT = YES

PROGRAM
    SPA=1000
```

The workflow management system general settings are extended by the SPA_SUPPORT keyword that indicates whether or not the workflow management system should provide scratch pad area support. When set to YES, support is provided.

The PROGRAM keyword that defines executables is extended with the SPA option. When SPA is set to a length greater than zero, a scratch pad area in the defined length will be maintained for the activity implementation. In the example, the program maintains a 1000-byte scratch pad area.

5.7   Performance Spheres

Applications that are carried out by a workflow management system use computing resources just as does any other application that is running on a system; *system* can be anything from a simple uniprocessor up to multiprocessor system such as an IBM S/390 Sysplex. All applications compete for these resources, so methods have been devised to assign more resources to time-critical applications. The simplest method is to assign priorities to applications. Based on these priorities, the operating system assigns appropriate resources.

However, this method does not help to specify performance goals for an application nor does it actively help applications to achieve those performance goals by dynamically reassigning resources from one application to another. This is the domain of *workload management systems*, such as the workload manager called WLM/MVS that is built into the OS/390 operating system. It allows the specification of performance goals and priorities for each service class, which is the abstraction of some service, and for collections of service classes, called an *enclave* in WLM/MVS. The workload manager performs periodic sampling of the resources assigned to services and enclaves. The workload manager makes processing resources available to enable services and enclaves to meet their goals. It withdraws or reduces processing resources from services and enclaves if (1) it becomes clear that a service or enclave will not meet its goal but another service will achieve its goal if given more resources, or (2) a higher priority service or enclave is in jeopardy for not making its goals because it lacks resources.

Not all parts of a business process are time critical; only certain sets of activities need to have some performance goals established. We call this set of activities a *performance sphere*, and we map a performance sphere to an enclave of the workload management system.

Ideal candidates for performance spheres are also processes with a small number of activities, which are all carried out automatically and which must be carried out very fast. An example is a simple inquiry process that provides a customer with the current amount of money in an account. The user's inquiry is possibly carried out via the Internet, using a Web browser. The process itself just consists of two activities that access backend systems to obtain customer and account information. Other candidates are atomic spheres, indicated in Figure 5.8 by AS-1, that must be executed very fast to be efficient.

All performance spheres do not necessarily need to be executed as fast as possible. In fact, a set of automatic activities is more likely to be carried out with low priority. For example, the printing and archiving of the letter sent in a loan process are done automatically and can be done with low priority and in the background.

Figure 5.8 also illustrates that the workflow management system can help in identifying performance spheres. A sequence of activities that are executed automatically, that is without user intervention, is a likely candidate for performance spheres.

Performance spheres fit nicely into the workflow management system's meta-model. Code Example 5.9 shows the definition of a performance sphere, using

Figure 5.8 Deriving Enclaves from Process Models

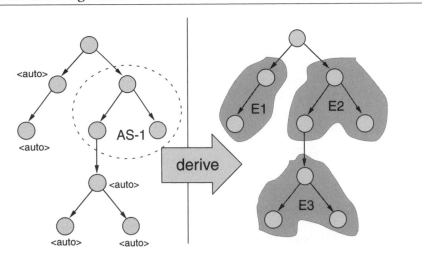

the flow definition language. It shows that the two activities `GetCustomerInformation` and `GetAccountBalance` need to be carried out in less than two seconds.

Code Example 5.9 Definition of Performance Sphere

```
PERFORMANCE_SPHERE GetCustomerInformation
   MAXIMUM_ELAPSED_TIME = 2 SECONDS
   PRIORITY = TOP
END GetCustomerInformation

PROGRAM_ACTIVITY GetCustomerAddress
   RELATED_PERFORMANCE_SPHERE GetCustomerInformation
END GetCustomerAddress

PROGRAM_ACTIVITY GetAccountBalance
   RELATED_PERFORMANCE_SPHERE GetCustomerInformation
END GetAccountBalance
```

A less-powerful but still efficient way of supporting a performance sphere can be implemented by the workflow management system itself. The workflow management system can achieve this by modifying the operating system priority of the invoked activity implementations, its own operating system priority, and the priorities of the communication mechanism that the workflow management system exploits, such as message queuing. We discuss how the workflow management system achieves this in section 10.9.2 on page 396.

5.8   Compile Spheres

The workflow management system carries out a process by interpreting the process model. For each request, such as starting a workitem, the workflow management system reads the appropriate process model and process state information from the database, performs the requested action, and stores the new process state information back into the database. This interpretative processing provides the flexibility that is needed to cope with the heterogenous environment in which the processes are carried out and the reliability that the workflow management system must provide. We had a short discussion on this subject in section 3.3.5 on page 70 and discuss it in great detail in Chapter 10.

When business processes are modeled, there is no definite point when one should stop using the business modeling tool and continue with another tool to model the individual activity implementations. In fact, modeling should be continued as long as possible so that the control and data flows are made as explicit as possible. This leads to very granular business processes, allowing the activities to implement only very small functions.

The interpretative nature of the workflow management system and the granularity of the business process can result in performance problems. The overhead of the workflow management system in navigating from one activity to the next is no longer a negligible portion of the overall processing but may, in fact, be a major factor. Most of the overhead comes from two sources. The first one is the reading and writing of data from and to the database. The second is the message traffic that goes on between client and server and within the server.

However, there are situations, in particular when the activities are very small, where some of the characteristics that workflow management systems are geared to are no longer an issue. A simple example is where one user consecutively carries out a set of activities at one place. In this case, activities can be combined into a *compile sphere*. Then, there is no need to be able to restart the set of activities at any point. Other candidates for compile spheres are atomic spheres, since atomic spheres are usually carried out without any user intervention and are carried out on a single instance of the workflow management system.

Figure 5.9 on the next page shows the steps in processing a compile sphere. In step one, the compile sphere is translated into a program by the *process compiler*. The process compiler generates a program in one of the major languages such as C++ or Java; the program is then handed over to the appropriate compiler to generate an executable. This step is performed when the process template is generated. Step two is also part of the translate process; when the process template is generated, the resulting process template logically replaces the compile sphere via a reference to the executable. Step three is run when the process is carried out. Instead of diving into the compile sphere and executing each of the individual activities, the workflow management system calls the generated program.

Figure 5.9 Processing a Compile Sphere

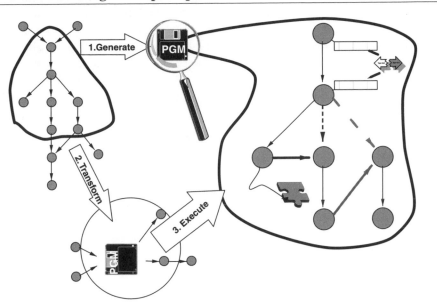

Compile spheres also fit nicely into the workflow management system's meta-model. Code Example 5.10 shows the definition of a compile sphere, using the flow definition language.

Code Example 5.10 Definition of Compile Sphere

```
COMPILE_SPHERE CollectCustomerInformation
    PROGRAM
        PATH_AND_FILENAME 'CCINFO.EXE'
END CollectCustomerInformation

PROGRAM_ACTIVITY CollectName
    RELATED_COMPILE_SPHERE CollectCustomerInformation
END CollectName

PROGRAM_ACTIVITY CollectLoanInformation
    RELATED_COMPILE_SPHERE CollectCustomerInformation
END CollectLoanInformation
```

The workflow management system can help in determining compile spheres by analyzing the appropriate staff assignment and the execution mode of the activities.

Translation of the compile sphere is made easy by the structure of the process graph. It allows an efficient mapping to the constructs of an object-oriented language, such as C++. Section 10.15 on page 421 discusses the architecture of such a process compiler.

Those who are interested in the mathematical foundation of PM-graphs, as provided in Chapter 4, should note that the compile sphere is to atomic and compensation spheres. It is just another hypergraph on top of the PM-graph.

Chapter 6

Workflows and Objects

In this chapter, we discuss the relationship between object technology and workflow technology. These technologies are related fundamentally by the facts that objects can provide implementations of activities in process models and that workflows can be manipulated as objects.

First, we review the notion of component-based software construction. The concept of a business object or component is introduced. Next, we discuss the role of scripting for building new application functions from components. Then, we present process models as scripts. This discussion reveals that software construction using components is basically a two-level programming paradigm.

Next, we discuss the problem of determining the most appropriate runtime environment for scripts. When should a script be specified as a process model and when should it be specified by a conventional scripting language (or even by a programming language)? We emphasize the importance of encapsulating scripts in separate objects to increase the robustness of object systems. Prerequisite for this encapsulation is identification of the different scripts. For this purpose, we describe a method for determining candidate scripts during the analysis or design phase.

Finally, after summarizing the basics of the common object request broker architecture (CORBA), we give an overview on the workflow management facility of the Object Management Group (OMG). It provides an object-oriented framework to manipulate workflows. In this framework, workflows are perceived as a special kind of script that exists in an object request broker (ORB) environment.

6.1 Component-based Software Construction

The notion of component-based software construction refers to the use of prefabricated software artifacts in building new application functions. These artifacts are often called "business objects." The means to build new application functions out of business objects is often called "scripting." In this section we explain both concepts.

6.1.1   Business Objects

As a software concept, objects represent things from reality, like customers, credits, response letters, but also polygons, circles, radio buttons, and list boxes, for example. This by itself is not unique, for example, the concept of an entity within the various entity/relationship-models does the same [Teo94]. But the coverage of features represented for an object is far-reaching. Not only the interesting observable properties of an object like its attributes and its relations to other objects are represented but also its behavior, that is the functions, called methods, which it can perform for others (see [JEJ95] for more details).

Furthermore, while an object exposes *what* can be done with it, it does not expose *how* this is internally achieved. Thus, a software object does not externalize any details about its internal data structures or the algorithms implemented to realize the exposed functions. This behavior is referred to as *encapsulation* of data and functional logic by an object. The advantage of encapsulation is that the internal details of an object can be modified without affecting the use of the object by others. As a consequence, objects can be perceived as self-contained entities.

Because of their self-contained nature, objects can often be exploited in many different application domains. To use an obvious example, a list box object can be used as an element in any end-user interface. Similarly, an account object might be generic enough to be used in managing savings, payments, or funds transfers. An object that can be exploited in many different situations, often even in situations not envisioned by the implementers of the object, is called *reusable*.

Reusable objects have been known and used for quite some time in the construction of end-user interfaces. Today, such interfaces are created with the aid of a GUI builder that is an integral part of a every state-of-the-art visual builder (such as the IBM VisualAge family). A visual builder encompasses objects like radio buttons, sliders, check boxes, scroll bars, etc., which are needed in many different applications. These objects can be used to build a huge variety of end-user interfaces. The degree of reuse of these objects is ideal since no application programmer would ever consider building such an object by himself.

At a higher, application-semantic, level, the business object is used to attain the same level of reuse as that achieved by objects in visual builders. A *business object* represents an artifact that has immediate meaning for a business, like a customer, a contract, or a ledger. It is not concerned with end-user presentation aspects of the corresponding artifact but with the business logic and constraints which govern it in a particular domain.

Business objects are reused to compose application-specific functions. This composition is done with a script (see section 6.1.2 on page 213). Often, scripting an application function requires not only business objects but also other reusable objects like GUI widgets, for example. It is normal to collectively refer to all objects that can be used for scripting application functions as *components*.

Typically, a script plugs multiple components together. These components are often provided by different vendors because each vendor might focus on particular business domains. To use components that fit their business needs best, users purchase components from multiple vendors. So, from the outset component-based software construction must deal with heterogeneity.

- Components must be language independent. The programming language in which they are implemented must be transparent. This is necessary because different vendors will use different programming languages to implement their components. If components were language dependent, the collaboration of different components from different vendors would be impossible or at least difficult.

- Similarly, components must interoperate with as many different tools as possible. Otherwise, a component is tied to particular tools for building application functions. This restriction limits the value of a component. For example, a component typically offers the capability to query metadata about itself, like the methods supported and their parameters. This feature can be used by a visual builder to present the component's properties in its environment.

- Also, components must interoperate across operating systems and networks. A component that runs only in a particular operating system environment limits its reuse. At the least a component must be accessible from other operating system environments and this accessibility must assume as little as possible of the underlying network that provides the necessary communication mechanism.

In addition, components (and business objects in particular) should support inheritance and polymorphism as objects known from object-oriented programming do. This support allows users to extend a component by subtyping it. We discuss in section 6.3 on page 224 an environment called object request broker that enables this.

In the following sections, we use the term "component" and "business object" interchangeably as a synonym for a software artifact with immediate business meaning. Besides the technical properties discussed, above a component can be considered a self-contained, shrink-wrapped piece of software that provides a subset of functions needed in a particular business domain. A component must be augmented by functions of other components to result in a complete application. This means a component is a marketable entity but not a complete application [OHE96].

Note that in practice, components of different granularity or different purpose are denoted as "business objects." Sometimes a business object includes corresponding presentation logic, sometimes it does not. Sometimes a business object includes data access logic, sometimes this logic is explicitly delegated to separate

objects. Sometimes a business object, such as a credit, is more like a business process, sometimes it is more like a resource, such as wage slip, required in performing
a business process.

In separating data access logic from the business object proper, a business
object becomes more flexible. Typically, data access logic is delegated to separate
data objects [IBM97]. A *data object* provides methods to manipulate persistent
data and hides any details of accessing this data in the underlying datastore. Thus,
a business object that maintains its persistent state by means of an associated data
object (see Figure 6.1), is isolated from changes and modifications applied to the
datastore. In supplying different data objects for different datastores, the same
business object can store its state data in different database systems or it can even
access other stores, such as shared file systems via TP monitor programs, without
making modifying the business object.

Figure 6.1 Component Granularities

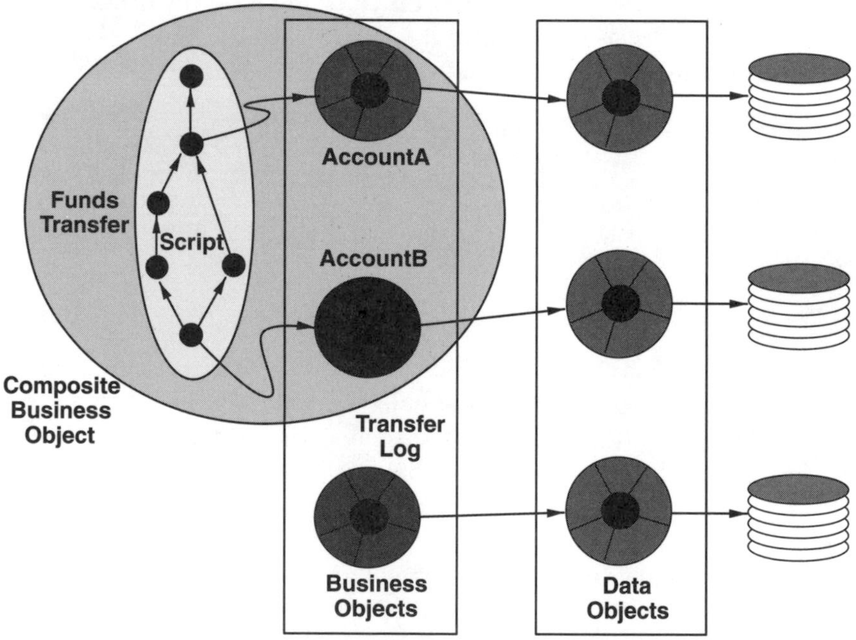

More complicated business logic may require the exploitation of other business objects in the implementation of a particular business object. Such a business
object is referred to as a *composite business object* [IBM97] in situations in which
the distinction is important. A composite business object is responsible for controlling the sequencing of the invocation of the used business objects' methods.
The composite business object is also responsible for managing any transactional

boundaries that are part of it. Typically, this logic is often performed by a separate control object or "script," as shown in Figure 6.1.

Figure 6.1 shows an example of a composite business object `FundsTransfer`. It provides business logic to transfer an amount of money from one account to another account. For this purpose, `FundsTransfer` exploits two other business objects, namely, `AccountA` and `AccountB`, withdrawing from one account the amount that is deposited on the other account. This transfer is done by an encompassed script that invokes the `withdraw` method on `AccountA` and the `deposit` method on `AccountB`. Furthermore, this script ensures data integrity by establishing transaction boundaries such that either both methods commit or both are aborted. The `TransferLog` business object offers functions to trace fund transfers. All three business objects—`AccountA`, `AccountB`, and `TransferLog`—use associated data objects to store their state in databases. An application can use `FundsTransfer` and `TransferLog` to transfer money between accounts and maintain a history of the corresponding actions.

6.1.2 Scripting

Component-based software construction means creation of application functions by means of scripts and components. A *script* specifies in a simple manner how the components used must behave. It also specifies how the components' methods and properties are used to build the application functions. The language used to write a script is called a *scripting language*. Scripting languages should be "simple" so that nonprogrammers can write scripts. For example, no declarations or definitions of variables or no complicated mechanisms such as pointer arithmetic are needed when a scripting language is used. A scripting language is geared towards nonprogrammers, allowing them to control components and plug components together. In contrast, a programming language is much more powerful (and complicated) and is used by programmers to build components themselves. In a nutshell, scripting languages are "usage languages," while programming languages are "implementation languages."

The difference between scripting languages and programming languages is fuzzy. In the previous example, the `FundsTransfer` business object made use of two other business objects; that is it includes a script for exploiting these two components and specifying their transactional behavior. Because of the latter, a programmer probably composed the `FundsTransfer` business object and this script was written in a programming language. Thus, the term "script" is also used for programs whose main purpose is to compose an application function from components.

Similarly, scripting and the specification of business processes overlap, as shown in Figure 6.2.

Figure 6.2 The Loan Request Implemented with Objects

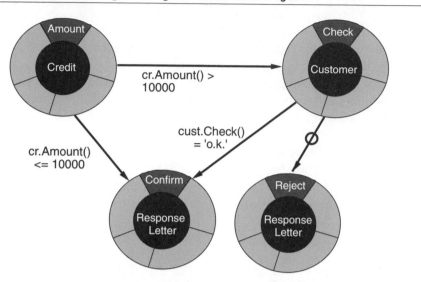

In the example, three business objects that represent a credit, a customer, and a response letter are used to realize the processing of credit requests. First, the amount of the credit must be determined. If it is a small amount of credit, less than or equal to $10,000, a confirmation letter can immediately be sent. For a credit larger than $10,000, the customer must first be checked. If the customer passes the check, a confirmation letter is then sent; otherwise a rejection letter is sent.

For performing the actions on the various business objects, the corresponding methods are invoked. For example, by invoking the Amount method of the Credit business object, the amount of the subject credit is determined; by invoking the Check method of the Customer business object, the respective customer's solvency is assessed. The business objects methods are used to specify the proper sequencing. For example, as a result of querying the amount of credit being requested from the Credit business object and comparing it with the corresponding limit, such as Amount() <= 10000, the confirmation letter for small credits is scheduled.

The fuzziness in the difference between scripting and process modeling becomes evident when the tools for scripting and process modeling are compared.

Using the VisualAge paradigm of graphical programming, one can envision a visual builder that supports the reuse of business objects to compose new application functions. The characteristics of this visual builder are discussed in the rest of the section.

As with most visual builders (see section 11.2.2 on page 432), the business objects that are available in the environment are presented on (or are at least accessible from) the tool palette of the visual builder, like business objects BO1, BO2,...BOn shown in Figure 6.3. From there, a business object can be selected, dragged to the main composition window, and dropped. Within this window, all of the methods provided by a business object are listed in its property window when the user clicks on the object with the mouse. By selection of a particular method from the property window, the invocation of this method is requested at runtime. One specifies the potential sequencing of method invocations by drawing directed edges from one business object to another so that the selected method of the target business object will be invoked after the selected method of the source business object. The condition under which the actual sequencing proceeds from the source business object to the target business object can be attached to the directed edge. The appearance of a visual builder clearly reminds one of drawing process models, with methods of business objects as activity implementations.

Figure 6.3 Objects as Implementations of Activities

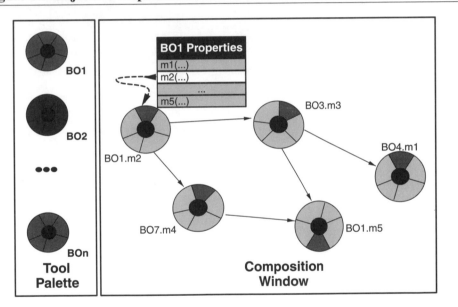

Thus, the question comes up of when to use a scripting language and when to use a process model to compose application functions. Assume that a script is run as a single executable and that a process model is interpreted by a workflow management system, then the first might be considered as *lightweight scripting* and the second as *heavyweight scripting*. This differentiation is based on the perception about the costs of the environment that is needed to support the running of the script. Thus, we must compare the run time environments for scripting languages and process models. This comparison leads to the question of how much overhead is perceived as "appropriate." From this information we can give an initial answer to our question. For example,

- Using a process model that is instantiated by a workflow management system to script an end-user interface based on GUI components would definitively be a misuse. A workflow management system is not built to control key strokes on a single desktop.

- When a script running as a single executable ends abnormally, human interaction is typically required to perform potential restart actions. A scripting language is not built to provide forward recovery; the activity must means interruptible at any point in its execution, and must be resumable where it left off, thus requiring a persistent state, for example.

The fact, that scripting languages, such as REXX or JavaScript, can be interpreted and that process models can be compiled as shown in section 5.8 on page 206, reveals that this first attempt at an answer is not really satisfying.

To understand what form to use for what situation, one must consider the purpose of the script. Obviously, if it is clear from the outset that a script represents a business process, it should be specified as a process model. In general, a script is a candidate for being specified as a process model if one of the following is true.

- The script must be forward recoverable, i.e., interruptible at any point in time of its execution, resuming execution where it left, thus requiring persistent state.

- The components invoked may run in parallel, distributed, in heterogeneous environments, and their parallel execution requires synchronization.

- The components invoked require different invocation methods or are based on different programming models. For example, they are written in different object-oriented and procedural programming languages, some are to be invoked by an ORB, some by messages, some others by a TP monitor.

- Parts of the script must be backward-recoverable in case errors are detected or signaled from the outside.

- The scripted components are not launched automatically but on explicit requests from external parties.

- The exploitation of components requires data flow facilities, for example the input parameters of a component are constructed from the output of several preceding components.

Figure 6.4 Micro Scripts in Components

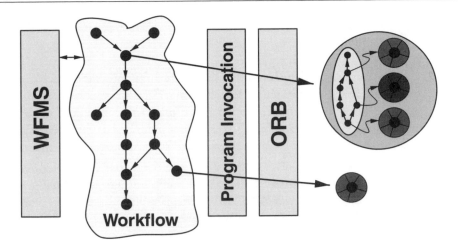

If the sole purpose of the script is to ensure (data) consistency of the joint state of a particular collection of components, it should be realized in a scripting language. Simple scripts are used to compose "small" components into a coarser granule. When such a script is invoked, it runs "very fast" and performs a single application function externalized to its user. Often, such a script is called a *micro script*. Programs that are used as scripts are micro scripts. The overhead one is willing to tolerate for a micro script is minimal. This is one of the reasons that it is called "lightweight."

Process models are referred to as *macro scripts*. As the term indicates a macro script typically operates "in the large." It may glue together components from different environments adhering to various programming models; it may be long running and allowed to be interrupted at any time, etc. (see the list above). The collection of properties a macro script provides lets users tolerate a higher overhead; hence the term "heavyweight" script is a synonym.

Note that in practice, micro and macro scripts are often used in the same application. As depicted in Figure 6.4, the workflow is run by the workflow management system. This represents the execution of a macro script, that is a process model. The program execution component of the workflow management system uses an ORB to invoke the method of a simple business object as one activity implementation, while another activity is implemented by a micro script that is invoked by the program execution component.

6.1.3 Two-Level Programming

Specifying a process model has many aspects in common with programming. Input and output structures of activities are defined, control and data flows between the various activities are furnished, and transaction boundaries are established. This kind of programming is sometimes called *programming in the large*, because it does not deal with low-level algorithmic aspects of an application but specifies "what happens when" in the overall environment. Note that creating a macro script is programming in the large.

In contrast to this, building an activity implementation is sometimes called *programming in the small*. All low-level algorithmic aspects of a business function must be dealt with, data accesses must be performed, and communication with an end user must be established. Programming in the small is the traditional notion of programming. Especially, creating a micro script is programming in the small.

Developing a complete application requires both programming in the large and programming in the small. Strictly separating both programming tasks is referred to as *two level-programming*. Two-level programming is applied when building workflow-based applications, as we show in section 9.10 on page 345.

Visual builders include graphical programming environments that support programming in the small in a graphical manner. We show this in Chapter 11. Not only is the construction of end-user interfaces with "visual components" (for example, list boxes, radio buttons) supported, but such a tool also allows the user to drag "nonvisual components" (for example, database tables, business objects) from its palette to its composition editor. Within the editor, the components can be connected by directed edges that specify what happens to the target component and the source component.

Figure 6.5 Visual Programming of Applications

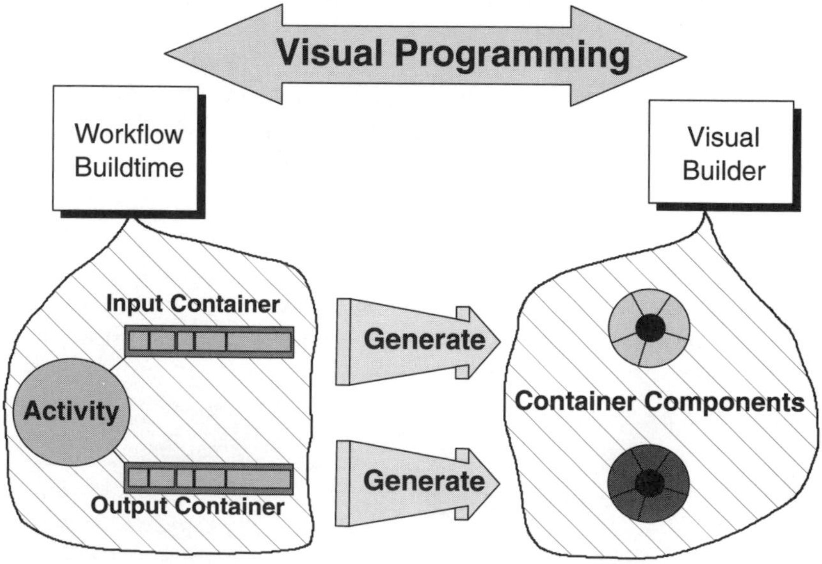

The buildtime component of a workflow management system or a business reengineering tool supports programming in the large in a graphical manner. In section 11.2 on page 431, we describe how components could be generated from the specifications of input containers and output containers (see also Figure 6.5). Because activity implementations and a workflow management system communicate by passing containers, these generated container components might be used within visual builders to graphically build programs that seamlessly plug into workflows as activity implementations.

As shown in Figure 6.5 the workflow buildtime or business reengineering tools on one side and visual builders on the other side together provide a visual programming environment for programming in the large and programming in the small. Both together provide a visual programming environment for two-level programming. Chapter 11 presents more details of such a visual programming environment and its role in the development of workflow-based applications.

6.1.4 Scripts and Robustness of Business Objects

Object technology strives to achieve robustness of systems against changes. If a system must be adapted to changing requirements or to necessary customization, as few components as possible should be affected. One of the underpinnings of object technology is the insight that this kind of robustness is normally achieved by encapsulating things that might be subject to changes. Thus, if the order in which business objects are used can change or if the use of certain business objects can be added or removed, the guidelines of object technology recommend a separate object encapsulating the usage of business objects. Since this use is specified by scripts, encapsulation of not only the function logic and data but also the scripts must be considered to achieve the robustness desired.

If the last proposition is ignored, then following the encapsulation paradigm tends to hide fragments of a script in a business object. Not only the business object itself becomes vulnerable to changes, but transitively each application using such a component becomes vulnerable too (see the discussion of "flow dependency" in Chapter 9.) This restricts the reusability and thus the widespread use of such a business object. Consequently, building business objects enforces a clear separation of the more stable aspects of the business objects, such as data and function logic, from the more dynamic aspects, such as their use in scripts.

The Business Application Architecture [OHE96] of the OMG encourages exactly this separation. This architecture introduces a separate object called a *business process object* that scripts collections of business objects into applications, as shown in Figure 6.6. Basically, an application consists of a business process (object) and a collection of business objects. Note that this is exactly the structure of workflow-based applications. The activities of the business process are implemented by methods of business objects. No assumption is made about the concrete implementation

Figure 6.6 Business Objects in Applications

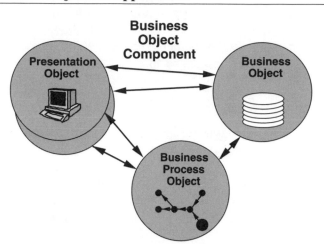

of the business process object. It might be realized through a program or through a process model instantiated by a workflow management system.

For interaction with end users, each business object may be associated with a multitude of presentation objects. A single presentation object often does not suffice because the aspects of a given business object that are of interest to an end user may vary from application scenario to application scenario. A presentation object and a business object typically communicate directly with each other to provide a particular business function. A separate control object (not shown in the figure) manages this interaction, encapsulating a micro script. The aggregate consisting of a business object, the appropriate presentation objects, and the necessary control object was vaguely called a "business object" when we introduced the Business Application Architecture above. To be more precise, the business process (object) invokes methods of business objects as well as associated presentation objects as appropriate.

6.2   Scripts in Object-Oriented Analysis and Design

Object technology provides many methods for capturing an application domain during the analysis or design phase. The derived object models represent the static representation of an application domain. To allow for an analysis of the dynamic behavior of an application, various techniques are proposed; these techniques include collaboration graphs [WBWW90], event flows [RBP$^+$91], timing diagrams [Boo91], interaction diagrams [JCJO92]. All of these diagrams reveal at the abstract level, a structure as depicted in figure 6.7. This structure can be appropriately called *message flow diagram*. On the x-axis of the diagram, all objects

Figure 6.7 Modeling Dynamics of Object Systems

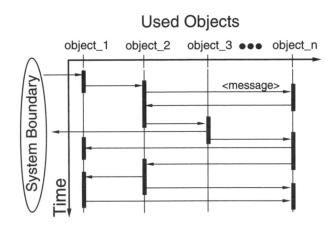

that are used in the application function and that are to be analyzed or designed are listed. The y-axis represents the passing of time. The time period during which a certain object is active is shown as a black-shaded rectangle at the x-coordinate representing the object. Interactions between active objects are specified by directed edges connecting the source of the interaction with its target. Directed edges are annotated with messages representing requests, responses, or simply data passed by an interaction.

Interactions between objects happen through method invocations. The time, as depicted on the y-axis of a message flow diagram, induces an order of the interactions between objects, that is induces a sequence of method invocations. Thus, a message flow diagram can be perceived as a specification of the control flow between method invocations. It can even be the case that additional conditions are associated with the edges describing the control flow [JCJO92], making the process model aspects of such message flow diagrams obvious. Based on this relationship between message flow diagrams and process models, a fundamental observation has been made in [JCJO92] on the structure of such diagrams. A message flow diagram is in general composed of two basically different structures called fork structures and stair structures.

Fork structures, as shown in Figure 6.8, are implied by centralizing responsibilities. Centralizing responsibilities occurs when the global control and data flow are placed in one object (object C in the figure). The remaining objects are used for inquiries, utilities, or interfacing with users. Using such kind of *control object* is an approach that workflow purists will prefer. A fork structure represents a script (the control object C) and the components used by the script (the "tines" of the fork).

indexStair structure *Stair* structures, as shown in Figure 6.9, are implied by delegating responsibilities. This delegation occurs when each object only knows

Figure 6.8 Fork Structure in Message Flow Diagrams

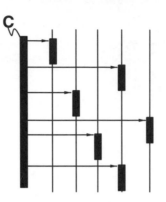

about and can exploit a few other objects (one, in the figure.) In such a decentralized structure, the responsibility for the local control and data flow is with each object. The delegation of responsibility as represented by a stair structure is the approach that object purists will prefer. Either each object in a stair structure together with its local flow knowledge is implemented as a separate component, or the complete stair structure results in a component. These components are thus flow dependent, which means that they may need to be adapted when control flow or data flow must be changed.

Not only must one consider encapsulating function logic and data, but one must also consider scripts; this proposition manifests itself in forks. A fork typically encapsulates ordering; it represents a script. In contrast, stairs express assumed stability of ordering (or collections of strongly connected operations—see [JCJO92] for more details); it represents separate components. In general, both fork and stair structures, will be found in message flow diagrams, yielding a stable and robust structure.

Figure 6.9 Stair Structure in Message Flow Diagrams

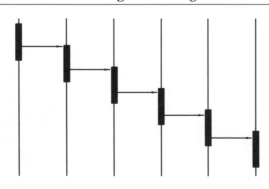

By analysis of message flow diagrams and determining fork structures, scripts can be identified. The control object of the fork structure may be a candidate for a macro script, in which case it will be specified as a process model. This process model describes the control and data flow between the objects whose methods implement its activities (the "tines" of the fork). At runtime the control object itself becomes an instance of this process model, a workflow. In terms of the Business Application Architecture of the OMG, this control object is the business process object.

The derivation of scripts from message flow diagrams could be supported by a tool. In the following steps, we briefly sketch a method that such a tool might implement to transform a message flow diagram into the skeleton of a process model [Ley95c]. We want to show the principle of this transformation, so we omit its details and ignore how to derive data flows from message flow diagrams.

1. **Identify all control objects**. To identify forks, all control objects must be determined. We characterize a control object as one having "many" outgoing edges. In practice, the quality of the method depends on the appropriate definition of what "many" means.

2. **Build all fork structures**. All objects that are targets of edges originating from a single control object are included in the associated fork. Objects receiving during their lifetime messages from more than one object need a special treatment (which is not covered in this sketch).

3. **Build all stair structures**. Each connected subgraph of the diagram that results when all outgoing edges of all control objects are removed is considered to be a stair structure. In particular, a control object receiving a message from a stair is added to the stair.

4. **Transform stairs**. A stair can be transformed into a process model; from this process model, source code could be generated (see section 5.8 on page 206). Otherwise, the diagram is transformed into a program or component with whatever tool is available.

5. **Transform forks into process models**. An object that is the target of an edge leaving a control object becomes an activity. Its associated implementation is the method specified in the message associated with the edge. If the target is a fork structure, its associated diagram is transformed into a subprocess. If the target is a stair structure and it has been transformed into a process model, then this process model becomes a subprocess. Otherwise, the stair structure is considered to be a single activity with the component as the implementation.

6. **Refinement of control flow structures**. Message flow diagrams in general hide parallelism. Thus, the resulting control flow structures should be reworked to enhance the degree of parallelism.

Figure 6.10 A Workflow Object and Its Activity Implementations

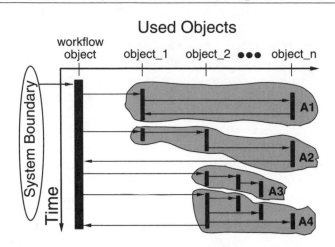

The example in Figure 6.10 shows how the leftmost object has been transformed into a process model.

The subgraphs A1,...,A4 are activities in this business process. A1, A2, and A3
are stairs that have been implemented as a component by a programming language.
The control object of the fork structure A4 has been identified as a micro script
which has also been implemented by a programming language; the other objects
belonging to A4 are called from within this program.

6.3   The Object Request Broker

The environment that enables the widespread usage of business objects is called an
object request broker, or ORB for short. This section sketches just the basics of an
ORB as it is related to business objects. Section 9.7 on page 339 discusses those
aspects of ORBs that are important from an application structure perspective. A
reader interested in an in-depth treatment of ORBs can refer to one of the many
excellent books on this area, like [OHE96] and [OH97]. We restrict ourselves to
the CORBA (Common Object Request Broker Architecture) approach to ORBs,
which has been standardized by OMG (Object Management Group), an industry
consortium with hundreds of members. Details on the other approach to ORBs
(namely Microsoft's COM/DCOM) are covered in [Ses98].

The most fundamental aspect of an ORB is that it enables objects to communicate with each other independently of their location. Objects that communicate
via an ORB can run in the same address space, in different address spaces, on different machines, or on different hosting environments. They can be implemented
with different programming languages. The ORBs that these objects use can even

be those of different vendors, and they can have any type of connecting network between them. This central functionality of an ORB is sometimes referred to as the *object bus*. Basically, it is the object bus that gives an object all the technical properties we assumed for a component in section 6.1.1 on page 210.

To make this approach work, each object which is to be available to other objects by means of an ORB must be described by metadata. The language used to specify this metadata is called *interface definition language* (IDL). The information that is specified to describe an object by means of IDL comprises all of its attributes, its methods, the exceptions that might occur when a method does not perform successfully, etc. Based on an object's IDL, an ORB understands how to mediate requests between objects. For example, an ORB can package a request to invoke a method of an object located on a remote machine into an appropriate data stream and transfer it to the other site. This results in interoperability across systems and networks as requested in section 6.1.1 on page 210.

Figure 6.11 depicts the building blocks of an ORB environment.

Figure 6.11 The Object Management Architecture of the OMG

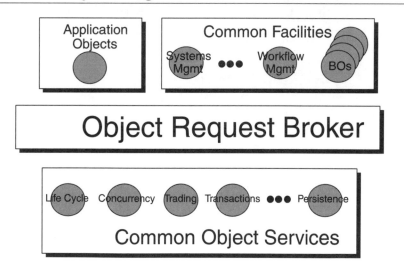

The object request broker represents the object bus. This bus is extended with *common object services* that provide generic functions, such as transaction management, at a system level. The *common facilities* provide groups of functions at the level of application semantics, for example, business objects or workflow management (see section 6.4 on the next page). The consumers of all of these services are called *application objects*.

Just to give an impression of the scope of features provided as common services, we will highlight a few of them. The *life cycle* services allow one to create, destroy, move, and copy a single object as well as a group of related objects. *Trading* services allow the dynamic registration of new objects. A registration includes a description of the services an object has to offer. By describing the services needed, a client can ask the trader for candidate objects satisfying its requirements; from the list of candidates a client can choose one object as target for its service requests. Trading services are supposed to be the "yellow pages" in an ORB environment. *Transaction* services provide all the functions needed to run distributed transactions in an ORB environment.

6.4   The OMG Workflow Management Facility

As discussed in section 6.1.4 on page 219, business process objects are the preferred mechanism to compose applications from business objects in an ORB environment. In ORB terminology, the business process object is an application object using the ORB to invoke methods of business objects as implementations of its constituent activities.

A business process object when implemented as a workflow provides application-level services. For example, the workflow management system that runs the business process object as an instance of a process model facilitates the monitoring of the business process or allows it to start its constituent activities. Being an object, the concrete implementation of a business process object is encapsulated, which means that the same services should be available for all business process objects independently of their concrete implementation (whether an implementation is based on a workflow management system or not). In ORB terminology, these services are building a common facility.

With the *workflow management facility* [Obj98], the OMG adds fundamental runtime functionality of a workflow management system to an ORB environment. Based on these functions, workflows can be started, suspended, or resumed, activities can be started or completed, and workflow-related events can be recorded. For this purpose, the OMG standard specifies a corresponding collection of interfaces in the interface definition language.

In this section, we sketch the workflow management facility at a conceptual level. In doing so, we interpret the constructs of the OMG standard according to the overall metamodel presented in this book. A reader who wants to understand the relation of the OMG standard to a particular workflow management system has to interpret the OMG standard in the context of this workflow management system. A reader who needs to understand all the details of the standard should, of course, refer to the standard document itself [Obj98]. This is because standards typically evolve, the actual version of the document should be consulted. For more information on the OMG Workflow Management Facility without consulting the complete standard document, refer to [Sch98].

6.4.1   Major Interfaces

Figure 6.12 shows the major interfaces of the workflow management facility and the relationships between them in Unified Modeling Language(UML) notation. For details on this notation, see [Rat97]. Note, that the figure does not depict the inheritance relationships of these interfaces to interfaces of other modules in the CORBA environment. See the standard document for all these details.

Figure 6.12 Framework of the OMG Workflow Management Facility

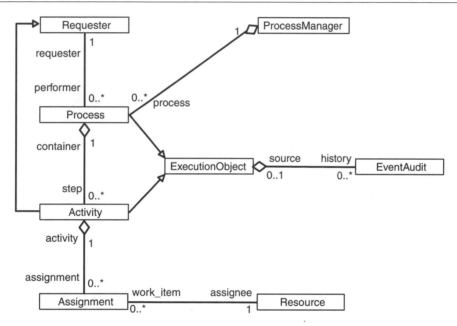

Process Manager Interface   A process model is represented by the `Process-Manager` interface. A process manager creates instances of a particular process model. For each process model, a separate process manager exists, so that a process manager is a factory for a particular process model. The name of a process manager is the name of the process model the process manager represents. The structure of the input and output container of the represented process model can be queried: `get_context_signature()` and `get_result_signature()` return a sequence of pairs, called `ProcessDataInfo`, representing the name and type for each member in the (input and output) container. This metadata can then be used to construct instances of the corresponding container. Navigating the relationship from `ProcessManager` to the `Process` interface locates all actual instances of the process model. Invoking the `create_process()` method creates a new instance of the process model. The only parameter of this method is an instance of `Requester`.

Requester Interface   A requester is the representation of a request for some work to be done. It is the object to which processes must signal their relevant state changes especially their completion. For this purpose, the corresponding interface `Requester` provides the method `receive_event()`. An instance of `EventAudit` is passed as parameter of this method. The collection of processes a requester has created can be retrieved by the `performer` relationship.

Process Interface   Once a process has been created, its input container has to be provided as a sequence of pairs. Each of these pairs consists of the name of a data member of the container and its associated value (so-called *name/value pair*). This information is provided by the `set_context()` method, which the `Process` interface inherits from the `ExecutionObject` interface. Then, the process can be started by invocation of the `start()` method. After completion, the output container of the process can be retrieved (again as name/value pair) by the `return()` method. The set of activities actually to be performed within a process can be accessed by navigating the `step` relationship.

Activity Interface   An activity is created by the process it is part of. The time at which activities are created and at which they are started is left to the implementation. This delegation reflects the fact that different implementations may use different navigation algorithms to discover what has to be done, when it has to be done, and by whom it should be done. There is no method available to start an activity. When an activity is started, it is assumed that the containing process passes the input container to the activity via the `set_context()` method. The `result()` method returns the output container of an activity. By use of the assignment relationship, all resources associated with an activity can be found. The corresponding relationship is established by the implementation of the workflow management facility, reflecting the fact that different implementations may realize different staff resolution policies. The `complete()` method completes an activity. This method is used with the `set_result()` method to pass the return data from the activity implementation back to the activity. This means that the implementation of an activity explicitly signals its completion to the activity and returns its result data.

Assignment Interface   An assignment represents the request of an activity for resources, for example, for certain people having the required skills to perform the piece of work represented by the activity, or a particular computer hosting a program to automatically perform the activity. From a high level, we call this piece of work a "workitem." It is left to the implementation to create instances of `Assignment` during its staff resolution processing. The method `assignment_status()` inquires whether the assignment has already been accepted by a resource (that is the resource will process the associated activity). A resource can accept an assignment by using the `set_assignment_state()` method.

Resource Interface   A resource is an object that can accept an assignment to an activity; that is it can signal that it will perform the associated piece of work. An instance of `Resource` has a name and a unique identifier associated with it. Navigating the `work_item` relationship fins all assignments associated with a resource. By use of the `release()` method, a resource can be informed that it is no longer needed for a particular assignment.

Execution Object Interface   An execution object defines the common behavior of activities and processes. Its internal state can be changed by using `resume()`, `suspend()`, `terminate()` and `abort()` methods. An execution object has a name and a unique identifier, and it has a priority that can be set by the `set_prior-ity()` method. The effect of setting a priority is not specified. The history relationship allows access to all of the audit records associated with an execution object.

Event Audit Interface   This interface provides auditing and monitoring capabilities. An event audit associates workflow-specific information with an execution object. The information is kept persistent and survives the execution object it is associated with. Thus, historic evaluations of workflow executions are enabled. The data recorded for all events includes the type of the event and time it occurred, the activity and process associated with the event, and the process model name. Additional data is recorded for special events, representing changes of state, resource assignments, and data. For this purpose specialized interfaces are provided. The `source` relationship locates the execution object associated with an event as long as this execution object is available in the environment.

The standard covers neither how to model business processes nor how to model of structures of resources, people, or organizations. The latter is simply abstracted in the `Resource` interface. No special mechanism is assumed for assigning resources and for navigation. The launching of programs as implementations of activities is also not covered. All of this is hidden in the implementation of the workflow management facility.

6.4.2 Some Usage Scenarios

The worklist for a particular user is materialized as follows. A user is represented as an instance of the `Resource` interface. Processing the `work_item` relationship of this instance results in all assignments the particular user is associated with as assignee. Following the activity relationship of each assignment results in the list of all activities associated with the user.

Based on his worklist, a user can start a particular workitem. The underlying worklist handler can determine all assignments for the activity associated with the workitem by processing the `assignment` relationship of this activity. Based on the `assignee` relationship of each of these assignments, the worklist handler determines all other resources assigned to the same activity. It deletes all of these assignments and invokes the `release()` method to inform the other resources about that fact. Then, it accepts the assignment on behalf of the particular user by a `set_assignment_state(accepted)` call. Finally, the worklist handler sets the activity into the active state by using the `change_state(running)` method call. Note that this whole processing might be implemented by a component different from the worklist handler and in a different environment.

Again, the standard does not specify how the implementation of an activity is launched when this activity is not another process (see below). One potential implementation might be that changing the state of an activity to `running` notifies a program execution agent appropriately. The program execution agent uses the `context()` method of the execution object corresponding to the activity to get the activity's input container. It then launches an executable, for example, the method of a business object, somehow passing input data to the executable. When the executable returns its output data, this data will be transformed by the program execution agent into the output container of the activity by means of the `set_result()` method. The invocation of the `complete()` method will end this processing.

When an activity is implemented as a subprocess, the standard provides a mechanism to start this subprocess. The `Activity` interface specializes the `Requester` interface. When an activity that is implemented as a subprocess is started, it locates the `ProcessManager` representing the corresponding process model and uses the `create_process()` method to create an instance of the process model, registering itself as requester for this process. Next, the activity uses the `set_context()` method of the process to copy its own input container to the input container of the process. Then, the `start()` method is used to start the process. If the subprocess is nested, the activity waits for the completion event signaled by the subprocess. When the subprocess completes it notifies its requester, the waiting activity, about this fact by invoking the `receive_event()` method. The activity in turn invokes the `result()` method of the process to get its output container. Next, the activity uses the `set_result()` method to pass the output container of the subprocess as its own result to its containing process. Finally, the `change_state(completed)` method is invoked indicating to the implementation that navigation can take place. If the implementing subprocess is chained, the activity immediately completes without waiting for the started process to return.

Note that the standard leaves a lot of freedom for different implementations. For example, one implementation may allow the input container of a process to be changed once the process has started, another may not. One implementation may allow the requester associated with a process to be changed, another may not. As a consequence, the functionality of the workflow management facility may vary from ORB environment to ORB environment. The validity and correctness of the presented scenarios should be checked for each environment.

6.4.3   Relation to Workflow Management Coalition Standards

The workflow management facility provides selected functionality of the client application interface (interface 2), the interoperability interface (interface 4), and the administration and monitoring interface (interface 5) of the reference model of the Workflow Management Coalition(see section 3.11 on page 117) as an object-oriented framework in an ORB environment. As mentioned, OMG's workflow management facility does not standardize a metamodel for modeling business processes or the exchange of models of business processes. Thus, interface 1 of the reference model of the Workflow Management Coalition has not been addressed. The invoked application interface (interface 3) is also not specifically addressed; in an ORB environment, it seems to be natural that the workflow management systems use business objects as activity implementations.

Chapter 7

Workflows and Transactions

A workflow management system coordinates the execution of the various activities constituting a single business process. As a result, activity executions of a given workflow share a common fate: they represent a unit of work. The corresponding activities are no longer independent of each other. The failure of one activity might impact other activities. Some activities may have a very strong influence on the overall success of the business process, other activities may have no influence at all. Sometimes, only certain groups of activities of a business process are related with respect to their successful execution.

For example, Traveluck may offer a conference service. This service allows a customer to simply specify a conference he wants to attend and Traveluck makes all of the corresponding reservations. Registrations for the conference, for a pre- or postconference tutorial and for the conference dinner are made, as well as corresponding reservations for flights and hotel rooms. All payments are made with the customer's credit card. It is interesting to note that the outcome of one activity can have different impacts on other activities. If no more participants for the tutorial are accepted, the reservations of hotel rooms and flights have to be modified accordingly. In this case, the outcome of one activity has impact on other activities. When no more seats are available for the conference dinner, the rest of the process should proceed. In this case, the outcome of one activity has no any impact on other activities. If checking the credit card of the customer reveals that the card has already expired or is invalid, or if no more participants are accepted for the conference, the complete reservation must not be processed. Thus, the outcome activity impacts a complete workflow.

Very early, the unit of work aspects of workflows attracted researchers with a background in transaction models and transaction processing. They coined the term *transactional workflows*. For business users, the business process aspect of workflows is in the foreground. When unit-of-work aspects become important to them, they use terms like *business transactions*. Both terms are used today nearly synonymously, and we will do the same. Nevertheless, one must bear in mind that this term is overloaded, having at least the following facets that are sometimes subsumed even in different combinations:

- Support a *run-and-gun* environment for performing workflows. This means that parts of a workflow once started are performed consecutively. The corresponding activities appear somehow assembled. We discuss this aspect in section 7.3 on page 246.

- Support an *all-or-nothing* semantics within workflows. This means that combinations of activities, each of which is implemented by a transaction, should be able to be run within a workflow as a single transaction. The workflow management system should glue together these transactions into a single distributed transaction. We discuss this aspect in more details in sections 7.4 on page 251 and 7.6 on page 274.

- Support a *business-oriented* unit of work model. This means that undo mechanisms have to be supported by the workflow management system which must reflect nontransactional activity implementations as well as potentially long duration of workflows and activities. Details are discussed in section 7.5 on page 259.

Today, only very few of the commercially available workflow management systems support one or more of these facets of transactional workflows. As a consequence, it is neither possible to explicitly define dependencies between activities expressing their "common fate," nor is the automatic correction of the associated failure situations supported. To provide some degree of support within existing workflow management system, [AKA+94] studied how to express such dependencies and automatic corrections based on advanced transaction models (see section 7.2 on page 241). In particular it has been shown how Sagas and Flexible Transactions can be realized without requiring the workflow management system to support additional constructs for this purpose. This endeavor turns out to be a quite cumbersome even in simple cases. A similar finding described in [EL96] shows how difficult it is to provide all necessary reactions for all possible transactional outcomes of activities directly in the encompassing process model without special constructs to specify transactional semantics.

In this chapter, we describe concepts and mechanisms that allow the workflow management system to support business transactions directly. The main constructs are atomic spheres and compensation spheres. Atomic spheres allow the specification of all-or-nothing semantics for selective parts of a process model based on distributed transactions. Compensation spheres represent a business-oriented unit of work model for any collection of activities within a process model based on compensation based backward recovery.

The concept of stratified transactions described in section 7.6.3 on page 279 provides a methodology that can be used in many practical situations to substitute a physically distributed transaction with a chain of collections of transactions running on the same machine. Stratified transactions are applied in section 7.6.4 on page 282 to realize the exactly once semantics of activity executions. This technique in turn ensures forward recovery of workflows.

7.1 Basic Transaction Concepts

We briefly sketch the basics behind transactions as needed in this book. A reader interested in this subject is referred to [GR93] for an in-depth treatment of transaction processing or to [BN97] for a detailed introduction.

7.1.1 The ACID Properties

The characterizing properties of what is usually called a transaction today have been defined in [HR83], and the acronym ACID (see below) has been coined to represent these basic properties. According to this definition, a *transaction* is a collection of operations like database updates or message actions, such that following characteristics apply.

- Either all of these operations finally succeed in having their intended effects or none of these operations have an effect at all. Such a collection of operations is called *atomic*, emphasizing the all-or-nothing semantics of the collection as a whole. When all operations of a transaction succeed, the transaction ends with *commit*; otherwise it ends with *abort* or *rollback*.

- When the transaction ends, its resulting manipulations produce a *consistent* state, assuming that the state at the beginning of the transaction was consistent. Thus, all operations comply with the constraints, such as integrity and business rules, associated with their manipulated state. While all other properties of a transaction are ensured by the environment hosting the transaction, the programmer must ensure consistency by writing a correct program, that is a program that complies with all affected constraints.

- The transaction is performed within the environment as if no other transaction is performed at the same time. This means the transaction is *isolated* from all effects of other transactions currently active within the environment. The results on the manipulated state are the same as if transactions were run one at a time, that means in a serial order. Because in practice many transactions are performed concurrently in the environment, performing transactions in isolation ensures equivalence to a serial order or *serializability*. Since each single transaction produces a consistent state, performing transactions in a serial manner finally results in a consistent state. Because a serializable execution of transactions is equivalent to a serial one, a serializable execution (that is an execution ensuring isolation) produces a consistent state.

- Once a transaction is committed all of its effects will survive failures of the environment. This means the new state created by a committed transaction is *durable* and will not be lost due to a system failure. Typically, the new state is stored on disk. Once the environment recovers from a failure, the newly created state can be accessed from the disk.

The four characterizing properties of a transaction—Atomicity, Consistency, Isolation and Durability—result in the mnemonic acronym ACID. It refers to the environment in which a collection of operation runs that ensures (especially by logging and locking techniques) atomicity, isolation, and durability of the collection of operations to become a transaction. The consistency property must be ensured by the programmer, although systems like database management systems allow the specification of integrity rules, such primary keys, referential integrity, or table constraints [BS95]. A violation of one of the rules is signaled to the program which can react either by correcting the erroneous operation or aborting.

The collection of operations that must run as a transaction are bracketed by a begin-of-transaction (BOT) request and an end-of-transaction (EOT) request. As the name indicates, the BOT request starts a transaction. Two different EOT requests specify the end a transaction. A commit requests that all changes performed by the operations are made durable. An abort requests that all changes made during a transaction be undone.

Establishing *transaction boundaries*, that is specifying BOT and EOT requests, is called *transaction demarcation* or *transaction bracketing*. Often, no explicit BOT request is required (or even supported). A new transaction is established automatically by the environment, for example, the database management system, when an application program issues its first modification request (*implicit* BOT). This first modification request is either the first request ever or the first request after a preceding EOT request. Furthermore, when a program ends normally without issuing an EOT request, some environments assume that the program wants to commit (*implicit* commit). Of course, when a program ends abnormally, the active transaction is aborted. Implicit BOT and EOT are bad programming practices, so we assume that each transaction is explicitly demarcated.

7.1.2 Distributed Transactions

The term *resource* is used to refer to what is manipulated by operations constituting a transaction. Each system that manages resources manipulated by transactions is called a *resource manager*. For example, resources can be tuples in a table or messages in a queue. The corresponding resource managers are a relational database management system or a message queuing system.

Often, transactions manipulate resources of only a single resource manager. For example, a transaction selects a tuple from a table to check the amount of an account, updates this tuple to reflect a deposit, and inserts a new statement tuple holding information about the source of the deposit. Another example is a transaction reading a persistent message from a queue that represents the order of a trip, analyzing the message and submitting corresponding persistent messages, representing hotel and flight reservations to the hotel's queue and to the airline's queue.

A transaction that manipulates resources in more than one resource manager is called a *distributed transaction* or a *global transaction*. The subset of operations of a global transaction that is performed by a particular resource manager is referred to as a *subtransaction*. For example, information about hotel rooms, flights, and rental cars are managed in different database management system, that is by different resource managers. The reservations of flights, hotel rooms, and rental cars for a trip are then performed in a global transaction. Either all reservations can be made successfully or none at all. The global transaction consists of three subtransactions, one reserving the hotel rooms, one reserving flights, and one reserving rental cars. If one of the subtransactions commits, the other subtransactions must commit too. Similarly, if one subtransaction aborts, all other must abort too.

The global transaction T in Figure 7.1, for example, contains operations (depicted by arrows pointing down) in three different resource managers, two different database management systems and one message queuing system. The operations that each affected resource manager has to perform are collected and depicted in the figure as three subtransactions named S1, S2, and S3.

7.1.3 Atomic Commitment

The resource managers affected by a global transaction are completely independent of each other. They do not share any memory or state. As a consequence, ending a global transaction cannot be as simple as sending a commit or abort request to each of these resource managers. An example of this would be the global transaction T in Figure 7.1 simply sent commit requests to one affected resource manager after another. It can happen that resource manager 1 and resource manager 2 succeed—that means subtransactions S1 and S2 end with commit—whereas resource manager 3 detects an error and must abort, and that means all effects of subtransaction S3 are undone. Thus, T is no longer atomic because some of its operations succeeded in having their effects (namely, the operations corresponding to subtransactions S1 and S2) while some other of its operations had no effects at all (namely, the operations corresponding to subtransaction S3). As a consequence, the global transaction T was not performed as a transaction, violating the atomic property of the ACID properties!

Obviously, we need a protocol that ensures that either each single commit operation of all affected resource managers succeeds (i.e., all subtransactions com-

Figure 7.1 Distributed Transaction

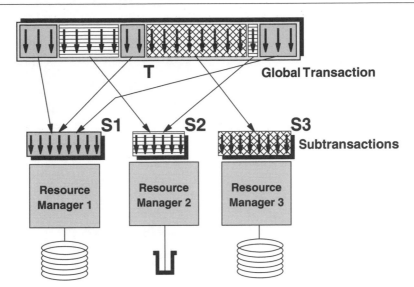

mit) or none at all, which means all resource managers will abort their associated subtransaction: the collection of commit operations must be atomic itself! The most famous way to achieve such an atomic commitment is the so-called *two-phase commit* protocol, or 2PC for short.

Because of its importance, the two-phase commit protocol has been made an integral part of the X/Open reference model for distributed transaction processing [X/O93], the OMG object transaction service [Obj97], and the Java transaction service [Sun99a, Sun99b]. We discuss the two-phase commit protocol in the context of the X/Open model because it is the underpinning of the other two.

An application that wants to run a global transaction performs transaction bracketing by means of a *transaction manager* (see Figure 7.2). For this purpose, the application first issues a `Begin` request to the transaction manager to start a global transaction (**1**). Next, the application performs its operations on multiple resource managers (**2**). Each resource manager used by the global transaction is registered with the transaction manager so that the transaction manager knows at the end of the global transaction which resource manager to involve in the two-phase commit protocol. Finally, the application issues a `Commit` request to the transaction manager (**3**). Here, the two-phase commit protocol begins.

When the transaction manager receives the `Commit` request for a global transaction, it first determines all resource managers that performed operations of this global transaction, that is that ran a subtransaction of the global transaction. The transaction manager sends a `Prepare` request to all of these resource managers

Figure 7.2 The Two-Phase Commit Protocol

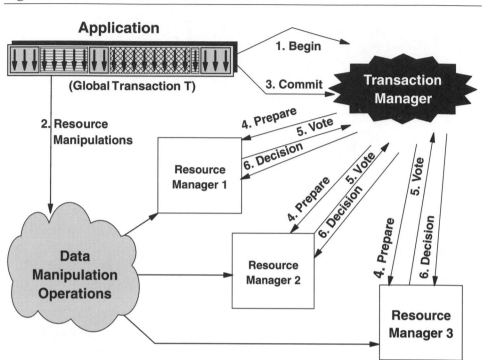

(**4**). When receiving the `Prepare` request, a resource manager determines whether it can commit its associated subtransaction. If it determines that it can commit the subtransaction, it prepares itself to run the commit under all circumstances when requested in future, but it does not perform the commit yet. If the resource manager determines an erroneous situation, it aborts the subtransaction immediately. Based on this processing, a resource manager responds to the transaction manager with a `Vote` (**5**) specifying that the resource manager will be able to commit its subtransaction in future or that the resource manager already aborted its subtransaction. The transaction manager waits for the votes of all resource managers. When all votes have arrived, phase 1 of the two-phase commit protocol has ended. If at least one vote indicates the abortion of a subtransaction, the transaction manager decides that the whole global transaction must be aborted. Thus, the abortion of a subtransaction is like a veto for committing the global transaction. If the votes signal that all resource managers are ready to commit their subtransactions, the transaction manager decides that the global transaction can commit. The corresponding `Decision` is sent to the resource managers (**6**). The resource managers will act according to the transaction manager's decision. If the decision is to `Commit`, each resource manager performs the necessary commit processing for its subtransaction and this processing finally succeeds because each resource manager has prepared for this in phase 1. If the decision is to `Abort`, each resource manager finally undoes the effects of its subtransaction. After processing according to the decision, each resource manager sends a corresponding acknowledgement to the transaction manager. When all acknowledgements have arrived at the transaction manager it can forget about the global transaction, thus ending phase 2 of the two-phase commit protocol.

The two-phase commit protocol ensures that all resource managers affected by a global transaction will eventually come to the same decision whether to commit or abort their subtransactions, and so the global transaction is atomic. Reflecting their roles in the two-phase commit protocol, the transaction manager is also referred to as *coordinator* and the resource managers are referred to as *participants*.

Some remarks on the overhead of the two-phase commit protocol: When the coordinator has to communicate with n participants, n `Prepare` messages have to be sent to the participants, each participant responds with a `Vote` message contributing another n messages, and finally the coordinator sends its `Decision` message to the participants, which amounts to another n messages. In summary, $3n$ messages are sent. The delay time of the protocol is strongly influenced by the 3 rounds that are needed: one round for broadcasting the `Prepare` messages, one round for communicating the `Votes`, and one round for broadcasting the `Decision`. Different variants of the two-phase commit protocol are known, resulting in different message complexities and numbers of required rounds (see [BHG87] for a discussion of this subject). In some environments, other transaction techniques substitute for global transaction techniques are substituted by other transaction techniques, as shown in section 7.5 on page 259 and 7.6.3 on page 279.

7.1.4 Transaction Trees

In practice, subtransactions of a global transaction are often implemented as separate programs which the application that represents the global transaction invokes. For example, a global transaction might directly include SQL operations on a relational database management system and also message operations in a message queue, and it might invoke a CICS transaction and a method of a business object, which, in turn, both update separate databases. This global transaction will consist of a subtransaction corresponding to the collection of SQL operations, a subtransaction corresponding to the message operations, a subtransaction realized by the CICS transaction, and a subtransaction corresponding to the resource manipulations the business object performs.

Especially when subtransactions are implemented as separate programs it might also be the case that subtransactions run at different locations, meaning the global transaction is distributed in a physical sense. This might mean that subtransactions leave the scope of the original transaction manager (then called *superior* transaction manager in the X/Open reference model). In this case, the subtransaction runs under the control of the transaction manager at the remote location (so-called *subordinate* transaction manager). From the superior transaction manager's point of view, the subordinate transaction manager becomes a participant in the two-phase commit protocol that the superior transaction manager will run as coordinator when the global transaction requests to commit. This coordinator-participant relationship between the affected transaction managers is typically established by the underlying communication manager when the global transaction calls (by means of the communication mechanism of the underlying communication manager) the remote program corresponding to the subtransaction. Establishing this relationship is also referred to as registering a *branch* of the global transaction at the remote location. Because a subtransaction might again invoke subtransactions at different locations, a tree structure results. The structure, shown in Figure 7.3, consists of transaction managers as nodes and edges representing coordinator-participant relationships. This structure is referred to as a *transaction tree*. For example, when the global transaction originating at location 1 commits the superior transaction manager TM1 runs a two-phase commit with the resource managers RM 1-1, RM 1-2, and RM 1-3 at location 1 and with the subordinate transaction managers TM2 and TM3 as participants. The transaction managers TM2 and TM3 will in turn run a two-phase commit at their location to come up with their votes. For this purpose, TM3 has to involve transaction manager TM4 at location 4 as participant.

Note that the structural complexity of global transactions supported in practice

Figure 7.3 A Transaction Tree

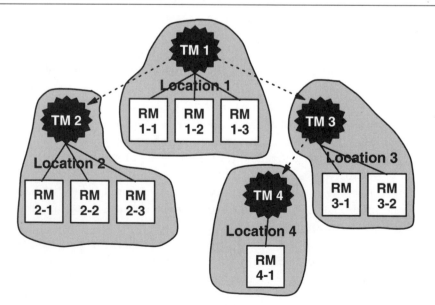

is heavily dependent on the concrete implementations of the transaction managers, resource managers, and communication managers used, and on how they interoperate. In some environments, global transactions can only consist of subtransactions whose operations are requested from the same thread that performs the transaction demarcation. In this case, a global transaction is restricted to a single node. Other environments, such as the ones that are based on implementations of the CORBA object transaction service, or the Java transaction service, in principle, allow global transactions that encompass subtransactions on multiple nodes. Some other environments allow global transactions spanning multiple nodes but the environment must be homogeneous, that is transaction managers, etc., from different vendors must not be mixed.

7.2 Advanced Transaction Concepts

When a transaction, whether it is distributed or not, becomes "complex", that means it contains many operations, it becomes advantageous to create groups of operations within a transaction and to establish a structure on the set of those groups. For example, those groups can reflect the modular structure of a transaction, or they can represent parallel pieces of work. In addition, the structure on the set of groups can reflect dependencies between groups which impact the recovery behavior of selective groups or the overall transaction.

A framework for defining such groups and associated structures together with the definition of the semantics behind groups and structures is called a *transaction model*. The most elementary transaction model considers a transaction to be just a single group of operations having ACID semantics and manipulating resources in just one resource manager. No grouping is foreseen, and, thus, no structures can be defined. Transactions built according to this model are called *flat* transactions; the overwhelming number of existing transactions comply with this model. Any transaction model (perhaps with the exception of global transactions) that goes beyond the flat transaction model is referred to as an *advanced* transaction model.

A lot of work has been done in the area of advanced transaction models, studying various kinds of dependencies between operations and ways to react in case of failing operations ([Elm92] and [JH97] present a lot of details on this subject). Much of this work is done from the point of view of a database management system or transaction manager. The business-related semantics of the operations, such as workitem processing based on staff assignments or escalation by means of notification processing, have been ignored in most cases. As a consequence, none of the proposed transaction models can be directly exploited for workflow management system, but some concepts developed in this area turned out to be of fundamental importance in the context of business processes. We discuss these concepts in this section.

7.2.1 Nested Transactions

Modularization or encapsulation recommends decomposing a "large" transaction into smaller functions. As a result, those decomposed transaction programs can manipulate resources by operating directly on the underlying resource manager as well as indirectly by invoking functions that manipulate resources, which in turn might invoke functions that do the same, and so on. Ideally, each function should best deal locally with failure situations, committing or aborting its part of the overall transaction without affecting the overall transaction's outcome. In failure situations, the surrounding function can try to correct the situation and go forward without aborting the overall transaction, so the amount of work to be undone and redone in case of failures is reduced. Furthermore, intra-transaction parallelism can be introduced by invoking functions to be executed in parallel possibly speeding up the response time of the overall transaction. Only if the overall transaction commits to the committed changes of the encompassed transactions finally become effective.

For example, the transfer of money from one account to another can be realized by two functions, a debit function and a credit function. The debit function accepts as input an account number and an amount. It will get the credit line for the account, get the current account value, and determine whether debiting the account would exceed the credit line. If the credit line will not be exceeded, the function reduces the amount from the account value, updates the database accordingly, and commits; otherwise, it rejects the debit and aborts. The credit function accepts an account number and an amount as input, too. It reads the current account value, increases it with the specified amount, and commits.

The application that performs the actual money transfer invokes the debit function with the number of the account from which money has to be withdrawn and the amount that has to be debited. In a parallel thread, the application can invoke the credit function with the number of the account to which the money has to be added and the amount to be added. It might happen that the credit function succeeds with commit, but the debit function aborts because the credit line of the specified account would be exceeded. To avoid the abortion of the complete funds transfer, the transfer application can retry the debit function with an alternate account of the customer to be debited; since the credit function already committed, it will not be aborted and redone. If the debit function now succeeds, the transfer application can commit, finally committing the effects of both the debit function and the credit function. If the debit function fails repeatedly, the transfer application will abort, finally aborting the credit function and undoing its effects on the target account.

The transaction model matching this processing is called a *nested transaction model* [Mos82].

Definition   A *nested transaction* is a collection of transactions with the following properties:

1. The collection has a tree structure.

2. Each transaction can commit or abort.

3. The root transaction has the ACID properties.

4. The commit of a transaction will only become effective if its predecessor transaction commits.

5. If a transaction aborts, all transactions of its subtree are aborted too.

6. Modifications on resources of a transaction become visible to its immediate predecessor transaction ("parent") if and only if the transaction commits.

7. Modifications on resources of a transaction are only visible to the transaction itself and to its immediate successor transactions ("children").

■

The following properties of a nested transaction are the result of the definitions. As a corollary of (**4**), all transactions can finally commit only if the root transaction commits. Thus, based on (**5**), if the root transaction aborts, all other transactions abort, too. This implies that the changes performed by the operations of a transaction will become durable if and only if the transaction committed and the root commits; as a consequence, a transaction other than the root transaction does not have the durability property at the time of its commit processing. Because of (**6**), a transaction is atomic from its parent point of view. A transaction is isolated from its parent transaction and its parent's "siblings" according to (**7**). In particular, a root transaction is isolated from other root transactions.

When intra-transaction parallelism is exploited, the average response time of a nested transaction may be reduced when compared with its nonparallel execution. This parallelism may improve the throughput in terms of number of transactions per time unit. As said before, a nested transaction as a whole (represented by the root transaction) is isolated from all other (nested) transactions. This property of nested transactions results in qualifying the model as a *closed* nested transaction model. Realization of the isolation property is typically based on locking mechanisms that reduce concurrent accesses to shared data. As a consequence, a dramatic increase of the overall throughput when using closed nested transactions must not be expected.

Giving up the isolation property while retaining intra-transaction parallelism promises to increase the throughput within the overall environment. To achieve the increase, a variant of the nested transaction model makes the effects of a transaction visible at commit to all other transactions of the environment and not just to the parent within its embracing nested transaction. What basically remains in this model is a tree structure of invocations between flat transactions. This kind of a nested transaction model is no longer closed, that is it no longer has the isolation property. It is thus sometimes called *open* nested transaction model [Tra83].

When a transaction in an open nested transaction aborts and this transaction has a child transaction that already committed, the child transaction cannot be simply undone. Its effects are durable and have already been made visible to the outside, so other transactions may already have used these effects to make their own decisions. Undoing already committed transactions requires the invocation of application-specific functions called *compensation* functions. A function and a compensation function often build a pair of mutual reverse functions, one logically undoing the effects of the other. For example, debit and credit, or reserve and cancel, is a pair of functions that compensate each other.

Even real-world actions can be more or less compensated. For example, an offer made to a customer by mailing a corresponding letter can be compensated by submitting a countermanding letter, or drilling a hole into a sheet metal can be compensated by throwing the part away. Compensation can be subtle. For example, compensating the deposit operation on an account after days by invoking the corresponding credit operation might fail because the money has already been spent. Compensation can be complex. For example, compensation of an order of a part that has already been delivered to a customer who is unwilling to pay requires a hortatory proceeding.

Nevertheless, when an application is built, many of the functions implemented can be paired such that one function compensates the other. In most applications, it is natural to build functions jointly with their compensation functions. Thus, choosing compensation as the underpinning of a transaction model is practical in the sense that it does not put the extra burden for creating compensation functions onto programmers.

7.2.2 Sagas

The open nested transaction model does not foresee any system services that automatically invoke compensation functions along a subtree of an aborting transaction. Thus, human beings have to find out what has happened and what compensation actions must be taken to create a new consistent state across the manipulated resources. This procedure is cumbersome and error prone and should be automated, or at least supported, by the environment.

The Saga transaction model adds the capability to automatically determine and start compensation functions to the environment. In its simplest version a Saga [GMS87] is a sequence of transactions that either all commit or that run compensation functions for all already committed transactions.

Definition A *Saga* is defined as a sequence $[(T_1, C_1), \ldots, (T_n, C_n)]$ that has the following properties:

1. $T_1,...,T_n$ and $C_1,...,C_n$ are two sets of transactions, such that C_i is the compensation function for T_i, $1 \le i \le n$.

2. $[(T_1, C_1), \dots , (T_n, C_n)]$ is executed as one of the following sequences:

   (a) $[T_1, \dots ,T_n]$ if all T_i committed (that means for $1 \le i \le$ n), or

   (b) $[T_1, \dots , T_i, C_{i-1}, \dots , C_1]$ if T_i aborts and $T_1, \dots , T_{i-1}$ committed before.

■

An environment that supports the Saga model starts the transactions of a Saga one after the other. When a transaction of the sequence aborts, the environment starts the compensation transactions of the already committed transaction of the sequence in reverse order. Otherwise, when the last transaction of a Saga commits, the whole Saga has run successfully.

In section 7.5 on page 259, we introduce the concept of compensation spheres that is based on the Saga model. It extends the Saga model from executing sequences of transactions to the execution of collections of possibly nested partial orders of arbitrary programs. In doing so, it reflects the structure of workflows as instances of process models.

7.2.3 ConTracts

The *ConTract* model [Reu89, RSS97] combines ACID semantics and compensation. Its supported target applications are long-running computations, that is applications that must tolerate (planned or unplanned) system outages in a reliable manner. A long-running application consists of multiple "steps," each implemented by a separate program. The control flow between these steps can be explicitly specified. In our terminology, the ConTract model supports a variant of what we called a control flow graph in section 4.6 on page 160.

Long-running computations must be forward recoverable, as we discuss in section 7.6.1 on page 274. When such an application is interrupted, the system must not redo steps that have already been performed successfully but it must resume the execution of the application where it left off because of the erroneous situation. Furthermore, it must be possible to recover from error situations to avoid the loss of work that has been correctly performed earlier. For this purpose, subsets of steps can be defined to have ACID semantics. Note that because steps can run anywhere in the environment, such a subset is in fact a global transaction. The concept of atomic spheres discussed in section 7.4 on page 251 resembles this idea.

Steps that already committed can be undone, based on compensation functions. This reflects the fact that long-running computations must release locks as early as possible to avoid throughput reductions. Groups of steps that are compensated collectively can be defined. At its heart, this is the Saga concept, which we extend in section 7.5 on page 259 when we discuss compensation spheres.

In its early version [Reu89] the ConTract model assumed a close cooperation between the ConTract environment and the available resource managers. Steps had to be implemented as transactions. Based on an evolution of the ConTract model, its actual version weakened this close relationship. Furthermore, steps can be any kind of program, and the recovery semantics have been adopted accordingly. But ConTracts still do not reflect workflows in our sense (instances of process models) since they omit things such as explicit data flows, staff assignments, or dead path elimination. In sections 7.4 on page 251, 7.5 on page 259, and 7.6 on page 274, we describe unit-of-work concepts that are geared toward workflows in our sense. These concepts are different from the ConTract model, but the fundamental ingredients (namely, compensation and distributed transactions) are the same.

7.3   Streams

The original meaning of the notion of transactional workflows was that of all-or-nothing semantics, discussed in the introduction, which was soon extended to incorporate business-oriented units of work. This is still the aspect of transactional workflows on which a lot of research work is focused. With the use of workflow management system in practice, the run-and-gun facet became of equal importance. Parts of a workflow must be assembled into a unit that, once started, is performed in a consecutive manner. We call such a unit a *workitem stream*.

7.3.1   Workitem Streams

A workitem stream, as shown in Figure 7.4, is a series of workitems with the following properties:

1. All workitems of the stream are assigned to a particular agent.

2. All workitems are created by the same workflow.

3. All workitems are the result of scheduling consecutive activities of the underlying process model.

4. All workitems of the stream are performed by the same agent.

Note that it is not required that the workitems of a workitem stream are assigned to only one single agent. Different agents might be assigned to the same workitem stream. What characterizes the workitem stream is that once a particular agent starts the first workitem of a stream, all other workitems of the stream are performed by this agent.

Figure 7.4 Workitem Streams

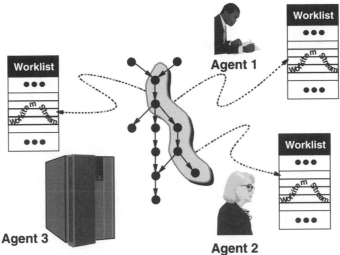

When processing workitems, the workflow management system must support in an "appropriate" manner "some" of the "relevant" functionality used from TP monitors. Behind the fuzziness of requirements, the following usage patterns of workitems are found in practice. These patterns can occur in any combination.

- **Micro script stream**. A workflow includes a series of automatic activities whose implementations do not require any end-user interactions. Each activity in the series is started immediately by the workflow management system as soon as it detects one of them.

- **Transaction stream**. A workflow includes a series of activities that are implemented by short-lived transactions. These transactions are often realized with the aid of a TP monitor. The workflow management system is then perceived as an extension of the TP monitor. Often, the activities are implemented with different TP monitors. In this case, the workflow management system is perceived as yet another TP monitor. When the transactions interact with an end user, theworkflow management system must support "screen navigation."

- **Work package streams**. A workflow includes a series of activities that represents a whole complete work package for agents. Often, an agent carries out the workitem stream consecutively and without any interruptions. No workitems of other workflows are performed in between. As soon as one workitem completes, the next workitem of the stream is started. Agents processing workitem streams in such a manner behave like "robots."

7.3.2   Micro Script Streams

The agent associated with a series of automatic activities is an abstract system agent that is assumed to perform each workitem of the stream immediately when the 1 is scheduled to the agent. Such a workitem stream is perceived to be performed "very fast", i.e., at "system speed." Typically, a workitem stream represents a micro script that would otherwise be implemented as a program.

Thus, the technique that most relates to micro script streams is that of compile spheres. The series of automatic activities corresponds to a micro script, which in turn can be defined as a compile sphere, as discussed in section 5.8 on page 206. A process compiler generates appropriate source code from this series of activities. At runtime, the workflow management system invokes the generated executable instead of the "substituted" compile sphere. In general, this procedure results in performance characteristics that are expected from micro script streams.

7.3.3   Transaction Streams

Two cases must to be distinguished in practice. In the first case, the series of transactions implements automatic activities without end-user interactions. If no additional transactional control is required from the workflow management system, such a stream is really more like a micro script stream and can be treated as outlined above. Otherwise, the transactional aspect is predominant, and what is mostly required is to run the stream as a single transaction. The workflow management system must make sure that either all transactions in the stream commit or all must abort. Such a stream is in fact an atomic sphere with "exactly once " semantics; the related techniques are discussed in depth in sections 7.4 on page 251 and 7.6 on page 274.

In the second case, the series of transactions encompasses interactions with the same end user and really represent navigation through menus or screens, as shown in Figure 7.5.

The stream reflects a classical programming technique, called *pseudo-conversation*, favored by TP monitors [BN97]. All end-user interaction and screen navigation could theoretically be implemented as a huge transaction. This huge transaction would last very long, thus locking resources for a long time. As a consequence, concurrency within the overall environment would be reduced, with the well-known negative impact on the overall throughput of the whole environment. Because of this, transactions of long duration are avoided and such huge transactions are split into a chain of smaller, short-duration, transactions. Typically, each of these transactions implements a logical end-user step, with the associated resource manipulations such as requesting input from a screen and updating a database correspondingly. To perform the same function as the original huge transaction, each small transaction within the chain passes the appropriate user data (and state data)

Figure 7.5 Screen Navigation

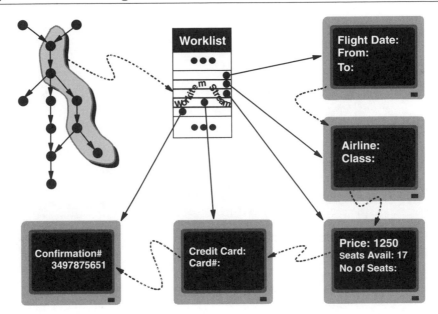

to its successor. Although the end user has the impression of having a conversation with the system, it is "just" a pseudo-conversation.

The fragment of the process model underlying this kind of stream in fact specifies some *dialog control*. The associated activities are automatic activities, which makes this type of stream similar to micro script streams. Nevertheless, the data-passing mechanisms require functions not necessarily assumed by a micro script. The pseudo-conversational style of the transactions typically needs a special kind of data sharing at memory speed. We will meet similar requirements of data sharing between activities next.

7.3.4   Work Package Streams

Work package streams are related to checkin and checkout techniques and the so-called floating storage, as shown in Figure 7.6. The activities of the process model resulting in the workitem stream are most often explicitly specified. For example, this specification can be simply supported via an appropriate staff query like "performed by starter of activity x" if x denotes the activity where the series of consecutive activities within the process model begins. The workflow management system has to provide the ability to check out complete workitem streams in advance, not just a single workitem, to allow their execution in a disconnected mode. When a workitem stream has been processed, it must be able to check in the complete stream.

Figure 7.6 Floating Storage

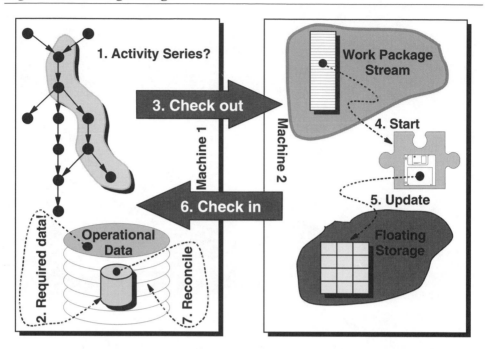

To execute the workitems of the stream in disconnected mode, the workflow management system allows the checkout of all operational data that is needed by the corresponding activity implementations. The resulting abstract container representing this data and the related services is sometimes referred to as a *floating storage* associated with the stream. When data is checked out and packaged into a floating storage, various lock modes can be specified to restrict concurrent accesses to the operational data (see [GR93] for an in-depth treatment on locking). The floating storage can be moved between machines and made persistent at its target locations; it allows access to and manipulation of its contained data by programs at its current location. When the floating storage is checked in, reconciliation must take place if updates of the operational data are allowed.

In summary, a user checks out a workitem stream and its associated floating storage. These workitems are carried out in disconnected mode, accessing the copy of operational data. When the workitems are checked in, the floating storage is automatically reconciled with the operational data if necessary.

For example, a customer asks his bank for a loan for remodeling his house. This request initiates a workflow comprising activities such as checking mortgages on the house and building plot, analyzing the customer's other debts, or checking the customer's solvency and credit rating. At some point, a representative of the bank may visit the customer to review the plans or to inspect the building plot.

These workitems of the bank representative build a workitem stream. The bank representative wants to check out the workitems and all customer related data (i.e., the related floating storage) to his laptop and process them during his visit. In particular, this process updates the floating storage. When the representative returns, he wants to simply check in the workitem stream as well as the floating storage. This action continues the workflow and updates the customer's data by reconciling it with the operational data.

Note the relation between floating storage and transaction streams representing dialog controls. The data sharing functions provided by the floating storage mechanism are similar to the functions needed by pseudo-conversational transactions. Since the floating storage associated with the transactions of a transaction stream representing screen navigation typically is not moved, its functionality can be restricted.

7.4 Atomic Spheres

In this section, we introduce the concept of atomic spheres. This concept is derived from the analysis of the reuse of transactions in the composition of other transactions. Then, we discuss the role of the workflow management system in running atomic spheres.

7.4.1 Reusability and Transaction Boundaries

Modularization or encapsulation fosters reuse of application functions. When such functions represent transactions, reusability requires that transaction boundaries be handled with care.

Let's recall the example from section 7.2.1 on page 242. Two reusable functions were built: a debit function and a credit function. Figure 7.7 shows these functions as methods of the `Account` business object, which is a reusable components itself (see section 6.1.1 on page 210).

In the withdraw application the debit method of the `Account` component is invoked. The method gets the credit line for the account and the current account value and then determines whether debiting the account would exceed the credit line. If the credit line would not be exceeded, then the method reduces the amount from the account value, updates the database accordingly, and commits. Otherwise, it rejects the debit request and aborts. The deposit application invokes the credit method of the `Account` object. The method reads the current account value, increases it with the specified amount, and commits. Note that it is vital that the transaction boundaries are established as described to make the changes on the account durable. Otherwise, either the bank or the customer will be disappointed.

Assume that a funds transfer workflow is built; the workflow uses the debit method and the credit method of the `Account` component as activity implementa-

Figure 7.7 Reuse and Transaction Boundaries

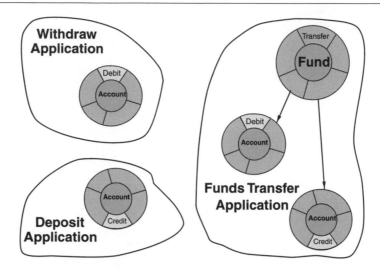

tions. When the transfer method of the Fund component completes, the workflow management system navigates through the underlying process model and determines that the debit method and credit method must be invoked. Because both methods establish their transaction boundaries independently of each other, it might happen that the credit method ends with commit but that the debit method aborts. This would leave the underlying databases in an inconsistent state!

How can this unacceptable situation be resolved? We saw in section 7.2.1 on page 242 that nested transactions allow one to specify transaction boundaries even around functions that demarcate their own transactions and that a root transaction finally can overwrite commit operations if erroneous situations are detected. Thus, if the workflow management system would somehow run the debit method and the credit method in a nested transaction, it could finally abort even the committed credit method once it detects that the debit method had failed. The underlying databases would be left in a consistent state!

Unfortunately, implementations of nested transactions are far from being pervasive. Only very few transaction managers or resource managers support nested transactions—none of the big relational database management system vendors does. Thus, a solution that is practical cannot rely on this technology.

But what if the workflow management system runs the debit method and the credit method within a global transaction? The workflow management system begins the global transaction before invoking the debit and credit method and ends the global transaction with commit or abort, depending on the outcome of both methods. This works as long as neither method demarcates its own transactions. This means they must not issue a commit or abort statement by themselves!

As a consequence, when fully reusable functions or components, etc., are built, no transaction boundaries must be established within the function or component. When transaction boundaries are established by the function or component, level of reuse is limited in practice. Of course, this fact is independent of whether the granule should be (re)used as an activity implementation within a workflow, as a component within a composite business object (as discussed in section 6.1.1 on page 210), or as a routine called by another program.

A function (or component or program) that does not establish its own transaction boundaries but requires demarcation of a transaction around it to achieve its effects is called a *transactional* function (or component or program). A transactional function is like a transaction except that it does not issue a commit or an abort request. Consequently, mechanisms are needed to establish transaction boundaries around transactional functions from the outside. In the following section, we describe such a mechanism that is based on workflow technology.

7.4.2 Concept of Atomic Spheres

The goal is that the workflow management system allows one to plug transactional programs into a new global transaction. Note that the transactional programs then become subtransactions of this global transaction. The global transaction paradigm assumes that an entity like a program represents the global transaction to the transaction manager. The main obligations of this entity are to demarcate the global transaction, to invoke the subtransactions, and to react to exceptions like a negative acknowledgment from a commit request submitted to the transaction manager. In traditional environments the global transaction is represented by a program that implements all these obligations. To simplify this task, that is to avoid the corresponding programming, the workflow management system (beside being able to invoke executables or transactional programs) has to provide the capability to demarcate transactions and to deal with associated exceptions in a generic manner. The corresponding support is associated with atomic spheres [Ley95b].

An atomic sphere is a collection of activities, all of them implemented by a transactional program (see section 7.4.3 on page 255 for the precise definition). Figure 7.8 depicts an atomic sphere consisting of activities B and C. When navigating through the process model, the workflow management system will make sure that either all activity implementations invoked within the atomic sphere commit or all abort. When all implementations commit, the atomic sphere itself is called committed; otherwise, it is called aborted. In Figure 7.8, if B and C are invoked and B aborts, C is aborted too. In that way the workflow management system ensures the atomicity of the collection of transactional programs corresponding to activities within the atomic sphere.

If an atomic sphere aborts, the workflow management system repeats the navigation through the atomic sphere by entering the atomic sphere at the same activities

Figure 7.8 An Atomic Sphere

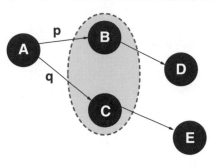

where the control flow entered it the first time. These activities build the "actual start set" of the atomic sphere. If the first execution of the atomic sphere of Figure 7.8 runs only B because the transition condition q has been false and the transition condition p was true, only B is redone if the atomic sphere must be repeated.

An atomic sphere has a variety of properties. One property specifies the number of times the workflow management system has to retry an aborted atomic sphere before finally declaring it failed. One can also be specified what has to be done when an atomic sphere finally fails. For example, a notification can be sent to recipients who are specified by a staff assignment query; or the workflow management system can set all activities within the atomic sphere into the dead or skipped state and perform dead path elimination to continue its processing.

For example, in Figure 7.8 activities B and C are defined to build an atomic sphere. Activity B is implemented by a CICS transaction and activity C by an IMS transaction. When activity A terminates successfully and both transition conditions p and q evaluate to true, the workflow management system will invoke both transactions. If the IMS transaction aborts, the workflow management system makes sure that the CICS transaction aborts too. After that, it starts the implementations of B and C again until both finally succeed or the retry threshold is reached. When both transactions commit, navigation continues as usual. The workflow management system determines whether D or E or both have to be carried out.

In another instance of this process model the transition condition p might evaluate to false while q evaluates to true. In this situation only the IMS transaction as implementation of activity C is invoked. If the transaction aborts it (and only it) is invoked again. When it commits, the next navigation step determines whether E has to be scheduled next.

The Flow Definition Language has to be extended to allow for an appropriate language representation of atomic spheres and their properties. Code Example 7.1 illustrates the necessary new constructs.

Code Example 7.1 Atomic Sphere Definition

```
ATOMIC_SPHERE 'My Sphere'
   RELATED_ACTIVITIES A, B
   RETRY 3 TIMES
   ON FAIL
      NOTIFY PROCESS_ADMINISTRATOR
END 'My Sphere'
```

An atomic sphere is defined by the ATOMIC_SPHERE section. The RELA-TED_ACTIVITIES keyword begins the list of all activities contained in the atomic sphere. The number of times the workflow management system should retry an aborted atomic sphere before it is considered to have finally failed is specified with the RETRY...TIMES keyword; in our example, the atomic sphere MySphere should be retried three times. The ON FAIL keyword defines how an atomic sphere that finally fails should be treated. In our example, the process administrator is notified, as specified by the NOTIFY keyword followed by the PROCESS_ADMINISTRATOR keyword. In general, any valid staff query may follow the **NOTIFY** keyword. Other options for ON FAIL are supported, such as TREAT AS SKIPPED which causes the workflow management system to perform dead path elimination for all control connectors leaving the atomic sphere.

Our discussion on atomic spheres is on a conceptual level and does not deal with idiosyncrasies of concrete implementations resulting from the functionality provided by the underlying environment. In particular, we assume that an implementation has as flexible an environment as its underpinning, allowing global transactions that span multiple locations. In more restricted environments that do not support subtransactions on different nodes, the corresponding functionality of atomic spheres is restricted accordingly. We tolerate restrictions on the functionality of atomic spheres based on environmental capabilities because our base assumption is that the workflow management system should use the available transaction manager and resource managers in the environment and not try to implement missing functions itself.

7.4.3 Mechanics of Atomic Spheres

Before discussing algorithmic details of atomic spheres, we have to define them more precisely. An atomic sphere is a collection of activities that must satisfy some additional conditions:

1. All activities within the atomic sphere have transactional activity implementations; that is their implementations accept transaction boundaries established from the outside.

2. Either all activities of the atomic sphere that have a predecessor outside of the atomic sphere have the same predecessor, or no activity at all has a predecessor outside of the sphere.

3. Either all activity implementations executing an activity of the atomic sphere commit or all abort.

Condition (1) allows implementation of atomic spheres with global transaction techniques. It is the workflow management system that establishes a transaction boundary around the transactional programs that implement the activities of an atomic sphere, and these transactional programs run as subtransactions of the corresponding global transaction (see later).

The semantics of our metamodel ensure that there is a point at which all activities are either completed or dead/skipped. At this point, it is then known that no more activities of an atomic sphere can become executable! Exactly at this time, the workflow management system will end the global transaction representing the atomic sphere. A two-phase commit protocol will make sure that either all completed activities commit or all abort. Thus, the all-or-nothing property of atomic spheres represented by condition (3) will finally be satisfied.

As long as any activity within the atomic sphere might become executable, the workflow management system does not end the corresponding global transaction. As a consequence, an atomic sphere should run "fast"! Otherwise, the corresponding global transaction lasts for a long time and the resource managers used by the activity implementations hold locks for the same long time, reducing the overall throughput of the environment. To furnish fast atomic spheres, one must ensure at least the following structural property (which is guaranteed by condition (2)):

- All control connectors entering the atomic sphere have the same origin, or no control connectors at all will enter the atomic sphere.

Activities having an incoming control connector originating from an activity outside of the atomic sphere, or a start activity of the process model being a member of the atomic sphere, are activities at which the atomic sphere might begin its execution. The set of activities at which an atomic sphere might begin its execution is called its "start set." The atomic sphere S in Figure 7.9 has the start set $\{A,B,D,G\}$. The condition above will ensure that all executable members of the start set will be detected at the same time, avoiding long delays for initiating independent paths within an atomic sphere.

Assume that this structural restriction is not satisfied. For example, activities A and D in figure 7.9 on the next page have different predecessors outside of the atomic sphere S. It may happen that the predecessor of activity D will complete hours after A has been started, resulting in an unacceptable duration of S. Furthermore, when A completes, the workflow management system must wait for the completion of

Figure 7.9 Structures to Be Avoided for Atomic Spheres

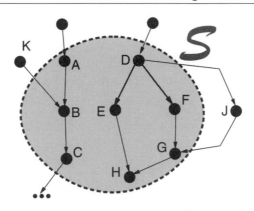

activity K to determine whether B becomes executable or not. Again, an unacceptable delay might result. Also, when D completes, the control flow might leave the atomic sphere and activity J might become executable. J might be long running, it might be assigned to an agent who is very busy and cannot start the activity within the next hours, and so on. The unacceptable impact on the duration of the atomic sphere is obvious because the workflow management system has to wait for the completion of J to determine whether G becomes executable.

There are other properties of an atomic sphere that are desirable but not necessary, so they are not enforced by our definition. For example, all activities of an atomic sphere should be automatic activities, to eliminate idle time on some end users' worklists before being started. Similarly, no activity implementation should perform a conversation with an end user, thus avoiding human think time.

The following is a formal definition of atomic spheres matching the prose version of the definition used before. Readers can skip the definition without loosing context.

Definition Let G be a process model graph and N its set of activities. A set $\mathcal{S} \subseteq N$ with $\mathcal{S} \neq \emptyset$ is called an *atomic sphere*:$\Leftrightarrow$

1. $\forall A \in S : \Psi(A)$ is a transactional program.

2. Exactly one of the following is true:

    (a) $\forall A, B \notin \mathcal{S} : A^{\rightarrow} \cap \mathcal{S} \neq \emptyset \wedge B^{\rightarrow} \cap \mathcal{S} \neq \emptyset \Rightarrow A = B$ or,

    (b) $\forall A \in \mathcal{S} \; \forall B \notin \mathcal{S} : A \notin B^{\rightarrow}$.

3. Let $\Phi \in$ with $\mathcal{S} \subseteq \lambda_i \cup \delta_i$ (such an i exists—see section 4.7.13 on page 179); then exactly one of the following is true:

(a) $\forall A \in \mathcal{S} \cap \lambda_i : \Psi(A)$ committed, or

(b) $\forall A \in \mathcal{S} \cap \lambda_i : \Psi(A)$ aborted.

$\mathcal{S}$ is then called committed or aborted, respectively. ∎

For our discussion of a possible implementation of atomic spheres, we need one more definition. The set of all activities of an atomic sphere S that have at most one predecessor outside of the atomic sphere is called the start set of S. Formally, this is the following set.

$$\mathcal{S}' := \{A \in \mathcal{S} \mid \exists B \notin \mathcal{S} : A \in B^{\rightarrow}\} \cup (N' \cap \mathcal{S}),$$

where N' denotes the set of all start activities of the process mode, that is all activities without any incoming control connector. Because of condition (2) exactly one of the two sets will contribute to the start set: the start set will either consist of activities without any incoming control connector, or it will consist of the activities having a single common predecessor outside of the atomic sphere. Thus, when the control flow enters the atomic sphere, it will be at a well-defined point in time, namely either the point in time when the common predecessor completes or when the process model is instantiated. ∎

At this time, the workflow management system determines all activities of the atomic sphere $\mathcal{S}$ that become executable. This set of activities is a subset of the start set $\mathcal{S}'$ and is called the actual start set of the atomic sphere. Next, the workflow management system begins a global transaction via the transaction manager of the environment (step 1 in Figure 7.10). Then, it registers itself as a resource manager participating in the established global transaction (step 2); we discuss the reason for this registration below. After that, the workflow management system navigates through the process model underlying the atomic sphere and determines all activities that become executable. The implementations of these activities are executed within the global transaction boundary; that is the implementations' resource managers , become participants of the global transaction (step 3). When the workflow management system determines that no more activities can become executable within the atomic sphere, it requests a commit of the global transaction from the transaction manager. If the commit succeeds, the atomic sphere is committed and navigation continues outside of the atomic sphere (step 4). Otherwise, the atomic sphere is aborted and the workflow management system runs the atomic sphere again by executing the original actual start set. If the retry threshold is exceeded, the corresponding specified actions are performed.

The workflow management system must always be aware of the outcome of the global transaction representing an atomic sphere because it must retry an aborted atomic sphere and it must continue navigation based on a committed atomic sphere. For this purpose, we assume that the workflow management system registers itself as a participant in this global transaction, as done in step 2, making the control of the atomic sphere straightforward.

Figure 7.10 Processing Atomic Spheres

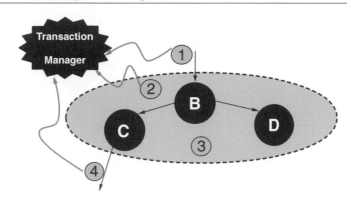

- When the workflow management system requests a commit for the global transaction it is asked as participant for its vote. By default, it votes for commit—had it encountered a problem, it would have requested an abortion of the global transaction before. If one of the executed activity implementations has aborted, the transaction manager decides to abort the overall global transaction and informs the workflow management system. The workflow management system then retries the aborted atomic sphere.

- If the workflow management system itself fails after requesting the end of the global transaction, it needs to ask the transaction manager for the state of the global transaction during its restart and process the atomic sphere accordingly.

- If the workflow management system fails during the usual execution of the atomic sphere, the atomic sphere might been aborted by the environment in the meantime. Thus, during restart the workflow management system needs also to query the transaction manager about the fate of the atomic sphere and react accordingly.

7.5   Compensation Spheres

Atomic spheres allow the process modeler to group activities with transactional implementations into a new unit of work, namely, a global transaction. This is not sufficient in many practical situations:

- In high-throughput environments in which it is clear from the very beginning that most atomic spheres will commit, the overhead of the two-phase commit protocol might be too high. In the rare case that an atomic sphere fails, compensation-based recovery may be tolerable.

- It should be allowed to group not only activities with transactional implementations into a unit of work but also activities with non-transactional implementations, and any mixture of both. In this case, an appropriate unit of work concept must be compensation based.

- Often, an incorrectly performed piece of work is detected long after the corresponding activity completed. Even if such an activity runs within an atomic sphere, only compensation can recover from the resulting erroneous situation.

In this section we introduce the concept of compensation spheres [Ley95a]. A compensation sphere allows the process modeler to group arbitrary collections of activities, transactional and nontransactional, into a unit of work. A failed compensation sphere is aborted by running appropriate compensation activities. The abortion of a compensation sphere can be requested at any time, even, if, for example, the control flow has already left the compensation sphere.

7.5.1   Completion versus Correctness

An activity of a process model is an abstraction of a piece of work that has to be performed within the represented business process. The actual performance of this piece of work is supported by the activity implementation associated with the activity, that is the activity implementation might be perceived as a tool helping in the execution of the piece of work.

It could happen that a tool has been used successfully, for example, the activity implementation returned without any error and the exit condition has been met, but the associated piece of work has not been performed successfully. Thus, completion of an activity does not mean its correct performance.

For example, the activity "Write a customer offer" has an editor associated as activity implementation. When the offer has been written, the editor is terminated. When the editor does not signal any error and the exit condition is met, the activity is considered to be finished (i.e., completed) and the workflow proceeds. The tool has been exploited successfully. But there is no guarantee that the offer is correct; the clerk could have offered the product with a wrong delivery date or price; the piece of work might not be performed successfully.

In other words, there must be a means to signal semantic failure even in case of syntactical success. Note that exit conditions can distinguish between the termination of the activity implementation and the completion of the associated piece of work. But completion is different from correctness!

7.5.2   How to Repair Pieces of Work

Usually, work that has been performed incorrectly must be repaired (or corrected). For example, "Write a customer offer" has been completed incorrectly, stating the wrong delivery date, and the letter has already been received by the customer. The work is corrected by writing and sending a new customer letter with the real delivery date (and some apologies, of course).

Most frequently, incorrectly completed work cannot be simply undone in the sense that it appears as it had never happened (for example, restoring before-images in a database management system). Repairing or compensating this type of work requires that the application and its real-world effects are kept in mind. For example, writing and sending the letter with the incorrect offer cannot be undone, since there is usually no way to get the letter out of the mail once it is on its way or, even worse, if it is already in the hands of the customer. Similarly, the dispension of money by an automatic teller machine or the drilling of a hole cannot be undone.

Sometimes, the compensation action to be performed is not obvious from the very beginning but has to be determined at runtime depending upon on the actual application context. For example, if sending a letter to a customer must be undone, the proper compensation action depends on whether or not the letter is still available. In the first case, it can be taken out of the mail. In the latter case, a corrective letter must be sent to the customer.

In general, collections of activities are coupled with respect to the correct execution of their associated pieces of work. The detection of the incorrectness of one of the coupled pieces of work invalidates the other pieces of work too. Consequently, the whole collection of pieces of work has to be repaired collectively. For example, reservations for hotel rooms, flights, and rental cars for a trip are tightly coupled. When one of the reservation fails, such as flight unavailability at a certain date to a particular destination, the reservations that have been already made must be changed.

An activity could be recognized as failed even after the time the associated activity implementation terminated successfully and the control flow continued. For example, production problems might lead to incorrectness of the promised delivery date weeks after the customer letter was sent. Of course, the workflow continued in the meantime, contracting a shipping agent and so on.

7.5.3 Concept of Compensation Spheres

A compensation sphere introduced in [Ley95a] is an arbitrary collection of activities, as shown in Figure 7.11. Activities with transactional implementations and activities with nontransactional implementations can be mixed within a compensation sphere. Putting a group of activities into the same compensation sphere specifies that the pieces of work corresponding to these activities are tightly related. If one of these pieces of work has not been performed correctly and must be repaired, all the other pieces of work that have already been performed must be repaired too. Thus, the activities of a compensation sphere share a common fate and define a new kind of unit of work.

Figure 7.11 Compensation Sphere

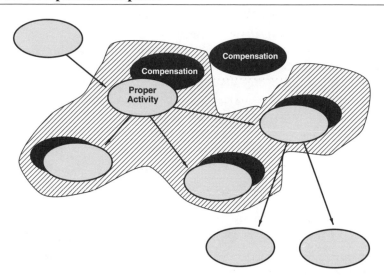

As the name already indicates, work performed in the scope of a compensation sphere is repaired by compensation actions. For this purpose, each activity within a compensation sphere can be defined as a pair consisting of the proper activity (i.e., the piece of work that is normally assumed to be performed correctly) and an associated compensation activity, as shown in Figure 7.11. Furthermore, a compensation sphere itself can be associated with a compensation activity. Note that a compensation activity is a usual activity. It has all properties of an activity such as an exit condition or a staff assignment. In particular, the implementation of a compensation activity can be a program or process model.

When an incorrectly performed piece of work is detected, the workflow management system can be requested to abort the including compensation sphere. At this point, the workflow management system determines all activities of the compensation sphere that had been activated until then. For all of these activities, the workflow management system invokes the associated compensation activities in reverse order. To be more precise, the workflow management system conceptually constructs a process model based on the actual state of the activities contained in the compensation sphere to be aborted; it then instantiates this process model to repair the work already performed within the compensation sphere. See section 7.5.4 on page 269 for more details on how this process model is derived.

The compensation sphere S depicted in Figure 7.12 consists of the activities A, C, E, and F. All four activities might have completed before S is requested to abort. The workflow management system first schedules the compensation activity associated with E. Once the compensation activity of E completes the compensation activities of C and F are scheduled because C and F can immediately be reached from E by traversing the original process model in reverse direction. When the compensation activity of C completed, A is reached from C by going backwards, so A's compensation activity is scheduled. After this compensation activity completes, the compensation sphere is aborted. So, one could perceive that the process model P(S) shown in Figure 7.12 is derived by the workflow management system, based on the actual state of S, and that this process model is instantiated to abort S.

Figure 7.12 Undoing Compensation Spheres

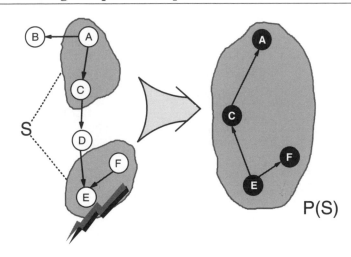

Figure 7.13 shows how this functionality would need to be modeled if the workflow management system does not support compensation spheres. The example we use is a subset of the running example presented in Appendix A. In this trip reservation process, a customer passes a trip itinerary and credit card information to a Traveluck representative. If the credit card passes a check, the reception of the trip to be reserved is confirmed, and different agents try to make the corresponding reservations for flights, hotels, and rental cars. If all these reservations have been confirmed, the trip schedule is built, and so on.

It is crucial that all reservations are confirmed so the trip can be made according to the itinerary. If one of the reservations fails, a new itinerary must be negotiated with the customer. For this exceptional situation, the trip reservation process foresees the contact customer subprocess. Within this subprocess, all already confirmed reservations are canceled and the customer is informed about the problems with the original itinerary. After that, the customer could submit a new itinerary, which is then processed as a new instance of the trip reservation process model.

All of this is cumbersome for the process modeler and often perceived as "unnatural." The process modeler has to reflect the exceptional situation "failing reservation" directly within the process model. As a result, the process model becomes more complex, mixing the proper business logic of the process with ex-

Figure 7.13 Foreseeing Failing Reservation in the Trip Reservation Example

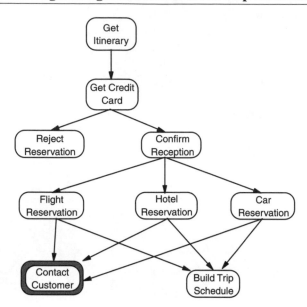

ception logic. Also, taking care of exceptional situations is often not considered to
be an aspect of process modeling at all, but an IT aspect such as ensuring atomicity
of collections of activities. Process modelers want to separate both aspects!

Figure 7.14 shows how this separation of normal and exceptional situations
can be achieved with compensation spheres. The modified process model no longer
specifies exceptional actions as activities within the model of the proper business
process. The contact customer subprocess has been removed. Instead, the activities Flight Reservation, Hotel Reservation, Car Reservation,
Confirm Reception, and Get Itinerary are specified to make up a compensation sphere. The reservation activities have corresponding Cancel activities
associated as compensation activities. To compensate the confirmation of a reception, the customer is informed about the overall failure of the reservations. The
Get Itinerary activity is not compensated (NOP = No Operation).

When a reservation fails, the workflow management system instantiates the
process model indicated in Figure 7.15. First, all reservations are canceled. Next,
the customer is informed about the failed itinerary. The Get Itinerary activity
is actually not compensated, so that the customer can immediately pass a new
itinerary to Traveluck.

Figure 7.14 Using a Compensation Sphere for Dealing with Failing Reservations

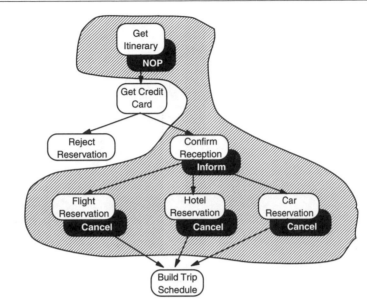

The additional advantage of taking care of failing reservations via a compensation sphere instead of additional constructs, such as activities or control connectors, is increased flexibility. Compensation can now be performed even when the airline calls the travel agent because of overbooking or the credit card company signals the insolvency of the customer when the payment is requested (see Figure A.1 on page 449), for example. If failed reservations are handled as in figure 7.13, then once the `Build Trip Schedule` activity has been scheduled, the customer can no longer be contacted, based on the process model shown.

The manner in which a compensation sphere is aborted is called the *compensation granularity* and is specified as a property for each compensation sphere. The granularity within the previous example is called *discrete*, because each activity is compensated separately. *Global* granularity specifies that a compensation sphere be aborted by invocation of the compensation activity that is directly associated with the compensation sphere itself. Global compensation applies in situations in which a compensation sphere cannot be undone by simply reversing the control connectors and invoking the compensation activities associated with the activities of the compensation sphere. For example, if a customer turns out to be insolvent once his order has already been delivered, separate hortatory processing must be done instead of a stepwise compensation in reverse order. In this case, the corresponding hortatory process model will be the compensation activity of the compensation sphere.

Figure 7.15 Performing Compensation when a Reservation Fails

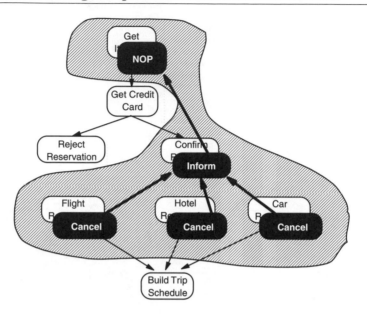

Another property of a compensation sphere is its *mode*. In the previous example, the mode of the compensation sphere was *retry*. After compensating the work, the workflow management system resumed its usual processing at the activities where the control flow entered the compensation sphere the first time (its "actual start set" —see section 7.4.3 on page 255). The *undo* mode specifies that compensation has to be run and, when finished, that the workflow management system should stop and inform a predefined agent, such as the process administrator. It is then the responsibility of the agent to decide which actions should be taken next. Aborting a compensation sphere in *rerun* mode means to stop processing any currently active activity of the compensation sphere and simply schedule the actual start set again. In this case, no compensation activities are run at all.

Work in different compensation spheres might interfere. For example, an activity of a compensation sphere which is actually aborted might have produced an output container that provided input for an activity in another compensation sphere. The latter compensation sphere might be aborted too because it presumably performed work based on incorrect data. Whether the abort of a compensation sphere should cascade to other compensation spheres in this sense is specified as the *proliferation* property of a compensation sphere.

Activities, too, have properties impacting the behavior of aborting compensation spheres. For example, an activity within a compensation sphere might be a process activity. Like any other activity, the process activity has a compensation activity assigned. The nesting property of a process activity specifies whether the compensation activity immediately assigned with a process activity should be run when discrete compensation is requested, or whether compensation of a process activity should be performed by pushing the abort request down into the subprocess. In the latter case, the abort of all compensation spheres of the corresponding subprocess is requested. The nesting is called *deep* if compensation is pushed down; otherwise, it is called *shallow*.

The Flow Definition Language must be extended to provide for the specification of compensation spheres and their properties. Code Example 7.2 shows the definition of the compensation sphere in the trip reservation example.

Code Example 7.2 Compensation Sphere Definition

```
COMPENSATION_SPHERE 'Reservations'
    RELATED_ACTIVITIES   'Flight Reservation',
                         'Hotel Reservation',
                         'Car Reservation',
                         'Confirm Reception',
                         'Get Itinerary'
    NO RELATED_COMPENSATION_ACTIVITY
    GRANULARITY DISCRETE
    MODE RETRY
    PROLIFERATION CASCADE

END 'Reservations'
```

The COMPENSATION_SPHERE clause defines a compensation sphere and gives it a name, Reservations in the figure. As in atomic spheres, the RELA-TED_ACTIVITIES keyword begins the list of activities that are part of the compensation sphere. In the figure, the Reservations compensation sphere contains the activities Flight Reservation, Hotel Reservation, Car Reservation, Confirm Reception, and Get Itinerary.

The GRANULARITY keyword indicates how compensation is being carried out. If DISCRETE is specified, as in the figure, discrete compensation is performed; if GLOBAL is defined, global compensation is performed. The MODE keyword specifies how the workflow management system should carry out the backout processing of the compensation sphere. Valid values are RETRY, UNDO, and RERUN. The PROLIFERATION keyword indicates how the workflow management system should treat dependent compensation spheres if the compensation sphere is aborted.

The name of a compensation activity that is associated with the compensation sphere is identified by the RELATED_COMPENSATION_ACTIVITY keyword followed by the name of the activity. The parameter NO preceding the keyword indicates that the compensation sphere has no associated compensation activity.

To associate compensation activities with the activities of a compensation sphere, the RELATE_COMPENSATION_ACTIVITY keyword is provided to be used within PROGRAM_ACTIVITY and PROCESS_ACTIVITY clauses. Code Example 7.3 shows the assignment of the Cancel Flights activity as a compensation activity to the Flight Reservation activity.

Code Example 7.3 Assignment of Compensation Activity

```
PROGRAM_ACTIVITY 'Flight Reservation'
  RELATED_COMPENSATION_ACTIVITY 'Cancel Flights'
END 'Flight Reservation'
```

For process activities, an additional keyword COMPENSATION_MODE can be specified, as shown in Code Example 7.4.

Code Example 7.4 Definition of Compensation Mode

```
PROCESS_ACTIVITY 'Contact Customer'
  COMPENSATION_MODE DEEP
END 'Contact Customer'
```

Compensation activities have input containers just as any other activities do. This container can be perceived as a separate *compensation container* associated with the proper activity. When the data flow is defined within a process model, data connectors might be used to specify the materialization of a compensation container in case the compensation activity is run. In particular, the output container as well as the input container of an activity might be used to pass data to the associated compensation container. For example, a debit function used to compensate a credit function may receive a copy of the input container passed to the credit function when invoked. Refer to [Ley95a] for more technical details.

Note that the same activities that make up an atomic sphere might also make up a compensation sphere, so that atomic spheres that have already been committed can be undone. A process model can include atomic spheres as well as compensation spheres, and some atomic spheres and compensation spheres might be identical. This mixture of global transaction technique and compensation-based recovery results in a flexible unit of work concept for workflows. Workflows that include such units of work are sometimes called *business transactions*.

Finally, note that in practice compensation actions—that is the abort of a compensation sphere—are most often explicitly requested by human beings. This reflects the fact that workflows often run for a very long time, possibly producing something with a high value for a company. If the workflow management system would trigger compensation by itself and perform compensation automatically, this value might be lost. A human being might be able to save a lot of this value by carefully specifying at runtime on a case-by-case basis what to compensate and how to compensate. What to compensate can be influenced by overwriting the retry mode property of a compensation sphere with rerun, or by overwriting the cascade proliferation property with restrict, for example. How to compensate can be influenced by overwriting the nesting property of a subprocess to deep, allowing for a much more fine-grained compensation than with shallow nesting, for example.

7.5.4 The Mechanics of Compensation Spheres

In this section, we define the notion of a compensation sphere more precisely. Note that we do not provide a comprehensive set of formal definitions covering all about compensation spheres. This would require us to replicate or modify a large part of Chapter 4. Instead, we focus on new formal aspects of compensation spheres, omitting subjects like data flow aspects of compensation.

Compensation spheres are nonempty sets of activities that can be requested to be collectively undone either by invoking their associated compensation activities in reverse order or by invoking the compensation activity associated with the compensation sphere itself. To define this more precisely we have to introduce the notion of reverse order and the pair structure of activities within compensation spheres.

Definition Let G be a process model graph with node set N and edge set E. We denote by $P^{-1} = (N, E^{-1})$ the graph with the following edge set:

$$(A, B, 1) \in E^{-1} :\Leftrightarrow (B, A, p) \in E$$

The graph P^{-1} is derived from P by reversing the edges and ignoring transition conditions. The transition conditions of the edges of P are ignored in P^{-1} because the edges of P are only needed to provide an order for scheduling compensation activities. No business rules (i.e., transition conditions) restrict the selection of which activities to compensate because all activities that run within the compensation sphere must be compensated.

Definition   Let $S \subseteq N, S \neq \emptyset$ be called *compensatable* iff each $A \in S$ consists of a pair $A = (A^p, A^c)$. A^p represents the proper activity, and A^c represents the compensation activity associated with A. $S^p := \pi_1(S)$ is the set of all proper activities of S, and $S^c := \pi_2(S)$ is the set of all compensation activities of S.

We denote by E_S the edge set induced on S^c by P^{-1}:

- $A, B \in S \wedge (A, B, 1) \in E^{-1} \Rightarrow (A^c, B^c, 1) \in E_S,$

  that means, two nodes of S^c which are already directly connected as activities in P^{-1} are also directly connected as compensating activities by E_S,

- $(A, B \in S \wedge (A, B, 1) \notin E^{-1} \wedge$
  $(\exists A_1, \ldots, A_n \notin S : (A, A_1, 1), \ldots, (A_n, B, 1) \in E^{-1})) \Rightarrow (A^c, B^c, 1) \in E_S$,

  that means that two nodes of S^c, which are not directly connected as activities in P^{-1} but which are reachable in P^{-1} via a directed path that does not include other activities from S, are directly connected as compensating activities in E_S,

- No other elements are in E_S.

  Then, $\overrightarrow{S} := (S^c, E_S)$ is called the *compensation graph* associated with S.

■

Figure 7.16 on the facing page illustrates this definition.

The left-hand side of Figure 7.16 shows a graph P together with a compensation sphere S. In the middle of the figure the graph P^{-1}, which results from reversing the edges of P, is depicted. The right-hand side shows the compensation graph $\overrightarrow{S}$ associated with S. Dark-colored nodes indicate the compensation activities S^c of S. This graph is induced by P^{-1} on S^c.

J and I are directly connected by an edge in P^{-1}, thus, a corresponding edge appears in E_S. The same is true for L and G. J is reachable from L via the directed path $L \to K, K \to J$, resulting in a corresponding edge in E_S. B is reachable from G via the path $G \to F, F \to E, E \to D, D \to C, C \to B$, which means that an edge (G,B,1) must be added to E_S. B is reachable from I via two different paths, namely $I \to H, H \to B$ and $I \to D, D \to C, C \to B$, resulting in an edge (I,B,1) in E_S.

Next, we have to define how to assign implementations to activities and compensation spheres; the implementations are to be used when a compensation sphere is requested to abort.

Figure 7.16 Inducing Graph Structures on Compensation Spheres

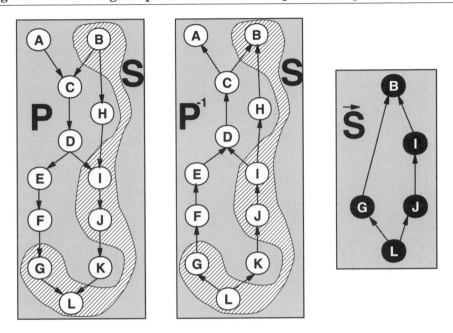

Definition   Let G be a process model graph and N its set of activities. The map

$$\kappa : N \cup (\wp(N) - \emptyset) \to \mathcal{E} \cup \{NOP\}$$

is called *compensation map*. It associates with each activity and each nonempty set of activities of G a so-called *compensation implementation*.

∎

Finally, we have to enhance the compensation graph $\vec{S}$ associated with a compensation sphere S to become a process model graph $P\left(\vec{S}\right)$ that can be instantiated by the workflow management system. For this purpose we do the following.

1. Define $\Psi(A^c) := \kappa(A)$; that means for each compensation activity A^c, the associated activity implementation is $\kappa(A)$.

2. Allow that an exit condition $\varepsilon(A^c)$ is assigned to each compensation activity.

3. Allow that a staff assignment $\Omega(A^c)$ is associated with each compensation activity.

4. Define the join condition assigned to a compensation activity in $\overrightarrow{S}$; the join condition is simply the disjunction of incoming transition conditions (which are constant true anyway).

5. Allow that a compensation container $\iota(A^c)$ is associated with each compensation activity, and so on.

Now, we are ready to define compensation spheres.

Definition   Let G be a process model graph and N its set of activities. Let $S \subseteq N$, $S \not\subseteq \emptyset$, and let $i \in \mathbb{N}$ denote a point in time. Then,

$$^iS := S \cap \omega_i^{-1}(\{\text{completed}, \text{terminated}, \text{activated}\})$$

denotes the set of activities of S that have been activated until time i. S is called a *compensation sphere* $\Leftrightarrow$

1. S is compensatable.

2. When S is requested to abort at time i, then either

    (a) $P\left(\overrightarrow{^iS}\right)$ will be executed, or

    (b) $\kappa(S)$ will be executed.

■

Note that if S is compensatable. then ^iS is compensatable too. Thus, the compensation graph $P\left(\overrightarrow{^iS}\right)$ is well defined and thus so too is the process model graph. It might be perceived that a compensation sphere S is aborted at time i by creating the process model $P\left(\overrightarrow{^iS}\right)$ on-the-fly and instantiating it (discrete compensation), or that simply the implementation $\kappa(S)$ is run (global compensation).

There are no syntactical constraints on compensation spheres. Compensation spheres might intersect, a compensation sphere might include other ones, the subgraph induced by the nodes of a compensation sphere S might consist of multiple connected components, and so on.

Because there are no restrictions in grouping activities into compensation spheres, the work performed in different compensation spheres might interfere. As a result, when one compensation sphere aborts, other compensation spheres might be affected and have to be aborted too. This is called *cascading abort*.

For example, if the compensation sphere S1 in Figure 7.17 is requested to abort, it might happen that B completed and that D has already been activated. In this situation, the abort of S1 should be cascaded to S4 because all work performed in S1 is detected to be incorrect and consequently, D was possibly given incorrect input data. If D has not been activated yet, there is no reason to cascade compensation. This means that whether an abort has to be cascaded cannot be determined simply on the basis of structural dependencies but must be determined at runtime.

Figure 7.17 Structural Dependencies Possibly Resulting in Cascading Abort

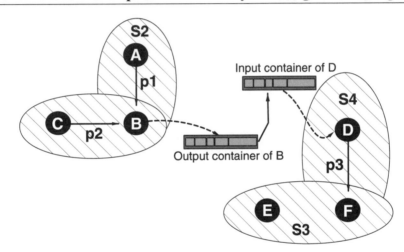

This determination may turn out to become complex. If B completed and transition condition p1 has been true, then the completion of A contributed to the activation of B somehow. Because S1 is requested to abort, B has been inferred to have performed incorrectly, and the work performed and represented by A possibly contributed to this incorrectness. Thus, A might have been performed incorrectly too, resulting in the need to abort S2 also. Similarly, depending on the state in compensation sphere S4, cascading to S3 might become necessary. More details can be found in [Ley95a].

Definition   If $G = (V, \iota, o, N, \Psi, \mathcal{C}, \Omega, \varepsilon, E, \Phi, \Delta, \vec{\Delta})$ is a process model graph, we denote by $\mathcal{R}(N) \subseteq \wp(N) - \emptyset$ the set of all compensation spheres and by $\mathcal{G}(N) \subseteq \wp(N) - \emptyset$ the set of all atomic spheres defined within G. To include business units of work or business transactions, respectively, we have to extend the definition of a process model graph to include the components $\mathcal{R}(N)$, $\mathcal{G}(N)$, and κ. A process model graph is then a tuple

$$G = (V, \iota, o, N, \Psi, \mathcal{C}, \Omega, \varepsilon, E, \Phi, \Delta, \overrightarrow{\Delta}, \mathcal{R}(N), \kappa, \mathcal{G}(N))$$

∎

The operational semantics must be adapted accordingly; this subject is outside of the scope of our book.

7.6   Phoenix Behavior

Ideally, when a workflow management system crashes for whatever reason and is restarted, all workflows active at the time of the crash resume their processing wherever they have been at the time when the crash occurred. The workflow management system has to provide all the necessary functionality to allow a workflow to "recover out of the ashes" after a restart (the similarity to phoenix in Egyptian or Greek mythology resulted in the nice name for this behavior—see [GR93]).

This kind of recovery has two major aspects. First, the workflow itself as an instance of a process model (i.e., the navigation processing itself) must be recoverable. Recoverability is achieved with persistent contexts for workflows, as discussed below. Second, the implementations of the activities must be included in the recovery processing of the workflow. The corresponding concept of safe activities is also introduced below.

7.6.1   Recoverable Workflows

In most environments such as database management systems or TP monitors, all units of work (i.e., transactions) active at the time of a crash are completely undone as part of the restart processing after the crash. This behavior is based on the assumption that the hosted units of work are short-running and the cost to repeat them after restart of the environment is low.

But workflows typically represent long-running units of work. Such a unit of work comprises many activities, each of which might involve human agents performing pieces of work contributing to the overall cost of a workflow. Thus, it is too expensive to undo a workflow as a whole whenever a system crash occurs. Undoing a complete workflow would force all the pieces of work already completed up to the time of the crash to be redone, which would mean this work would have to be performed twice. Besides the associated labor costs, performing work twice might jeopardize integrity since some activities are non-redoable because of their effects on the real world; for example, successful transfer of money should not be repeated.

The underpinning that eliminates the need to redo workflows is a persistent context that the workflow management system maintains for each workflow. This context is stored in the database management system used by the workflow management system (i.e., it is persistent), and it represents all relevant data about each workflow (see Figure 7.18). Whenever a workflow relevant event occurs, such as the completion of an activity, or the creation of workitems, the workflow management system updates the context database accordingly. Because the components of the workflow management system are typically distributed, the workflow-relevant events must be signaled in a recoverable manner, for example by using reliable messaging for communication between the components of the workflow management system (see sections 9.5 on page 323 and 10.2 on page 364). The context database is updated within transactions, and these transactions must process events and their corresponding context updates within the same transaction boundary. (See again section 9.5 on page 323 for the related technique of "message integrity"). This technique makes sure that each workflow-relevant event of which the workflow management system is aware (see below!) is finally reflected appropriately in the context database (**1**).

Figure 7.18 Persistent Contexts of Workflows Used in Recovery

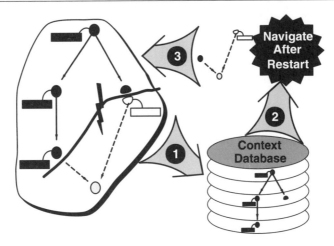

In case of a system crash, the context of each workflow is available in the workflow management system's database after restart. Thus, it is known for each single workflow which activities have already been completed, which activities are currently active, which activities are on whose workitems awaiting execution; the output containers of all completed activities are available as the base for materializing input containers of activities to be scheduled in the future. (**2**). The workflow state is recoverable. In particular, none of the already completed activities of a workflow have to be redone, and none of the activities awaiting execution have been lost. After restart, navigation resumes where it has been left (**3**).

But what about an activity that has been active at the time of the crash, such as the activity torn apart in Figure 7.18? When the workflow management system recovers, the state of the activity is still "activated" in the context database. Two main cases need to be distinguished:

1. The activity implementation is also affected by the crash.

   If the implementation is not a transaction, the presumably partial effects the implementation already had made must be analyzed. Depending on this analysis, the activity might be compensated and redone, or might be resumed, or some other action taken.

   If the implementation is a transaction, it automatically aborts during restart of its underlying resource manager, recreating the last consistent state of the underlying resources. Thus, the activity could be redone without jeopardizing any consistency of the resources manipulated by the implementation.

   In any case, the workflow management system must be able to force changes in the state of the activity to allow its restart, compensation, or resumption.

2. The activity implementation is not affected by the crash.

   If the execution component that launched the implementation is still running, processing can simply proceed. Otherwise, if this execution component failed, the following distinctions must be made:

   - As before, if the implementation is not a transaction, the effects the implementation had in the meantime must be analyzed and appropriate actions must be taken.

   - If the implementation is a transaction, it must be determined whether the transaction whether has committed or aborted while the execution component was down. If the transaction had committed, it must not be redone; if the transaction had aborted, it must be redone. When it is still active it should be forced to abort because the whole environment is suspicious. After that it can be redone.

   Again, the workflow management system must be able to request the appropriate state changes to proceed appropriately.

None of the interventions that are required for activity implementations that are not transactions can be avoided. Transactions were invented to avoid such interventions! If the activity implementation is a transaction and is affected by the crash, the recovery behavior is well defined from the very beginning. So, the situation that remains and that requires support from the workflow management system is the failure of the execution component that launched the transaction implementing the active activity.

In theory, this situation can be resolved by including the user-provided transaction into the internal transaction processing of the workflow management system resulting in a single global transaction (see section 10.5.8 on page 384). If the internal transaction fails, in particular if the execution component fails, the user transaction is automatically aborted and must be redone.

In a nutshell, within this global transaction the workflow management system materializes the input container for the implementation to be launched, changes the state of the activity to "activated.", and communicates with the responsible execution component to launch the user provided transaction. Then, the transaction itself runs. Upon completion, the output container is sent to the workflow server. The workflow server stores that container into the workflow management system's database, checks the activity's exit condition, updates the state of the activity accordingly, if appropriate it continues navigating through the underlying process model, and produces workitems. Because of the negative impact of such a long transaction on the overall throughput this approach cannot even be considered in practice. Instead, as we show in section 10.5.8 on page 384, the required transaction can be run as a "stratified transaction."

7.6.2 Atomicity Versus Ensured Execution

The basic idea behind what is called a *stratified transaction* is the following one. The atomic property of a collection of operations can be satisfied by different subsets of the collection at different points in time. This means that in many situations it is not necessary that all operations are carried out at the same time. It is sufficient if guaranteed that eventually all operations have been carried out, perhaps at different points in time.

In fact, this situation occurs frequently in practice. When money is transferred between two accounts at different banks, the money is debited from the source account at a different time than the money is credited to the target account. What happens is that the first bank runs the debit transaction and sends a message to the second bank, requesting it to credit the amount to the target account. When the message is received by the second bank, the credit transaction is run against the target account.

To make this work recoverable, a reliable messaging system, as discussed in section 9.4.2 on page 319, is needed. Such a messaging system makes sure that a message eventually arrives in its destination queue once the messaging system acknowledged the reception of the message. Furthermore, the messaging system behaves as a resource manager allowing messages to be manipulated in queues

Figure 7.19 A Sample Stratified Transaction

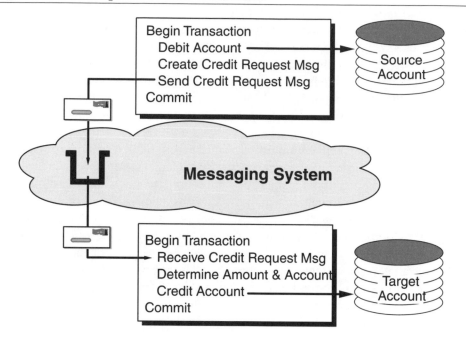

within global transactions. This allows the combination of database operations and message operations into a single transaction, as exemplified in Figure 7.19.

The example in Figure 7.19 shows the transfer of money. The transfer is realized by two programs chained together by a reliable message queuing system. The program at the top establishes a global transaction, and within this transaction, it debits the source account and submits a message to the input queue of the program at the bottom, requesting the matching credit action.

Both the database management system holding the source account and the message queuing system responsible for message delivery are resource managers participating in the global transaction. Thus, when the debit program ends the transaction, it is guaranteed that both transactions—the database update debiting the source account and the submission of the credit request message—commit or abort. For example, If the database management system detects an error when asked to prepare for commit, it aborts its subtransaction. As a result, the subtransaction run by the messaging system aborts too, and the credit request message is not delivered. Or, if the message queuing system detects that it cannot deliver the credit request message, it aborts, and as a consequence the debit update is undone by the database management system. When the global transaction commits, the source account has been debited and the message queuing system has acknowledged that it can deliver the credit request message.

Once the message arrives in the input queue of the credit program at the bottom of Figure 7.19, this program receives the credit request message and performs the corresponding updates on the target account within another global transaction. If, for example, the database management system fails to perform the update of the target account, the subtransaction associated with the message retrieval is aborted too. The credit request message is restored in the input queue of the credit program, and the program retries to process the message until it finally succeeds.

Delivering a message to its destination queue may take some time: seconds, minutes, or even longer. Thus, there is no guarantee how long the delivery process takes. However, there is the guarantee that the message is eventually delivered once its reception is acknowledged by the messaging system. See section 9.5.1 on page 323 for details and exceptions. This guaranteed delivery behavior is used in the example to chain the two transactions together.

From an abstract point of view, the technique behind this idea is the following one. The set of all operations of both transactions must be performed or none of the operations at all. This all-or-nothing property can be achieved by splitting the operations into two sets, as discussed later, and guaranteeing that whenever one set of operations is successfully performed, the other set of operations succeeds also. The guarantee is based on two premises. First, the request to execute the second set of operations is issued as a message that is guaranteed to be delivered to the second set of operations if and only if the first set of operations committed. Second, both sets of operations guarantee to maintain message integrity; that means the submission of the message is part of the first set of operations and the reception of the message is part of the second set. This technique of tying two transactions together based on guaranteed message delivery and maintenance of message integrity is sometimes referred to as *transaction chaining*.

7.6.3 Stratified Transactions

In this section, we generalize the concept of transaction chaining to *transaction stratification* [Ley97]. The situation we are dealing with is a given set of transactional programs that must be tied into a unit of work with all-or-nothing behavior; within the definition below, $T = \{t_1, \ldots, t_n\}$ is this set of transactional programs. One possible way to achieve this tie is to build a global transaction with the elements of T as subtransactions. As discussed before, this solution is not always possible in practice.

Thus, based on various criteria, the set T of given transactional programs (transactions, for short) is partitioned into smaller sets of transactional programs; within the definition below, $\mathcal{T} = \{T_1, \ldots, T_k\}$ represents such a partitioning (conditions 1.a, 1.b and 1.c), where each T_i is a subset of transactional programs from T (condition 1). Each set of transactions T_i is run as a global transaction (condition 1.5), called a *stratum*. These global transactions are tied together by means of transaction chaining. For this purpose, each stratum T_i has an input queue associated with it (condition 1.4). From this input queue, one subtransaction receives a request message (condition 2.a.b) that has been submitted by another global transaction (condition 2.a.i). The structure induced on the global transactions is that of a tree (condition 2.b). Figure 7.20 depicts a possible stratification of a given set of transactions.

Figure 7.20 A Stratified Transaction

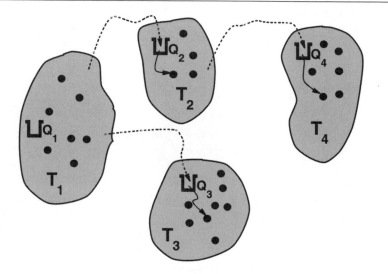

Definition   Let $T = \{t - 1, \dots, t_n\}$ be a set of transactions. $\mathcal{Z} = (\mathcal{T}, \mathcal{M})$ is called a *stratification* of T (or a *stratified transaction* with basis T) $:\Leftrightarrow$

1. $\mathcal{T} = \{T_1, \dots, T_k\} \subseteq \wp(T)$ with

    (a) $\forall\, 1 \leq i \leq k : T_i \neq \emptyset$,

    (b) $\forall\, 1 \leq i, j \leq k : i \neq j \Rightarrow T_i \cap T_j = \emptyset,$

    (c) $\bigcup\limits_{i=1}^{k} T_i = T,$

    (d) $\forall\, 1 \leq i \leq k : T_i$ is associated with a queue Q_i ,

    (e) $\forall\, 1 \leq i \leq k : T_i$ is a global transaction.

2. $\mathcal{M} \subseteq \mathcal{T} \times \mathcal{T}$ with

    (a) $(T_i, T_j) \in \mathcal{M} \Leftrightarrow$

        i. $\exists!\, t \in T_i : t$ puts a message into Q_i,

  ii. $\exists! \, s \in T_j$: s gets a message from Q_j,

(b) $\mathcal{M}$ induces a tree structure on $\mathcal{T}$.

A global transaction $T_i \in \mathcal{T}$ is called a *stratum*.

∎

Note that because of property (1.5), either all transactions of a stratum commit or all transactions of a stratum abort. We assume that the transactions of a stratum are controlled by an atomic commit protocol. In particular, the put and get operations on the queues Q_j in property (2.a.i) and (2.a.b) are operations that are included within the transaction boundaries of the corresponding stratum. This means they are committed or aborted with all of the transactions of a stratum, and thus message integrity is ensured.

If the root stratum commits, all other strata commit too; that means a stratified transaction has all-or-nothing behavior. This conclusion is reached inductively. When the root stratum commits, the request messages sent to its child strata will finally be delivered. Once such a message gets delivered into a child stratum's input queue, it is eventually retrieved from that stratum by a transaction and processed; if the processing fails, the message reappears in the queue of the stratum and processing will be retried. When the child stratum commits its processing, the original request message is gone from its input queue and the request messages it sent in turn to its children will finally be delivered, and so on. Eventually, all leaf strata commit, and the overall stratified transaction succeeds. Note that this proof depends on the assumption that each stratum eventually commits. This assumption could be false in practice. A request message could be "poisoned" so it could not be processed at all (see section 9.4.2 on page 319). This exceptional situation must be resolved manually in a way similar to in-doubt situations that can occur in distributed transactions in practice today.

There are many situations where stratifying a given set of transactions is beneficial. For example:

- The transactions to be run in all-or-nothing behavior are located on different nodes. The transaction managers available on these nodes might not be able to participate in a two-phase commit protocol. A stratified transaction in which the transactions on each node are grouped into a stratum can resolve this situation.

- Although the environment supports two-phase commit, the global transactions across machine boundaries result in network traffic caused by the message complexity of the two-phase commit protocol might not be tolerable. A stratified transaction with strata not spanning machine boundaries might be appropriate.

- The number of transactions per stratum is less than the total number of transactions that must be run together in all-or-nothing mode. Thus, each stratum commits sooner, resulting in earlier releases of locks by the underlying resource managers. As a consequence, the overall throughput might be better than when the overall collection of transactions is run as a single global transaction.

- The response time that a requestor experiences is that of the root stratum. If requester response time is critical, stratifying a collection of transactions so that the root stratum commits very fast helps. For example, the root stratum simply transforms the request into a message, submits it to the messaging middleware, and commits.

7.6.4 Safe Activities

An activity is called a *safe* activity if its implementation is a transactional program that is included in the internal transaction processing of the workflow management system. This inclusion can be achieved by appropriate stratification of the set of transactions consisting of the activity implementation, the message manipulations of the execution component that launches the activity implementation, and the corresponding internal transactions of the workflow server. This is discussed in detail in section 10.5.8 on page 384.

Recall that a transactional program manipulates recoverable resources and does not establish its own transaction boundaries, and especially does not itself request a commit. When the workflow management system crashes during the execution of a safe activity, the activity implementation will be automatically aborted, and the activity can be redone after the workflow management system has restarted. As consequence, a workflow that has only safe activities has phoenix behavior. After a crash, the workflow can resume processing where it was interrupted.

Chapter 8

Advanced Usage

We have already sketched in Chapter 1 how workflow can add some attractive features to project management. There are many more examples where workflow technology could supplement or even improve other information system technologies. In this chapter, we show more examples where workflow technology could add value.

8.1 Monitoring Dynamic Integrity Rules

The integrity of data [FSW81] is vital for all enterprises. Inconsistent data may result in wrong decisions and eventually the loss of significant amounts of money. Integrity has three different aspects: (1) *operational* integrity deals with the synchronization of concurrent access to the data, (2) *physical* integrity protects from loss of data due to media failures, and (3) *semantic* integrity ensures that the data complies with the appropriate business rules.

Small and large enterprises have for many years relied on the industrial strength and robustness of commercial database management systems [BS95a] to ensure the operational and physical integrity of their data. A few years ago, commercial database management systems also started to support the means to specify and ensure a broad range of semantical integrity rules (from entity integrity over referential integrity to check-constraints and triggered actions [BS95a]. As shown in Figure 8.1 semantic integrity rules can be categorized as static, transitional, and dynamic semantic integrity rules.

Static semantic integrity rules ensure the validity of each single database state; for example, an employee's salary must not exceed the manager's salary.

Transitional semantic integrity rules refer to two consecutive database states thereby ensuring the validity of the transition from an existing particular database state to the next one; for example, an employee's salary must always increase.

Figure 8.1 Classification of Semantic Integrity Rules

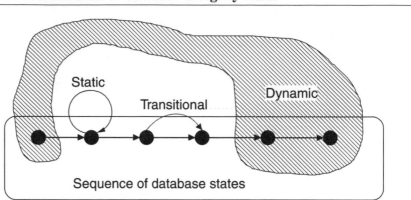

Dynamic semantic integrity rules refer to two or more database states out of a whole series of database states, ensuring the validity of the corresponding transitions; for example, an employee can only be promoted if the appropriate job code has been increased before.

State changes of databases are typically performed by running transactions. A transaction is a unit of database manipulations that together transform the database from one consistent state to another consistent state [BN97]. Static and transitional integrity rules both deal with *single* transactions. Static integrity rules determine whether the database state produced by the transaction is valid; transitional integrity rules control the relation between the database state when the transaction began and the database state when the transaction ended. Dynamic integrity rules deal with *multiple* transactions; they control the ordering of the set of transactions as well as the corresponding collection of database states. Based on the number of affected transactions, static and transitional integrity rules are collectively referred to as *intra-transaction* integrity rules and dynamic integrity rules are referred to as *inter-transaction* integrity rules.

For monitoring intra-transaction integrity rules, only the database state at the beginning of the transaction and the data modified by the transaction are needed to perform the required validations. The appropriate implementation techniques, such as locking and logging [BN97], are well understood and can be considered mature. This maturity of understanding is by far not true for inter-transaction integrity rules. They are not well understood; their implementation requires extensive modifications to the internals of the database; they can be bypassed easily by the application programmer. Database management systems therefore focus today on integrity issues related with single transactions.

8.1.1 How Workflow Can Help

Workflow management systems can easily help the database management system in the support for inter-transaction semantic rules. The necessary changes to the database management system are minimal. It involves just the addition of a few exits to the database management system that hook the workflow management system to the database management system.

Figure 8.2 shows the three entities that are involved in checking the semantic integrity rule; that means checking whether sequences of transactions are valid or not.

Figure 8.2 Components

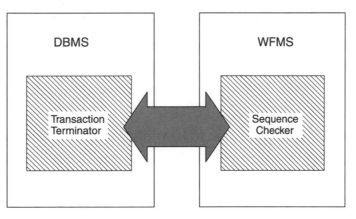

First, a system is needed to decide on the outcome of a transaction (*transaction terminator*). This means the system decides if a transaction terminates successfully (commit) or not (rollback). If it is detected that committing a transaction would produce an invalid sequence of transactions, the transaction is aborted. A transaction that does not run successfully is treated as if it has never run.

Examples of such a system are database management systems, TP monitors, or transaction managers; the last are needed in the case of global transactions. We use a database system as the transaction terminator because most transactions manipulate data as part of their transaction.

Second, a system is needed to check about valid sequences of transactions (*sequence checker*). This requires that the system knows about all valid sequences of transactions and that it keeps a history of all relevant transaction executions so that it can check that a particular transaction forms a valid sequence together with all associated past transactions.

This role is subsumed by the workflow management system since it provides exactly the desired functionality, such as controlling the sequence of executables according to a prescribed model. In addition, it offers tools to easily make that definition.

Third, a *communication mechanism* is needed to manage the communication between both systems on the state of transactions and the validity of their sequencing.

This mechanism depends on the functional capabilities of the transaction terminator. We have chosen a database management system as the transaction terminator, so appropriate database management functions are used.

This set of components allows to provide inter-transaction integrity rules support for database management systems. We show in the remainder of the section how this approach can be made to work by solving the following three major problems that need to be solved.

First, how can process models be used to check the validity of transaction sequences? Second, which protocol must be established between a transaction terminator and sequence checker to ensure only valid sequences of transactions? And third, how can existing database management systems and workflow management systems be exploited to make checking of valid transaction sequences as seamless as possible without assuming extensions to the database management system that would touch the kernel of the engine?

We assume the following notion of a transaction as a unit of work. A transaction consists of all data manipulations performed between its begin (BOT) and its end (EOT), which may be either commit or rollback. This definition of a transaction rules out the notion, sometimes found in practice, of a transaction as a series of data manipulations that can include any number of synchronization points. Each synchronization point is an EOT, and if more manipulations are to be performed by the same program, the first manipulation after an EOT (implicitly) establishes a BOT before performing the remaining manipulations ("chained programming model"). We therefore treat a collection of manipulations with multiple synchronization points as a series of transactions, where each synchronization point finishes a transaction and starts another one.

8.1.2   Inter-transaction Integrity Rules

An inter-transaction integrity rule actually defines a dependency between instances of services where each is realized by a transaction. A service, for example, that implements the funds transfer from account X to account Y with the amount Z can be requested to transfer 100 dollars from account 12345 to account 67890; the service in turn will perform the proper transfer by executing a corresponding transaction. Instead of talking about dependencies between instances of transactional services we will the common usage and ignore the difference between the service and the proper transaction, simply talking about dependencies of transactions.

As pointed out, we link the monitoring of intra-transaction integrity rules to workflow. To do this, we need to introduce an abstract model. As a first step, we define the concept of predecessor dependency between transactions. Finally we discuss the situation in which a particular transaction is governed by multiple inter-transaction integrity rules.

Predecessor Dependency

We assume the specification of dependencies between transactions t' and t, which we call predecessor dependencies. A predecessor dependency is of the abstract format (t',p,t). The semantics of such a dependency are that t cannot be started before t' has been performed successfully, which means terminated with commit, and the Boolean predicate p has been evaluated. Note that this condition is only a necessary condition for "it can be started" but not a sufficient condition: all predecessor dependencies having t in its third component are relevant.

The predecessor dependency (t',p,t) can be interpreted as a fragment of a directed graph. Both t' and t are two nodes of the graph, and a directed edge originating in t' and targeting in t exists in this graph; that means t' precedes t. In addition, the edge from t' to t is associated with the Boolean predicate p, called a *transition condition*; that means the graph is weighted.

Specification of a Rule

In general, a transaction t will depend on more than one single other transaction; that means there will be a whole set of predecessor dependencies $\{(t_i, p_i, t) | 1 \leq i \leq n\}$ with t as target. Of course, some of the predecessor transactions t_i will depend on other transactions, and t might be a predecessor transaction for another set of transactions. As a result, a whole graph will be specified, representing a complete inter-transaction integrity rule D.

Definition An inter-transaction integrity rule D is a collection of (semantically related) predecessor dependencies (t_i, p_{ij}, t_j): $D = \{(t_i, p_{ij}, t_j) \mid t_i, t_j \in T\}$, where T denotes the set of all transactions governed by the rule D and p_{ij} is a Boolean predicate. Thus, the set of all nodes of the graph D is the set of transactions **T** governed by D, and the set of weighted directed edges E of the graph D is a set $E = \subseteq T \times P \times T$, where P is the set of Boolean predicates called *transition conditions*.

■

It is obvious that D=(T,E) is equivalent to the control flow part of the PM graphs we introduced in Chapters 3 and 4. The operational semantics of PM graphs can be simply applied to the interpretation of the rule by use of transactions as the nodes (instead of activities). That means a transaction t can only be started if all transactions preceding t have committed or clearly will never run. If a predecessor t_i of t will never run, the associated transition condition is automatically set to false (we called this action "dead path elimination" in Chapters 3 and 4); otherwise, its value is computed base on the actual parameters of the dependency rule. Next, the *start condition* of t is relevant. This is a Boolean condition in the transition conditions associated with the incoming edges of t; that means it is a Boolean condition in the predicates $\pi_2(\{(t_i, p_{ij}, t_j) \in E \mid t_j = t\}$. As usual, if the start condition evaluates to true, the transaction t is allowed to be executed. The notion of exit conditions, which is available in the PM graphs is trivial in the case of inter-transaction integrity: if the transaction commits, the exit condition evaluates to true, if the transaction aborts, the exit condition evaluates to false. We assume that the transactions that are part of an inter-transaction rule D have the corresponding exit conditions assigned; that means exit conditions are implicitly specified.

Monitoring

We have shown that the specification of an inter-transaction integrity rule is equivalent to the specification of the control flow aspect of a process model. The workflow management system instantiates and manages the corresponding simple workflow triggered by the database management system. Each transaction is represented as an activity in the workflow. We call the workflow simple, since only the logic dimension is used and not the other two dimensions, the organization and information technology dimension. The database management system checks the validity of transaction executions by calling the workflow management system to inquire about the corresponding states of activities. If the activity that represents the transaction is ready, the transaction is allowed to run; if the activity is not ready, the transaction must not commit.

This description allows us to identify the components in Figure 8.2 as follows. The transaction management component of the database management system is the transaction terminator and the navigation of the workflow management system is the sequence checker.

Since many transactions belonging to many instances of the rule, can be carried out at the same time, each workflow instance needs to be identified uniquely by a rule instance identifier. The rule instance identifier must be supplied by each of the transactions that is part of an inter-transaction rule, A typical rule instance identifier could be an account number or a license plate number.

How exactly the inter-transaction integrity rules are enforced depends on the environment in which these transactions are executed and controlled. Figure 8.3 shows the three possible environments.

Figure 8.3 Transaction Invocation in Different Environments

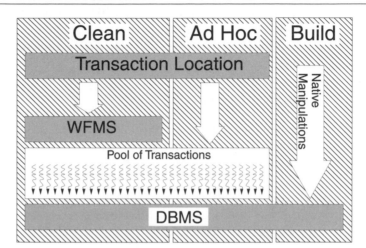

8.1.3   Clean Environment

In the *clean* environment all programs that modify a particular database are available from a pool of "precanned" transactions and are started by a workflow management system. The inter-transaction integrity rules for this database are therefore automatically enforced by the workflow management system. The worklists represent exactly all programs that are valid to be started; validity especially covers compliance with the control flow. The clean environment is the traditional processing mode of workflow management systems.

The database management system and the workflow management system must not establish any special relationship. Since all accesses to the data are initiated by the launching mechanism of the workflow management system, the only execution histories that will be produced by the workflow management system are the ones satisfying the inter-transaction integrity rules.

Clean environments exist today in many standard application areas. Vendors like SAP [SAP96] deliver their applications as a workflow-based application. All data access is performed through functions that are determined and presented by the workflow management system. More and more enterprises are implementing this paradigm. Since the associated databases are only accessed through functions controlled by the workflow management system, inter-transaction integrity monitoring is performed automatically.

8.1.4   Build Environment

A clean environment is rigid in the sense that it predefines the manipulations that can be performed on the database. The other extreme is a *build* environment. In such an environment, (sufficiently authorized) users can exploit native manipulations of the database management system, such as SQL, to access the database. In this case, transactions are built on-the-fly. In such an environment, it is not meaningful to monitor inter-transaction dependencies, since the transactions are not known in advance and thus cannot be constrained in advance.

8.1.5   Ad Hoc Environment

In the *ad hoc* environment, users are allowed to manipulate the database by directly invoking transactions from the pool of precanned transactions. Transactions are invoked without involving the launching facilities of the workflow management system. By use of interface outlined in Figure 8.2, inter-transaction integrity rules can nevertheless be enforced. Incidentally, it is possible to run a *mixed* environment; that means user can start precanned transactions directly from the pool or via the workflow management system.

8.1.6   How Transactions Work

Code Example 8.1 shows the function that the database management system invokes when a transaction is started. For simplicity, we assume that a transaction is only associated with only one rule and that the same transaction appears only once in a rule.

Code Example 8.1 Transaction Start

```
returnCode startTransaction(transaction t)
{
  returnCode = isHistoryValid(t, activity)
  select(returnCode)
    when returnCode = invalidHistory
       return 'invalid sequencing'
    when returnCode = noRule
       run t
    when returnCode = validHistory
       do
           checkOutInstance(activity)
           run t (syncpoint, outputData)
           checkInInstance(activity, synchPoint, outputData)
       end
  end
}
```

The function first verifies whether the transaction produces a valid execution history; that means it is allowed to be run. This verification is done by calling the function `isHistoryValid()`. If the transaction could not produce a valid history, the request is rejected, If the transaction is not bound by an inter-transaction rule, the transaction is allowed to run. Otherwise, `CheckOutInstance()`

checks out all activities that represent this particular transaction by using the check-out function of the workflow management system. This function puts the activity in the workflow management system into the running state, and the transaction is allowed to run. When the transaction completes, CheckInInstance() checks in the activity, passing into it synchronization point information and some output data produced by the transaction.

The passed synchronization point is the value for the exit condition to be checked by the workflow management system. As pointed out earlier, the exit condition checks whether the transaction has committed or rolled back. It is defined implicitly as SYNCPOINT = 'COMMIT'. When the transaction commits, the database management system passes in the value COMMIT for the sync point. Thus, the transaction can no longer be started again and the workflow management system continues navigating through the inter-transaction integrity rule. If the transaction rolls back, the database management system passes the value ROLLBACK for the sync point. This causes the activity to be put back into ready state, so that the transaction can be started again.

The function IsHistoryvalid(), shown in Code Example 8.2, determines whether the transaction produces a correct execution hsistory.

Code Example 8.2 Checking for Valid History

```
returnCode isHistoryValid(transaction t,
                          activity a)
{
  associatedRule R = GetRule(t)
  if associatedRule = empty
     return noRule

  returnCode = BindInstance(transaction t,
                            associatedRule R,
                            activity a)

  if returnCode = noRuleInstance
     return invalidHistory

  state = getState(a)

  if state not equal 'ready'
     return invalidHistory

  return validHistory
}
```

The first step is to use GetRule() to determine whether a rule is associated with the transaction. That means this function determines (implicitly) whether the transaction is a node in such a rule. If not, no further checking is necessary.

If the transaction is part of a rule, the database management system requests through the `BindInstance()` function to return the activity that is associated with the transaction. If no associated rules instance can be found, the transaction cannot be carried out. Otherwise, the state of the activity is determined by the function `GetState()`. If the activity is not in the ready state, then the transaction cannot be carried out; if in the ready state, the transaction can be started.

The function `BindInstance`, shown in Code Example 8.3, determines the instance of the workflow that represents the appropriate instance of the rule.

Code Example 8.3 Locate and Bind to Appropriate Workflow

```
returnCode BindInstance(transaction t, rule r, activity a)
{
  id = GetIdentifier(t);

  if t is startActivity(r)
     do
        instantiateWorkflow(r, id)
        a = startActivity
        return instanceBound
     end

  rc = matchId (id) ;

  if rc = notFound
     returnCode = noRuleInstance

  a = findActivity ()
  returnCode = instanceBound

}
```

The `GetIdentifier` function obtains the rule instance identifier as supplied by the transaction. If the transaction is a start activity in the rule, a new workflow is created by the `instantiateWorkflow()` function This function calls the appropriate create process function of the workflow management system with the rule name as the process template name and the identifier as the process name. This request causes the start activity to be put into the ready state. If the transaction is not represented by a start activity, the appropriate workflow with the identifier as name is looked up. This lookup is done by using the workflow management system's query process function. If no process can be located, an appropriate code is returned to the caller. If the activity is found, it is returned to the invoker together with a successful indicator.

8.1.7 The Ingredients Needed

The support of inter-transaction integrity rules in a database management system by means of a workflow management system can be implemented in several ways. In any case, the following three mechanics are needed:

- A mechanism that allows the database management system to detect that a transaction is part of an inter-transaction integrity rule. This detection can be done, for example, by representing a transaction as a plan within the database management system. The catalog then can associate all inter-transaction rules that affect the plan. This information is accessed by the `GetRules()` function. The relationship between the transaction and the activity can be kept in the workflow management system.

- A mechanism that identifies to the database management system which parameters need to be passed to the workflow management system. Those parameters are the parameters that are used in the transition conditions and the fields that make up the rule instance identifier. Several alternatives could be used to implement this mechanism. For static SQL, one could flag the appropriate host variable in the `DECLARE SECTION`; for dynamic SQL one could introduce special parameter markers or extend the SQLDA.

- A mechanism that calls the workflow management system for each transaction that is part of an inter-transaction integrity rule. This mechanism can be implemented in several ways. One way would be that the database management system provides appropriate exits that are invoked at appropriate points when a transaction is carried out. This is the approach we assumed earlier. Another way could be to generate appropriate triggers from the inter-transaction integrity rules.

8.1.8 Summary

We have already sketched the importance of making applications data and flow independent; we provide an in-depth discussion in Chapter 9. Extending the scope of the integrity rules that can be monitored in practice will very likely push the importance of the notion of *rule independence*. The benefits of extracting static and transitional integrity rules monitoring from applications and managing and enforcing them with a database management system has been traditionally argued as a means for making application development more productive. In addition to extracting these rules, extracting another broad class of rules—the inter-transaction rules—from the application and have these rules managed and enforced by a workflow management system will make application development even more productive. This productivity

Figure 8.4 Application Structure

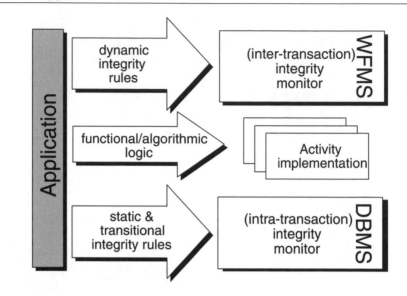

increase is mostly realized because rule-independent programs are more reusable, more stable, and more flexible. Figure 8.4 provides a different view of the application structure of workflow-based applications that we discuss in Chapter 9.

8.2   Software Distribution

Even in small enterprises, installation and update of software cannot be done without the support of some other software. The chances that the different workstations and servers are on different software levels and so can cause all kinds of problems are just too great. This is the domain of systems management systems, such as Tivoli's TME-10 [Incb] product. Incidentally, we use it in this chapter as the prototype of a systems management system. A systems management system performs, among many other system-related activities, the distribution and installation of software on any number of heterogenous target processors. This task includes not only full installations of software components but also upgrades. The specified target can be a single workstation to which the software must be distributed or can be sets of workstations that must be updated simultaneously.

To support this task, the systems management system maintains an asset database. It contains all users who have registered their software requirements, the actual software state on the appropriate processor, plus all the software that needs to be distributed as illustrated in Figure 8.5.

Figure 8.5 Software Distribution

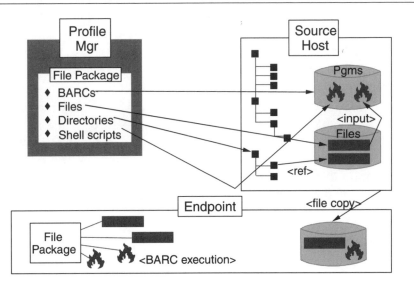

Figure 8.5 shows the fundamental entities and operations that are involved in the distribution and installation of software. Each piece of software that needs to be distributed is described by a file package. This package contains the BARC (Begin Action Rollback Commit) script that identifies the systems management system actions that need to be performed, the layout of the directory structure of the software, references to the files that need to be distributed, and appropriate shell scripts that perform the appropriate operating-system-specific installation. These file packages are managed by the profile manager, which also maintains profiles for each user and group. These profiles identify all the software components that a particular user or group needs and has installed. This profile is set up and maintained by the user or an administrative person. The actual software (code and data files) are maintained by the source host.

For example, if it is then the case that, for example, a software update needs to be applied, the systems management system queries all user profiles and determines those users that have it installed. Then, the appropriate data (code and data files) are copied from the source host to the target processor (end point), where they are installed by the appropriate installation facility, such as Install Shield when installing on a Windows NT system.

One of the difficulties is that there is no simple method to determine which piece of software at which level is needed by which user. Even though systems management systems provide the capability for users to maintain their own profile, this may not be a great help unless the users have the appropriate computer literacy. Things are further complicated if substitutes might perform work assigned to another user or if an authorized user transfers work form one user to another user by transferring the associated workitems. And things really get bad if users are engaged in many applications, changing jobs frequently, or if larger numbers of users are hired.

If applications are written as workflow-based applications, this situation can be solved by the combined knowledge maintained by the systems management system and the workflow management system. Figure 8.6 shows how the process information managed by the workflow management system is transformed into the software requirements that make up the user's profile in the systems management system so that the appropriate software can be copied onto the user's workstation.

Figure 8.6 Workflow-Controlled Software Distribution

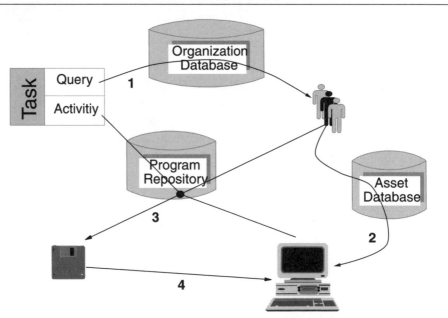

As shown in Figure 8.6, four distinct steps are needed to determine the users and appropriate software requirements for a particular activity within a process model. These steps must be repeated for each of the activities in a process model as well as for all process models.

Step **1** finds the users that can be selected to perform the activity. This selection is made by performing staff resolution for the activity, which is done by running the staff assignment query against the organizational database. Included in the query are also all substitutes, to make sure that they are also considered when software is distributed, and all users to whom the selected users can transfer workitems.

Step **2** uses the asset database of the systems management system to obtain the operating system and hardware address of the work station of each user that will be selected.

Step **3** determines the program object that is defined for the activity. Then, for each of the users, the appropriate executable that would be used by the user to carry out the activity is determined. The executable that is used to carry out the activity is determined by operating system installed on the user's work station as a determinate.

Step **4** assigns the selected executable to the user's profile.

The software requirements derived for one particular activity are combined with the software requirements of all other activities for all processes. This results in the total software requirements for all users.

The following small example is illustrates the described method for distributing software based on process models. We use the credit check activity within the loan process of a bank.

Code Example 8.4 shows the definition of this activity; the appropriate name is `Credit Limit Check`. The activity needs to be performed either by a `Corporate Credit Expert` or by a `Credit Expert` in the `Credit Check` department. The activity is performed by means of the program `Check Credit Limit`.

Code Example 8.4 Activity Definition with Staff Assignment

```
PROGRAM_ACTIVITY 'Credit Limit Check'
    PROGRAM 'Check Credit Limit'
    DONE_BY MEMBER OF ROLE  'Corporate Create Expert' OR
                            'Credit Expert'
    DONE_BY ORGANIZATION    'Credit Check'
END 'CreditLimitCheck'
```

As pointed out earlier, step 1 performs staff resolution for the specified staff assignment. Code Example 8.5 shows the definitions for the Credit Check department and the associated roles.

Code Example 8.5 Organization Database

```
ORGANIZATION 'Credit Check'
    MANAGER      'Thomas'
END 'CreditCheck'

PERSON 'Smith'
    LAST_NAME    'Smith'
    FIRST_NAME   'John'
    RELATED_ROLE             'Corporate Credit Expert'
    RELATED_ORGANIZATION  'Credit Check'
END 'Smith'

PERSON 'Taylor'
    LAST_NAME    'Taylor'
    FIRST_NAME   'Jack'
    RELATED_ROLE             'CreditExpert'
    RELATED_ORGANIZATION  'Credit Check'
END 'Taylor'

PERSON 'Thomas'
    LAST_NAME    'Thomas'
    FIRST_NAME   'Sally'
    RELATED_ROLE             'Manager'
    RELATED_ORGANIZATION  'Credit Check'
END 'Thomas'

ROLE 'Credit Expert'
ROLE 'Corporate Credit Expert'
ROLE 'Manager'
```

The department has three members: the manager Sally Thomas; the corporate credit expert, John Smith; and the credit expert, Jack Taylor. Based on the staff assignment, John and Jack qualify for the activity and may have the task assigned during process execution.

For Jack and John, step 2 is performed. The asset database is queried to determine their workstations, including the operating system that is installed on them.

Code Example 8.6 on the facing page shows the definitions for John's and Jack's workstation. The workstations are identified by the names PC4713 and PC4714, respectively.

Code Example 8.6 Workstation Definitions in Asset Database

```
WORKSTATION 'PC4713'
      TYPE            PII
      MEMORY          128
      USER            'Smith'
      OPSYS           'NT'
      SERVER          'PC4712'
      CONNECTION      'TCP/IP'
END 'PC4713'

WORKSTATION 'PC4714'
      TYPE            Power
      MEMORY           128
      USER            'Taylor'
      OPSYS           'AIX'
      SERVER          'PC4712'
      CONNECTION      'TCP/IP'
END 'PC4714'
```

Using the operating system information, the workflow management system's repository is queried to determine which executables are needed. This is step 3 of the described approach.

Code Example 8.7 shows the definition of the program `Check Credit Limit` in the program registry. `123.EXE` is used for the Windows NT environment; `ABC.EXE` for the AIX environment.

Code Example 8.7 Program Registry

```
PROGRAM 'CheckCreditLimit'
   WINNT
      EXE
            PATH_AND_FILENAME '123.EXE'

   AIX
      EXE
            PATH_AND_FILENAME  'ABC.EXE'
END 'CheckCreditLimit'
```

In the final step, the two executables are registered in the appropriate user profiles that are managed by the systems management system's profile manager.

The described method is applicable to a wide range of scenarios, adding a new process, adding a new user, or modifying a process. In fact, the method could even be used if an application can be described by workflow technology; it is not required that the application itself be deployed as a workflow-based application.

8.3   Security Management

We showed in the previous section that workflow technology can be used to provide efficient code distribution. The same technique can be used to grant the correct access rights to the right people.

Figure 8.7 shows an example of the relationships between the activities in a process model, the roles performing the activities, the implementations associated with the activities, and the privileges a role must have to carry out these implementations.

Figure 8.7 Security Management

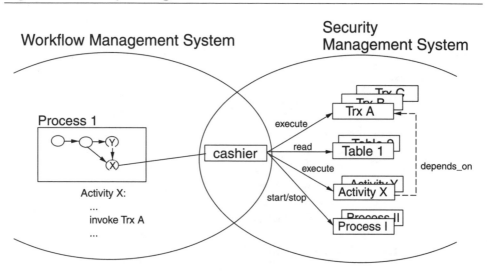

As shown, activity X in a process is carried out by the role of cashier and the invocation of transaction A. This means that transaction X represents the activity implementation of activity A. To allow the transaction to be executed, the role must have appropriate privileges defined in the transaction system. If the transaction system does not support the notion of roles, the appropriate users must be authorized.

It is obvious that the activity implementations are carried out by a multitude of systems. These include the native operating systems such as Windows NT or AIX, TP monitors such as CICS or IMS, or object request brokers. Most of them supply their own security facility; only a few rely on some external security system such as DCE.

A user must therefore be defined to a number of systems with the proper security privileges. This task is cumbersome because each system provides its own proprietary way of requesting changes such as registering users, updating passwords, or changing access privileges. Note that this is true regardless of whether the applications are workflow-based or not.

Security management systems have been developed to ease this task. They provide for the definition and maintenance of groups to which individual users are assigned. Typical groups are organizational structures such as roles. For each group, the appropriate access rights to the various applications are registered. When a new user is added to a group, the security management system derives from the group information, those systems to which new security information must be added.

Creating the groups, the programs, and the association between the groups and the programs is a difficult task. This information however can be easily derived for workflow-based applications.

Staff assignments are typically expressed in organizational units, such as roles. Those organizational units can automatically become groups in the security management system. The programs associated with the appropriate activities are also made part of the security management system repository. Then, the staff assignments provide the security management system with the linkage between the program information and the group information.

Whenever changes are made to information maintained by the workflow management system, the information is propagated to the security management system, which in turn updates the appropriate security systems.

The approach we have shown allows the workflow management systems and security management systems to work together by exchanging information. This working together can be improved significantly if the workflow management system manages its security information in the security management system rather than in its own repository. Figure 8.7 shows, for example, that the security management system maintains the information which role can start which process.

If no security management system is available, deriving security information and managing this information for the underlying security systems could be made part of the workflow management system itself.

8.4   Business-Process-Oriented Systems Management

The availability of systems, including all hardware and software, is controlled and monitored by systems management systems; that means the systems management system makes sure that the systems are available. A system is available if it is up and running and produces correct results. System in this context means the combination of hardware and software that performs a user-specified task, such as bookkeeping or loan processing. In general, a system is distributed; that means the individual software components are running on different processors.

Controlling the availability of systems is the major task of a systems management system; other tasks include functions such as the distribution and installation of software. We discussed in section 8.2 on page 294 how workflow management systems can assist systems management systems to handle this task very efficiently. In this section, we continue to use TME-10 as the prototype of a systems management system.

The detection of errors is outside the scope of the systems management system and is done by special instrumentation code injected into the executables to be monitored or by some other program that monitors the execution of an executable. When such an error occurs, a set of steps is carried out by the entities shown in Figure 8.8.

Figure 8.8 Processing an Error

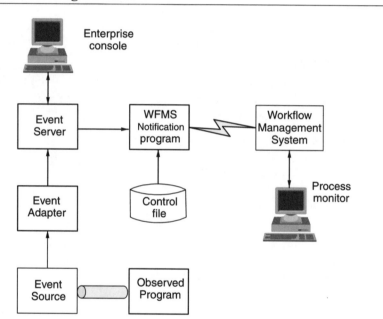

Suppose the observed program causes an error, then the appropriate monitoring program, called the *event source*, sends the raw information to the *event adapter*. The event adapter consolidates the raw information and generates an appropriate standardized message to the *event server*. The event server then carries out the actions that have been previously defined by administrators. One of the actions is to send an alert to the *enterprise console*. This alert prompts an operator to initiate appropriate actions. Which actions need to be taken depends on established procedures. Incidentally, one of the resulting actions, whether system or operator initiated, could be the start of a business process.

The view that the systems management system exhibits is that of a set of hardware components and pieces of software. It is therefore difficult for the people designing the proper actions and for the master console operator to come up with the proper set of actions. The providers of systems management systems try to address this issue by providing different levels of abstractions. Figure 8.9 shows the different levels of abstraction. The lowest level represents the network; management of the network is done via the simple network management protocol (SNMP), the standard protocol for managing networks. On the next level are the individual software components, such as the different pieces of the operating system, the middleware components, such as database management systems or workflow management systems, or individual pieces of application software. The third level addresses the fact that application systems are made up of different components; a bookkeeping system, for example, may use a database system to store data.

Figure 8.9 Business-Process-Oriented Systems Management

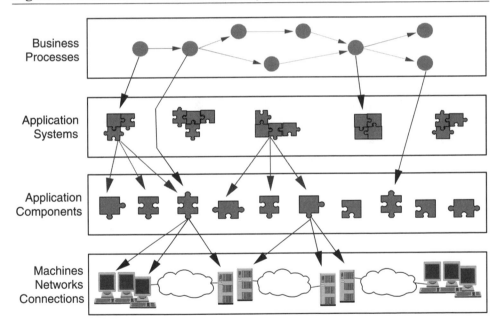

The approach of having different levels allows us to understand the impact of any error situation by propagating errors from the lower levels to the higher levels. For example, the enterprise console operator can then see the impacted application systems.

Even with the notion of application systems, the level of abstraction is still below what is needed to understand the dependencies between the different pieces of software that are involved. This level of abstraction can only be achieved by looking at the system from a business process point of view, as shown in Figure 8.9. Instead of looking at the individual components, the system is viewed as a collection of business processes, where each of the business processes is connected to a set of application systems and application components.

One solution is to enhance the systems management system enterprise console with a business process view. The systems management system would need to access the workflow management system's repository and use the appropriate process structures to present the managed system in the structure of business processes. If an error occurs, the appropriate activity would be shown in the *inError* state. The console operator could then dig deeper into the structures managed by the systems management system and find out exactly what needs to be done.

This approach of presenting the managed hardware and software in a business-process-oriented view still suffers a problem: it only reflects the relation between the infrastructure and the business processes. It does not reflect other types of resources that are important for the processing of business processes, such as people working on the business processes. This aspect of business processes is only known to the workflow management system; it is the organizational dimension of workflow.

As we discussed in section 3.7.2 on page 108, the workflow management system's process monitor helps to manage the business process, monitoring the execution of business processes and taking appropriate actions by means of the provided application programming interface.

If defined properly, either explicitly or by defaults, all errors, either hardware or software, are eventually detected by the process monitor. If, for example, a connection breaks for a program, the break show up as a problem in the throughput of the activity that is associated with the particular program. The process monitor would now help the process administrator find out whether this is a people related problem or not. If the problem is not people related, the GUI could query the workflow management system, using the workflow-management-system-supplied application programming interface to identify the related activity implementation. With this information, the systems management system could be contacted for further analysis.

This approach is also not completely satisfactory for two reasons: (1) it may take too long until an error manifests itself as a problem that is detected by the process monitor and (2) the appropriate setup lacks usability (two APIs). This tight integration can be achieved by providing a bridge between the two systems, as shown on the right-hand side of Figure 8.8 on page 302.

When an error that cannot be completely resolved by the event server automatically is encountered, the event server sends an appropriate notification to the workflow management system. The notification is sent by the workflow notification program that is invoked as a normal action by the event server. The shown control file allows the program to determine which workflow management system the notification should be sent to.

The workflow management system accepts the notification, uses the sent information to locate the affected process model, and then determines the affected activities. This information is then made available to any interested party via the process monitor API. This can then be used to graphically represent this information in the process monitor's console.

The process administrator can then determine the cause of the problem and take appropriate actions. In fact, the process monitor could propose appropriate actions, based on the information maintained in the workflow management system's repository.

Chapter 9

Application Topologies

This chapter discusses the impact of various middleware technologies on the structure of applications for production use. The most fundamental notion of this chapter (presumably of this whole book) is that of flow independence. Just as the insight into the importance of data independence for production applications resulted into the overwhelming use of database management systems, the discovery of the benefits of flow independence will foster the use of workflow management systems for building flexible production applications. A flow-independent application has the structure of a workflow-based application that we discuss in section 9.10 on page 345. Standard application vendors provide applications complying with this structure today.

We review the evolution of location transparency of the parts constituting an application by discussing various client/server topologies, three-tier structures, and n-tier distributed applications. Various supporting technologies are sketched. The role of TP monitors for scalability and robustness of vital application parts is emphasized. Based on an abstraction of the core functionality of a TP monitor, we show that various middleware technologies such as object request brokers and message monitors can be perceived as some kind of TP monitor.

We discuss messaging more extensively than other middleware technology. The reason for this bias is that messaging is the underpinning for the architecture both of workflow management system which we outline in Chapter 10, and of a message broker, that is an environment for integrating applications, sketched in section 9.6 on page 331. We discuss the role of workflow technology in message brokering.

9.1 Dependent Applications

In this section, we discuss the two fundamental origins of application inflexibility. Inflexible application systems often correspond to inflexibility within companies supported by these applications. Consequently, providing flexibility of application systems from the very beginning may turn out to be vital for companies' competitiveness.

9.1.1 Data Dependency

Many applications that exist today show a structure similar to the one shown in the upper-left corner of Figure 9.1.

Figure 9.1 Removing Flow and Data Dependencies from Applications

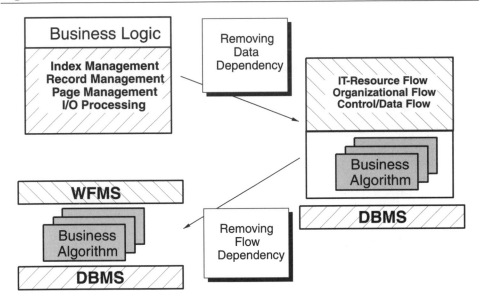

In addition to implementing the business logic, the application also contains a lot of code dealing with managing the associated data. For example, the application knows about the following:

- The various access paths to the data the application manipulates. It might explicitly select an index and traverse it to locate a particular record, and it might even depend on the particular implementation, such as a B-tree for the index.

- The structure of the records holding data fields of interest. The application may, for example, depend on the order of fields in some record it manipulates, or it must know explicitly how variable length fields are encoded.

- The grouping of records and their storage in files. If records of different applications are stored in the same file, the application has to determine which records to ignore and which records to process. The application could also depend on a particular ordering of records or interleaved storage of different record types.

- The movement of data between volatile storage and disks. It might be necessary that the application has to explicitly flush modified data from memory to disk or has to provide buffer space to hold loaded data.

The situation gets even worse when the business logic aspects of such an application are not clearly separated from its data management aspects.

Applications that deal with data management aspects in addition to business logic are called *data dependent*. Data-dependent applications are very volatile against changing data requirements, which fact in itself is known to be the origin of many problems. For example, if new functional requirements result in changes to the structure of the records manipulated by the application, the application must be modified to cope with the new record structures. But changing the application may itself be a problem because there is no time to change the application, the skill is no longer available, or it is impossible to find out all of the applications that are affected by the data structure changes.

One typically resolves this situation by making a copy of the original file, applying the necessary structural changes to this file, and running the new application function against the new file. Keeping these different copies consistent then becomes a problem, and procedures must be established to periodically synchronize the files. Over time, things get worse because more and more requirements result in more and more copies of the "same" data, and finally, very complicated procedures must be established to keep the whole collection of data consistent (Incidentally, this is an interesting problem for the applicability of workflow technology.) As a result, tremendous effort is spent because of the rigidity of data-dependent applications.

To reduce the rigidity of data-dependent applications, database technology is used. When applications manage their data via database management systems, the structure of the data is defined as a database schema to the database management system; data is manipulated as instances of this schema based on the database management system's functionality. Consequently, the applications have only minimum knowledge about access paths or record structures. Ideally, the code does not deal at all with low-level data management. To a large degree, applications get rid of their data dependencies. For example, if relational database management systems are exploited, access paths to the data are not known by the application. Access paths can be dropped, and new ones can be created at any time. Similarly, the view concept of relational database management systems helps in shielding applications from changes to the structure of the manipulated data. As a consequence, applications become *data independent*. They are now much more flexible.

9.1.2 Flow Dependency

The application structure that is typically found when database management systems are exploited, is the one shown on the right side in Figure 9.1. The business functions of an application are implemented by collections of business algorithms and the specification of the flow between these business algorithms appropriate to the performance of a particular business function. This flow defines the following: (1) the correct sequencing of business algorithms, depending on the context in which the business function is processed; (2) the data that is needed by each affected business algorithm; (3) the programs that need to be invoked in order to perform a business function; (4) the people that need to carry out the individual business algorithms; and (5) privileges or duties that are needed for performance of the business algorithms. The properties we have described for the flow are the properties of a business process. The flow is nothing else than a process model.

Applications that contain implementations of process models (i.e, the applications contain which manages control and data flows, flow through organizational units, and flow through the IT environment) are called *flow dependent*. Flow-dependent applications are very volatile with respect to changes in business processes. The problems associated with flow-dependent applications are similar to the ones outlined for data-dependent applications. When a business process must be changed, all applications implementing some of the affected parts of this business process must also be changed.

This situation is seen more and more as a major inhibitor for staying competitive in a rapidly changing business environment. This dynamic originates from new competitors appearing with innovative products on a global scale. As a consequence, business processes must be changed for the following reasons:

1. From an internal viewpoint, products are often equated with the processes used to "manufacture" them. For example, from an insurance company's view, life insurance is not the corresponding contract signed by the customer but the business processes that define how to accept a new application or how to manage it over time.

   Thus, new or modified products require new or modified business processes. The faster existing business processes can be modified or new business processes can be introduced, the faster new products can enter the market place, which translates immediately into increased competitive advantage.

2. Mergers or acquisitions result in changes of business processes. For example, two companies merge to offer a more diverse or more complete product spectrum to their customers. Based on what has been said before, the impact on the business processes is obvious.

3. Companies may want to outsource parts of their business, with an obvious impact on the affected business processes. For example, if certain aspects of a business can be done more efficiently or cost effectively by a business partner or if a company has to concentrate on its core competencies to stay competitive, outsourcing takes place.

Note that mergers and acquisitions often have an aspect of outsourcing too. Common business tasks are combined or mutually exploited to gain cost savings.

Workflow technology eliminates problems that result from flow-dependent applications. All flow aspects of the application domain—the covered parts of its underlying business processes—are defined as process models to the workflow management system. The resulting application has no knowledge of and makes no assumptions about appropriate sequencing of the business algorithms, privileges or duties related to their invocation, or IT-specific issues. As a consequence, applications become *flow independent*.

When both data dependencies and flow dependencies of an application are removed the resulting situation is the one depicted in the lower-left part of Figure 9.1. The application consists of a collection of business algorithms that manipulate their data via database management systems; the appropriate invocations of the business algorithms are proactively managed by workflow management systems according to corresponding process models. We discuss applications of this structure in more detail in section 9.10 on page 345.

9.2   Client/Server Structures

Structuring applications according to the client/server paradigm results in increased flexibility in terms of location transparency that is based on a simple role model. A client part of an application requests a service from the server part of an application; the server performs whatever is needed to satisfy the service request and typically sends a response back to the invoking client. Neither the client nor the server needs to know the physical location of its communication partner.

Furthermore, the role that a particular application part assumes is not fixed, and an application part can even play both roles at the same time. When a client requests a service, the server that satisfies the request might need additional services that are provided by another server. Thus, a server becomes a client of another server.

9.2.1   Client/Server Topologies

Based on the following well-known analysis, different client/server topologies can be identified. Figure 9.2 shows the three major parts of a typical application: the

Figure 9.2 The Different Client/Server Topologies

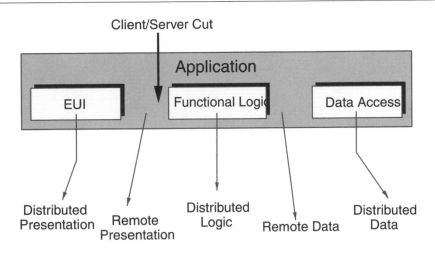

end-user interface (EUI) used to communicate with people working with the application, the functional logic implementing the business rules and business algorithms of the application, and the data access part performing the data manipulations corresponding to the modifications resulting from the functional logic.

By cutting an application vertically at any of the five points shown in the figure (so-called client/server cuts), we define the following client/server topologies:

- The *remote presentation* topology is one of the two "classical" client/server structures. It results from cutting an application between its EUI part and its functional logic part. In this topology, the EUI is put on a machine that is separate from the proper application. This machine could be a usual PC, where the EUI is implemented as a GUI based on the environment's windowing system or based on a browser, a network computer running a browser, or a terminal presenting a 3270 screen. The remote presentation topology thus covers "modern" browser-based applications as well as "old" TP monitor applications. It represents the well-known terminal/host structure.

- The *remote data* topology is the other one of the two "classical" client/server structures. It is the result of cutting an application between its functional logic part and its data access part. It is a characteristic property of this topology that the functional logic (running on the same device as its associated EUI) directly uses client interfaces of its exploited database management system to access data. For example, the functional logic runs on a PC and uses embedded SQL to access data on a remote database server, or it runs on a network computer and uses JDBC (Java Database Connection—see [OH97]) for its data manipulations on a remote machine.

- The *distributed presentation* topology results from cutting the EUI into two parts. The X Window System well known from UNIX environments, is the famous representative that exploits this topology.

- The *distributed logic* topology results from cutting apart the functional logic itself. This client/server structure is becoming more common. For example, commercially available database management systems support stored procedures and triggers that allow to run parts of the function logic to be run on the same machine as the database engine. Similarly, distributed object technology facilitates the placement of different parts of an application on different machines (see section 9.6 on page 331). Frequently, this topology is used to put data-intensive application code "close" to its data to avoid network latency because of massive data movements, and to leave compute-intensive application code on the client machine to avoid this load at the database server.

- The *distributed data* topology results from cutting the data access part in two pieces. This client/server structure is typically exploited by means of appropriate database management system functionality such as distributed databases or client caches. The manipulated data resides on different machines, and the database management system manages the associated required modifications at the various locations to maintain consistency of the data and to provide location transparency for the application.

9.2.2 Multitier Structures

Applying a simple client/server cut to an application typically puts two different pieces of the application on two different machines; that is the application is structured in two tiers. This is the famous *two-tier* structure for applications derived as an immediate corollary of the client/server paradigm. Based on this structure, it is common to call the device running the EUI (and some or all of the functional logic) simply a *client* and the machine running the database management system (and some or all of the functional logic) simply a *server*. Although this terminology does overload the terms "client" and "server," it does not result in confusion. It is clear from the context whether the software role model of a client or server is meant, or the hardware location.

In a two-tier structure where all of the functional logic runs on the same machine as the EUI, remote SQL (in one of its variants, for example, embedded SQL or CLI) is typically used to manipulate data located on a different machine. This configuration requires a client machine with enough resources to run the EUI, the functional logic, and the database client; the required client is referred to a *fat client*. In some situations, fat clients are not desirable because they are too expensive.

The remote presentation topology is often chosen to reduce the resource prerequisites for the client machine, This choice means that no function logic runs on the client. When the EUI is based on browser technology, the client can even become a diskless device such as a network computer. Clients that have only a few resource prerequisites are referred to as *thin clients*.

A thin client typically assumes that the functional logic runs on a separate server machine. We discuss exceptions to this assumption in section 9.8 on page 341. As a result, the server must be able to run the functional logic of many clients in addition to the database system. If the server is not a very powerful machine scalability become an issue in this two-tier structure.

To solve this problem, the function logic and the database access can be split up, as shown in Figure 9.3.

Figure 9.3 The Three-Tier Application Structure

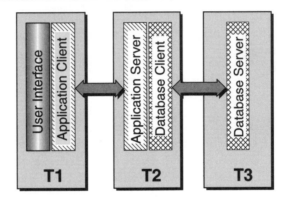

In the figure, all three parts of an application may run on different machines. The user interface is run on the client machines, the functional logic runs on a separate machine, and the database management system runs on yet another machine. This is the famous *three-tier structure*. Many standard applications are architected according to this structure. In section 3.10 on page 114 we discussed this structure as the underlying software structure for a workflow management system. A more detailed discussion of how it applies to a workflow management system is provided in Chapter 10.

Because the functional logic is seen as the heart of the application, and because clients request services from the functional logic pieces, it is usual in the context of the three-tier structure to talk about *application servers* instead of functional logic. This term also encompasses the fact that application servers provide interfaces (so-called *application clients*) that run on the client machines and that are used by the user interface component to invoke services from the application servers (see Figure 9.3). Application servers in turn use database clients provided by database management systems to request data accesses from database servers. It is usual, as shown in Figure 9.3, to denote the tier representing the clients simply as tier one (T1 for short), the tier representing the application servers as tier two (T2, or sometimes mid-tier or application server tier), and the tier representing the engine of the database management system as tier three (T3 for short).

An application server can be structured in such a way that some of its services are located on different machines. For example, putting resource-intensive services on separate machines could improve performance of the application. Another example is the case where a service is already bound to a certain environment by its very nature, such as being bound to an existing host transaction. It should also be noted that any number of these services might depend on other services which could be located on other different servers. As a result, the proper function logic can be realized as a complicated network of application pieces that are related according to the client/server paradigm. As a whole, the resulting application structure is sometimes called multitier structure, or *n-tier structure* for short.

The motivation for three-tier structures arose directly from scalability concerns. We next discuss different middleware components that provide for scaling applications and show the associated impact on application architectures.

9.3   TP Monitors

The most important property of a transaction processing monitor (a TP monitor) is scalability. To be more precise, a TP monitor provides an environment for scaling applications. This means that each application function can be written with only a single client at a time in mind, but running an application function in a TP monitor scales it up to serve hundreds and even thousands of clients concurrently. A TP monitor makes efficient use of the available system resources on its host machine, ensuring scalability. From this perspective, a TP monitor is an appropriate environment for building application servers.

The other important property of a TP monitor is robustness. A TP monitor provides an environment in which the TP monitor itself and the application functions running under its control can recover from system or application malfunctions. For this purpose, TP monitors support transaction services, and application functions usually run as transactions (see section 7.1 on page 234) in a TP-monitor environment. Because of the latter, application functions performed under the control of a TP monitor are called *transactions*.

Figure 9.4 depicts the main conceptual elements of a classical TP-monitor environment. Readers interested in in-depth information on TP monitors are referred to[GR93]; readers looking for a detailed overview are referred to [BN97].

Figure 9.4 Basic Elements of Transaction Processing

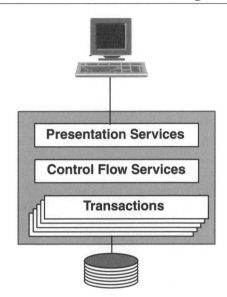

The *presentation services* encapsulate an application from a concrete device used to communicate with end users. They gather the input from an end-user device, perform an initial validation of the input, and construct the proper request message. This request message is then passed to the control flow services. Also, the presentation services prepare the device for the appropriate screen layout, allowing for the input data related to a request and the output data representing the response of a request.

The *control flow services* route a request to the correct target program, that is the transaction responsible for servicing the request. For this purpose, control flow services decode incoming request messages, determine the transactions to invoke, and invoke the programs. They establish the necessary transaction context and ensure message integrity (as discussed in section 9.5.1 on page 323). Finally, they handle exceptions.

The *transactions* implement the application's functional logic. Each transaction is responsible for executing the appropriate business algorithms and for manipulating the related data (typically, through a database system). Note again that this actions are done within the transaction context established via the control flow services.

9.3.1 Stored Procedures

Today's relational database management systems support stored procedures[BS95a, Cha98]. Basically, a stored procedure is a program that runs on the same machine as the database engine, perhaps even within the database engine itself. When a client calls a stored procedure, the database engine invokes the corresponding program on behalf of the client. Because the stored procedure may include SQL statements, it can perform all the data manipulations for the client local to the database engine before returning to the invoking client. When the stored procedure returns, it simply passes the result to its invoking client. Client 1 in Figure 9.5 uses a stored procedure.

Figure 9.5 Stored Procedures and Network Traffic

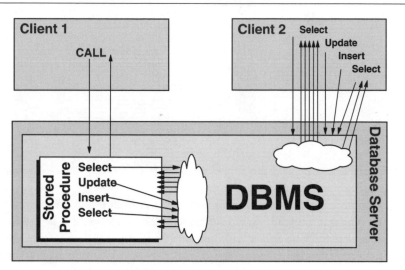

In contrast, client 2 performs the same functions, but instead of using a stored procedure, it invokes all the SQL statements itself, i.e., remotely. As a result, many different messages corresponding to the SQL requests and the results of these requests are exchanged via the network between the client and the database system. The difference in network traffic generated by each client is obvious. Even worse, in some application scenarios most of the result messages sent to the client are not directly needed; for example, they are somehow aggregated by the client to produce the proper result of the implemented application function. This means the network might be swamped by superfluous messages. If the aggregation had been computed in a stored procedure, just the aggregation value would have been returned.

Whenever a stored procedure issues an SQL statement, the underlying operating system switches between the address space running the stored procedure and the address space running the database engine. When the stored procedure runs within the same address space as the database engine, even this processing is avoided, further reducing the overhead. The variant of stored procedure that runs in a separate address space is called a *fenced* stored procedure; a stored procedure that runs within the address space of the database engine is called a *non-fenced* stored procedure.

Database management systems that support stored procedures can be seen as a kind of TP monitor. First of all, a database management system provides a scalable and robust environment. Next, the database client is responsible for handling messages related to stored procedure invocations and returning responses. Control flow services are provided by the database server, for example determining the program that implements the called stored procedure and invoking that program. A stored procedure can be implemented as a self-contained application function, or as a transaction in the above sense.

Nevertheless, conventional TP monitors provide many more functions than we have discussed, such as forms builder, sophisticated security, and access control mechanisms [GR93, BN97]. Those additional functions are not part of the functionality that the database management system provides. so the use of database management systems as TP monitors is referred to as the *TP-lite* approach; the use of "full blown" TP monitors is referred to as the *TP-heavy* approach. We show in Chapter 10 how the TP-lite approach can be used to build a workflow management system.

9.4 Communication Paradigms

Communication between the various pieces of an application can happen in two inherently different manners: synchronously and asynchronously. *Synchronous* communication requires that both communication partners are available for the duration of the communication, that both are connected to each other during the communication, and that one partner cannot continue its processing until the other has responded to its request. *Asynchronous* communication requires none of the above. One partner can submit a request or return a response while the other partner is unavailable; thus, there is no need for a connection between the partners at all, and a partner can continue its processing as soon as its request or its response has been sent.

In this section, we discuss these two different paradigms, using representative components of a client/server system. Remote procedure call (RPC) is used in the discussion of synchronous communication and messaging is used in the discussion of asynchronous communications. Remote procedure call is discussed here only briefly but is covered extensively in computer literature.

9.4.1 Remote Procedure Call

From an application's point of view, calling a stored procedure is like calling any other program. The calling application simply issues an SQL CALL statement that includes the name of the stored procedure and its parameters. The stored procedure call is a special case of the more general mechanism of a *remote procedure call*. It enables the invocation of a program to be performed independently of its physical location. This means that the program being invoked can run on the same machine as the caller or it can run on a remote machine.

In Figure 9.6, the invoking program P1 simply calls the other program P2 and passes input parameters to P2 as if P2 were in P1's own local address space. While P1 is waiting for P2 to return, P2 processes the request and on completion returns its output parameters to P1 as if P1 and P2 were running in the same address space.

Figure 9.6 Remote Procedure Call

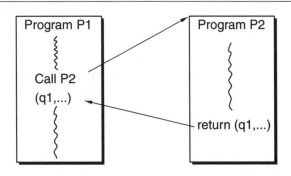

A separate middleware layer is needed to enable remote procedure calls [Mul93, BN97]. This middleware requires the definition of an interface to the program that is to be invoked via the RPC mechanism. This definition is done with a special language, the Interface Definition Language (IDL). Based on this definition, a corresponding client stub and a server stub are generated. The invoking program, P1 in Figure 9.6, calls the client stub, which transforms the input parameters into a request message (marshaling). This message is passed to the RPC transport layer, which sends the message to the server stub on the remote machine to invoke the called program, P2 in Figure 9.6. The server stub extracts from the request message the input parameters (demarshaling) and uses them to invoke P2, using a normal program call. When P2 returns to the server stub, the server stub marshals the output parameters and passes the corresponding response message to the RPC transport layer which sends the message to the client stub. Finally, the client stub demarshals the response message and returns the extracted output parameters of P2 to P1.

While the mechanics of simply invoking a program are the same in using an RPC and a normal program call, the calling program must be aware of which mechanism to use. In the local case, when the hosting environment fails, both the caller and the callee fail. This is obviously different in the remote case because the caller and the callee can fail independently.

As a consequence, special care must be taken to cope with this situation. For example, when the caller fails and recovers, it must detect whether or not it has to deal with an outstanding RPC. Next, it has to determine the state of an outstanding RPC, is such as whether the RPC is active or whether it has completed successfully.

If an RPC has not completed, the caller must determine what to do to complete the call. The correct implementation of this restart behavior is a nontrivial undertaking.

To ease this processing, a transactional RPC has been proposed; it treats the RPC as a normal resource manipulation, that is the call is part of the caller's transaction. For example, if the caller aborts (which includes an unsolicited abort due to a system failure from the scenario above), the call is "undone" in the sense that the callee is informed about this fact and can initiate the appropriate recovery actions.

9.4.2 Messaging

The main idea of message-based communication between programs is that programs exchange requests and responses as messages via queues. A program sends a request to a queue, not to a specific "partner" program. A program can put a message into a queue even if no program is currently available to retrieve the message from the queue and process it. The underlying middleware (*message-oriented middleware*, (MOM) or simply *messaging middleware*) manages queues and the messages contained or manipulated in queues, and it guarantees the delivery of messages to their target queues. For more details than are presented in this chapter on this subject refer to [BHL95].

Each message encompasses a message body and a message header. The message body represents the information that has to be delivered to the target queue, for example the name of the requested service and its required input parameters, or the output produced by a former service invocation. The message body is constructed by the sending application. The message header includes descriptive information, such as the name of the queue to which replies should be sent, as well as context information about the origin of the message to enable authorization. The message header is constructed by combining information that the messaging middleware derives from environmental settings and information that the sending application specifies by appropriate parameter settings as part of requesting the service.

Messages have many properties. A message, for example, can require confirmation of arrival or confirmation of delivery; that is, the messaging middleware is asked to generate a report message when the message arrives at its target queue or when the message is read from this queue. These reports are sent to the reply-to queue specified by the application (which is part of the message header). Although messages are guaranteed to be delivered to their target queues, once *transient* messages arrive, they do not survive failures such as system crashes. Messages which are *persistent* do survive these failures because they are subject to the recovery actions of the messaging middleware.

Queues are the basic resources that are managed by the messaging middleware. A queue has properties like its name, the maximum number of messages in the queue allowed to be awaiting processing, or the maximum size of a single message in the queue. Note that another property of a queue is whether by default a message sent to the queue is persistent or transient. Besides explicitly specifying for a particular message whether it is persistent or transient, the property of a message depends on the corresponding setting of its target queue. Typically, queues are predefined (*static* queues), although applications can define queues dynamically during execution (*dynamic* queues).

All services that a program needs to exploit message-based communication are provided by a *message queue manager* (MQM) as shown in Figure 9.7. Such services include administrative functions to manage queues and to control the execution of an MQM itself, and the services to manipulate messages in queues. Each queue is managed by and resides in a particular MQM. Applications manipulate messages through a messaging client that provides an interface to all relevant operations. This allows an application to run on a machine different from the one that hosts the MQM. An application must be connected to an MQM to manipulate messages. A queue that is managed by the MQM to which a particular application is connected is called a *local queue*; all other queues are *remote queues* from the application's perspective. An application can put messages into both local and remote queues, but it can get messages from local queues only.

Figure 9.7 The Client/Server Structure of the Messaging Services

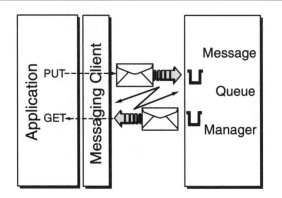

All messaging middleware implementations support conceptually similar operations on messages and queues, but the syntax of the corresponding interfaces differs. To give an impression of what these operations are, we briefly sketch the subset of the message queuing interface (MQI) of MQSeries that is relevant for the discussion to follow. For the detailed functionality, correct syntax, and all parameters of the MQI, refer to [IBM94c].

- First, an application uses the CONNECT operation to establish a connection to a message queue manager; the name of the MQM is a parameter of this operation. A corresponding DISCONNECT operation breaks this connection once the application finishes its manipulations on messages and queues.

- When an application wants to manipulate messages in a particular queue, first opens the queue by using the OPEN operation and specifying the name of this queue. The application can signal that it has finished manipulating the queue and the messages in the queue by using a corresponding CLOSE operation. Note that multiple applications can have opened a queue at the same time. Concurrent accesses to a queue and the messages within the queue are managed by the MQM that owns the queue.

- Messages are sent to a particular queue by the PUT operation. The target queue of the message is one of the parameters of this operation. If the queue is a remote queue, it is managed by an MQM different from the one to which the sending application is currently connected; the connected MQM ensures the delivery of the message to the remote queue (see section 9.5.1 on page 323).

- Receiving a message from a particular queue is done by means of the GET operation. The queue from which a message should be retrieved is one of the parameters of this operation. If no message is currently in the queue the issuing application can specify by a corresponding parameter of the operation whether it is willing to wait for a message to arrive in the queue and how long it is willingly to wait. Another parameter allows the application to determine whether the GET operation should return the message and immediately remove it from the queue or whether the message should remain in the queue (browsing).

- The properties of a queue (as well as properties of other objects such as its connected MQM) like its name or default message persistence can be retrieved with the INQUIRY operation. Furthermore, selective dynamic attributes, like the actual number of messages in the queue and the number of applications that have currently opened a particular queue (for PUT or for GET), can be retrieved by this operation. The SET operation allows the alteration of some selected properties of a queue.

- Any collection of put and get operations can be grouped into a transaction (see section 7.1 on page 234 for the concept of a transaction). The BEGIN operation starts such a transaction, and the COMMIT operation or the BACKOUT operation. ends a transaction. Messages that are sent to queues do not become visible in the target queues until the transaction commits. If the transaction ends with BACKOUT none of the messages sent ever appear in a queue. Similarly, messages that are retrieved from queues are removed from the queue once the transaction commits; all messages retrieved are restored in their queues when the transaction is backed out.

Program P1 in Figure 9.8 bundles three PUT operations and one GET operation into a single transaction. Program P2 ca not retrieve the messages sent by P1 until P1 commits the transaction. As depicted in the figure, manipulations of messages in multiple queues can be bundled into a single transaction.

Figure 9.8 Queuing-based Communication

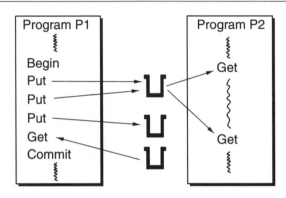

It is even possible to mix PUT and get operations with manipulations of resources managed by other resource managers, such as database management systems into a single transaction. This means that an MQM can behave like a resource manager, and can be tied into a global transaction that is coordinated by a two-phase commit protocol (see section 7.1.2 on page 235 for the concept of global transactions). Thus, if the MQM or one of the other resource managers detects that it cannot successfully complete its part of the transaction, the overall global transaction is undone. In this way, an application can ensure *message integrity*.

The application receives request messages via its input queue. The application processes the request by beginning a global transaction and retrieving the request message from the input queue. Within this transaction, the application manipulates resources corresponding to the request, for example, it updates tuples in tables of a relational database management system. When finished with these manipulations, the application creates a response message, if appropriate, and puts it into the reply queue of the originator of the request—still within the same global transaction. Then, the application commits, causing the request message to be deleted from the input queue, the manipulations performed on the other resources are made permanent, and the response message finally appears in the reply queue.

If something goes wrong during this processing, the overall transaction is aborted. Then, the original request message reappears in the application's input queue, the manipulations of the resources (for example, the updates performed in the relational database management system) are undone, and the response message is withdrawn from the response queue if already sent. Subsequently, the application can simply start processing the request again. In Chapter 10 we discuss the role of message integrity in building a scalable and highly available workflow management system.

There are situations in which an application cannot process a particular message successfully. If, for example, the parameter combination in the message body represents an invalid request, such as division by zero, or the request results in integrity violations, such as key uniqueness, within the database that must be updated, then, the overall transaction is aborted. The ensured message integrity causes the request message to reappear in the application's input queue. The application tries to process the message again. This attempt fails as it did earlier, causing the process to abort again. This message thus fails forever and is referred to as a *poisoned message*. To deal with poisoned messages, the messaging middleware typically maintains a backout count for each message. An application can check this count, and when a certain threshold is exceeded, the application can simply assume that the message is poisoned and transfer it to a special queue without attempting to process it.

The message queuing interface (MQI) also allows put and get operations to be performed outside of the current transaction, as is necessary in certain cases, for example, when the application is not able to complete a transaction successfully. In that case, the put operations would signal the error by sending a corresponding message into a special queue before aborting the transaction. Without being able to put a message into a queue outside of a transaction, the error message would be undone as part of the backout processing and the signal would be lost.

Messaging middleware has many of the attributes associated with database systems. Data can be stored in queues as persistent messages, concurrent accesses to queues and messages are managed by the messaging system, and collections of message manipulations can be grouped into transactions providing for data recovery. In Chapter 10 we will see how to use queues as databases for building a workflow management system.

9.5 Message Monitors

As discussed in section 9.3 on page 314, a TP monitor can be perceived as a robust environment for scaling applications. In this section, we describe how messaging middleware can be extended to a similar environment for message based applications. Because of the similarities to a TP monitor, we call this extended middleware a *message monitor*.

9.5.1 Message Queue Manager

The centerpiece of any messaging middleware is the message queue manager (MQM). As described in section 9.4.2 on page 319, the MQM provides the services needed to send and receive messages, to manage queues, and to include message manipulations in global transactions. Two other important areas that are covered by the MQM are hiding all details of the network underlying the message exchange from the applications and guaranteeing delivery of messages. We cover both subjects next.

When an application sends a message to a remote queue, the local MQM initiates the submission of the message to its final destination. Obviously, the first step is that the local MQM detects that it does not manage the target message queue. For this purpose, the local MQM consults its queue directory, which contains all queues to which messages can be sent. For each of these queues the directory entry consists of the queue name as known to the local MQM (*alias name*), the name of the MQM to which the message is to be submitted (*adjacent* MQM), and the queue name by which the adjacent MQM knows the target queue. The alias name is used in put and get operations that are initiated by the local MQM. Note that in using an alias name applications become independent from the physical location of the target queue. This independence allows queues to be moved to different locations without affecting a sending application.

Once the local MQM detects that the target queue is remote, it puts the message into a so-called *transmission queue* (see Figure 9.9). A transmission queue is a local representation of the adjacent MQM (not for the remote queue). At least one transmission queue is needed for each adjacent MQM to which the local MQM wants to pass messages. Putting the message into the transmission queue has the advantage that the actual transmission of the message to the remote MQM can take place at a later time. The remote MQM may not be currently available, or messages should be sent in batches instead of one message at a time, for example. The transmission queue is used as a temporary store for messages destined for a remote MQM. Figure 9.9 illustrates this concept.

When program P1 wants to send a message to queue Q1, it sends a PUT operation to the local message queue manager MQM1. Consulting its queue directory, MQM1 determines that Q1 is not a local queue but a queue managed by message queue manager MQM2, and that MQM2 knows Q1 as Q7. Thus, MQM1 puts the message sent by P1 into the transmission queue representing the adjacent message queue manager MQM2.

A *channel* must be defined so a message from a transmission queue can be transferred to the represented adjacent MQM. A channel represents a connection and its properties between two message queue managers. In particular, it abstracts the underlying physical network and protocol used for the communication between the two MQMs. Applications simply address messages to queues without any considerations about the underlying network or protocols.

To be more precise: a channel ties a transmission queue and a message queue manager together. Multiple transmission queues can be defined for the same adjacent MQM, resulting in multiple channels between two MQMs. To support this, the queue directory is extended to allow the specification of which transmission queue,

Figure 9.9 Delivering Messages Across Message Queue Managers

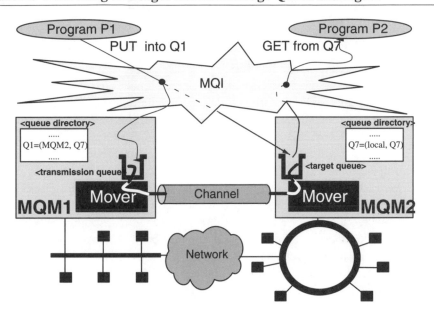

or channel, should be used for submitting messages to a particular remote queue at the adjacent MQM. Thus, multiple channels can be defined between two MQMs, each with possibly different operational characteristics, for example, whether the associated transmission queue has to be flushed continuously or periodically or whether messages should be flushed in batches. This definition of multiples channels allows the traffic of message transmissions destined for different remote queues to be separated.

Communication between two MQMs is actually performed by components called *message channel agents* or *movers* for short. There is one mover at each end of a channel. The mover at the local MQM establishes the communication with the mover at the adjacent MQM and sends the message over the channel. When the mover at the receiving end of the channel gets the message, it puts the message into the target queue and informs the mover at the sending end of the channel about the successful reception. The mover at the sending end of the channel does not erase the message from the transmission queue until it gets this positive acknowledgment. When a transmission fails, the sending mover repeats the transmission until it succeeds or until a policy declares the transmission as failed. This behavior guarantees that a message is eventually delivered to its destination.

As an example, Figure 9.9 shows that once MQM1 stores the message into the specified transmission queue, the mover at MQM1 initiates the actual submission of the message to MQM2. The receiving mover informs MQM2 of the reception of a message for target queue Q7. From its queue directory, MQM2 determines that Q7 is a local queue, and the message is stored into Q7. The receiving mover informs the sending mover of this fact, and the sending mover deletes the message from the transmission queue. The submission of P1's message to queue Q1, alias queue Q7 at MQM2, is now successfully finished. Finally, program P2 receives the message from its local queue Q7.

When the message is delivered to the adjacent MQM through the appropriate channel, this MQM could also detect that the target queue of the message is not managed by itself but is an alias for another remote queue. As described above, the MQM determines the next adjacent MQM as recipient of the message and puts the message into its corresponding transmission queue. This technique is called *multi-hopping*. It allows an administrator to define a network of MQMs without having to connect each MQM with all the other MQMs. It is sufficient to distinguish for each MQM only an appropriate subset of all MQMs as "adjacent," ensuring the connectedness of the graph-structure defined. Multi-hopping results in reachability of remote queues independently of the number of intermediate MQMs that need to be traversed to deliver a message to a remote queue. Overall, this behavior simplifies the definition of the underlying topology of MQMs.

When a message finally arrives at its destination it can happen that the message is longer than allowed for the target queue or that the target queue has been deleted from the MQM. As a result, messages might be undeliverable. To handle this possibility, each MQM maintains a so-called *dead letter queue*, on which stores all messages that cannot be delivered. By having a program that monitors dead letter queues, on can detect undeliverable messages and take appropriate actions.

9.5.2   Message Monitor

Because the various pieces of an application communicate through messaging, the messaging middleware contributes to the robustness of the overall environment by guaranteeing delivery of messages and by treating messages as recoverable resources. An application client requests a service from an application server by simply sending a corresponding request message to the input queue of the application server. The request reliably arrives in the input queue because the messaging middleware ensures the delivery of the message. Furthermore, a persistent request message is recoverably stored in the queue, awaiting its final processing. The application server processes the request while maintaining message integrity. It is ensured that the client's request is eventually serviced once the messaging middleware has accepted the client's operation. This technique dramatically simplifies the recovery processing of clients and servers and shortens to a minimum the time needed for restarting a failed application piece. Chapter 10 shows how this technique improves the availability of the application.

The notion of an application server as introduced in section 9.2.2 on page 312 needs to be refined in the context of messaging. As already mentioned, an application server maintains message integrity. This means that an application server exploits transactions to manipulate *all* resources that are involved in the correct processing of a request. It further means that all these resources are manipulated in a single transaction and that this transaction includes the reception of the request message and the submission of the response(s). To emphasize these facts, such an application server is called a *transacted* application server. In addition, if a transacted application server has to maintain state information between invocations, it must use resources in a database to manipulate this state. Consequently, the resources reflecting state information are manipulated in the same transaction as all of the other resources related to a request. This ensures that all state is recoverable. It is usual to qualify such an application server as *stateless*. No special care must be taken to synchronize state manipulations and end-of-transaction processing of the other resources. A stateless application server does not maintain local state, that is it does not hold state information in volatile storage or file systems. Consequently, state will never be lost or corrupted because of system failures. Often, stateless transacted application servers are meant when one simply is talking about application servers; we follow this convention from now on and note explicitly when "simple" application servers do suffice.

An application server processes one request message at a time. Having multiple application servers receiving request messages from the same input queue allows multiple requests to be processed concurrently. A collection of application servers that provide the same services and receive the request messages from the same input queue is called a *hot pool*. An application server running in a hot pool is called a *member* (of the hot pool); the number of members in the hot pool is called the *cardinality* of the hot pool. A hot pool allows the implementation of application servers that support only a single client at a time. Running these application servers as a hot pool allows many clients to be serviced at a time. Hot pools thus ensure the scalability and multiuser capability of application servers.

Thus, the first component that needs to be made part of the message monitor is a hot pool manager (see Figure 9.10). The *hot pool manager* is responsible for starting up and shutting down complete hot pools of a particular application server or selective members of a hot pool. It ensures workload management by monitoring the activity of a hot pool and by automatically taking actions such as starting or shutting down hot pool members depending on the depth of the input queue. This too contributes to scalability. As the cardinality of a hot pool is increased, finally all resources (like CPU, etc.) can be exhausted. Thus, the more resources the hot pool gets, the more requests it can service.

When a member of a hot pool fails, its currently processed request message reappears in the input queue of the hot pool because message integrity is maintained by each member. The next available member of the hot pool takes up this message

Figure 9.10 Basic Elements of a Message Monitor

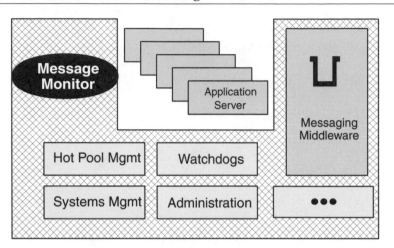

and processes it. Thus, the ability to process service requests is available as long as a single member runs in the hot pool. Grouping application servers in a hot pool increases the availability of the corresponding services.

If the last member of the hot pool fails, the service is no longer available. The turnaround time for service requests is sensitive to the cardinality of the hot pool. Therefore the time a request message has to wait in the input queue before it is picked up by a hot pool member for processing adds up with the actual processing time to result in the turnaround time visible to the client. Loosing members from a hot pool typically increases the turnaround time for client requests. Obviously, this statement is only true if enough processing resources are available for each hot pool member, i.e., there is a threshold beyond which adding members to a hot pool will of itself increase turnaround time. Thus, maintaining a certain cardinality of a hot pool is important.

To maintain cardinality, we add watchdogs to the environment we will finally call a message monitor. A *watchdog* is responsible for detecting failing members of a hot pool as soon as possible and for re-creating a failed member immediately. As a consequence, the cardinality of a hot pool is constant when measured over time. Various fault-detection mechanisms, such as heartbeats, semaphore waiting, or queue inquiries can be applied [GR93]. We discuss the various mechanisms in detail in section 10.1.2 on page 353.

An *administration* component is needed for the message monitor. This component defines hot pools, for example, the kind of application server that is implemented by the members of a particular hot pool, the initial cardinality of the hot pool, which fault-detection technique is to be used by the watchdog. The *systems management* component of the message monitor, shown in Figure 9.10 can monitor the environment itself and to take corrective actions from a central site.

The message monitor provides a robust structure for scaling message-based applications. In Chapter 10 we show how to build a production workflow management system in a message monitor environment.

9.5.3 Application Clustering

The environment hosting a message monitor on a given machine can become resource bound or can fail. As a result, the message monitor and thus the application server hot pools managed by it become resource bound or will fail too. Thus, the environment on the hosting machine might turn out to be a limiting factor in scalability and availability.

To overcome this limitation, a technique similar to one used in building hot pools can be applied. Replicating components and connecting them via messaging, further improves scalability and availability of the application.Putting hot pools of the same application server on multiple machines enhances scalability as long as the application servers can share data via a common database. Then, if these machines fail independently, the application is still available on the other machines and its availability of the application is thus further increased. This configuration, an *application cluster*, is illustrated in Figure 9.11.

Figure 9.11 Structure of an Application Cluster

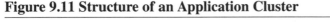

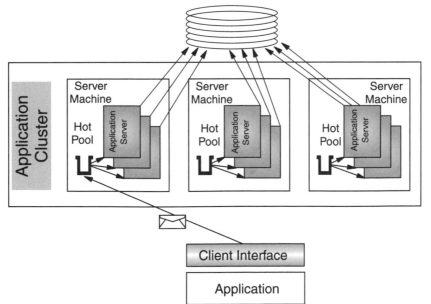

An application cluster is described as follows.

- It is a collection of machines, which fail independently.

- Each of these machines hosts a hot pool of application servers of the same kind.

- All members of these hot pools share the same database.

- The input queues of these hot pools can be used by potential clients of the application server for receiving service requests.

From a client's perspective an application cluster is a single resource servicing its requests. The interface component of the application server used by the client selects an input queue, and thus a machine hosting a hot pool, and submits the service request. When the messaging middleware indicates that the input queue is not available, the interface component chooses a different hot pool, and so on. So, as long as a single hot pool is available on some machine, the service request can be processed; this increases the availability of the application server's services. Similarly, when the application cluster becomes resource bound, an additional machine with a corresponding hot pool can be added and more requests can be processed; this, too, increases the scalability of the application server's services.

The definition of application clusters is supported by the administration component of the message monitor. It maintains information about the different machines that host hot pools of application servers and makes this information available to other components of the environment. This information management provides the basis for realizing various methods of workload management across server machines within an application cluster. It even provides the base for hot plug-in of new server machines. When a server machine is added to an application cluster as mentioned above, it can immediately receive requests from application clients without any further administrative actions.

Furthermore, selective server machines can be taken out of service in a controlled manner: one can ensure that enough server machines remain to process requests. This service control is important to allow maintenance of the hardware or software of a server machine, such as release upgrades of the hosting operating system or of the application servers of the hosted hot pool. Thus, application clusters isolate the overall environment from planned outages, that is they contribute to continuous operation of the environment (see [Pfi95] for more about this subject). As discussed at length before, application clusters also isolate the overall environment from unplanned outages by providing high availability. Altogether, application clusters increase what is called the *continuous availability* of the environment.

In Chapter 10, we show how to build a production workflow management system system based on application cluster techniques.

9.6 Message Broker

A message monitor provides a TP monitor like environment for message-based applications. Most importantly, this environment can scale up message-based applications and ensure their availability.

In addition to having these important operational properties, message-based applications can easily be integrated. They can be grouped in unpredictable combinations of communication partners. This capability is different from RPC-like communications, where a request is sent to a queue and not to a program. As long as the receiving program understands the message format, it can process the request. This simple fact is the reason why message middleware has become so popular as the underpinning for application integration (see [Pat98, Yan97] for examples).

In this section, we describe the fundamental technology and functionality to be added to messaging middleware to further ease the integration of applications based on messaging. In doing so, we introduce an environment that is referred to as a *message broker*[Sch96].

9.6.1 Application Bridging

The fundamental step in application integration is to enable two particular applications to exchange data and requests. Based on messaging middleware, this goal is achieved by defining message sets and by providing adapters. That solution has the following implications.

For each application, a collection of messages that represents all logically related services the application supports is defined. This requires the definition of all data that has to be passed to the application when a service is requested, as well as the data that is returned as response to a request. Such a collection of messages is called a *message set*. An application, A1. that wants to invoke a service of another application, A2, has to create the corresponding request message from the message set that A2 supports, and then A1 has to put the message into an input queue of A2. If A2 is a message-based application, it gets the message from its input queue and processes it; on return, it submits a corresponding response message.

If the invoked application or the invoking application is not message based, special programs called *adapters* have to be provided. If the invoked application is not message based, an adapter gets the message from the queue on behalf of the application and invokes the application appropriately. This procedure requires that the adapter decodes the message, determines the proper function to invoke, and maps the data according to the invoked application function's input data structure. Note, that sequence is similar to the invocation mechanisms of the workflow management system, as discussed in section 3.4.4 on page 89. On return, an adapter catches the output data, encodes it into the corresponding response message, and puts it into the invoking application's response queue. If the invoking application is not message based, it does not create a request message itself but invokes an adapter that creates the corresponding message and puts it into the target application's input queue. If appropriate, this adapter also waits for the associated response and returns it to the invoking application in the format expected. Note the similarity to the RPC mechanism discussed in section 9.4.1 on page 317.

It is usual to use the term *front-end* adapter for adapters provided for invoking applications, and the term *back-end* adapter for adapters provided for invoked applications. Then, *application bridging* denotes the provision of a front-end or back-end adapter for a particular application or generic application subsystem. An example of an application bridge is a back-end adapter that allows CICS transactions to be invoked by simply putting messages into a queue. Another example is a back-end adapter to invoke functions in SAP R/3 by means of message submission.

Because of the importance of message sets for application integration corresponding standards, such as S.W.I.F.T. or EDIFACT, have been established for a multitude of application areas. Application bridging often encompasses the transformation between the different message formats of the applications to be integrated.

9.6.2   Message Routing

The next important step in application integration is to enable more complicated patterns of message routing than simply passing a message from one application to another.

For example, in Figure 9.12, an application sends (**1**) a request message into an input queue using, for example, an appropriate adapter. A service called a message

Figure 9.12 Message Routing

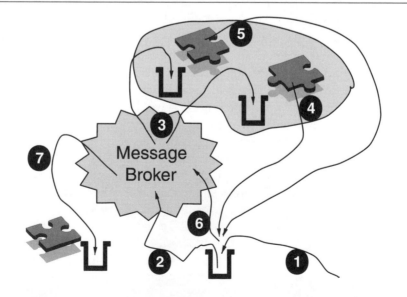

router picks up the message and determines (**2**) that it has to pass the message to two different applications (**3**); it might even be necessary to transform the message to two different formats, one format for each application to be invoked. When finished, the invoked applications send response messages to the message router (**4**, **5**). The message router determines that it has to combine both messages (**6**) before sending it to yet another application (**7**).

Message routing allows one to define a script that specifies sequences of application invocations, including invocations of necessary transformation steps for the messages involved. Considering message transforms as applications, a message routing script simply defines the control flow between applications. Thus, such a script can describe a complex transformation of a particular incoming message, or the order of invocations of applications that have to process an incoming request, or both in an intermixed manner.

9.6.3 Message Brokering

In simple application bridging environments, adapters and message transformation routines are often handcrafted. They are built specifically for particular applications or for pairs of applications that need to be integrated. When each application has to exchange requests and data with any other application of the environment, a simple application bridging approach requires that $N \times (N - 1)$ adapters and message set transformations be provided to integrate N applications.

As usual in those situations, the introduction of a neutral hub reduces the complexity. The message set of each of the N applications of the environment must be transformed into a neutral format and vice versa. The neutral hub in an application bridging environment is called a *message broker* (see Figure 9.13). A message broker introduces additional components and features to the overall environment as we discuss next.

First of all, a message broker environment maintains a message repository. The *message repository* contains all information needed to transform the messages of a particular message set into messages of another format. This information includes the definition of the structure of all messages of all supported message sets, rules for mapping messages between different formats, and transformation functions for special semantic mappings like data cleansing functions. For example, the message repository could contain the structure of EDIFACT messages, rules on how to translate them into XML format, and a special transformation routine to compute net prices. This routine would require to take care of different VAT rates of various countries based on country code fields of an input messages. The content of the message repository is maintained by corresponding tools.

The message repository is also used by the adapters to map message sets of the applications they support into the neutral format of the message broker, and vice versa. This information can then be used at runtime by generic adapters, which

Figure 9.13 The Message Broker Environment

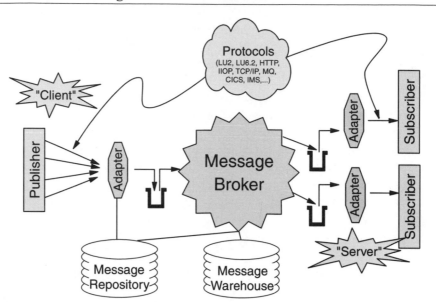

dynamically transform messages on-the-fly, or at buildtime to create a transformation function for each supported message, which is then simply invoked at run time by a static adapter. Routing scripts can be stored in the message repository too. These scripts are used by the message broker itself at runtime to determine for each incoming message which applications to invoke and how to perform complex message transformations.

The routing mechanisms discussed so far—application bridging or routing scripts—define statically the applications that are invoked for an incoming message. By additionally supporting a publish/subscribe mechanism, a message broker environment gains a lot of flexibility. An application that wants to submit a message does not use the put operation to send a message to a specified input queue of a particular application, but it *publishes* a message via the message broker, externalizing selected fields from the message. Applications that want to receive messages published in this way do not just use the get operation to fetch messages from their input queue, but they additionally *subscribe* to messages of a particular content. A subscription can be perceived as a query on some fields of the published message. The message broker delivers a published message to the input queue of a subscribing application if the message qualifies under the query of the subscription request.

Subscriptions can be done statically or dynamically. Static subscription means that a subscription request that is associated with an application (that means its input queue) is specified in a separate step. For example, an administrator might subscribe a particular application to direct specific messages to the application's input queue. Dynamic subscription means that the application itself subscribes to specific messages at runtime. For example, a stockticker application might allow the specification of company names for which stock quotes are reported. For this purpose, it subscribes to messages for stock quotes of exactly the requested companies.

A message broker may provide support for *message annotation*. This means that a message can be combined with operational data from databases or with data from other messages (or both). Those annotations can be defined in the subscription request or in a routing script. In the same way, a message broker allows the specification of the exact data fields to be delivered from a published (and possibly annotated) message. The similarities to a join operation and a project operation as known from relational databases are obvious. It is, therefore, usual to talk about "joining" messages with operational data or other messages and about "projecting" fields from messages. Finally, the format in which the message has to be delivered, such as an XML message, can be specified in a subscription request. In a message broker environment, subscription requests and routing scripts are stored in the message repository.

For example, an application periodically publishes messages containing stock quotes, externalizing the name of the company the stock quote is for and the associated stock value. Another application subscribes to stock quotes of the company named "Traveluck" in case the value is above $100. It further requests that the message be annotated with the industry segment of the company and the number of employees. Each published stock quote is analyzed by the message broker, and only the messages containing quotes for Traveluck exceeding $100 are filtered out for the subscriber. The additionally requested data is retrieved from the underlying database and combined with the message before the message is delivered to the subscribing application.

The *message warehouse*, as shown in Figure 9.13, is used by the message broker to permanently store messages of certain predefined types. Of course, these message might be annotated and projected. Most importantly, messages are held in the message warehouse to allow for analytical processing, for example. Also, the message warehouse stores messages that have to be replayed periodically for a certain period of time. This period, as well as the time when a message to be replayed expires and can be removed from the message warehouse, can be defined with corresponding tools.

A message broker supports in a straightforward manner the *hub-and-spoke* paradigm for application integration. Applications (called "clients" in figure 9.13 on the facing page) submit messages to the message broker via published requests or simple put operations. The message broker as a "hub" determines the applications to be invoked (called "servers" in Figure 9.13), based on routing scripts or subscription requests. The invocation requests are delivered by submitting the corresponding messages to the applications' input queues, that is along the "spokes." The actual invocation might be performed by associated adapters in case servers at the end of some spokes are not message-based application, for example. Similarly, "clients" might use adapters to pass messages to the "hub."

9.6.4 Complex Requests

A message routing script can be perceived as a process model for handling an incoming message. The activities of this process model represent message transformation functions as well as applications to be invoked for performing message-related business functions. The control connectors of this process model manage the order in which these functions are invoked, and data connectors manage the accompanied data flow, like passing parts of the original message or newly produced messages to their target functions. Since no human beings are involved, no staff resolution needs to be performed. Furthermore, all activities are defined as automatic; they are started by the workflow management system once navigation reaches them. The resulting workflows are often referred to as *complex requests*.

Complex requests are typical for hub-and-spoke environments. Often, they represent or contain units of work, making use of atomic spheres or compensation spheres, we discussed in Chapter 7. Also, the activity implementations are often existing applications that must be invoked with the data format they expect. The transformation into the appropriate data format can be specified explicitly as part of the process model or can be performed implicitly by the workflow management system. The latter is done by the program execution components (see section 10.5 on page 378) that realize the various invocation mechanisms supported by the workflow management system (see section 3.4.4 on page 89). Of course, these components may use the transform functions available in the message broker environment.

Figure 9.14 depicts the processing of a complex request. The incoming message represents a funds transfer from account B to account A. The message broker detects that the message must be processed as a workflow. It transforms the original message into a corresponding message for the underlying workflow management system and submits it to the workflow management system's input queue. As a result, the process model specified in the request message is instantiated. The process model specifies that a CICS transaction is used to increase account A and an IMS transaction is used to decrease account B. Before these transactions can be invoked, the data passed to the workflow system must be transformed into the two different formats that are expected by these two transactions. Next, these transactions are invoked in parallel, and both must commit to achieve a new consistent state, which means they run in an atomic sphere. After that, accounting operations are initiated, which in turn are implemented as a subprocess.

The decision whether or not message transformations need to be described as (part of) process models and run as workflows depends on several issues. For example, simple message transformations, especially transforming a message into the storage structure immediately required by an application, can be performed implicitly by the program execution components of the workflow management system. Note that in this sense, program execution components can be perceived as

Figure 9.14 Complex Requests

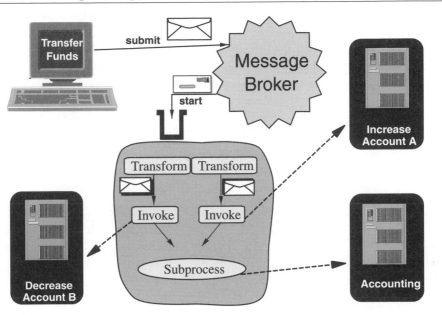

adapters (see section 9.6.1 on page 331). Transformation functions available in the environment are exploited by these components.

Complex message transformations, such as transformations that require a series of invocations of different message transformation functions, are typically not performed by program execution components. They are explicitly specified as routing scripts and run separately before the consuming application is invoked. If the message transformation is a relevant aspect of the business context it can be specified as a process model.

If a complex message transformation is specified as part of a process model, one could consider extracting it into a separate process model. Another option is to generate source code out of it by treating it as a compile sphere, as shown in section 5.8 on page 206. Treating message transformation as a separate process allows its reuse in different process models. Treating it as a compile sphere might improve performance.

Using compile spheres even allows one to generate message transformation scripts that are executed by a generic message transformation engine geared toward performing such scripts. At runtime, the wfms can simply invoke this engine as an activity implementation to perform the required message transformation. A message transformation engine is another component of the overall message broker environment.

Figure 9.15 Message Broker Stack

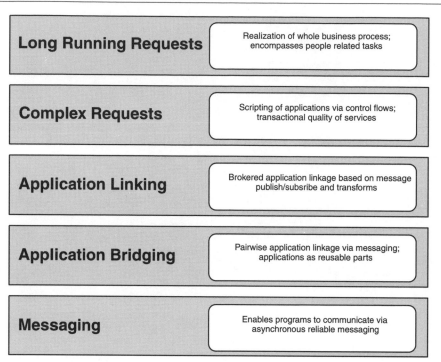

9.6.5   The Message Broker Stack

The overall message broker environment can be arranged as a stack as shown in Figure 9.15.

    The bottom of the stack represents messaging middleware that enables programs to communicate, connectionless, in an asynchronous manner by reliably exchanging messages, (see section 9.4.2 on page 319). Based on messaging, the next level represents application bridging functionality that supports pairwise application integration with adapter technology (see section 9.6.1 on page 331). Next, brokered application linkage functions offer flexible and dynamic application integration features based on message transformation and routing services as well as message publication and subscription (see section 9.6.3 on page 333). Above that, complex requests allow message transformations and application scripting to be combined, adding transactional quality of services (see section 9.6.4 on page 336). At the top level, long-running requests allow the realization of whole business processes, including people-related tasks, or general-purpose workflows.

9.7 Object Brokers

In section 6.3 on page 224, we briefly sketched the architecture of an object request broker environment according to the Object Management Group (OMG). In this chapter we briefly highlight the role of an object request broker (ORB) for application structuring. A reader interested in details about the technologies that we mention in this section is referred to [OH97, OHE96].

9.7.1 Client/Server Structures in ORBs

Each object can provide services as methods that can be called by any other object. An object that invokes methods of another object assumes the role of a client and is thus called a *client object*, whereas an object that provides methods that are invoked by another object assumes the role of a server and is called a *server object*. Note that a server object is not necessarily a "real" object; it might be a huge monolithic application wrapped as an object and externalizing its functions as methods. The object bus provided by an ORB allows one to make method calls independently of the actual location of the server object. It is transparent to a client whether the server object runs in the same address space as the client or in a different address space, and can even run on a different node. Consequently, an ORB facilitates the creation of distributed client/server applications.

To make that facilitation happen, each server object has to be described to the environment by an interface definition language (IDL). Based on the definitions stubs are generated for use by clients of the server object to call the needed methods. The stub deals with all the details required to exchange requests and their responses with the object bus. Note the similarity to what has been briefly discussed for remote procedure calls in section 9.4.1 on page 317. Stubs are generated on a per-language base. Clients written in C++ or Java use the C++ or Java stub of the server object. As a result, the language used to implement the server object is transparent to its clients; that means server objects are language independent.

Of course, a server object can use methods of other server objects to implement its own services, that is a server object might itself be a client. Because the location of the server objects used is transparent, an application with an arbitrary multitier structure typically results.

As within other applications, the three-tier structure has a canonical role. The end-user interface runs on the client node, the application server is realized via business objects hosted on the mid-tier; and the data resides at the backend (see section 9.6.1 on page 331). Recall that data objects that might be associated with the business objects (see section 6.1.1 on page 210) perform all data manipulations. For this purpose, so-called *connectors* can be used. Connectors hide the idiosyncrasies of backends. For example, if the values of a data object have to be retrieved or stored by invocation of appropriate CICS transactions, a corresponding connector hides the protocols used to call the associated programs. To a certain degree, connectors are comparable to adapters (see section 9.6.1 on page 331) since they allow access to programs that are not immediately usable in an ORB environment. In particular, connectors are a means to integrate non-object-based applications and object applications.

9.7.2   TP-Monitor Aspects of an ORB

A business object (or server object, in general) implements business functions; it does not deal with any system aspects. Nevertheless, answers to questions like the following ones are important in practice. How is the server object activated when a client object calls a method of a server object? How is scalability achieved when multiple clients request services from a server object? In an ORB environment, the *object adapter* deals with these kinds of aspects.

The object adapter informs the ORB about the presence of a particular server object on a node. When a client makes a method call, the object adapter invokes the method of the server object in its address space and passes the results back to the ORB. The object adapter decides whether to create and run multiple replicas of a server object to cope with many concurrent client requests and balances such requests across these replicas. Thus, with object adapters, an ORB environment achieves scalability of server objects. A server object can be written with a single client at a time in mind and the ORB scales the object up to serve many concurrent client requests.

Recall from section 6.3 on page 224, one of the common object services provided by an ORB is the so-called object transaction service (OTS) [Obj97]. This service allows transaction boundaries to be established around the invocation of methods of possibly multiple objects. Because these objects can run on any node in the environment, OTS facilitates physically distributed transactions. At the end of such a transaction (be it explicitly requested or unsolicited because of a crash), OTS runs a two-phase commit protocol between the resource managers used by the objects. Thus, with OTS, an ORB environment facilitates applications that can recover from system or application malfunctions.

In summary, an ORB provides a scalable and robust environment. Clients invoke services via stubs that generate request messages corresponding to method calls. The ORB determines an available server object that implements a particular method, selects one of these objects, and invokes the method on the selected object by means of object adapters. Altogether, these functions reveal that an ORB can be seen as some sort of a TP monitor.

9.8   Distributed Applications

An object request broker supports the construction of applications whose various components might run on different nodes. The components might be written in different programming languages and even according to different programming models.

Also, a message broker facilitates the construction of a similar kind of application. In a message broker environment, the communication between components is based on asynchronous message exchange, in contrast to the synchronous style of communication predominant in ORB environments.

The abstract application structure facilitated by both object broker and message broker environments, is called a *distributed application* structure. A distributed application consists of various parts that can run in different environments and even on different nodes, and the parts can be written in different programming languages. Most frequently, a distributed application has a multitier structure.

Figure 9.16 depicts a nondistributed application. It consists of a collection of tightly coupled modules that are written in the same programming language with predetermined formats and protocols of how and when to exchange parameters, and so forth. In contrast, a distributed application is a collection of loosely coupled programs. When an application is built with a distributed application structure in

Figure 9.16 Distributed Application

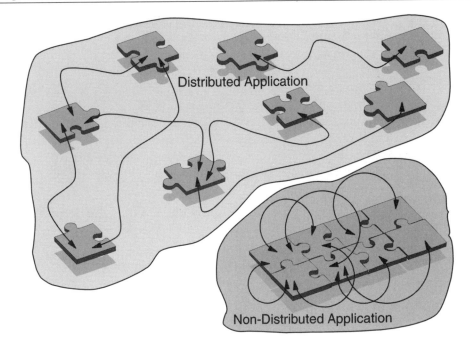

mind, it is very flexible with respect to component placement. It can be adapted to a multitude of hardware and software configurations.

A component-based application that is implemented with business objects on top of an ORB becomes automatically a distributed application. This is some sort of side-effect when object broker technology is used. When existing applications are integrated by message broker technology, the resulting application is automatically a distributed application. Since component-based software construction and message-based application integration are two major trends found in practice, distributed applications will become a frequently exploited application structure.

9.9   Web Applications

The integration aspect we focused on in this chapter until now was integration of applications. Another aspect of integration becoming more and more important is stimulated by Internet technology in general and web technology in particular: the integration of processes and people.

At the beginning browser technology provided the capability to access static web pages only. These pages were Hypertext Markup Language (HTML) documents with fixed content that could be retrieved and rendered. In the next step, web pages and their content could be dynamically constructed with CGI (Common Gateway Interface) scripts and, more recently, servlets. Basically, the browser requests from the web server the invocation of a particular program that returns a web page as result. Such a program can be simple, such as composing a web page out of fragments locally available on the web server, or more complicated, such as a program that invokes a transaction on the next tier to get the required data from an operational database (see Figure 9.17).

By exploiting Java technology, a browser can even load applets, which are "little" programs that perform local functions such as the verification of user input. An applet can use the object bus of an ORB to access server objects. For this purpose, the client machine either has an ORB installed, or the required part of the ORB is loaded as an applet (then called "ORBlet") to the browser. Figure 9.18 shows some of the possible combinations. For example, a browser first loads a simple HTML page offering the user a menu. When the user selects a menu item, another HTML page is loaded together with Java code that verifies user input and finally invokes services from server objects via the object bus. The server objects in turn access data at the backend.

The browser thus performs some sort of presentation services. The web server or the ORB acts as a control flow service, determining which CGI script, servlet, server object, etc., to invoke. At the backend, transactions can be invoked to manipulate operational data. Comparing Figure 9.17 and figure 9.4 on page 315 reveals the similarity between the sketched web environment and a TP monitor. Based on

Figure 9.17 The Web as TP-Monitor Environment

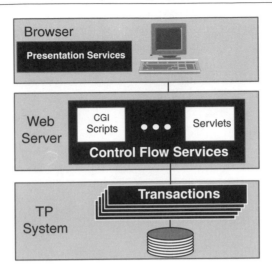

this combination of web technology with Java, ORB, and transaction technology, the Web can be perceived as a gigantic TP monitor.

Browsers are ubiquitous. Theoretically, this ubiquity enables access to all functions and data available in an enterprise. What is needed to make the theory real is that an enterprise provides appropriate functions accessible from the Web. For

Figure 9.18 Three-Tier Structures on the Web

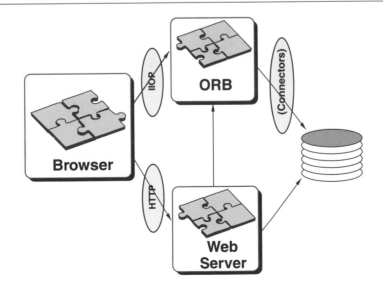

this purpose, servlets or ORB server objects can be used from within appropriate web pages, as sketched above. With this approach, people can be closer to the services provided by an enterprise, customers can browse through online catalogs and place orders from the Web, sales persons can check availability of goods and their delivery dates even if at customer sites, employees can manipulate their worklists and start workitems even if off site, and so on. Also, people can be better connected with processes and processes between enterprises can be better coupled: for example, a customers can check the state of their orders, a company can start a delivery process at a supplier and monitor its state, and so on. Applications from the areas of customer relationship management, sales force automation, value chains, supply chains, etc., are obvious. These are only a few sample applications from the area of "electronic commerce."

Figure 9.19 depicts a "virtual enterprise" scenario, a refinement from the one given in section 1.3 on page 4.

Figure 9.19 Virtual Enterprise

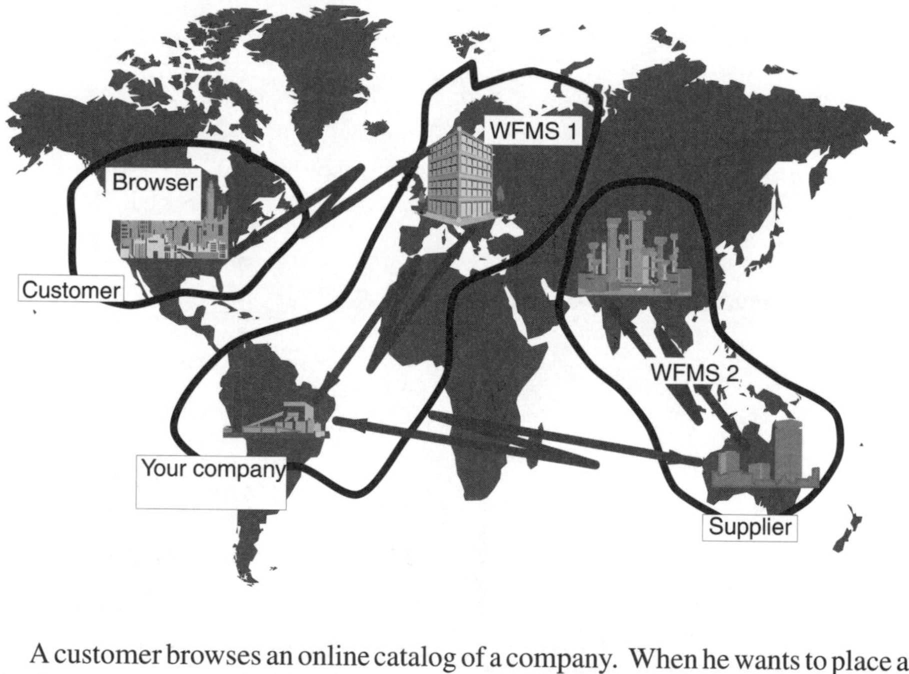

A customer browses an online catalog of a company. When he wants to place an order, he starts an associated order process. For this purpose, the browser may make available an applet that uses server objects at the company's ORB, implementing the OMG workflow management facility, discussed in section 6.4 on page 226. The order process may be distributed, involving people from organizations in different locations of the company. One of the subprocesses of the order process may be outsourced to another company. To start and monitor this process, the workflow management system of the company uses an implementation of the WfMC interface 4 to communicate with the workflow management system of the company to whom the process has been outsourced. This process again can be distributed.

9.10 Workflow-based Applications

In section 9.1.2 on page 309 we discussed the relevance of flow independence for an application. By separating its business process aspects from its business algorithm, an application becomes very flexible. Instead of determining all applications affected by changes of a business process and modifying the corresponding application code (including all related efforts like compiling, testing, etc.), the business process itself is directly modified by changing the corresponding process model in the underlying workflow management system.

The resulting application structure is shown in Figure 9.20. The application consists of a collection of process models, such as credit applications, order placements, or trip reservations, and a collection of activity implementations, that is programs that encode business algorithms that support users in performing activities (e.g., entering customer data, computing interest rates, editing letters, etc.). Running the application means that the workflow management system navigates through the process models and invokes the activity implementations of the appropriate activities of the process models. Such an application is called a workflow-based application. A workflow-based application has all the benefits of flow-independent applications discussed in section 9.1.2 on page 309.

Figure 9.20 Structure of Workflow-based Applications

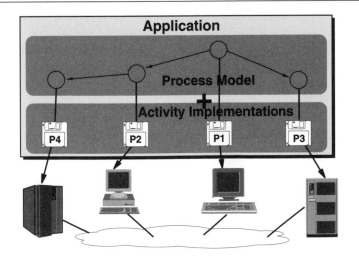

Furthermore, workflow-based applications have a lot more properties that are automatically inherited as the result of exploiting workflow technology and that are cumbersome to achieve an application is implemented completely with a programming language. A workflow-based application has the following characteristics:

- **Distributed**. The workflow management system invokes an activity implementation wherever it is located. With activity implementations placed on different machines, the resulting application consists of pieces that run at different locations.

- **Heterogeneous**. Different activity implementations can run not only on different machines but the hosting environments on these machines can be very different. For example, the operating system can differ from machine to machine; the activity implementations can run in native operating system address spaces or in TP monitors or on an ORB, they can be written in any programming language, they can comply with a variety of programming models; and so on. The workflow management system invokes the activity implementations independently of any of these aspects. Thus, the resulting application consists of heterogeneous pieces.

- **Parallel**. Activities on many different paths can be active within an instance of a process model. This is simply achieved by specifying multiple start activities of a process model (see section 4.7.6 on page 169) or by specifying an activity with multiple outgoing control connectors whose transition conditions evaluate to true (or are simply specified to be constantly true). Thus, the resulting application runs multiple pieces in parallel.

- **Recoverable**. Activities can be grouped into compensation spheres (see section 7.5.3 on page 261), and activities with transactional implementations can be grouped into atomic spheres (see section 7.4.2 on page 253). By using these unit-of-work concepts, the resulting application becomes backward recoverable. By simply using a workflow management system, the resulting application has a persistent context (see section 7.6.1 on page 274). This persistence automatically provides forward recoverability of the application to its latest context, and by exploiting safe activities (see section 7.6.4 on page 282) full forward recoverability is achieved.

In particular, a workflow-based application is a distributed application in the sense described in section 9.8 on page 341. Finally, recall the other properties that the workflow management system provides for a workflow-based application, such as enforcing constraints like durations by means of notifications, or tracking the history of application executions with the aid of auditing and monitoring. A workflow-based application is much more than just a coded script invoking business algorithms!

Chapter 11 discusses the development process for workflow-based applications. Finally note that the structure introduced in section 6.1.4 on page 219 for object-oriented applications is that of a workflow-based application.

9.10.1 Customization

Often, the business process aspects of an application must be changed if the application is used at different locations. For example, a company wants to use an application at different sites or countries it operates in, or an application is an off-the-shelf application offered to a variety of companies. The origin of these changes is that different companies or sites of the same company follow different business processes even when deploying the same application (e.g., companies process orders differently), or that business processes are affected by country specific law (e.g., tax rates or auditing regulations vary from country to country).

Workflow-based applications allow companies to easily customize their business processes. To adapt a workflow-based application according to different business processes, the affected process models of the application are simply changed by use of the graphical buildtime features of the underlying workflow management system. As a result, no coding efforts (and resulting tasks) are required for this aspect of customization. Consequently, the introduction of an application within different companies or at different sites of a particular company is (often dramatically) accelerated. Because of this inherent benefit, standard applications are build as workflow-based applications. It is interesting to note that depending on the coverage of a standard application, the overall system can be made up of many hundreds of process models and many thousands of activity implementations.

An activity implementation of a workflow-based application is flow independent. This means that (ideally) it makes no assumptions about its position in a series of invocations of activity implementations, about privileges related to its invocation, etc. Such an activity implementation can be used in a variety of process models, that means it is a granule of reuse. This kind of reusability is independent of object technology. When object technology is used for activity implementations, the activity implementations are methods of business objects; even business algorithms can be customized according to an individual company's need by overriding selective method implementations of particular business objects. Because this capability further increases the flexibility of a workflow-based application, some vendors of standard applications operate with business objects in this way.

9.10.2 Integration

The workflow-based application paradigm also supports application integration. It is the result of the capability of a workflow management system to invoke many different kinds of executables and to manage data flow between application pieces.

Figure 9.21 shows a workflow-based application that integrates a variety of applications into a new application.

Figure 9.21 Integrating Applications Based on Workflow Technology

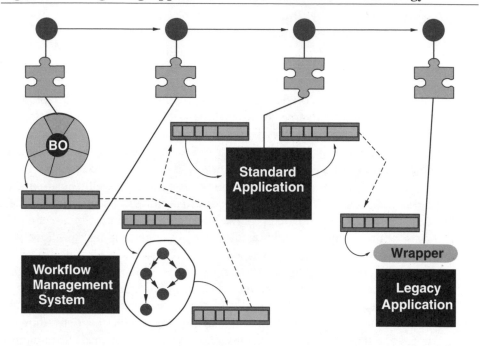

The scenario assumed in Figure 9.21 is the following. A company wants to build a new application system with a minimum programming effort. They use existing applications as well as newly purchased standard applications. The functionality offered by the standard applications has to be modified and extended according to the company's needs. Extensions to the standard applications are provided by existing functionality of legacy applications, by business objects that are newly written or purchased, and by other workflow-based applications that the company already built. These functions are composed into the required application system by specification of appropriate process models. The activity implementations of these process models are methods of the business objects, subprocesses matching other workflow-based applications, functions or processes provided by the standard applications, and functions externalized by legacy applications. When this application system is run, the workflow management system navigates through instances of the underlying process models and invokes the corresponding executables. It calls methods, starts subprocesses, invokes transactions or workflows within the standard applications, and calls legacy applications. The data needed by the different executables is passed, based on the specification of the data flow in the process models.

9.10.3 Wrappering

To exploit legacy applications in other applications (like workflow-based applications) the functions implemented by legacy applications must be invocable from the outside. The standard technique to furnish this requirement is to use so-called wrappers or gateways [BS95b]. A wrapper is a program that provides callable interfaces for selective functionality of the legacy application, as shown in Figure 9.22.

Figure 9.22 Preparing Existing Applications for Exploitation in Workflows

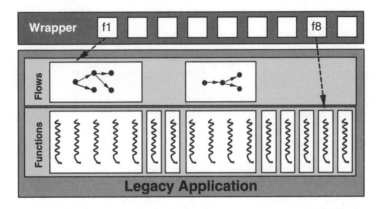

Such an interface can externalize a simple function, such as interface f8 in the figure, or a micro script implemented within the legacy application that already ties a collection of simple functions together, such as interface f1. The reason for not externalizing all simple functions is that in many situations only a certain invocation sequence of simple functions maintains consistency (see the related discussion in section 6.1.2 on page 213). This means, that the invocation of an arbitrary subset of simple functions of a legacy application is not meaningful.

Note that a similar argument applies for standard applications. Although many simple functions of a standard application may be callable from the outside, separate interfaces are sometimes provided for integrating a standard application with other applications. Using these separate interfaces guarantees consistent manipulations of the underlying resources. In this sense, these separate interfaces are wrappers for a standard application.

Finally, wrapper techniques are often used for a lazy migration of legacy applications. By use of a wrapper, one externalized function after the other can be rewritten. Once a function callable via a wrapper has been rewritten, the new implementation can be called instead of the old interface provided by the wrapper. With workflow technology, this result is achieved by changing the specification of the program associated as an activity implementation. A program activity simply refers to the name of the program that implements the activity. The properties of this program (like the name of the executable to be called) is specified separately.

Changing the name of the executable to be invoked applies to all referring activities at once if the workflow management system binds programs late to activities; for programs bound early the affected process models must be translated.

Thus, the workflow-based application paradigm helps in reengineering legacy applications over time. Without time pressure functions of the legacy application can be rewritten and intermixed with functions that have not yet been rewritten yet. If all needed functions are newly implemented, the legacy application can be switched off.

Chapter 10

Architecture and System Structure

In section 1.17 on page 24, we specified the operational and enterprise requirements for a production workflow management system. We show in this chapter that the structure of message monitors and application clusters, as presented in Chapter 9, are the appropriate base for building a production workflow management system that meets the specified requirements. In particular, these structures help to address the requirements for availability and scalability. We then further refine the system structure and show how relational database technology, message queuing, and transaction management are exploited.

10.1 Architectural Principles

The most important operational criteria for a production workflow management system are availability and scalability. These characteristics are provided by the message monitor structure we discussed briefly in section 9.5 on page 323. In this section, we show in detail how the message monitor achieves both availability and scalability.

10.1.1 Availability

A system is considered *available* if and only if it is up and running and producing correct results. One can then define the *availability* of a system as the fraction of time it is available. A system is then *highly available* if the availability is close to 1. Thus *high availability* is the property of a system that is up and running all the time, always producing correct results. This is in essence the famous 7×24 requirement, which means that the system should be up 7 days a week, 24 hours a day. All mission-critical systems, such as database management systems, TP monitors, and workflow management systems must be highly available.

A system *fails* if it gives a wrong answer or no answers at all. Thus, the more a system fails and the longer it takes to repair the system after it fails, the less it is available.

We call the average time a system runs before it fails its *Mean Time Before Failure* (**MTBF** or ψ). The MTBF measures the *reliability* of the system. We call the average time it takes to repair the system after failure the *Mean Time To Repair* (**MTTR** or ρ). The MTTR measures the *downtime* of the system. We can now define the availability α as :

$$\alpha = \frac{\psi}{\psi + \rho}$$

Thus, availability can be improved by:

- Improving reliability; that means MTBF $\psi \to \infty$: $\lim\limits_{\psi \to \infty} \frac{\psi}{\psi+\rho} = 1$

- Decreasing downtime; that means MTTR $\rho \to 0$: $\lim\limits_{\rho \to 0} \frac{\psi}{\psi+\rho} = 1$

Systems are assigned to availability classes. Each availability class defines an appropriate availability. The availability class name defines the number of nines in the appropriate availability. For example, class 2 has two nines in the appropriate availability (99%), class 4 has four nines in the appropriate availability (99.99%). The scale starts at the low end with commodity uni-processor systems (class 2) and ends at the high end with in-flight aircraft computers (class 6); in between are standard open system clusters (class 3), clusters with special hardware/software (class 4), and, systems like IBM S/390 Parallel Sysplex HW (class 5).

There are numerous causes for computer failures; however, all indicators show that software is the problem. As with hardware, there are two types of errors: hard errors that must be fixed before the system can continue to operate and soft errors that go away when the function is retried or switched over to a backup process.

As said before, two options exist for improving availability: improving MTBF or reducing MTTR. MTBF can be improved by having multiple implementations for the same function possibly developed by different development teams. When the function needs to be carried out, all implementations are run and then the results are compared. If the results are different, one approach is to take the majority of the votes and keep on running. This is unrealistic in practice.

Thus, the only reasonable approach is to reduce MTTR. The downtime of a system is made up of two different times: the time to detect that an error has occurred (*fault detection time*) and the time that is needed to bring the system back to life (*restart time*). Thus one reduces MTTR by improving the fault detection time and reducing the recovery time.

10.1.2   Fault Detection

Detecting faults is the responsibility of the *fault detection monitor*; for obvious reasons also called a *watchdog*. Figure 10.1 shows the different mechanisms that the watchdog can use to detect that a particular process is no longer executing. These mechanisms exploit the capabilities offered by the underlying operating system and messaging middleware.

Figure 10.1 Fault-Detection Monitoring

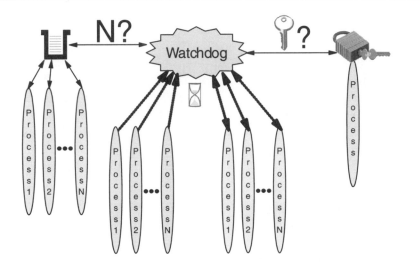

The fastest way to detect that a process has died is to exploit shared operating system locks. Which mechanism is actually used depends on the functions that are provided by the operating system, such as semaphores in Windows NT. When the observed system starts in an operating system process, it creates a lock and puts a hold onto the lock. It then returns the lock identifier to the watchdog, which then tries to acquire the lock. As the lock is still held by the process, this request is not honored. If the process terminates, the lock is released and the lock is granted to the watchdog which then knows that the process has terminated.

The message queue manager provides an administrative function that allows programs to query the number of participants that are attached to a queue. The watchdog periodically invokes this function to find out the number of processes that are attached to the queue. If the number has changed, the watchdog knows exactly how many operating system processes have terminated.

In the case of heartbeating, the process itself plays the active role. It periodically sends an "I'm alive" message to the watchdog

periodically. If no message arrives as scheduled, the watchdog treats this a failure: the process may have terminated or may be looping.

Pulse requires the exchange of messages between the watchdog and the monitored process. The watchdog sends out a message and the process returns an appropriate message. This exchange of messages is typically done periodically or on an explicit request by the watchdog.

If heartbeating and pulsing are active and neither a heartbeat arrives nor a pulse is honored, the watchdog may be isolated or malfunctioning. In this case, the watchdog "commits suicide" and forces a complete shutdown of the system. This action is called the *dead man switch*.

The fault recognition time of each of the methods is different. The fault recognition time for the operating system lock approach is practically zero. All others have a well-defined fault recognition time, which is the time period between two inquiries to the queue—the heartbeat interval, or the pulse interval. Thus, these intervals are customizable to allow an optimal MTTR.

However, fault recognition time is not the only criteria for selecting a method. The operating system lock, for example, in general only works on a single operating system image; the pulse method on the other hand works in heterogenous distributed environments, provides the greatest flexibility, but needs the most resources as two messages need to be exchanged. Generally, a combination of these methods is used. The makeup of the combination is determined by the particular setup and environment.

10.1.3   Client Recovery

In a client/server environment, the client has typically to perform a series of actions when it restarts after the connection between the client and the server has been broken. A broken connection could be the result of many things: the connection itself broke, the server went down, or the client went astray. First, the client has to locate all outgoing calls that were active, when the connection broke. Then, it has to determine the appropriate state of the calls and, based on the state, take the necessary actions to finish the calls.

If the client/server communication is based on persistent queues, recovery is trivial. All outstanding calls are still in the queue. If not yet processed, they are in the server's input queue and will be processed by the server automatically. If processed, the appropriate output can be found in the client's response queue. Thus, client recovery is very easy and very fast, which results in an improved client MTTR. Using persistent queues for client/server communication provides for high availability of clients.

10.1.4   Server Recovery

Unless persistent queues are used, it is the client's job to find out whether a request has completed. Thus, the server must provide information that allows the client to determine whether the request has completed, otherwise the client might submit the request twice. This is no problem for simple inquiry type requests but creates a severe problem if the server has performed a *non-redoable operation* such as crediting an account or dispensing money. Reissuing the request might result in executing a non-redoable operation twice.

In the case of persistent queues, the client does not reissue the request a second time. However, the server still must make sure that it does not process the message in the queue twice because doing so causes the same problem.

Recovery of a server must ensure (1) that a request that is active at the time of failure is not reexecuted and (2) that the request is completed and an appropriate result is returned. In other words, the issue in server recovery is the non-redoability. To recover then, the server must re-create the state it was in *after* the last completed non-redoable operation.

One approach is to save the state on a nonvolatile device, such as a disk drive, before executing a non-redoable operation; that means the server performs *check-pointing*. At restart, the server restores the last checkpoint, checks whether the last non-redoable operation actually ran successfully, and depending on the outcome, reruns the operation or not. The implementation effort associated with checkpointing is, in general prohibitively high, and is only used for resource managers, such as database management systems or message queuing systems.

A much simpler approach can be taken if all clients requests can be mapped to transactions, in particular, if no non-redoable operations are requested. In this situation, if the server is restarted after a failure, the server state includes all committed transactions but no residues of transactions that have aborted or were active at time of failure. This means that the server performs implicitly the two actions needed to come up with a valid state. First, it performs a checkpoint at each commit. This is a very efficient form of checkpointing; database management systems, for example, are optimized to make this operation very fast. Second, it recovers by discarding all effects of active and aborted transaction. This is a fast restart method; database management systems, for example, carry out the restart with modest effort. MTTR is improved as all operations are redoable.

Resource managers are servers which *directly* manipulate resources that are shared by a transaction. Typical resource managers are database management systems and message queuing systems. In contrast to this, application servers manipulate resources only through resource managers and use transactions (see section 9.5 on page 323). For example, the message monitor is an application server that uses shared resources but uses a resource manager for this purpose. Furthermore, application servers are *stateless*. They execute each client request within a transaction and maintain all state information through resource managers; that means there is no need to maintain any other local state. So the only remaining difficulty with respect to restarting in an application server environment is client recovery, something that we addressed earlier with the aid of persistent queues.

Figure 10.2 Transaction Boundaries

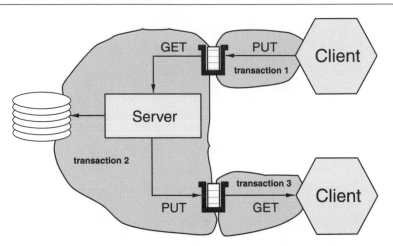

Thus we end up with an overall system structure as show in Figure 10.2. Each client request is carried out as three individual transactions. The client puts its request into the server's persistent input queue within transaction 1. In transaction 2, the server reads the message from the queue, performs appropriate processing including reading from and writing information to the database and puts an appropriate result message into the server's persistent output queue. When the transaction finishes, the message in the input queue has been removed. In transaction 3, the client retrieves the message from the server's output queue. Upon completion of this transaction, the message is removed from the server's output queue.

10.1.5   Hot Pooling

Availability of a single server can be further improved by having a hot pool of servers, as shown in figure 10.3 on the facing page. The concept of hot pools is particularly suitable for application servers. It is the generalization of the warm backup concept, where a *primary server* is doing the real work and a *backup server* performs the function of the watchdog and takes over when the primary server fails. This approach reduces MTTR because no time is needed to create the backup server process.

A hot pool is a collection of application servers that share a common persistent input queue to which the clients send their requests. Whenever a *member* of the hot pool has finished processing a particular request, it immediately gets the next request from the pool's input queue. When a member of the hot pool fails, the others continue processing the requests in the input queue. The hot pool appears as a "virtual application server." As long as one member of the hot pool is active, the "virtual application server" is available. Thus, MTTR is further reduced.

Figure 10.3 Hot Pool

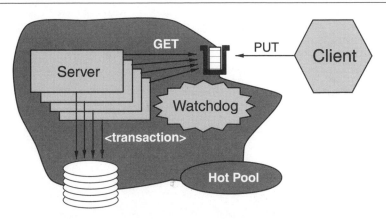

Failure of a member of the hot pool is recognized by the watchdog; it is automatically restarted. On the average, the number of members in the hot pool is constant.

10.1.6   Calculating the Availability Class of a Hot Pool

Let us assume that an event occurs with a probability P. When we carry out the same experiment N times independently, for example, in parallel, and count how often a particular event occurs, then the probability that the event occurs exactly k times is

$$P_k = \binom{N}{k} P^k (1 - P)^{N-k}$$

The availability of hot pool members can be computed using the above formula (binomial distributed). Each member in the hot pool runs a copy of the same software, so availability is the same for each member. The N independent experiments consist of running N hot pool members in parallel, and the event observed is "member available." The probability that *exactly* k members are available of a hot pool having N members is

$$P_k = \binom{N}{k} \alpha^k (1 - \alpha)^{N-k}$$

The probability of *at least* k members being available is

$$P_{\geq k} = \sum_{i=k}^{N} P_i = \sum_{i=k}^{N} \binom{N}{i} \alpha^i (1 - \alpha)^{N-i}$$

For k = 1 we get the probability that an event occurs at least once. Thus, the service provided by its hot pool members is available as long as at least one member of the hot pool is available; that means $P = \alpha$:

$$\alpha_{\text{hot pool}} = P_{\geq 1} = \sum_{i=1}^{N} \binom{N}{i} \alpha^i (1 - \alpha)^{N-i}$$

$$= \sum_{i=0}^{N} \binom{N}{i} \alpha^i (1 - \alpha)^{N-i} - (\binom{N}{0} \alpha^0 (1 - \alpha)^N)$$

$$= (\alpha + (1 - \alpha))^N - (1 - \alpha)^N$$

The availability $\alpha_{\text{hot pool}}$ of a hot pool with N members where each member of the hot pool has the same availability α_{member} is

$$\alpha_{\text{hot pool}} = 1 - (1 - \alpha_{\text{member}})^N$$

If an event has a probability much less than 1 and if it is memoryless, which means its occurrence is not influenced by previous occurrences of the same event, then *the mean time to such an event is the reciprocal of the probability of the event.*

The failing of a hot pool is such an event having the probability $1 - \alpha_{\text{hot pool}}$, thus

$$\text{MTBF}_{\text{hot pool}} = \frac{1}{(1 - \alpha_{\text{hot pool}})}$$

We can now use these formulas to determine the availability of a hot pool. Let us take an example with really bad values for each of the members: MTBF 24 hours, MTTR 6 hours. These values result in a member availability of 80 percent. However, with eight members, a hot pool achieves very good results, as shown in Figure 10.4.

Figure 10.4 shows that the MTBF of a hot pool with eight members is 44 years. Similarly, the downtime has improved, as shown in Figure 10.5.

In other words, a hot pool with eight members gets availability class 5.

10.1.7   Clustering Hot Pools

The availability calculations are correct under the simple assumption that the environment never fails, which means the availability of the environment is 1. This is a rather unrealistic assumption: the hardware can fail, the operating system can fail,

Figure 10.4 Hot Pool MTBF

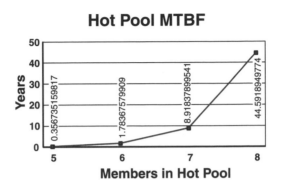

Figure 10.5 Hot Pool Downtime

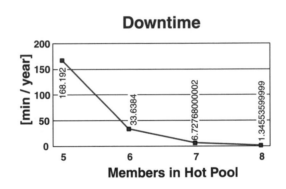

the message queueing system can fail, and so on. If any of these components fail, the hot pool fails.

This situation can be solved by taking the hot pool concept further. Instead of having a hot pool running on a single machine or node, we have a set of nodes each running a hot pool. The set of nodes then again form a hot pool. We called this arrangement an application cluster in section 9.5.3 on page 329.

All systems have access to all of the data. Thus the database management system becomes critical with regard to availability, and appropriate measures must be taken, such as running the database management system in a cluster itself.

10.1.8 Takeover of Hot Pool

If a complete hot pool fails, for example, as the result of an operating system failure, an automatic reroute of the requests to another hot pool is performed automatically as shown in Figure 10.6.

Figure 10.6 Taking Over Hot Pool

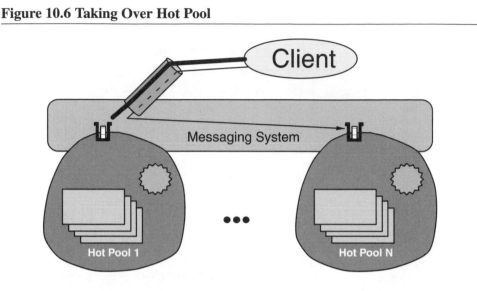

The automatic reroute can be implemented in different ways: (1) the cluster architecture performs it, (2) the messaging system supports reroute directly, or (3) the client performs this specifically for each application.

Thus the client behaves as if nothing has happened.

10.1.9   Spraying

There is a problem associated with the hot pool takeover approach we just discussed. If an error is encountered with a request that has been sent to the hot pool, one cannot know for sure the state of the request. One knows that the request sent to the hot pool arrived in the hot pool's input queue because of the reliability of the message queuing system. However, one does not know whether the request was processed or whether it will be processed when the system recovers. Consequently, when the hot pool takeover mechanism switches to another hot pool the requests sent (and acknowledged by the message queuing system) to the failed hot pool cannot be simply resubmitted to the new hot pool without taking care that the requests are not executed twice. As knowing this information is not possible in most cases, those messages will not be processed until the system comes up again.

If this delay is not acceptable, the client could send out the same message to all hot pools. If it does so, either the client either must be sure that the environment will take care that from an application's perspective the same effects will result as if only a single message was sent, or the client indicates that performing the same request multiple times will not hurt. The first case means that application servers have to be built with request multicasting in mind, this means they have to check whether or not the represented request has already been performed (by an application server of a different hot pool). The second case means that the corresponding request is "repeatable."

From an application server perspective, the application client has to indicate whether or not a request is repeatable. If a request is flagged as repeatable, the receiving application server can perform the corresponding actions immediately, without any further impact on its usual behavior. If a request is not repeatable, the receiving application server must check whether the corresponding actions have already been performed or not. If the actions have already been performed, the application server ignores the request and continues with a new request; otherwise, the requested actions are performed.

Various mechanisms enable an application server to detect that a request has already been performed: for example, each request message may contain a unique request identifier. The identifiers of all requests already performed or currently under processing are persistently stored in a database that is accessible by all application servers within the cluster. Before executing the actions associated with a request, the performing application server checks the existence of the request identifier in this database; if it is already there, the request is not performed; otherwise, the identifier is inserted into this database and the actions corresponding to the request can be executed. Garbage collection of the request identifiers stored can be done according to a protocol that limits the maximum lifetime of request messages within the messaging system. For example, MQSeries allows one to set the maximum lifetime of each message. Request identifiers can be discarded from the database if they are older then the maximum lifetime of the associated message. Because all messages with the corresponding request identifier will be discarded by the messaging system, no application server will ever retrieve this request message again.

10.1.10   Continuous Availability

When maintenance tasks, such as software release upgrades, or replacement of failed hardware components, are required, the affected hot pool or even the whole hosting server must be shut down. In this case, users attached to this hot pool or server typically get an error message when sending a request message to the hot pool or server.

Thus, these users realize the reduced availability of the requested service by experiencing the outage. Typically during an outage, an affected user has to find a hot pool or a server that can service his requests. This search is often done by querying a directory, by calling an administrator, or by calling a help desk. Once the available service is located, the user must logon to it.

Figure 10.7 depicts an application that requests services through an application client.

Figure 10.7 Shutdown

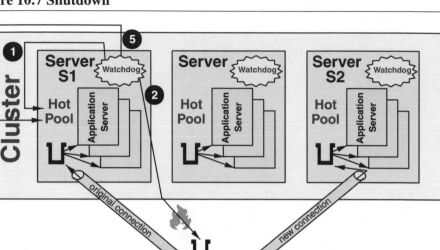

The application client is connected to a hot pool on server S1. Assume that the hot pool on server S1 must be shut down for some maintenance task. Then, the following protocol ensures that the hot pool can be shut down without the application noticing it. This protocol is not initiated as long as one other hot pool is active, thus making sure that this is not the last hot pool that is shutting down.

1. When the watchdog negotiated a shutdown, the hot pool it makes sure that no new connections to this hot pool can be established by any application client.

2. The watchdog determines all application clients that are connected to the hot pool need to be shut down. It sends a message to each of those application clients, indicating that they have to switch immediately to another hot pool. As an optimization option, this message could contain all currently available hot pools providing the same services. Such information can be used in the next step.

3. In response to the request message, each receiving application client selects another available hot pool and logs on to it. From this time on, all new request messages created by that application client are sent via the new connection. The list of available hot pools providing the same services helps the clients to efficiently determine an available hot pool.

4. When the application client establishes its new connection, it closes (all of) its existing connection(s) with the hot pool awaiting shutdown. To assist the hot pool, the application client could inform the hot pool that it is going to close the connection.

5. When all connections to the hot pool awaiting shutdown are closed the watchdog shuts down the hot pool.

Numerous modifications can be implemented to cope with error situations, such as clients that are not responding or clients that cannot find another hot pool.

10.1.11 Scalability

Scalability is the ability to sustain increasing workloads without decreasing an agreed on service level when the underlying resources are also increased.

What we would like to have is *linear scalability*. In this case the formula

$$\text{performed workload} = \gamma \times \text{resources}$$

holds, where the factor is ideally close to one : $\gamma \lesssim 1$.

As Greg Pfister [Pfi95] nicely phrases it, linear scalability can, in principle, be achieved in three different ways. The first one is to work harder by having faster processors. The second way is to work smarter by using better algorithms. The third one is to get help by introducing parallelism.

The structure of stateless application cluster servers implements the third method, introducing parallelism. Thus, the structure not only provides for availability but also for scalability.

10.1.12 Using Stratified Transactions

A request from a client is processed as a transaction. As long as the transaction runs, the database management system needs to hold locks. These locks should be released as early as possible. Holding locks for longer times reduces concurrency since other transactions may be locked out for some time. This issue increases the amount of code that needs to be serialized. In other words, the hot pool members can no longer execute independently and can no longer exploit the capabilities offered by SMP machines or clusters.

Figure 10.8 shows how the message monitor structure can be enhanced by use of stratified transactions a discussed in section 7.6.3 on page 279.

The user puts the request into the server's input queue (IQ). This request is then processed by the server by means of two transactions T_1 and T_2. The first transaction, T_1, reads the message from the input queue, performs the appropriate activities

Figure 10.8 Exploiting Stratified Transactions

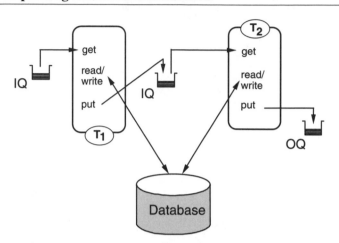

against the database including managing state and then inserts a continuation message into the input queue again. This continuation message is then processed in the second transaction, T_2. The transaction reads the message, performs the remaining activities against the database, and then inserts a message into the output queue (OQ). The user then obtains the reply as usual from this queue.

10.2   System Structure

The message monitor structure is ideally suited for addressing the operational characteristics of a workflow management system and therefore is the preferred structure for building a workflow management system. This preference is particularly true since the natural structure of a workflow management system is that of a stateless application server that operates in a client/server environment.

A major advantage of the message monitor structure is the fact that the workflow management system does not need to exploit operating system functions. Code is thus highly portable, so that deploying it on different platforms is a minor effort unless one wants to exploit the strengths of the various operating systems on which the code is deployed. A typical example of such an exploitation is the support of a workload management system.

The concept of message queuing as the underlying communication mechanism is used for communication not only between clients and the server but also between the servers. All requests are carried out as transactions. Thus we provide the workflow management system with a communication bus for the workflow management system that is similar to the hardware bus of a personal computer, as shown in Figure 10.9.

Figure 10.9 Message Queuing as Communication Bus

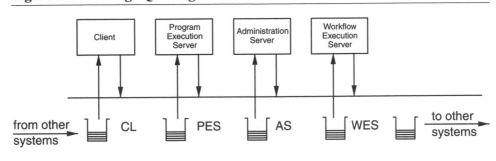

Message Queuing System

When a component needs services from another component, it sends a message, using the queue name of the appropriate component. The targeted component receives the message as soon as it is ready for processing. Correlation identifiers are associated with messages if a response is expected from a component. It is immaterial where each of the components resides, whether on the same processor or on a different processor. With message queuing as the only communication bus, components can be placed wherever they are suited best.

The workflow management system is implemented as a client/server structure as shown in Figure 10.10.

The client exposes the application programming interfaces (API) that allow applications to invoke services offered by the workflow management system. It also hosts the program execution agent that invokes activity implementations to be carried out on the client. The server carries out the functions offered by the workflow management system. For ease of use and maintenance, the server is made up of several independent, individual servers, each of which is responsible for a particular task. The workflow execution server performs the processing of the business process instances, which includes navigating from activity to activity, determining the set of users to perform the activity, and requesting from the program executor the execution of the activity implementations. The program execution server invokes the activity implementations that are carried out on the server. The administration server controls the operation of the workflow management system.

When a client needs services, a message is sent to the server's input queue. For example, if the client wants to make a request to the administration server, it sends an appropriate message to the administration server's input queue (AS). The administration server sends back its response by inserting a message into the client input queue. The client then picks up the message from this queue. Correlation identifiers associate the request with the appropriate reply.

As can be seen, the workflow management system does not access the message queuing system directly but uses its own message layer. This allows it to hide the differences of different message queuing implementations so that different message

Figure 10.10 System Structure

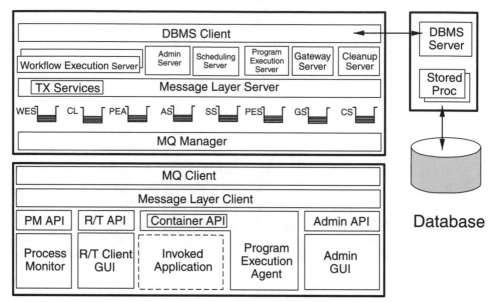

queuing implementations can be supported.

The individual server components access the workflow management system's database by calling the database management system via the database management system client that resides on the server.

The availability and reliability of the workflow management system depends greatly on the availability and reliability of the database management system in which the database is managed. Therefore the database is maintained in a relational database because only relational database management systems address those requirements. However other factors also make relational databases the only choice.

When designers and implementers build the workflow management system, they do not know which properties are most often used by user when making queries against the objects in the database. In fact, users may want to query properties that the workflow management system did not foresee. With a relational database, these query capabilities can easily be implemented by just transforming the user's query into an appropriate SQL statement. To make these queries perform efficiently, the objects that are to be queried must be found with the aid of an index so that objects need not to be scanned. Thus the database management system must provide the option to create and drop indices without requiring changes to the workflow management system's implementation.

New versions of the workflow management system typically require new fields to be made persistent. The database management system must support the notion of a view mechanism that allows the addition of those fields with the old workflow management system version running unchanged. In addition, moving from one version to a newer version must not require that the database be unloaded and reloaded to accommodate a new table schema.

10.2.1 Tier Structures

The different parts of the system structure—the client, the server, and the database management system—can be deployed onto different processors. Figure 10.11 shows the two prominent system structures. In the two-tier structure, the server, the message queuing system, and the database management system are placed on the second tier. In the three-tier structure, the server and the message queuing system are placed on the second tier; the database management system on the third tier.

Figure 10.11 Tier Structures

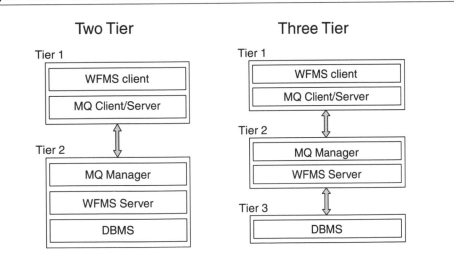

Which system structure provides the best performance depends on a number of factors, such as the availability and power of the different processors, the bandwidth of the communication mechanism between the different processors, the performance of the message queueing system and the database management system, and the usage of stored procedures.

The system structure shown in Figure 10.11 is the simplest structure that the workflow management system can implement. More complex structures can be implemented if desired. An option, for example, is to distribute the different server components across multiple processors. Another option is for the client to have its own message queue manager, which allows the workflow management system to implement safe applications. We discuss safe applications in section 10.5 on page 378.

This system structure can also be extended to the structure of an application cluster and a collection of application clusters. We discuss this extension in sections 10.6 on page 386 and 10.7 on page 388. However before that discussion, we want to dig deeper into the various parts of the workflow management system, the server, the client, and the program execution component.

10.2.2 Accessing the Database

All state data is made persistent in a relational database management system. All operations that the workflow management system carries out are reflected as state changes in the database. The workflow management system can use two options to implement this concept.

The first option, the more traditional one, is to implement the workflow management system on top of the relational database management system. For each request, the appropriate implementation makes multiple calls to the database management system. The second option is to implement the individual actions as a set of stored procedures. For each request, the server just calls the stored procedure. Section 9.3 on page 314 discussed the two types of implementation in detail.

Both setups have their advantages and disadvantages. From these, one can establish guidelines for when to use one instead of the other. Naturally there is no choice if the underlying database management system does not support stored procedures.

In a two-tier setup, there is no reason for not using stored procedures. Because all processing is carried out on one processor, the appropriate savings in processing are not offset by other effects. With this approach, we are saving all processing that is incurred as the result of crossing the firewall between the workflow management system and the database management system.

In a three-tier structure, the use of stored procedures depends on the processing power of the processors on the second and third tier as well as on the bandwidth between the second and the third tier.

If the third tier is a very powerful processor with high availability, such as an S/390 mainframe, then the option of stored procedures should be used. In this case, the processors on the second tier can be made rather small because the processor just has to sustain the load that results from message processing.

If the bandwidth between the second and the third tier is rather low, then a stored procedure set up should be used as well.

If the processors on the second and third tier provide the same processor power and the communication bandwidth is high, then probably a setup without stored procedures should be selected.

What makes the selection of the best setup difficult is that it is determined not only by the raw processor performance and communication bandwidth, but also by the processes that are executed. For example, the size of the containers and the number of work items generated are important factors.

10.3 Servers

As we showed in the previous section, the workflow management system server is made up of a set of server components, each of which performs a particular function. This structure provides for greater flexibility. We discuss each of the server components in detail in this section (except for the distribution server, which we discuss later). For simplicity, we call server components also servers, using their particular function as their identifier, such as administration server.

10.3.1 Transactions

All servers are implemented as stateless application servers that maintain their state in a relational database. It is the structure we showed in section 10.1.4 on page 354. Each request is run as a transaction. For each request, the server performs the processing that is shown as a code snippet in Code Example 10.1.

Code Example 10.1 Running Requests as Transactions

```
BEGIN TRANSACTION
    READ MESSAGE FROM INPUT QUEUE
    ANALZYE REQUEST
    PERFORM REQUEST
    SAVE STATE IN DATABASE
    WRITE MESSAGE(S) TO REPLY QUEUE
COMMIT TRANSACTION
```

The number of accesses of the database depends on the type of request that is carried out. If the transaction makes a large number of SQL calls, the transaction is implemented as a stratified transaction. A typical example where this technique is applied is the generation of workitems when an activity is processed during navigation. In this case, the navigation step is divided into two transactions. The first transaction determines the workitems for the activity and stores these workitems as a single object in the database. The second transaction retrieves this object and generates workitems for each of the users who should receive a workitem causing an access of the database.

A simple example illustrates the advantages of this approach. Let us assume that we perform 10 access of the database to navigate the activity and that 10 workitems are generated. If everything is handled in one transaction, the transaction makes 20 accesses to the database. If the transaction is split into two transactions, the first transaction makes 11 accesses of the database, and the second transaction makes also 11 accesses of the database. In this case, each transaction only takes half of the time of the overall transaction. The time that a transaction waits for resources held by another transaction (transactions are thus serialized) is reduced because locks are held by the transactions for a shorter time. Thus, reducing these conflicts improves scalability of the workflow management system.

10.3.2   Hot Pooling

Most servers are available as hot pools. They read from the same server input queue. The number of members in the hot pool when the workflow management system is started is defined when the workflow management system is set up. The number of the members in the hot pool can be changed by an authorized person by an explicit request or it can be changed dynamically through workload management facilities. This automatic workload management can either be provided by the workflow management system itself or by special workload management facilities. We discuss workload management in detail in section 10.9 on page 396.

10.3.3   Multiple Instances

The operating system maintains an operating system priority for all member of a hot pool. This operating system priority defines the amount of processor resources that are assigned to the each of the members. This has then a direct effect on how fast requests are carried out. However, some of the requests do not need to be carried out as fast as other requests. For example, a query may not be as urgent as a navigation step.

This prioritization can be achieved by having multiple instances of a server, each running with a different operating system priority. Depending on the request, the corresponding message would be inserted into the input queue of the appropriate server. Incidentally, each instance could be running as a hot pool.

10.3.4   Administration Server

All servers are controlled and managed by the *administration server*. Server management and control is not the only task of the administration server. The administration server is responsible for all operational aspects of the workflow management system, such as managing user sessions or performing error management.

Most of the functions are exposed through an API which allows the implementation of a graphical user interface (GUI) to control and monitor the workflow management system. In certain operating system environments, such as OS/390, the administration server functions are also exposed through the operating system console.

The administration server is also the interface to the operating system. On Windows NT, the administration server is defined as a Windows NT service. As such, it honors the appropriate control requests and automatically writes all important information into the Windows NT event log.

The following list summarizes the functions that are provided by the administration server. Some of them were already discussed in Chapter 3.

- The administration server is the first server brought up when the workflow management system starts. Based on information that it maintains in the database, the administration server starts the appropriate servers, each of them with the predefined number of members in the hot pool. The administration server uses trigger services offered by the message queuing system to start a particular server. Using the trigger services avoids the need for the administration server to use operating system services. If the previous running of the workflow management system had terminated abnormally, the administration server performs the appropriate cleanup processing and returns the system to its previous state. When the workflow management system is terminated, the administration server stops each of the servers before shutting itself down.

- The administration server plays the function of the watchdog, we have discussed in the previous section. If it detects that a server or a member in a hot pool has died, it takes a set of actions. (1) It collects any error information that has been emitted by the terminating server to allow post-mortem diagnosis. (2) It restarts the server automatically to keep the number of hot pool members as defined. (3) It sends an appropriate notification to the administrator console so that appropriate actions can be taken.

- The administration server allows the operation administrator to change the state of any server, such as shutting down or starting anew. The operation administrator can thus shut down servers or start them to adapt the number of servers to the needs of the current situation.

- All sessions are maintained by the administration server. When a user wants to establish a session, the request is routed to the administration server. After appropriate authentication information is exchanged, the session is established. If the user cannot provide correct authentication information, the user's access to the workflow management system is blocked. If the session exceeds a specified time limit, the administration server automatically closes the session.

10.3.5   Workflow Execution Server

The main work of the workflow management system is carried out by the *workflow execution server*. It starts and finishes processes, navigates from one activity to the next, performs staff resolution, and sends appropriate requests to the program execution server or program execution agent for launching the activity implementation. It manages work items and the associated work lists. It also writes the audit trail.

It is the workflow execution server that implements the Workflow Management Coalition's interfaces 2 and 5.

10.3.6   Scheduling Server

The scheduling server makes sure that all actions that are time based happen. This action could be the generation of a notification if a specified deadline is exceeded, the deletion of processes or workitems whose retention time has expired, or the resumption of a process that has been suspended long enough.

The scheduling server actually only determines that an action needs to be carried out. The actual actions are taken by the execution server. The scheduling server informs the execution server by sending appropriate messages.

To determine which actions need to be carried out, the scheduling server periodically looks into the database to determine whether actions are overdue. Since this operation could be time consuming, options are available to specify the time window and the frequency in which this lookup should be carried out. Typical examples are every day at 12 P.M. or every hour.

10.3.7   Cleanup Server

Physically removing all data that is related to a particular business process is an expensive and time-consuming task because of the amount of data involved. During its lifetime, a process accumulates quite a lot of data. When the process is immediately removed when the process finishes, performance of the currently running business processes is impacted. It is desirable to perform the removal of business processes from the database at times of low activity. This is the responsibility of the cleanup server.

Options are available to specify the time window in which the cleanup server operates. A typical example is every day from midnight to 4 A.M. This window is divided into periods where the cleanup server is idle, and periods where the cleanup server performs its operation. Having some idle time allows the database to cool down. Without this, other servers could be locked out when they want to access the database.

10.3.8 Modeling Server

The modeling server delivers the functions that are needed by the workflow management system buildtime and the business engineering tools. These function are the ones we have discussed in detail in section 3.3 on page 64 and include Import, Export, Translate, Lock, Unlock, Checkin, Checkout, and all the individual object functions, such as the functions to deal with persons, roles, processes.

The modeling server implements interface 1 of the Workflow Management Coalition.

10.3.9 Gateway Server

The gateway server supports the communication of the workflow management system with another workflow management system if message queuing cannot be used as the communication mechanism. This is the case, for example, on the Internet, where the communication is usually done via e-mail. E-mail typically uses the Simple Mail Transfer Protocol (SMTP) for communication with the message itself provided in Multi-purpose Internet Mail Extensions (MIME) format.

The gateway server transforms the workflow management system internal messages into a MIME format and causes the transformed messages to be sent to the target destination. Figure 10.12 shows how this task is performed by the gateway server in conjunction with a POP3 server.

Figure 10.12 Gateway Server

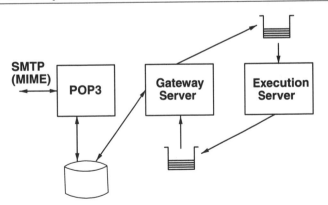

The POP3 server provides access to the network and maintains an in-basket for all incoming messages. The gateway server periodically checks this basket for incoming messages. If a message is found, it is transformed into the workflow management system's internal format and put into the input queue of the server that is responsible for handling the request.

Messages can be lost in an SMTP environment. The gateway server must be able to handle this situation.

Support of this type of communication between workflow management systems can be used not only between two different workflow management systems but also between different instances of the same workflow management system, using the Internet as the carrier.

The gateway server implements interface 4 of the Workflow Management Coalition.

10.3.10   Event Server

The event server implements the processing of events. As such, it keeps track of awaited and posted events, as discussed in Chapter 5.

When the execution server processes an event activity, it sends an appropriate request to the event server. This is similar to sending a request to a program execution component to carry out an activity implementation. When the event server receives the request, it looks to see whether a matching entry already exists in the "posted events table." If so, it fills the output container with the stored information and sends an appropriate message back to the execution server. The execution server uses this message to complete processing of the event activity and to continue navigation. If the event server could not find an entry, it stores an appropriate entry in the "awaited event table."

The occurrence of an event is signaled to the event server via the event API. The event server verifies the correctness of the event by checking for an appropriate entry in the "awaited event table." If an entry is found, an appropriate message is sent to the execution server together with the output container. Otherwise, the event is inserted into the "posted event table."

10.3.11   Dead Letter Queue Server

Messages that cannot be delivered by the message queuing system to the designated queue are stored in a dead letter queue. There are a number of reasons why a message cannot be delivered. The main reason is incorrect setup of the different message queuing system managers in a larger network. The dead letter queue server reads these messages and sends them to the administration server that manages the system from which the message was sent. This procedure allows the appropriate actions to be taken to resolve the problem. Note, that no messages must be discarded. The messages are an integral part of the workflow management system's execution of a business process.

10.4 Client

It is the client that delivers the functions of the workflow management system. The actual functions such as the displaying the worklist are delivered by applications that sit on top of an API. The API is the only means by which functions of the workflow management system can be controlled from the outside. This interface allows the workflow management system to hide its internals from the exploiters and to make changes to the internals without impacting the applications that use the services of the workflow management system.

10.4.1 Interface Styles

The API differentiates the three modes : synchronous request, asynchronous request, and unsolicited messages.

For synchronous requests, control returns to the application program request after the request has completed. All requested data is also returned. This is the typical style used by programs that do not interact with the end user.

For asynchronous requests, the application program specifies the function that should be called after the request has been completed. When the request has been completed by the workflow management system, the specified callback routine is invoked, and the result of the request is passed to it. This style is being used for writing GUIs since it fits well with the message-driven approach used in constructing these interfaces.

To receive unsolicited messages, an application program must register functions for each unsolicited message type that may be received. These functions are then called when an unsolicited message is created by the workflow management system. This style is used for supporting the push model of user interaction and for modeling system consoles.

10.4.2 Languages

The API is supplied in different language bindings, such as C, C++, or Visual Basic. The structure shown in Figure 10.13 allows different language bindings to be implemented easily.

The main interface is the C language interface because it is completely independent of compiler implementation. All other languages are implemented on top of this C language interface. Another advantage of this interface structure is that language bindings can be developed in parallel development teams, so that new language bindings can be added rather quickly. It should be noted that not only language bindings can be implemented on the C language interface but also other bindings, for example, for Lotus Notes.

Figure 10.13 API Layers

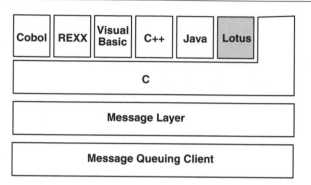

10.4.3   Components

Instead of just providing a simple API, the workflow management system supplies the API as a set of components. The components are implemented in all of the different component models, such as ActiveX controls, Java Beans, or VisualAge parts. Application programmers can easily implement applications that need to access the workflow management system API. Figure 10.14 illustrates a component set.

The client applications that the workflow management system delivers are also made up of components. These components are higher-level components. A typical component is the component that is available for displaying and managing process models. These components are used in buildtime and runtime, providing a consistent end user-interface. These components can then be used quite efficiently to build customer specific GUIs.

Figure 10.14 Client Component Ware

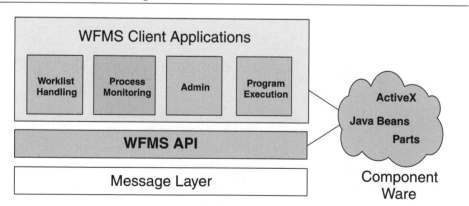

10.4.4 Ultrathin Clients

In the structures we have discussed so far, tier 1 was delivered via a client processor that was able to handle the GUI as well as the API. This type of client is too fat to be used in Internet and Intranet applications. In this case, users are using a Web browser to communicate with applications.

Figure 10.15 shows the structure of the workflow management system client if users interacting via a Web browser. The Web browser typically runs HTML scripts or JavaScripts that implement the user interface and provide the functions that a user can carry out. The workflow management system functions are provided by servlets running on the Web server. The servlets communicate with the workflow management system server using the standard workflow management system API. Communication between the Web browser and the Web server is via HTTP.

Figure 10.15 Ultrathin Clients

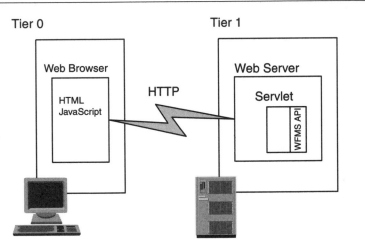

10.4.5 Object Environment

A similar client structure can be implemented if the underlying infrastructure is an object environment, as defined by the OMG.

Figure 10.16 shows the components that are involved. The workflow management system provides its API as a set of objects with appropriate messages, as described in section 6.4 on page 226. Access to the objects managed by the ORB are through the client ORB that talks to the server ORB through IIOP.

Figure 10.16 Client in an Object Environment

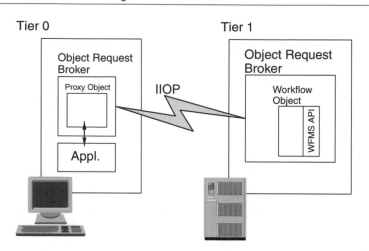

10.5   Program Execution

Program activities are associated with activity implementations that are carried out when the appropriate activity is processed. Two options are provided by the workflow management system to process the activity implementations. The first option is to launch the activity implementations on the client. The appropriate workflow management system component is the *program execution agent* (PEA). The other option is to launch the activity implementations on the server. The appropriate workflow management system component is the *program execution server* (PES). Even if the basic functions are the same, different names are used because PEA and PES have different operational characteristics. The PEA is a more lightweight implementation, whereas the PES is managed like any other server components. It can be run as multiple instances as well as a hot pool of server instances. For simplicity, we use the word *program execution component* (PEC) when we talk about the common functions.

An activity implementation is launched on the client if the activity implementation needs to interact with the user.

The activity implementation can be launched on the server if no interaction is required with the user. This capability not only avoids the sending of messages between the client and the server, but also does not require that a user be logged on.

10.5.1   Request Processing

When a workflow execution server determines that a particular program execution component (PEC) should process an appropriate activity implementation, it inserts a message into the PEC's input queue.

This message contains all information that is required for the execution of the implementation, such as the name of the executable, the input and output container including the appropriate metadata that describes the structures of the container and the command line to be passed to the executable. Only the information that is required for a particular platform is sent to the PEC.

The PEC reads this message and invokes the implementation. It honors all container and process control requests issued by the invoked implementation. When the implementation completes, the PEC sends an appropriate message to the execution server. This message contains the return code from the implementation plus the output container if it has changed.

10.5.2   Internal Structure

Figure 10.17 shows the overall structure of a PEC.

Figure 10.17 Program Execution Component Structure

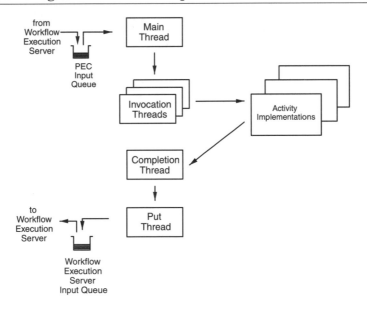

The PEC is made up of at least four independent threads. The main thread reads the messages from the server input queue and determines which actions need to be taken. The invocation thread calls the activity implementation. The completion thread is required for certain invocation mechanisms, which do not support an RPC type invocation, to detect when the activity implementation has completed processing. The put thread sends completion messages back to the workflow execution server, which causes the workflow execution server to continue navigation for the associated process instance.

An installation option allows the system administrator to specify whether the PEC should process multiple requests in parallel or not, and if processing multiple requests in parallel is active, how many requests should be processed in parallel. If multiple requests are supported, a thread is created for each request for execution of an activity implementation and deleted after the activity implementation has completed. This approach provides for greater throughput in particular if the creation and deletion of threads is a cheap operation. It is, however associated with a more complex recovery scenario, in the case of the PEC terminating abnormally.

10.5.3 Program Execution Agent

The program execution agent (PEA) is started when the user logs on to the workflow management system and is stopped when the user logs off from the workflow management system.

As shown in Figure 10.10 on page 366, the PEA's input queue is managed on the server. The PEA accesses the queue via a remote API offered by the message queuing system. Thus, no message queue manager is needed on the client and limits the amount of memory needed.

10.5.4 Program Execution Server

The program execution server (PES) is a server like any other server. As such, it must have local access to its queue. This requires that the appropriate queue manager is on the same processor. The PES is controlled by the administration server. A PES is typically implemented as a hot pool. The hot pool provides better recovery than does the use of threads. In addition, multiple PES instances can be defined. Each instance has a name by which it is addressed in the process model. Each instance has certain operating system properties assigned to it that define operating system parameters, for example, the operating system priority with which the PES is executed.

If the execution of an activity implementation is not time critical and the server is resource constrained, a PES instance could be moved to a completely different processor. Figure 10.18 illustrates this case. This approach should only be used for applications that are not critical since the administration server cannot use the options that help it to recognize PES failures immediately. For example, the option of operating system locks cannot be used. If immediate recognition is required, a system must be installed on the target server. In this case, the local administration server can manage the PES.

Figure 10.18 Remote Program Execution Server

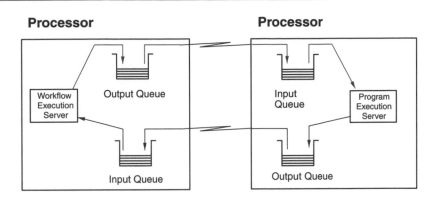

10.5.5 User-Supplied Program Execution

Even the sophisticated service invocation implementation in the program execution server does not help if the particular service cannot be reached. For example, when the program execution server is not available on an operating system or the operating system does not offer an implementation for a supported one.

For those cases, users can build their own program execution server. It is only required that the appropriate message queuing system be available on the desired platform. The program execution server is registered with the workflow management system with an indicator that the program execution server is user supplied. This information is necessary so that the workflow management system can ship the correct data to the program execution server.

So that a wide variety of different operating systems can be supported, the data must be supplied in a format that can be processed easily. A good example of such a format is XML because XML parsers are available on many different platforms.

10.5.6 DLL Support

Dynamic link libraries (DLL) are typical activity implementations on workstations running UNIX, Windows, or OS/2 operating systems; they are less common on mainframes. They are executed in the same process as the program execution component itself. Any misbehavior of those DLLs could cause the program execution component to terminate abnormally. To avoid abnormal termination, the program execution component can run DLLs in fenced mode as shown in Figure 10.19.

When a DLL needs to be executed, the program execution component starts a stub program in another operating system process, which in turn launches the DLL. A DLL failure, therefore, does not do any harm to the program execution component itself. The program execution component recognizes the failure and performs appropriate error recovery.

Figure 10.19 Fenced DLL Support

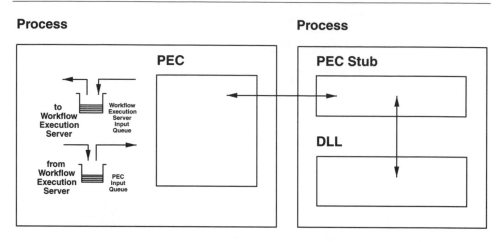

Another option can specify whether the program execution component should keep a DLL loaded or not. Keeping a DLL loaded saves the time it takes to retrieve the DLL from persistent storage.

10.5.7   Ensured Invocation

The program execution agent (PEA) has its input queue on the server and accesses the queue via a remote API. This results in the transaction boundaries shown in Figure 10.20. Scheduling of the request for execution of the activity implementation is performed within a transaction. This transaction is carried out as the result of a user selecting a workitem. When the server receives this request, it determines the PEA that needs to launch the activity implementation and inserts a message into the PEA's input queue. The PEA then reads this message within a second transaction. In this transaction the message is pulled from the queue. This gives an overall transaction shown as the outer transaction in Figure 10.20. The invoked application is executed in a separate transaction.

When the PEA has read the message, it launches the activity implementation and waits until the activity implementation completes. When the activity implementation returns, the PEA inserts the completion message into the workflow execution server's input queue and then deletes the message in the PEA input queue. If everything goes well, the activity implementation is invoked once and only once.

Problems occur if the activity implementation terminates abnormally. In this case, the status of the invoked application is unclear. If the abend occurs after the application committed, the application must not be reexecuted. If the abend occurs before the commit, the application must be reexecuted. Since the actual state of the application is not known, the workflow management system offers several options

Figure 10.20 Ensured Invocation

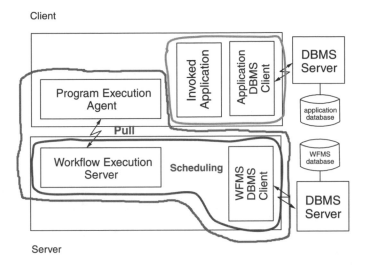

to cope with the situation. These options can be specified when the appropriate processes, activities, or programs are modeled.

When the *at least once* option is active, the program execution agent deletes the message from the input queue after the invoked application returns. If a failure occurs, the application is launched once more. This action could cause the application to perform the same operation multiple times, depending upon whether the application has committed the first time. If the application just performs queries, repeated operation is no problem. If the application performs updates against the application database, the application must make sure that the changes in the database are made only once.

When the *at most once* option is active, the program execution agent deletes the message from the input queue before activity implementation is invoked. If a failure occurs, no actions are taken. This means the application is not launched again. Thus the application is not executed at all if the application terminates before it has committed the changes.

When the *set InDoubt* option is active, the program execution agent sets the activity in doubt. The must determine the state of the invoked application and then take appropriate actions.

10.5.8   Safe Applications

To make sure that an activity implementation is executed *exactly once*, the execution of the activity implementation and the appropriate state changes in the database of the workflow management system must be performed as a transaction, as shown in Figure 10.21. We call such an application a *safe* application.

Figure 10.21 Safe Application

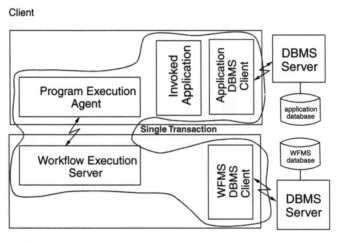

Running all operations a as a regular transaction is not possible because it would require holding long locks in databases. The notion of stratified transactions helps here.

Figure 10.22 shows how the whole transaction is divided into a set of transactions. The first transaction is the generation of the request for the program execution agent. The next transaction is the transport of the message from the server queue to the program execution agent queue. The third transaction is the execution of a global transaction, which includes reading the message from the program execution agent input queue, the activity implementation performing its database operations, and the completion message being put into the output queue. The fourth transaction is the transport of the message to the workflow execution server input queue.

Note that it requires a message queue manager on the workstation. In the case of the program execution server, the workflow execution server and the program execution servershare the same message queue manager, when they are placed on the same processor. So, the program execution servercan run safe applications without any additional software requirement.

Figure 10.22 Implementing Safe Applications

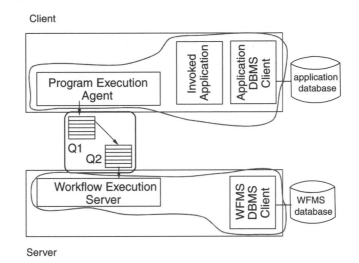

Figure 10.23 shows the steps that are required to have the execution of the activity implementation as a global transaction. These steps are performed for each activity implementation execution request message that the program execution component—a program execution agent or a program execution server—processes.

Figure 10.23 Running the Application as a Transaction

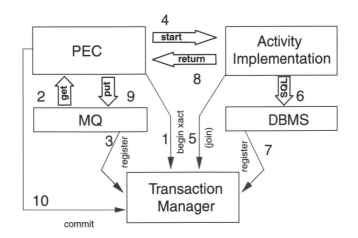

First, the program execution component (PEC) begins a global transaction by calling the transaction manager (**1**). Then, the PEC gets the message from the message queuing system (**2**), which registers with the transaction manager (**3**) when it receives the request. The PEC agent then starts the activity implementation (**4**) using the appropriate invocation mechanism. The activity implementation optionally joins the global transaction through a request to the transaction manager (**5**). When the activity implementation performs the first SQL call (**6**), the database management system registers itself with the transaction manager (**7**). When the activity implementation has finished its task, it returns to the PEC without committing its changes to the database (**8**). The PEC puts the result into the workflow execution servers input queue (**9**) and then calls the transaction manager with a commit request (**10**). The transaction manager then performs its two-phase commit protocol for the two involved resource managers: the message queuing system and the database management system. If successful, the changes made by the PEC and the activity implementation are made persistent.

10.6   System Group

The system structure discussed so far is that of a single system with a single database. It is therefore limited in the number of users it can support. Physical limitations include CPU power, I/O capacity, and communication line bandwidth. Some of these limitations are leveraged to a certain extent through appropriate hardware upgrades, such as multiprocessor systems that help to better exploit hot pool support or the three-tier structure that separates communication resources from database resources.

The introduction of system groups allows for a further dispersion of resource requirements. A system group allows multiple systems to be attached to the database as shown in Figure 10.24. This is the structure we previously termed an application server cluster. The system group provides all the availability characteristics we discussed earlier.

Each system contains at least an administration server (AS) that controls and manages the various servers, program execution servers that are part of that system, and a dead letter queue server (DS) that manages messages that went into the dead letter queue. All other servers are optional on any of the systems. System A, for example, provides support for buildtime and thus contains only a modeling server (MS). System B runs process instances and interacts with other workflow management system and thus contains a gateway server (DS) and a workflow execution server (ES). System C performs all housekeeping, tracking of information, and the interacting with other workflow management systems; it contains a cleanup server (CS) and a scheduling server (SS).

Figure 10.24 System Group

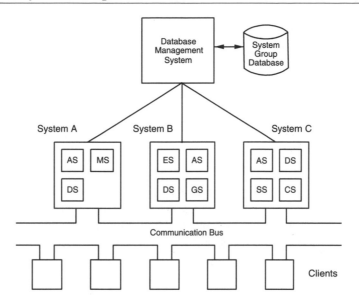

At least one scheduling server must be available in a system group. If only one scheduling server is defined for the system group, the scheduling server is responsible for all systems in the system group. If more than one scheduling server is defined, each scheduling server is responsible for a set of systems, but under the premise that all systems are covered by the scheduling servers. The same is true for the cleanup server.

No communication between workflow execution servers on different systems is necessary for supporting workitem processing for users of the various systems. For process instances that implement the pull user interaction model, no special actions need to be taken. When the user requests a workitem, the system just gets it from the database. If the process instance implements the push user interaction model, the workflow execution server puts the workitem directly into the client input queue of the appropriate users, depending on the system the user is currently logged on.

Communication between execution servers on different systems is only required for requesting the execution of a *remote subprocess* and for signaling the completion of subprocess.

The structure of a system group allows to have attached to it, as many systems to it as the database management system can handle.

Each client in a system group is assigned to one server, the *home server*. When this server is not available, the client tries to connect to another server. The server is selected on the basis of some predefined sequence.

The client also implements the failover mechanisms we discussed in section 10.1 on page 351.

10.7   Domains

For a large enterprise, a single system group may not be sufficient to handle the available work load. Even if it could, the necessary bandwidth for connecting the clients may not be available. The workflow management system allows system groups to be grouped into a domain. All system groups within a domain maintain a common set of information. The information includes topology, staff, data structures, programs, process models, lists, and groups.

All systems within a domain are also connected by the communication bus implemented through message queuing, as shown in Figure 10.25. The system groups are completely independent of each other. Thus, systems in different system groups must always use the communication bus to exchange information.

Figure 10.25 Multiple System Groups

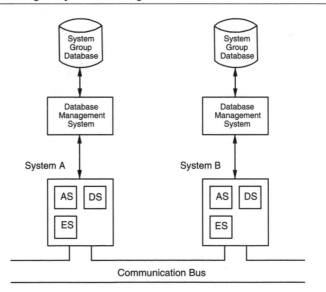

10.7.1 Domain Management

Because it is totally impracticable to manage the data individually for each system group, the workflow management system must support a mechanism to distribute information entered at one system group to all other system groups within the domain. We call this process *distribution*.

Figure 10.26 shows a topology that allows distribution to be easily implemented by a *primary copy* approach. Primary copy means that for a set of identical copies of data, all changes are applied to one copy of the data, the primary copy, and then distributed to all other copies.

Figure 10.26 System Group Hierarchy

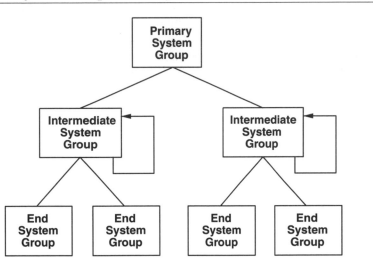

The *primary system group* holds the master copy. All changes to topology, staff, data structures, programs, process models, lists, and groups must be made at the primary system group either by the import function or by the buildtime API. Attempts to execute these functions at systems that are not part of the primary system group are rejected.

All changed data is then transmitted to the *intermediate system groups*, which apply any received changes to themselves and propagate the changes to other system groups—either end system groups or intermediate system groups. System groups without children, called *end system groups*, apply the received changes only to themselves.

The distribution of changes to the individual system groups and the application of changes to the system groups's repositories must be carried out as a distributed transaction. Only running the task as a transaction makes sure that all system groups have the same information. The transaction is realized as a stratified transaction.

The distribution server performs the task of distributing the changed data to all system groups and applying the changes to the database associated with each system group within the domain.

The information to be distributed is in FDL format. FDL format has been chosen for two reasons: (1) The data must be database independent as the database schemes on the various platforms are quite different, and (2) the function implementing the import of FDL is available on each of the different platforms to load the data into the workflow management system database.

Figure 10.27 shows the interaction between the modeling server and the distribution server when data is imported at the primary system group. The modeling server reads the FDL information, writes the data into the database, and copies the FDL information into the distribution log. After completion of import processing, the modeling server puts a message into the distribution server's input queue, indicating that data needs to be distributed. The distribution server then takes the information from the distribution log and distributes it to the distribution servers defined as children of the primary system group.

Figure 10.27 Import Processing with Later Distribution

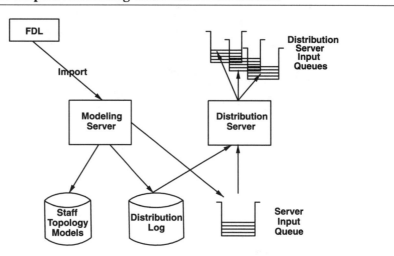

For easier recovery, the modeling server supports the notion of mini-batches. Each batch is called an import transaction. The end of such an import transaction can be specified by the user by means of special FDL constructs. Within such a transaction, the modeling server performs the following actions.

- Writes a checkpoint that allows the restart of the import of the FDL stream at the checkpoint in case a severe error condition caused the abnormal termination of the import

- Decomposes the FDL in the import transactions into the various FDL constructs

- Performs the requested action, such as inserting the object into the database, for each construct

- Copies the FDL information to the distribution log

- Inserts a message into the distribution server input queue to signal the completion of an import transaction

An import transaction is a regular ACID transaction. This means that either all of the above listed actions are performed or none of them are performed. Thus, the distribution log always contains the complete set of changes applied to the database.

Multiple modeling server instances on the same system or multiple modeling servers on different systems of the primary system group can perform modifications to the database. Therefore it is important that the distribution log follows an order that records the changes in the exact order in which they were applied in the database. This means that the distribution log maintains the time of commit of a transaction as the primary sort sequence and the time of the database access as the secondary sort sequence. This task is achieved by means of two tables: one table keeps an entry for each transaction commit, and one keeps an entry for each object.

The FDL information in the distribution log is stored in compressed format to reduce the amount of data that needs to be sent via the communication bus.

The distribution server of the primary system group then transmits the data from the distribution log to the input queues of the distribution servers of the system groups that are designated as children to the primary system group. This transmission via the communication bus is also a transaction.

Figure 10.28 shows the actions of the distribution server at an intermediate system group. The distribution server reads the data from its input queue, decompresses the sent data into standard FDL format, wraps the decompressed data into an import request message for the modeling server, sends the message to the input queue of the modeling server, puts, if an intermediate system group, the sent data into the input queue of the distribution servers on the next level, and then deletes the message from the input queue. All actions are performed under transaction control.

Figure 10.28 Distribution Processing

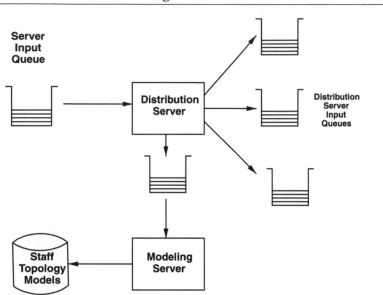

10.7.2   Remote Subprocesses

A subprocess that is carried out by a different system group is called a *remote subprocess*. When the owning system determines that the subprocess should be carried out by a system in another system group, it sends an appropriate message to the system. The message contains the name of the process model, the input container including the appropriate metadata, and the metadata for the output container.

The receiving system then creates and starts a process using the supplied information, and processes this process as it would any other process. When the process completes, the appropriate output container is shipped back to the originating system. No audit trail information is shipped back.

10.7.3   Remote Workitems

If staff resolution returns a user whose system is on a different system group, communication with the workflow execution server of that system must make the workitems available to selected users *remote workitems*. The actual processing depends on whether the selected users all belong to the same system or whether they belong to different systems.

If only users of one system are selected, a single request is shipped to the remote system workflow execution server. This request contains the input container, the output container, the list of users, and any other processing-relevant information. The remote system workflow execution server manages this request by creating the appropriate workitems. When processing has completed, the remote system workflow execution server sends back the output container and all audit trail information that was created. The local system workflow execution server places the audit trail information into the audit log, saves the returned container in the database, and continues navigation through the process.

If users on multiple systems are selected, a request is sent to each target system. In this case, the following protocol is executed to make sure that only one user processes the workitem.

- The local system sends a request to each of the remote systems containing a list of selected users and all processing-relevant information.

- Each remote system creates a workitem for each of the specified users and inserts it into their worklist.

- When a user selects a workitem, the associated system disables the workitem on the worklist of all other users attached to the system and then informs the local system that the workitem has been selected.

- The local system determines whether this is the first request, and if so the remote system is informed to continue processing of the workitem. The local system also informs all other systems that they don't need to honor any workitem processing requests from their users.

- The nonselected systems disable the workitem on the worklist of all users. In a user has already selected the workitem, then the user is informed that somebody else has selected the workitem.

- After the workitem has finished, the remote system ships back the output container and the audit trail information.

- The local system inserts the audit trail information into the audit trail.

- All systems are now informed that processing of the activity has completed so that they can perform the proper cleanup processing.

- The local system continues navigation through the process instance.

This approach of handling workitem processing has the advantage that the process is owned by one system. That ownership allows the system to know the exact state of the process and makes the support of queries fairly trivial. In another approach, one could envision that the process is routed itself through the workflow management system. This approach makes queries rather complicated because the state of the process must be constructed by querying all involved workflow management systems.

The number of messages between the different workflow management systems is rather high. The number of messages can be reduced by assigning those users to a system group that are typically involved in a business process. Section 11.8 on page 447 presents a method to minimize the number of messages to be exchanged between the different system groups.

10.8   System Tuning

The structure of the workflow management system allows for many different optimizations based on the actual environment. The workflow management system offers a number of tuning parameters that help to optimize the consumption of resources. We present here some of the tuning options that MQSeries Workflow offers. Another set of tuning parameters can be specified as part of modeling business processes. We discuss these tuning parameters in section 11.7 on page 445.

The robustness of the workflow management system stems its implementation as an application server. It uses persistent messages, stores all state information in the relational database, and performs all actions under transaction control. This means that the reading of the request message, the management of state data in the database, and the sending of messages is under transaction control. The option that controls the overall operational behavior is controlled by the OPERATION_MODE parameter. The standard operation mode that we just described is called ROBUST. There are situations where this rock-solid behavior is not required. If, for example, the workflow management system just processes complex requests that are performing inquiries, then there is no need to be able to restart the complex request. In this case, there is no need to run the workflow management system actions as transaction, which saves running the two-phase commit protocol. This operation mode is called PERSISTENT. In an even lighter mode, all messages are processed as nonpersistent messages saving the associated reading and writing to disk. This mode is called OPTIMISTIC.

The data that is returned as the result of user queries can be quite substantial. A parameter MAXIMUM_MESSAGE_SIZE allows one to specify the maximum size of the message that is returned to the user. If the size is exceeded, the user is told that the query would return too much data and that the query should be rephrased. This procedure avoids unintended queries that impact the processing of other messages and cause the overloading of communication lines.

Messages that the workflow management system sends to a client stay in the client input queue until the designated client picks them, which may never happen. The parameter CLIENT_MESSAGE_EXPIRATION_TIME allows one to specify how long the message should stay in the message queue. If the specified time is exceeded, the message is removed. This procedure helps to keep the number of messages in the client input queue as low as possible.

When something goes wrong with the execution of a business process or the workflow management system itself, messages are sent to the administration server, which stores them in the workflow management system database. The MESSAGE_RETAIN_PERIOD parameter specifies how long a message should be kept in the workflow management system's database. If the specified time is exceeded, the message is removed. This procedure helps to keep the number of messages that are maintained in the workflow management system database to a minimum.

Sessions are held until the user explicitly logs off from the workflow management system. If this was not done, a session could hang around indefinitely. To avoid this situation, the parameter SESSION_EXPIRATION_PERIOD defines how long a session may last before it is automatically closed by the workflow management system. Incidentally, this feature can also be used to tighten security, requiring the user to establish a new session. A new session requires the user to enter the password again. The administration server is responsible for checking whether a session has expired. This check has to be done periodically. Because each check of expired session takes up resources, the parameter SESSION_EXPIRATION_CHECK_INTERVAL defines the time interval for checking for expired sessions.

It is not necessary for all of the servers to be up and running all of the time. The cleanup server, for example, may only be needed for a few hours during the night. The running time is defined via two parameters START_TIME and STOP_TIME. The parameters can be defined for all server types. The administration server initiates a server at start time and terminates a server at stop time. That way, no resources are needed when a server does not need to be active.

The administration server is the watchdog within a system and periodically controls whether the other servers are still active. The CHECK_INTERVAL specifies the time interval in which the administration server should carry out this function.

Some of the servers run as a hot pool. The parameter NUMBER_OF_INSTANCES indicates how many hot pool members should be started when the workflow management system is started.

DLLs are kept loaded in memory by the operating system as long as they are used by a running application. If the last application terminates, the DLL is removed from memory and must be loaded from disk the next time it is required. It is useful to keep frequently used DLLs loaded. One does this by setting the DLL_MODE parameter for the program execution component. Valid settings are NO, which causes no DLLs to be kept loaded; LIMITED, to keep a specified number of DLLs loaded; and UNLIMITED to keep an indefinite number of DLLs loaded. If the number of DLLs is limited, the program execution component keeps as many DLLs loaded as specified by the MAXIMUM_DLL_LOADED. If the maximum specified are already loaded, and a new one needs to be loaded, the DLL that has not been used for the longest time is removed.

10.9   Workload Management

In a system group environment, the workload must be controlled so that the available hardware resources are optimally used. The hardware is optimally used if all specified goals, such as performance spheres, are met.

10.9.1   Hot Pool Management

The simplest form of workload management is the dynamic adaption of the number of members in the execution server or program execution server hot pools. If the number of messages in the queue exceeds a specified limit, the administration server starts a new hot pool member. If the number of messages in the queue falls below a specified level or the number of messages that are to be processed in a specified time period is reduced below a specified limit, the administration server shuts down a member of the appropriate hot pool to reduce resources consumption.

This function of automatically bringing up and shutting down members of a hot pool can also be handled by a workload manager if one is available on the particular operating system. In the case of the WLM/MVS (see section 5.7 on page 203), the workflow execution server and the program execution server are instrumented to honor appropriate WLM startup/shutdown requests.

10.9.2   Performance Spheres

In both cases, discussed above, only the workflow management system processing is considered for workload management. The processing of the invoked activity implementations is completely neglected. This is not the case if the workflow management system implements the notion of performance spheres as discussed in section 5.7 on page 203. The function can be supplied by the workflow management system itself, or the workflow management system can exploit the services of a workload manager.

If workload manager support is available, the goals of the performance sphere have been defined to the workload manager, so the workload manager can take appropriate actions such as reassigning the resources. When the workflow management system enters a performance sphere, it indicates this entry to the workload manager to establish an instance of an enclave. The workload manager returns an enclave identifier that the workflow management system hands over to each of the invoked activity implementations. The invoked activity implementations use this identifier to join the enclave. When the control flow leaves the enclave, the workflow management system indicate this departure to the workload manager. This processing guarantees that the workflow management system and the activity implementation processing are taken into account for workload management. This approach of using the workload management support is typically limited to homogeneous environments. In fact, it is typically limited to a single processor or a cluster.

If no workload manager support is available or if the performance sphere is carried out in a heterogenous environment. the workflow management system must implement the performance sphere by using other techniques. This implementation can be achieved by means of the following three different mechanisms:

- Setting the execution priority of the activity implementation. The appropriate mechanism depends on the invocation mechanism that is used to invoke the activity implementation. For an executable, this is the operating system priority of the process in which the activity implementation is carried out. For a message, this is the priority assigned to the message and the operating system priority of the invoked activity implementation. The execution priority can be set by the workflow management system itself, handed over to the activity implementation to be handled by the activity implementation, or by a combination of both.

- Setting the execution priority of the workflow management system itself.

- Setting the priorities of the messages that the workflow management system exchanges between workflow execution server and the program execution server and between workflow execution servers of different system groups.

Code Example 10.2 shows the processing that is carried out when an activity within a performance sphere is processed. The code without asterisks in front of a statement is the code that is executed when an activity implementation is carried out without being part of a performance sphere. We discussed this procedure in some detail in section 10.5 on page 378. The statements with the asterisks show the additional code that is carried out when an activity is executed that is part of a performance sphere.

The code example assumes that the activity implementation is carried out by the local program execution server. This assumption is not true if the activity is carried out by a server in another system group. In this case, the workflow execution server not only assigns the appropriate priority to the message it sends to the other workflow execution server but also puts the appropriate priority into the message. This priority is immediately honored as shown in statement **2**. This priority setting allows performance spheres to run even in a distributed and heterogenous environment.

Code Example 10.2 Processing an Activity Within a Performance Sphere

```
1      Workflow execution server reads message
2  *   Workflow execution server sets operating system priority
         according to the priority specified in the message
3      Workflow execution server locates activity
4  *   Workflow execution server sets operating system priority
         according to the execution priority of the
         performance sphere
5  *   Workflow execution server sets message priority
         according to the execution priority of the
         performance sphere
6      Workflow execution server inserts request message
         into program executor input queue
7      Program execution server reads message from
         queue according to message priority
8  *   Program execution server sets its operating
         system priority according to execution priority
         of the performance sphere
9  *   Program execution server launches the activity
         implementation with appropriate execution
         priority
10     Program execution server waits for completion
11 *   Program executor server resets operating system priority
         to default
12 *   Program execution server sets message priority according
         to the execution priority of the performance
         sphere
13     Program executor inserts completion message
         into the workflow execution server input queue
```

10.9.3   Load Distribution

In the case of a system group, workload balancing can be used to make sure that each of the systems in the system group is used the same way. This workload balancing is performed by the administration server. When a user logs on to the workflow management system, the administration server determines the server that has the least load. The name of this server is returned to the client, which then logs on to the specified server.

10.10   Systems Management

We showed in ´Chapter 8 how workflow technology can help systems management to improve the functions delivered by the systems management system. In particular we showed how a business-process-oriented systems management helps to provide the desired total management view. In this section, we discuss additional support that the workflow management system provides for the systems management system.

10.10.1 Code Distribution

Code distribution is one of the tasks that is part of systems management. We showed in section 8.2 on page 294 how the workflow management system can help the systems management system to distribute activity implementation code. However, the workflow management system code itself, the servers, program execution agent, and client must be distributed by the systems management system. This means that various components of the workflow management system itself must be enabled for code distribution. This enabling is achieved by defining the components of the workflow management system to the code distribution component of the systems management system.

10.10.2 Automatic Restart Management

Some operating systems provide for the automatic restarting of operating system processes if the program executing in the operating system process terminates abnormally, if the operating system for whatever reason terminates, or if the processor goes dead. The restart of the processes may be on the same processor or even on a different processor. Restarting on a new processor just requires that disks which hold the queues are attached to the new processor. Typical examples of such a facility is the Automatic Restart Manager (ARM) on OS/390 or HACMP on AIX. The sophistication of the restart ranges from user initiated to fully automatic. In the case of an OS/390 SYSPLEX, the automatic restart manager can even restart the running processes automatically on a new processor if the current processor goes out of order.

If an automatic restart manager is available, it can restart the administration server. If the administration server has been restarted successfully by the restart facility, the administration server in turn starts the other servers.

10.10.3 Enterprise Console Support

Figure 8.8 shows how an error is detected and handed over to the event server either for display on the systems management system's enterprise console or for taking appropriate actions. The figure shows that an observed program is monitored by an event source that sends the appropriate information to the event adapter.

The outlined mechanism can be implemented by the workflow management system to support the systems management system. The administration server provides the functions that are the responsibility of the event source. Whenever one of the observed server components encounters problems, those problems are recognized by the administration server and the necessary information is sent to the event server for the appropriate actions.

10.10.4   Application Response Measurement

The *Application Management Specifications* are part of Tivoli's framework (TME-10) for systems management. They are partially a defacto standard for systems management, because the OMG has adapted it as their standard for systems management. These specifications are complemented by the *Application Response Measurement* API, which assists distributed applications passing to the systems management environment information that is considered critical for performance management in terms of business operations. Based on this information appropriate tools can measure service level agreements or signal early warnings of poor performance in terms of business functions.

The application response measurement functions assume that the managed application is a self-instrumented component. This means that the application itself has to use the application response measurement API to exchange information with the systems management environment.

The problem with this approach is that it requires that every application required to convey data must have instrumentation added to it. In the case of workflow-based application, this function can be provided by the workflow management system. All activity implementations are launched by the program execution component, which can then provide the appropriate information via the application response measurement API. Figure 10.29 shows how the program execution component (PEC) implements this function.

The PEC performs the following functions in addition to the function it already carries out when launching an activity implementation. The PEC tries to keep to a minimum the amount of its own work that falls into the measurement period.

- The PEC determines whether response measurement should be made on the activity implementation. Since application response measuring is time consuming, it may not be necessary to measure all activity implementations, but only selected ones. Selection is done by a new parameter ARM_MEASURED, added to the activity definition to allow the process modeler to specify whether the activity should be measured.

- If the activity response is to be measured, the program execution component introduces the application to the ARM by the following API call:

  ```
  appID = arm_init(Application_Name, [User_ID],...)
  ```

  The next call then establishes a systemwide unique name for the running instance of the application that is to be created by the program execution component.

Figure 10.29 Supporting Application Response Measurement

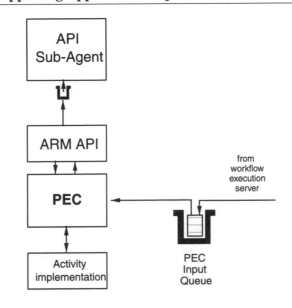

```
tranID = arm_getid(ApplicationName,applID,...)
```

- The program execution component starts the activity implementation.

- The program execution component signals, possibly in parallel with the starting of the activity, to the systems management environment that the instance of the application introduced before has started. This signal is done by the following call:

```
instance = arm_start(tranID,...)
```

- When the activity implementation has completed, the program execution component immediately informs the systems management environment about the termination of the application by issuing the following calls:

```
arm_stop(instance, status,...)
arm_end(...)
```

10.11   Exploiting Parallel Databases

The workflow management system uses a relational database management system to store all information. Advanced relational database management systems, such as IBM DB2 Universal Database Version 5 [Cha98], can support parallel databases. A parallel database is a database in which multiple actions can take place at the same time. We discuss in this section how the workflow management system can exploit the inter-partition parallel database support to provide better performance.

10.11.1   Characteristics of Parallel Databases

Parallelism has been available for many years in relational databases. It allows multiple users to be connected to multiple databases while giving each user the impression that he is the only user working with a single relational database management system. This result is achieved by the standard techniques of time-sharing. Each user is given a certain slice of the processor time to get the work done. Each user is assigned one operating system process; that means at most one processor can be busy with performing work for a particular user. For differentiation, such a database system is called a *serial system*.

In a *parallel system*, a database can be split into several separate parts, called *partitions*. Each table in a database can be split into partitions. Each partition can run on a separate machine; it has its own log and its own set of indexes.

Two kinds of parallelism can be applied to the processing of an SQL statement. *Intra-partition parallelism* refers to simultaneous processes within a single partition, and *inter-partition parallelism* refers to simultaneous processes in multiple partitions. Both types of parallelism are orthogonal to each other.

Intra-partition parallelism is typically used on symmetric multiprocessor (SMP) machines, in which multiple processors share common memory and disks. Intra-partition parallelism is completely managed by the database management system and does not require any particular action on the user side except that the database management system must be told to exploit intra-partition parallelism.

Inter-partition parallelism works with a set of processors, each of which has its own memory and disks. Nothing is shared among the different processors. This hardware configuration is called a *shared nothing* system [Pfi95]. Some or all of the processors themselves may be symmetric multiprocessors that can then exploit intra-partition parallelism. A typical machine that implements this architecture is IBM's RS/6000 SP2. The processors of different nodes talk to each other via the cluster's internal high speed network.

Each of the different partitions, which DB2 UDB calls a node, is assigned a unique identifier; in DB2 UDB an integer starting with 0. Each node is then assigned to the processor that holds the partition.

The tables that are assigned to different partitions (called *partitioned tables*) must each have a *partitioning key*, which determines how the rows of the table are distributed among the partitions. The values of the partitioning key are then mapped to the set of partitions by a hash function. This hash function may be supplied by the database management system or even by the user.

A client connects to a specified node. This node, the *coordination node*, is responsible for all client requests. The coordination node distributes these requests to other individual nodes, which process the requests. Thus, from a user perspective, there is no difference between the request being processed by a serial database or by a parallel database.

Figure 10.30 shows the conceptual structure of a database management system using parallel databases.

Figure 10.30 Structure of the Database Management System

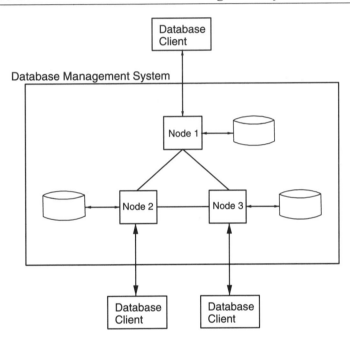

10.11.2   Exploiting Parallel Database Support

No actions are required by a workflow management system to exploit intra-parallelism. This exploitation is handled transparently by the relational database management system. It is different for exploiting the inter-parallelism of parallel databases. Exploiting parallel database support requires that the tables that make up the database be split into multiple parts. Using inter-parallelism provides for better performance because of to reduced database size, reduced contention, and better exploitation of CPU resources. Best performance results are achieved if a request made by the workflow management system just touches one node.

Most of the data in the database is runtime information; the size of the build-time information can almost be neglected. The size of the runtime information depends on a few factors: the number of process instances, the amount of audit trail information that is written, and the number of workitems that a user has.

The database consists of a set of tables. The layout of the tables reflects the structure of information that the tables are holding. We show the rudimentary structure later when we discuss how navigation is carried out on the tables (see section 10.13 on page 412.

The process information, for example, is kept in several tables, that reflect the structure of the process metamodel. One table holds an entry for each process instance, and another table holds an entry for each activity. All constructs, such as activities and processes, are identified by a unique object identifier that is generated by the workflow management system. These object identifiers are used to relate the tuples in the individual tables; this is the way that the tuples in the activity table are related to the tuples in the process table, for example. The audit trail, on the other hand, is a simple table in which the individual entries are written.

All information about a process must be kept at least until the process has finished. However. there are many reasons to keep the information for quite some time; legal obligations sometimes require that information be kept for several years. These obligation cause the size of the workflow systems database to grow quite considerably, with obvious impacts on performance.

It is important to find good partitioning columns that can be used to split tables. These columns are made part of each table that is split. Two approaches are available to define these columns: internal properties and external properties. Internal properties are properties that are always available to the workflow management system; external properties need extra definition from the user and can provide greater control over the distribution among the different partitions or nodes.

10.11.3   Internal Properties

Typical internal properties are the creation/start time of a process or the system identifier of the system that created a process. These properties are just prototypical for internal properties; other properties could also be used.

Start Time

Each process has an associated creation or start time property. This property allows the tables to be divided by time frames such as decades, years, or months.

System Identifier

In a system group, each system is identified by a unique identifier. This property allows the tables to be split by the system. This property is ideal for exploiting parallel databases for multiple reasons.

1. The system that creates a process owns that process until the process finishes. Thus there will be no contention on the tables the different systems share. This setup is particularly attractive for the audit trail, since there will be a discrete table for each of the systems.

2. Each system knows its name without accessing the database and thus can easily include the name in all queries.

3. A particular system can attach to the node that holds all of the runtime data for the system.

Definition

Code Example 10.3 illustrates how the support for parallel databases can be specified for internal properties. This code example defines the system group Stuttgart so that the audit trail is split, using the SYSTEM_ID column, and all process related tables are split using the CREATION_TIME column. Thus, the workflow management system must maintain a SYSTEM_ID column in the audit trail table and a CREATION_TIME column in all process-related tables.

Code Example 10.3 Specifying Parallel Database Support for Internal Properties

```
SYSTEM_GROUP Stuttgart
  PARALLEL_DATABASE_SUPPORT
      AUDIT_TRAIL   SYSTEM_ID
      PROCESSES     CREATION_TIME
  END Stuttgart
```

10.11.4 External Properties

External properties are specifically defined by the user and associated with constructs of the metamodel. A simple method is to associate each process model with a unique identifier that identifies in which part of the table appropriate process instances should be put. The workflow management system then manages a particular column within the appropriate tables. Typical external properties are the user on whose behalf an activity is carried out, the starter of a process, or the name of a process model.

Code Example 10.4 illustrates how this support for parallel databases can be specified.

Code Example 10.4 Specifying Parallel Database Support for External Properties

```
SYSTEM_GROUP Stuttgart
  PARALLEL_DATABASE_SUPPORT
    PROCESSES      STARTER
    AUDIT_TRAIL    USER
END Stuttgart

PROCESS Loan
  PARALLEL_DATABASE_SUPPORT
    AUDIT_TRAIL    Node1
    PROCESSES      Node2
END LoanProcess

PROCESS TravelExpense
  PARALLEL_DATABASE_SUPPORT
    AUDIT_TRAIL    Node3
    PROCESSES      Node3
END TravelExpense
```

This example specifies three things:

1. It defines that for the system group `Stuttgart` the process related-tables and the audit trail table are to be split, using the `USER` field. Thus the workflow management system maintains a column for the audit trail table and the process-related tables; the table contains the user identification. This is default definition for all processes. This definition can be overwritten for particular process models by the `PROCESSES` keyword.

2. It defines that for the `Loan` process the audit trail should be managed in `Node1` and the process instances in `Node2`. Whenever the workflow management system works with an instance of the loan process, it will set the appropriate column value in the audit trail table to `Node1`, and the appropriate columns in the tables associated with processes to `Node2`. Note, that the user must make similar definitions to the database management system. Certainly the workflow management system could help to generate the appropriate entries.

3. It defines a similar entry for the `TravelExpense` process.

10.11.5   Setup

Setting up the workflow management system and the database management system requires some user actions.

- The user needs to provide a special hash mechanism if the hash mechanism(s) supplied by the database management system are not appropriate. A random hash mechanism would not help, for example, if one wanted to use the creation data to partition the tables by create-date time frames.

- The user needs to define how the workflow management system connects to the database management system. One option is to have all systems connect to one node, have this node hold all buildtime information, and have the runtime information split across the other nodes. Another option is to attach each system to the node that holds most of the data, an approach that may prove particularly useful when the system identifier is used.

10.12   Server Implementation Aspects

The server part of a workflow management system consists of a set of servers. Despite the fact that each of the different servers performs different tasks, they all implement the same behavior. Each server, for example, must understand a common set of messages, such as a shutdown request issued by the administration server or each server must access the database by use of the same mechanisms. These requirements are met by a common server framework that is used for the implementation of each server. In this section we discuss the structure of this server framework. We also show how requests are processed in this frame work as well as how data is accessed.

10.12.1   Server Framework

Figure 10.31 shows the overall structure of a server. The upper part of the structure is the part of the server that performs the actual processing of requests. The lower part of the structure implements the accesses to the database.

The core of the server is the actual implementation. This part implements the actions that are taken for a particular request. Each request coming into the server is a message, where the message type uniquely identifies the request. The implementation just performs the appropriate action. All other actions are handled automatically by the server framework from which all servers inherit.

The server framework performs all functions that are common to all servers. The server framework consists of the server request handler, the server manager, and the server reply handler.

Server Manager

The server management component sets up the server and controls the individual requests submitted to the server. Setup and control includes the following actions.

Figure 10.31 Server Structure

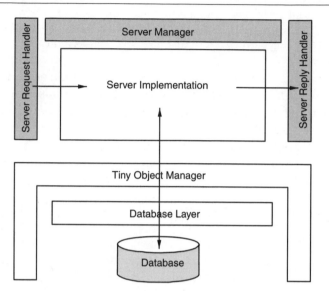

- When the server (actually, a member in the hot pool), is started, the server context is set up. All system parameters are retrieved from the database and stored in memory so that they are available when requests are processed. If requested by the administration server, the server context is updated.

- All messages are inspected. If a message is a request from the administration server, it is handled immediately. A typical administration request is a request to shutdown the server. Messages with other requests are left for the server implementation to be carried out.

- The server management component performs if processing of the request fails. One reason for this could be a "poisoned" message. Error processing typically includes the sending of a message to the administration server to inform the process administrator or operation administrator about the problem.

- Some servers, such as the cleanup server, divide their time between being idle and performing work. The server management component control this division automatically, based on the server context that was established when the server was brought up.

Server Request Handler

The server request handler obtains the requests for the server. Requests typically come from the server's input queue. However there are other sources of requests to the server.

A server has not only just queue, but two queues. The main queue is the server's input queue. All client requests go into the server input queue, which is shared by all members of the hot pool. In addition, each member in the hot pool has a control queue to allow the administration server to selectively address members of the hot pool. For example, this selective addressing is required, if a server setting has changed and each member in the hot pool has to know about it.

Another source of requests is the operating system console. Support for the console is mandatory in some operating system environments such as OS/390, where it must be possible to control the system by the operating system console. Then all functions that the administration server offers must also be offered by the operating system console.

Another source of requests is the workload manager. The workload manager controls the execution of the servers.

Server Reply Handler

The server reply handler replies to requests as well as forwards requests to other servers or clients. It provides the same set of functions as the server request handler. For example it supports replies to the operating system console.

Server Implementation

The server implementation carries out the actual processing of request messages, including processing the message, taking appropriate actions, maintaining state in the database, and generating new messages.

10.12.2 Request Processing

Each message type causes a particular action to be taken. In fact, each message type is associated with an implementation that implements that message. For example, the "activity implementation complete" message is associated with an implementation that continues navigation.

This association allows servers to be vertically sliced by message type and to have new requests easily added to them. The top module is just a big CASE statement, as shown in the code snippet of Code Example 10.5. This CASE statement is part of the server framework.

Code Example 10.5 Dispatching Requests

```
CASE message_type
    WHEN activity_implementation_complete
        CALL Navigate
    WHEN get_workitems
        CALL GetWorkItems
    OTHERWISE
        CALL ErrorProcessing
END
```

Figure 10.32 shows the processing of a client request. The client issues the request via the workflow management system's API. The client translates the request into a message and sends it to the server, using the message layer that encapsulates the underlying message queuing system. The server reads this message from the queue. As we have pointed out, this processing is done by the server framework.

Figure 10.32 Request Processing

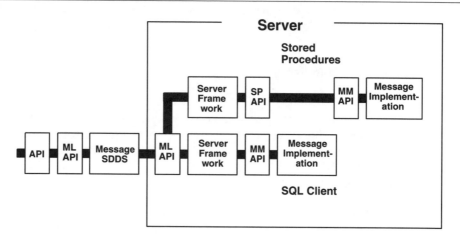

If the server uses stored procedures, the server framework calls the stored procedures API of the database management system. The database management system then calls the stored procedure which calls the message implementation via an API that encapsulates the implementation. If the server does not use stored procedures, the server framework just calls the message implementation. The message implementation is thus not aware of whether it executes as a stored procedure or not.

Figure 10.32 shows only the flow of control from the client to the server. When the server replies, control flow is basically the reverse of what is shown. The server inserts a message into the reply queue, using the message layer API. The message is then retrieved by the client via the message layer API. One should note, however, that issuing a request does not require the use of the workflow management system

API. The request could also be sent as a message using the message layer API. This is, in fact, the way that other servers request services.

From an architectural viewpoint, each server is made up of a set of towers, each of which implements a particular request. Adding a new request to a server requires that the following pieces are implemented :

- A message of a new message type must be defined. This definition includes defining the common properties of the message, such as the type identifier or whether the message should be made persistent. Then, the fields that are passed in the message, must be specified.

- The API must be adapted to allow the programmer to build the request. This request must then be translated into the message.

- The request processing must be implemented. The implementation may include additional functions that must be provided by the database layer.

- Last, the dispatcher must be adapted to understand the new message type.

10.12.3   Message Layer

We have not shown in the server framework the message layer we showed in Figure 10.31 on page 408. The message layer is used by the server request handler and the server reply handler as well as by the APIs. It encapsulates the underlying message queueing system to allow it to provide support of any message queuing system by using different invocation mechanisms in the message layer.

10.12.4   Database Access Layer

The server structure in Figure 10.31 on page 408 showed two layers that were used by the server implementations to access the database. The two layers together form the database access layer, which provides the server implementations with an object-oriented access to the database.

The database layer (DB layer) encapsulates the actual access method to the underlying database, such as embedded SQL or ODBC. This ensures portability of the components that are running on top of the DB layer to different operating system platforms and database management systems.

The tiny object manager (TOM) layer encapsulates the mapping of objects used by the server to the relational database management system schema. For example, it maps a person object to a set of tuples in tables and vice versa. It is the component that hides the impedance mismatch between the object-oriented implementation of the workflow management system and the tuple orientation of the relational database management system. For performance reasons, it offers a caching and noncaching interface.

In the caching interface, the TOM owns the objects and deletes them when the cache is deleted. This deletion happens normally at the end of the transaction. The caching interface is the interface for objects that are accessed multiple times within a request. A typical object that is accessed multiple times during a transaction are process instances or activity instances.

The noncaching interface retrieves, inserts, updates, and deletes objects in the database without caching them. Besides these functions this interface is used for objects for which set oriented processing is required, such as retrieving all workitems for a user.

10.13   Navigation

All persistent state information is stored in the relational database. All server classes are mapped to appropriate tuples in the relational database. All operations on the objects are then operations on tuples in tables. We use two functions of the workflow execution server to illustrate this approach. First, we show how a process instance is created; second, we show, how navigation is performed after an activity is completed. The examples are simplified; only the most important fields and processing steps are shown. The actual processing is far more complex.

Code Example 10.6 shows the main buildtime table, the `Process` table, which serves as the anchor point for all other build time tables. The key of the table is the model identification (`PMID`), which uniquely identifies a process model. This key is used by other buildtime tables to reference particular process models. `Name` contains the name of the process model, which also uniquely identifies a process model. Both the name and the key can be used to identify the process model when a process instance is created.

Code Example 10.6 Process Table

```
statement =   CREATE TABLE Process (
              PMID                CHAR (32)      NOT NULL ,
              Name                CHAR (32)      NOT NULL ,
              CONSTRAINT Process_pk
                PRIMARY KEY (Name)
              )
```

Code Example 10.7 shows the activity table. For each activity in a process model, an entry is managed in the table. The `PMID` column is a foreign key, pointing to the appropriate process table entry. Each activity is uniquely identified via the `AMID` column. The value of this field preserves the topological order (breath-first) of the activities within the process model. Using this technique in conjunction with a clustered index on (PMID,AMID) causes related activities to be stored together providing efficient I/O behavior. The ActivityPos field contains an indicator about the relative position of the activity within the process model, such as whether the activity is a start or an end activity. This indicator helps to quickly determine start activities when a process is started and to determine the end of navigation when an activity ends. The NrInCC field contains the number of incoming control connectors and provides an easy way of determining when navigation can continue at a join node. Implementation identifies the executable or process that implements the activity. The StaffAssignment field contains an SQL statement that is the SQL representation of the staff assignment. At execution time, the SQL statement is executed dynamically to obtain the appropriate users.

Code Example 10.7 Activity Model Table

```
CREATE TABLE ActivityModel (
   AMID              CHAR (32)        NOT NULL ,
   PMID              CHAR (32)        NOT NULL ,
   NrInCC            SMALLINT         NOT NULL ,
   ActivityPos       SMALLINT         NOT NULL ,
   Implementation    VARCHAR (256}    NOT NULL ,
   StaffAssignment   VARCHAR (256)    NOT NULL ,
   CONSTRAINT Activity_pk
     PRIMARY KEY (AMID)
)
```

Code Example 10.8 shows the table holding the control connectors. Source-Act contains the identifier (AMID) of the source activity; TargetAct, the AID of the target activity; and TransCond, the transition condition. The table has a clustered index on (PMID,SourceAct,TargetAct) that causes all control connectors for an activity to be grouped together. This grouping provides for efficient I/O processing, because all outgoing control connectors for an activity are most likely fetched with one physical I/O operation.

Code Example 10.9 shows the table that contains an entry for each process instance. Each process instance is uniquely identified by the process identifier PID. The appropriate identifier for the associated process model is stored in PMID, which is maintained as a foreign key to the process model table. The field State contains the actual state of the process instance.

Code Example 10.10 contains an entry for each active activity instance. AID uniquely identifies the activity instance. This field locates an activity instance. AMID identifies the associated activity in the associated process model. State contains the current state of the activity instance; NrInCCProc the number of control connectors that have entered the activity instance and whose transition con-

Code Example 10.8 Control Connector Table

```
CREATE TABLE ControlConnector (
  PMID            CHAR (32)      NOT NULL ,
  SourceAct       CHAR (32)      NOT NULL ,
  TargetAct       CHAR (32)      NOT NULL ,
  TransCond       VARCHAR (254) ,
  CONSTRAINT ControlConn_pk
    PRIMARY KEY (PMID,SourceAct,TargetAct)
)
```

Code Example 10.9 Process Instance Table

```
CREATE TABLE ProcessInstance (
  PID             CHAR (32)      NOT NULL ,
  PMID            CHAR (32)      NOT NULL ,
  State           INTEGER        NOT NULL ,
  CONSTRAINT ProcInstance_pk ,
    PRIMARY KEY (PID)   ,
)
```

Code Example 10.10 Activity Instance Table

```
CREATE TABLE ActivityInstance (
  AID             CHAR (32)      NOT NULL ,
  PID             CHAR (32)      NOT NULL ,
  AMID            INTEGER        NOT NULL ,
  State           SMALLINT       NOT NULL ,
  NrInCCProc      SMALLINT       NOT NULL
                  WITH DEFAULT 0 ,
  CONSTRAINT ActivityInstance_pk
    PRIMARY KEY (PID,AMID)
)
```

dition evaluated to true. The number of incoming control connectors is set to 0 if no value is supplied. The table uses a clustered index on (PID,AMID) to keep related activities together.

Code Example 10.11 shows the table that maintains workitems for users. A tuple is maintained for each user who is assigned a workitem. AID identifies the activity instance, for which workitems are generated. User contains the user identification of the assigned user, and Implementation contains the identification

Code Example 10.11 Workitem Table

```
CREATE TABLE WorkItem (
  AID              CHAR (32)      NOT NULL ,
  Implementation   CHAR(256)      NOT NULL ,
  User             CHAR(32)       NOT NULL ,
  CONSTRAINT WorkItem_pk
    PRIMARY KEY (User,PID,AID)
  )
```

of the activity implementation used by the program execution components to carry out the activity implementation. The table uses a clustered index on (User,AID) to keep the workitems of a user together. The index allows all workitems of a particular user to be efficiently fetched.

The workflow execution server navigates through the process graph by executing appropriate SQL calls. A simplified notion of SQL is used in the pseudocode of the following examples. For details about SQL, see any book about relational databases could be used, for example [Dat93]. For further simplification, no checking for SQL return codes is shown.

Code Example 10.12 shows the appropriate code fragment to start a process. Statement 1 retrieves the appropriate process model information from the process buildtime table using the supplied process name. Statement 2 inserts an entry into the ProcessInstance table, using a generated PID. The process state set is set to running. Statement 3 declares a cursor to retrieve all start activities (ActivityPos = 0) for the appropriate process model; statement 4 opens this cursor. Statement 5 starts a loop over all start activities. Statement 6 retrieves for each activity the appropriate activity information, including the staff assignment. Statement 7 creates an activity instance for the selected activity by inserting a tuple into the activity instance table. The appropriate activity state is ready. The staff resolution is maintained in the form of an SQL statement to access the staff database. This statement is then prepared for execution in statement 8. An appropriate cursor is defined in statement 9 to retrieve the assigned persons, then opened in statement 10. Statement 11 starts a loop to retrieve all assigned persons. Statement 12 fetches the appropriate resource identifier and statement 13 inserts an appropriate entry into the worklist table. Statement 15 closes the cursor for retrieval of the assigned persons. The procedure of starting a process terminates with closing the cursor for retrieving the start activities.

Code Example 10.12 Start Process

```
1    SELECT PMID
        INTO :pmid
        FROM Process
        WHERE Name = :processModelName

2    processState = running
     INSERT INTO ProcessInstance (PID, PMID, State)
        VALUES (:pid, :pmid, :processState)

3    DECLARE startActivities AS CURSOR FOR
        SELECT AMID, Implementation, StaffAssignment
        FROM Activity
        WHERE PMID = :pmid AND ActivityPos = 0

4    OPEN startActivities

5    DO UNTIL allStartActivitiesRetrieved
6       FETCH startActivities
           INTO :amid, :implementation, :staffAssignment
7       activityState = ready
        INSERT INTO ActivityInstance (AID, AMID, State)
           VALUES (:aid, :amid, :activityState)
8       PREPARE staffResolution FROM :staffAssignment
9       DECLARE staffResolutionCursor
           AS CURSOR FOR staffResolution
10      OPEN staffResolutionCursor
11      DO UNTIL assignedAssignedStaffIsRetrieved
12         FETCH staffResolutionCursor INTO :user
13         INSERT INTO WorkItem
              (AID, User, Implementation)
              USING (:aid, :user, :implementation)
14      END
15      CLOSE staffResolutionCursor
16   END

17   CLOSE startActivities
```

After an activity has been completed, navigation needs to continue. For navigation, the next set of activities needs to be determined. For those activities, staff resolution is performed and workitems are generated. These actions are initiated by an "activity implementation complete" message that is sent by the program execution component. This message contains the appropriate activity identifier that allows the workflow execution server to locate the activity. Code Example 10.13

Code Example 10.13 Navigate Process - Part 1

```
1    SELECT AMID
        INTO :amid
        FROM ActivityInstance
        WHERE (AID = :aid)

2    activityState = finished
     UPDATE ActivtyInstance
        SET state = :activityState
        WHERE AID = :aid

3    DELETE FROM WorkItem
        WHERE (AID = :aid)

4    DECLARE selectTargetActivities AS CURSOR FOR
        SELECT TargetAct FROM CONTROLCONNECTOR
           WHERE (SourceAct = :amid)

5    OPEN selectTargetActivities
```

shows the code that the workflow execution server executes to continue navigation. For simplicity we assume that the activity has no exit condition and that exit mode is automatic.

Statement 1 determines the activity in the process model that is associated with the activity instance that just completed. Access to the activity instance in the activity instance table is made through the activity instance identifier that is supplied by the completion message. This step also checks for an exit condition. Statement 2 updates the state of the activity to `finished`. The activity instance is identified by the activity instance identifier in the completion message. The activity instance cannot be deleted since it may be needed for process monitor queries. Statement 3 deletes the associated workitem information from the worklist table. Statement 4 defines a cursor that allows all control connectors having the completed activity as their source activity to be retrieved. The cursor is opened in statement 5.

In Code Example 10.14, part 2 of the `Navigate Process` processing, statement 6 starts a loop to retrieve all outgoing control connectors. Statement 7 retrieves the target activity identifier of the selected control connector. Statement 8 then retrieves the target activity information, such as the number of incoming control connectors, from the activity table. Statement 9 checks whether the target activity is a join activity by determining the number of incoming control connectors.

Code Example 10.14 Navigate Process - Part 2

```
6    DO UNTIL allControlConnectorsProcessed
7        FETCH selectTargetActivities
            INTO :activityId
8        SELECT NrInCC
            INTO :nrInCC
            FROM ACTIVITY
            WHERE AMID = :activityId

9        IF (nrINCC > 1) THEN
            DO
10               SELECT NrInCCProc FROM ActivityInstance
                    INTO :nrInCCProc
                    WHERE (AMID = activityId)
11               IF notFound THEN
                    INSERT INTO ACTSTATE
                     (AMID,AID,NrInCCProc)
                     USING (:activityId,
                      :activityInstanceId,1)
12               nrInCCProc = nrInCCProc + 1
13               IF nrInCCProc < nrInCC THEN
                    DO
14                      UPDATE ActivityInstance
                          SET nrInCC = :nrInCCProc
                          WHERE (AID = :activityInstanceId)
15                      activitySelectable = FALSE
                    END
16               ELSE
                    activitySelectable = TRUE
            END
17       ELSE
            activitySelectable = TRUE
```

If the activity has only one incoming control connector, it is no join condition and it can be selected immediately for processing. This status is indicated to the processing code by having statement 17 set the variable `activitySelectable` to true.

If the number of incoming control connectors is greater than one, the activity is a join activity. In this case, this activity can not be dispatched until all incoming control connectors have been evaluated. This processing is performed in statements 10 to 17. Statement 10 checks if an instance of the target activity has already been created by accessing the activity instance table. Such an instance of the target activity exists, if any one of the other control connectors entering the activity has been processed earlier. If not, statement 11 creates an activity instance by inserting the appropriate tuple into the activity instance table. Statement 12 increases the number of control connectors that have already entered the join activity. Statement 13 checks whether all control connectors have entered the join activity. If not all control connectors have yet entered the activity, statement 14 updates the activity instance tuple with the new number of control connectors that have entered the join activity. Statement 15 then sets the activity as not selectable by setting the `activitySelectable` variable to false. If all control connectors have entered the join activity, statement 16 sets the activity as selectable by setting the `activitySelectable` variable to true.

If (see Code Example 10.15, part 3 of the `Navigate Process` processing) statement 18 determines that the activity is selectable, then statement 19 checks the start condition. If the start condition evaluates to `TRUE`, statement 20 performs staff resolution and generates workitems. If the start condition evaluates to false, then statement 21 causes the activity to be skipped and dead path elimination to be carried out. Statement 22 ends the loop that fetches the target activities. Statement 23 closes the cursor that was used to retrieve the target activities.

Code Example 10.15 Navigate Process - Part 3

```
18        IF activitySelectable THEN
              DO
19                Check start condition
20                IF TRUE THEN
                      EXECUTE staff resolution and
                          workitem assignment
21                ELSE
                      Skip activity and perform dead path
                      elimination
              END
22   END
23   CLOSE selectTargetActivities
```

10.14 Message Queuing Usage

All components in a domain communicate via a communication bus that is implemented by message queuing. The underlying message queuing system topology must support the workflow management system topology.

The setup of the message queuing network is optimized for system groups. It is assumed that most communication is performed between the systems in the same system group and that only limited traffic occurs between different system groups.

Each system has an associated MQ manager. Within a system group, each system is connected to each other system by a MQ channel. This scheme provides efficient communication between the systems of a system group. One system in each system group is designated as the system whose MQ manager talks to the MQ manager of the appropriate system in another system group. For simplicity, the

MQ manager on that designated system is called the primary MQ manager in the system group. A3, B3, C2, and D4 are the primary MQ managers in Figure 10.33. The channel between the MQ manager of a system and the primary MQ manager is defined as a default channel. Any request which is not for a system in the system group is routed to the primary MQ manager.

Figure 10.33 Routing Messages in a Domain

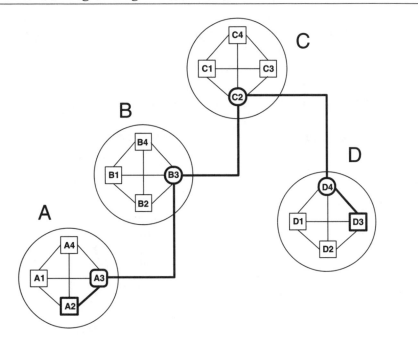

The primary MQ manager at the primary system group is called the root MQ manager; C2 in our example. The root MQ manager keeps information about all MQ managers in the domain. All other primary MQ managers keep only data for the MQ managers that are farther away from the root of the tree. All messages that cannot be resolved within a system group are sent up the tree until either an MQ manager recognizes the target system or the root MQ manager, which has knowledge about all MQ managers and their queues, is reached. Default channeling provides the routing of messages for unknown MQ managers up the tree.

Figure 10.33 highlights the path being taken if a server on system A2 sends a message to a server on system D3.

Some message queuing system, such as MQSeries, facilitate this setup by providing clustering functions. In this case, all message queuing systems know about each other. There is then no need for the particular setup we just described.

10.15   Process Compiler

The process compiler allows an executable to be created out of a process (see section 5.8 on page 206). Creation of such executables is particularly easy when the language of the executable is an object-oriented language. Executables are created by object-oriented language constructs that represent the constructs of the workflow management system. Activities and fields in the input and output containers are represented as instances of classes. Data connectors are represented as class methods. Regular language expressions are used to represent conditions such as transition, start, and exit conditions.

We use C++ to show how the translation process works. First, we discuss the classes and their methods, then the implementation of control and data connectors, and finally the expressions for start, exit, and transition conditions.

Each activity of the process graph is represented by an instance of the activity class shown in Code Example 10.16. Data member `actualNumberCCIn` holds the number of incoming control connectors that evaluate to true at execution time. Data member `activityState` holds the state of the activity instance. An encoded form is used, such as 1 for the finished state.

Code Example 10.16 Activity Class

```
class activity {
    int         actualNumberCCIn ;
    int         activityState ;

public :

    int         getNumberCCIn () ;
    int         getActualNrCCIn () ;
    void        setActivityState (int activityState) ;
    int         activityState () ;

}
```

`getNumberCCIn()` obtains the number of incoming control connectors. `getActualNrCCIn()` obtains the number of control connector that have entered the activity during execution. `setActivityStatus()` allows to set the activity state, `activityState()` to query the state of the activity.

Each field (item) in the input and output container is an instance of a data-type specific container item class. Those container item classes inherit from the base class specified in Code Example 10.17. The member `valueSet` indicates whether or not the class instance holds a value. The class instance holds no value when no value has been assigned to the class instance. `testForValue()` returns true if the class instance contains a value; false, if the class instance contains no value.

Code Example 10.17 Container Item Base Class

```
class contItem {

protected :
   int       valueSet ;

public :
   int       testForValue () ;

} ;
```

For each of the basic types, a type-specific class that inherits from the base class as shown in Code Example 10.18 is used for a container item with data type LONG.

Code Example 10.18 Container Item Long Class

```
class contItemLong : public contItem {

   long      value ;

public :
   void      copyValue (contItemLong* sourceDataItem) ;
   long      getValue () ;
   int       testForTrue (int compOperator, long compValue) ;

} ;
```

`copyValue()` populates the member of the class with the value of another container member. The method first tests whether the source member contains a value, using the `testForValue()` method against the source field. If the field contains a value, the value is copied and the member `valueSet` is set to indicate that the field holds a value. If the source field contains no value, nothing is done. `GetValue()` obtains the stored value, and `testForTrue()` compares the value with a specified value, using a specified comparison operator.

The start condition is checked by one of the statements in Code Example 10.19.

Code Example 10.19 Check Start Condition Statement

```
01      if (activityName->getActualNrCCIn() > 0) {

02      if (activityName->getActualNrCCIn () == numberCCIn) {
```

Line 01 is generated if the start condition is defined as "At least one control connector is true." The data member `actualNrCCIn` contains the number of incoming control connectors that evaluated to true; method `getActualNrCCIn()` returns this number. The start condition is therefore true if this number is greater than zero; that means at least one incoming control connector evaluated to true.

Line 02 is generated if the start condition is defined as "All control connectors must be true." If the number returned by `getActualNrCCIn()` and the number of control connectors specified via `numberCCIN` are equal, then the start condition is met. `numberCCIn` is filled with the actual number of control connectors. For example, if the activity has three entering control connectors, then `numberCCIn` has a value of 3.

The data for an input container item is copied from a container item of a previous output container item with the statement shown in Code Example 10.20. It is checked that the source activity has been executed, that is it has not been skipped. If the activity has been processed, an output container has been allocated for the source activity. If an output container has been allocated, data to be copied. If the activity has been skipped, no output container has been allocated. In this case, the attempt to copy would reference invalid storage and the program would terminate.

Code Example 10.20 Container Item Mapping Statement

```
if sourceActivity->activityState(finished){
   containerItemName -> copyValue
                        (sourceContainerItemName) ;
}
```

The code fragment listed in Code Example 10.21 implements the exit condition for an activity. In the generated code, the `exitConditionStructured` symbol is replaced with the actual exit condition. Each field name together, the comparison operator, and the comparison value are replaced by an appropriate method invocation of the `testForTrue` method on the class instance that represents the field.

Code Example 10.21 Check Exit Condition statement

```
01   exitCondition = FALSE ;

02   while (exitCondition == FALSE) {

03      exitCondition = exitConditionStructured ;

04   }
```

Lines 01 and 02 are executed before the activity implementation is invoked; lines 03 and 04 are executed after the activity implementation has been invoked.

The code generated for the program invocation depends on the implementation of the program. Code Example 10.22 shows the invocation of an OS/2 program in a separate OS/2 session.

Code Example 10.22 Sample of Program Invocation

```
sd.PgmName = "d:\\pgma5.exe" ;

rc = DosStartSession (&sd, &ulSessionId, &pidProcess) ;

if (rc==0) {
   rc = DosReadQueue (termQueue, &request,
                      &dataLength, (PVOID*) &dataAddress ,
                      elementCode, noWait,
                      &elemPriority, semHandle) ;
}
```

The code fragment in Code Example 10.23 checks the transition condition. In the generate code, the `transitionConditionStructured` symbol is replaced with the actual transition condition. Each field name, the comparison operator, and the comparison value are replaced by an appropriate method invocation of the `testForTrue` method on the class instance that represents the field.

Code Example 10.23 Statements to Check Transition Conditions

```
01   otherwise = ON ;

02   if (transitionConditionStructured) {
         otherwise = OFF ;
         targetActivityName->incrActualNrCCIn() ;
         }

03   if (otherwise == ON) {
         targetActivityName->incrActualNrCCIn() ;
         }
```

Line 01 is generated if at least one outgoing control connector is defined with `otherwise`.

Line 02 is generated for each control connector leaving the activity. The expression `transitionConditionStructured` is generated before the code for invoking the activity implementation is generated. If the transition condition is true, the number of incoming control connectors in the target activity that evaluate to true is increased by executing the member function `incrActualNrCCIn()` on the target activity object.

Line 03 is generated for the `otherwise` control connector. It is executed if none of the other control connectors evaluates to true and, therefore the variable otherwise was never reset to OFF.

Code Example 10.24 through 10.26 on page 427 show the generated code for the `Assess Risk` activity in the loan process. For simplicity only the essential parts are shown.

Statements 1 through 4 (Code Example 10.24) form the initialization part of the generated program. They define the appropriate activity states used in querying and setting the state of an activity, operators that are used in transition and exit conditions, and the truth value returned in operations (`comparisonResults`). An instance of the activity class is created for each activity in the process model.

Code Example 10.24 Compiled Code for Assess Risk Activity - Part 1

```
1     enum activityStates {finished,
                           running,
                           executed,
                           skipped}

2     enum operators {EQ,
                      NE}

3     enum comparisonResult {TRUE,FALSE}

4     activity* AssessRisk = new activity ;
```

In Code Example 10.25. statement 5 checks whether a control connector has entered the activity. If the defined control connector has not entered the activity, the incoming control connector has evaluated to false and, therefore, the activity must be skipped. If the activity is skipped, processing continues with the `else` branch in statement 29 with statement 30 setting the activity state to skipped (see Figure 10.26.

Code Example 10.25 Compiled Code for Assess Risk Activity - Part 2

```
5      if (AssessRisk->getActualNrCCIn() > 0) {

6          dataItemString* AssessRiskInFirstName =
                            new dataItemString ;
7          dataItemString* AssessRiskInLastName =
                            new dataItemString ;
8          dataItemString* AssessRiskInAmount =
                            new dataItemLong ;
9          dataItemString* AssessRiskOutFirstName =
                            new dataItemString ;
10         dataItemString* AssessRiskOutLastName =
                            new dataItemString ;
11         dataItemString* AssessRiskOutAmount =
                            new dataItemFloat ;
12         dataItemString* AssessRiskOutRisk =
                            new dataItemString ;
13         dataItemLong* AssessRiskOut_RC =
                            new dataItemLong ;

14         if (CollectCreditInformation->activityState()
              == finished){
15            AssessRiskInFirstName->
                copyValue(CollectCreditInformationOutFirstName) ;
16            AssessRiskInLastName->
                copyValue(CollectCreditInformationOutLastName) ;
17            AssessRiskInAmount->
                copyValue(CollectCreditInformationOutAmount) ;
           }
```

Statements 6 through 8 allocate the fields in the input container, statements 9 through 13 allocate the fields in the output container. The field allocated in statement 13 allocates a system field that holds the return code that is filled with the appropriate code returned by the activity implementation.

Statements 14 through 17 copy the fields from the output container of the Collect Credit Information activity into the appropriate fields in the input container of the Assess Risk activity. The fields are only copied if the Collect Credit Information activity was carried out and therefor an output container has been allocated. The statements implement the data connector that is drawn from the output container of the Collect Credit Information activity to the input container of the Assess Risk activity.

In Code Example 10.26, statement 18 sets the activity instance into the running state. Statements 19, 20, and 23 implement the exit condition. The exit condition evaluates to true if the return code set by the activity implementation evaluates to true. This check is performed in statement 23. The activity implementation, in the example, an OS/2 program, is carried out in statements 21 and 22.

Statement 24 is carried out when the exit condition has evaluated to true. It sets the activity instance into the executed state.

Statements 25 through 27 check the transition condition of the outgoing control connectors. Statement 26 is processed if the risk is determined to be low. Thus the control connector to the `Accept Credit` activity is followed as indicated by increasing the number of incoming control connectors for this activity. If the risk is not low, the otherwise connector to the `Request Approval` activity is taken. Statement 27 indicates this by increasing the number of incoming control connectors for this activity.

As a final step, statement 28 sets the activity instance into the `finished` state.

Code Example 10.26 Compiled Code for Assess Risk Activity - Part 3

```
18         AssessRisk->setActivityState(running) ;

19         exitCondition = FALSE ;
20         while (exitCondition == FALSE) {

21             sd.Pgmname = "arisk.exe" ;
22             rc = DosStartSession (....} ;

23             exitCondition =
                   (AssessRiskOut_RC->testForTrue(EQ,0)) ;
           }

24         AssessRisk->setActivityState(Executed)

25         otherwise = ON ;
26         if (AssessRiskOutRisk->testForTrue(0,"Low"}){
               otherwise = OFF ;
               AcceptCredit->incrActualNrCCIn()
               }
27         if (otherwise = ON) {
                   RequestApproval->incrActualNrCCIn() ;
               }

28         AssessRisk->setActivityState(Finished) ;
       }

29    else {

30         AssessRisk->setActivityState(Skipped) ;

       }
```

Chapter 11

Development of Workflow-based Applications

We discussed in previous chapters the structure of workflow-based applications as a combination of process models and activity implementations. We also discussed some of the aspects of the construction of those applications, such as the engineering of business processes or the relationship between object technology and workflow technology.

This chapter presents a development method, a blueprint, for the construction of workflow-based applications. It addresses all aspects in the design, implementation, testing, and monitoring of this type of application. We call this approach *process-based CASE* (computer-aided software engineering) to indicate that the goal of the outlined CASE method is to create applications that are workflow-based, thus implying that the underlying business process is externalized and managed by a workflow management system [LR97]. This approach is different from the notion of *process-centered CASE*, where processes are used to develop applications and coordinate development teams [BSK94]. In fact, process-centered CASE could also be applied to process-based CASE.

All process relevant components that make up the development environment have been discussed in one form or another in the previous chapters. We have even discussed some of the relationships between these components. We concentrate, therefore, on those parts that have not been discussed. In particular the aspects of constructing and testing workflows and activity implementations are discussed in great detail.

11.1 Development Environment Blueprint

Figure 11.1 shows the architecture of the development system. It shows those components users are dealing with. It does not reflect internals, such as how the individual components exchange information.

Figure 11.1 Development Components

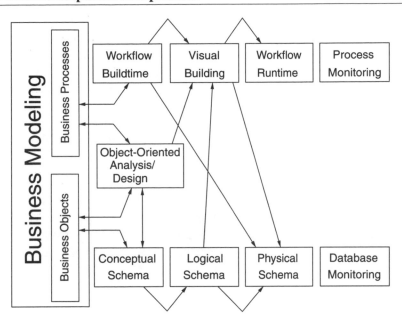

The flow of actions in the figure is from left to right. Thus the development of workflow-based applications starts with the high-level modeling of business processes and business objects. This modeling is performed either by means a business modeling tool as discussed in Chapter 2 on page 30 or by an object-oriented analysis/design tool as discussed in Chapter 6.

Neither business modeling tools nor OOA/D tools define the business processes and business objects at such a level of detail that they can be used immediately by workflow management systems, database management systems, or object brokers. They must be refined and enriched with information-technology-specific information. The upper half of the figure shows the refinement of the business processes; the lower half shows the refinement of business objects into appropriate database structures.

The development of workflow-based applications does not stop when the processes, activity implementations, and associated data have been handed over to the appropriate systems for running the developed business processes. As outlined, monitors observe the operation of the workflow management system and the database management system.

The refinement of business processes so that they can be carried out by the workflow management system is typically performed by the workflow management system's buildtime. Input to the buildtime is in the form of business process skeletons as delivered by the business modeling tool or the OOA/D tool. The output of the buildtime is executable business processes with all interfaces defined for the activity implementations. These interfaces constitute the contract between the process logic and the activity implementations.

A visual builder is typically used to create the activity implementations. Visual builders provide a programming environment that allows the programmer to visually construct applications and create objects. The programmer constructs applications by arranging objects on a drawing board and manipulating the objects. This method makes visual builder ideal companions to business modeling tools, OOA/D tools, and the workflow management system's buildtime since they all provide a GUI. The visual builder together with this set of tools implements the two-level programming paradigm that we mentioned in Chapter 6.

The runtime component of the workflow management system then controls the execution of process instances, as discussed in Chapter 3. It allows users to start, terminate, suspend, and resume processes. It determines who should perform a particular activity and puts the resulting workitems onto the worklist of the selected user(s). When a workitem is selected, it schedules the proper program. When the activity has completed, it determines the next activities. All actions are recorded in an audit trail.

The process monitor ensures that the business processes are carried out as expected and that actions are taken if the specified goals are not as expected. We discussed the functions of this component in great detail in Chapter 3.

The business objects identified during business modeling or object-oriented analysis are input to conceptual data modeling. They represent the local conceptual schema of the application implemented via a business process. In general, these objects form the kernel entities of the enterprise data model and thus provide the basis for the creation of an enterprise data model through view integration [EN94, BCN92].

The conceptual schema is transferred into a logical schema, the schema of the database in which the data is stored. [BCN92] outlines the rules to transfer an entity-relationship schema into a relational schema.

A physical schema is created from the logical schema by choice of specific storage structures and access paths to achieve the best performance for the various applications. Input to the physical schema design is the transaction load and the database load. Transaction load represents the amount of requests that the database must sustain; database load, the amount of data that the database holds. Both pieces of data can be derived from information collected during business modeling, workflow definition, and application building. We discuss this later in detail.

The activities in the databases must be monitored to detect performance bottlenecks. This monitoring could trigger modification of the database schemes and the structure of the business processes.

11.2   Component Generation

As pointed out, visual builders use predefined or user-defined components to construct applications. The components are represented as icons on the builder's icon bar. The application developer drags these icons from the icon bar and drops them on the builder's surface. Then, she connects the different icons to specify what a component should do as the result of the action of another component.

Different visual builders use different component models. Conceptually, they all try to achieve the same result, namely to facilitate the reuse of components in different applications. The different component models differ mainly in the way the individual components interact with each other. The more prominent examples of these components are ActiveX controls, Java Beans, and VisualAge Parts.

An important element in the development of workflow-based applications is that the process logic and the activity implementations are clearly separated by the activity's input and output containers. From the structure of those containers, the workflow management system can generate appropriate components that then can be used directly in the visual builder, allowing tight integration between the visual builder and the workflow management system's buildtime. Additional parts can be generated to reflect the structure of the business objects in a relational database so that these parts can access the data by using the appropriate database accesses.

We show in this section how container parts can be generated for the parts architecture as implemented by IBM's VisualAge for C++ product. The interested reader should see the appropriate IBM VisualAge literature for details [IBM95b, IBM95a].

11.2.1   Characteristics of Parts

A VisualAge part in VisualAge C++ is a software object implemented as a C++ class that supports a simple, standardized protocol. This protocol supports the interconnection of parts to form higher-function parts or entire applications. The part interface is composed of three distinct features: *attributes*, *actions*, and *events*. These features correspond to a natural way of viewing parts (and objects in general) in terms of what properties (*attributes*) they have, what behaviors (*actions*) they can perform, and what unsolicited information (*events*) they can notify other parts about.

A part is made up of a header file and a code file for a C++ class that supports the parts architecture. The part's interface must be made known to the visual builder either via the built.in parts editor or via a *part information file* or .vbe file. This file must be imported into the visual builder.

11.2.2   Parts Usage

Figure 11.2 shows the composition editor of VisualAge as used to construct the
activity implementation for an activity within a loan process. The activity implementation displays the customer name, which was obtained in a previous activity,
and collects the address and credit amount.

Figure 11.2 Parts Usage

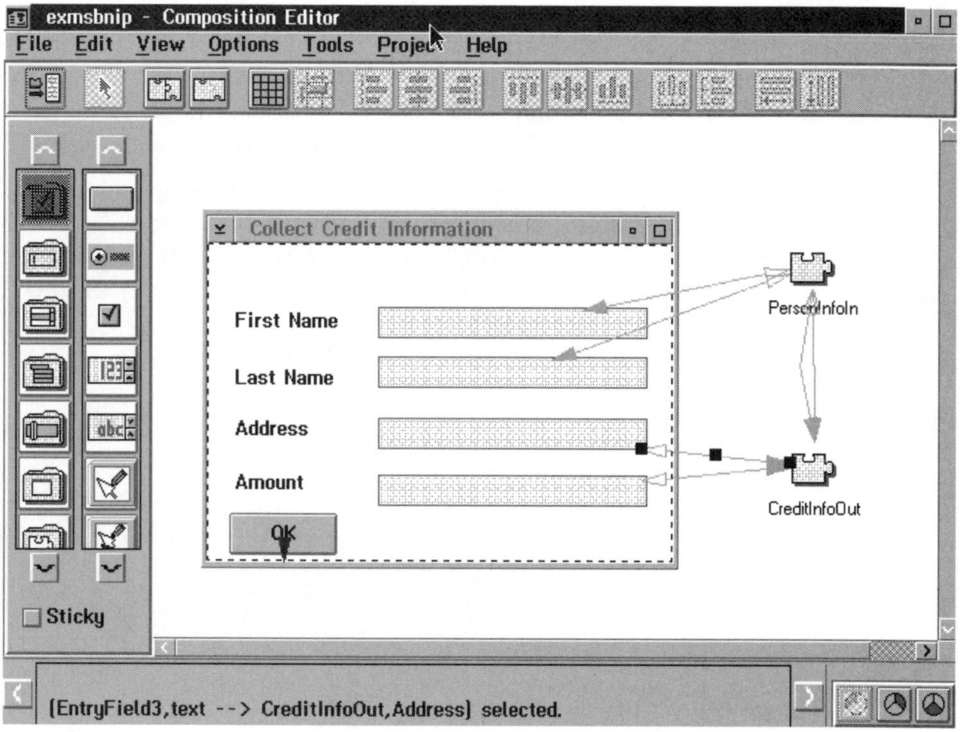

The rectangle with the heading Collect Credit Information represents the screen
that the program will display when invoked. The appropriate fields allow entry and
display of the required data. The OK button, when pressed, causes the program to
terminate and return control, in this case to the workflow management system. The
two parts that are not part of the screen are parts that represent the containers of
the associated activity; the PersonInfoIn represents the input container with the two
fields First Name and Last Name; the CreditInfoOut represents the output container
with four fields: First Name, Last Name, Address, and Amount.

The fields in the input container part are filled when the program is started;
that means the contents of the container are copied from the workflow management
system to the program storage that holds the values of the part. Copying is done by
invoking the appropriate container API. The arrows from the input container part to

the two fields First Name and Last Name cause the contents of these two fields to be copied from the input container. The arrows from the input container part to the output container part cause selected fields to be copied from the input container to the output container. The arrows from Address and Credit to the output container cause the contents of those fields to be copied to the output container whenever the field value changes. When the program terminates, the contents of the output container is copied back to the workflow management system via the container API.

11.2.3 Container Parts Generation

Container parts can be automatically generated from the information that the workflow management system maintains. Thus, input and an output container parts are created for each data structure. The data structure information is augmented by the predefined field information to make up the input and output containers. For each part, an .hpp file for the header information, a .cpp file for the part implementation, and a .vbe file for the part information file to be imported into the visual builder are created.

When an input container part is created, the following steps are performed:

1. For each field in the data structure, an attribute is created. The name of the attribute is the name of the field. For nested data structures, the name is constructed by prefixing the field name with the names of the data structures in the path. Field type and length are taken from the field information in the data structure.

2. For each field in the predefined data structures contained in the input container, an attribute is created.

3. A get method is created for each attribute. No set method is created for the attributes, because there is no requirement to set the values of the fields in the input container. If the field has no value, the attribute is populated with a default value.

4. A constructor is created for the part. This constructor is called when the program is started. It obtains the container via the appropriate programming interface calls and stores each container field into the appropriate parts field. If the field has no value, the attribute is populated with a default value.

When an output container part is created, similar steps are performed:

1. For each field in the data structure, an attribute is created. The name of the attribute is the name of the field. For nested data structures the name is constructed by prefixing the field name with the names of the data structures

in the path. Field type and length are taken from the field information in the data structure.

2. For each field in the predefined data structures contained in the input container, an attribute is created.

3. A set method is created for each attribute. No get method is created for the attributes, because there is no need to get the values from the output container. A notification is sent out if the value of an attribute is set. This notification informs other parts, that the field has changed, so that they can take appropriate action.

4. A constructor is created for the part. The purpose is to set a control indicator for each attribute; the indicator shows whether a value has been supplied for the attribute via the attribute's set method.

5. A destructor is created for the part. It is invoked when the program terminates. It stores the values of all attributes in the output container via the container API. Only those attributes, for which a value has been set, are stored in the output container.

11.2.4   Database Access Part Generation

The generation of the conceptual, logical, and physical schema of the application databases as shown in Figure 11.1 on page 429 is oversimplified. Each business process and, in some cases every activity, in a business process may have its own conceptual scheme. These local conceptual schema must then be combined into the global conceptual schema, from which logical and physical schemes are then derived as shown in Figure 11.3.

Figure 11.3 Database Access Part Generation

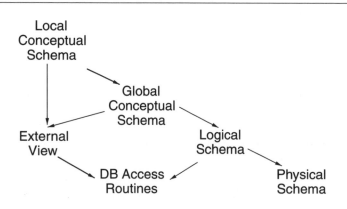

In the next step, the local conceptual schemes are represented as external views, as subsets of the global conceptual schema. Each external view then represents a business object in the global conceptual schema.

From the external view and the logical scheme, the appropriate part that represents the business object can be generated. Each part then contains the fields as attributes. The appropriate get and set methods are used by these parts to obtain and set the value of the individual fields. In addition, the typical database operations—create, retrieve, update, and delete—are created. Similarly to the container parts, the constructor could retrieve the business object from the database, whereas the destructor could perform the necessary updates.

11.3 Testing

Testing is an important step in the development of every application; actually, for every computer system. They need to be tested to make sure that they perform the way they are intended to. The amount of testing depends on many factors, such as the amount of code reuse or the design methodology that is used. One very important aspect is the quality of the requirements that are input to the development of the application and against which the created application must be tested.

Unless the application has been built as a workflow-based application, everything must be tested together, the application logic as well as the built-in business process. The testing of such an application reflects the construction of the application as one monolithic application. Individual components cannot, in general, be tested separately unless an appropriate test bed that provides the correct infrastructure is written.

We have discussed several times the advantages of the two-level programming paradigm that underlies workflow-based applications. This two-level programming also facilitates the testing of workflow-based applications. First, the application's business process is created and tested; second, the individual activity implementations are created and tested. Integrating the different pieces and finally testing the complete application becomes a simple task that can be carried out in a very short time. This testing is different from the usual testing of applications, where the integration and the system test make up a large portion in the development of an application.

Ensuring the correct execution of an application is only one of the objectives of testing the application. Another important aspect of testing is the performance tuning of the application, the setting of the tunable parameters of the application to their optimal value. In workflow-based applications, discovery and setting of these parameters is facilitated also by the two-level programming approach. Tuning of the business process, including the underlying workflow management system, can be done separately from the tuning of the individual activity implementations. In particular, the distributed nature of the implementation allows deployment of the individual activity implementations and individual parts of the business process to different processors for optimal throughput.

Another aspect mostly neglected by non-workflow-based applications is the monitoring of the actual execution performance of the application after it has been released for production. A simple reason for the neglect is the amount of instrumentation required to perform the appropriate collection of runtime data. The audit trail written by the workflow management system, along with the built-in process monitor, provides a solid base for performing runtime performance analysis.

Figure 11.4 shows schematically the individual steps that are carried out in the testing and monitoring of business processes. It does not show the appropriate testing of the corresponding activity implementation.

Figure 11.4 Testing and Monitoring Business Processes

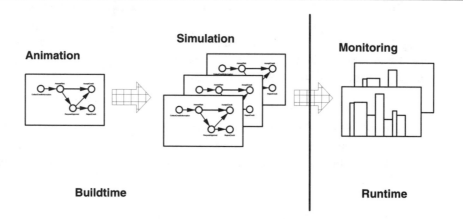

The first step is the testing of the business process and its interfaces to the individual activity implementations. This testing requires that a debugger be available to step through the business process. Animation, as first implemented by IBM FlowMark [IBM96], is a powerful method for debugging. We describe animation next in section 11.4.

The second step is the simulation of the business process to determine the necessary information technology environment that is needed to carry out the estimated number of business processes. In addition, this step helps in designing the databases that are accessed by the individual activity implementations. The business aspects, such as the number of people needed to carry out the business processes, are usually handled in the business modeling tool. If no business modeling tool has been used or the business modeling tool does not provide this function, simulation of the business aspects must also be carried out here.

The third step is to monitor the execution of business processes. We described monitoring in detail in Chapters 2 on page 30 and 3.

Debugging and testing of the appropriate activity implementations, which is not shown in the figure, requires a particular because activity implementations are invoked by the workflow management system and not as usual via the execution of a command. Thus, we need a test tool that simulates the launching characteristics of the workflow management system. This tool is described in section 11.5 on page 441.

11.4 Animation

Recall creating business processes is a high-level form of programming (programming in the large). Thus, business processes must be tested as any other program; errors must be located and removed. Locating errors is usually carried out by running the supplied debugger, stepping through the code, and displaying and altering the data managed by the program. This function is realized for business processes by animation. Animation helps to address the following requirements for debugging business processes.

- Discover modeling errors in the process graph, such as the following:

  { Passing of data from one activity to a subsequent activity is incomplete and incorrect. Incomplete information, for example, can result in the wrong evaluation of a transition condition, which causes the process to take unanticipated paths through the graph, or wrong data is passed to the activity implementations. This error is deleterious in the case of join nodes, when data from the output container of multiple activities is mapped to the same field in the input container of the join activity. In this case, the value of the target field could depend on the time the source activities were executed, resulting in possibly erratic behavior.

  { The transition, start, and exit conditions are defined incorrectly. A trivial error is the incorrect use of the OR in Boolean expressions. In everyday language OR generally expresses an either-or (XOR) as in the simple question: "Would you like to rent a small or a large car ?" In this case, the question asks for a decision. The logical OR in a question asks whether at least one of the pieces of the question is true.

- Test that the invocation of programs is correct. This means that the data passed to the activity implementations is correct and that the returned data is processed correctly by the workflow management system. This testing must be possible even though the activity implementation has not been written. If the activity implementation has been written, the activity implementation must be called correctly. In this case, it is desirable that the activity implementation could be invoked by a version of the activity implementation that was compiled in debug mode.

- Determine not only that the right persons are getting the workitem but also that the distribution of work is correct. At the least, a first indication about worklist distribution should be provided. A final statement about workitem distribution and the appropriate workload for each of the participants is only possible after simulation has been performed.

- Carry out testing even if the process model is not complete or still contains errors. This capability allows the process modeler to recognize design errors and to analyze different design alternatives at an early stage. This early problem solving is particularly advantageous for modeling processes by use of a top-down mode.

- Visualize the verification results in the typical form used during modeling. Because modeling is performed with a graphical editor, it is desirable that the verification is visualized with the same editor. In addition, an audit trail of the verification should help to trace the various actions performed during the verification.

- Select the optimal test strategy. It should be possible to verify process models in different operational modes. First, it should be possible to step through a process model, preferably not only in forward but also in backward mode. In particular, this stepwise navigation through a process should also be available also for processes that do not interact with the user. If the process modeler encounters an error, the system should allow the process modeler to store the current process state, make the appropriate modifications to the process model, and continue at the interruption. The stored information should also be available for regression testing. In any case, the system should write a protocol to provide some documentation.

The basic idea behind graphical animation is to show how control and data flow through the process graph, how data is exchanged between the activities and the appropriate activity implementations, and how work is distributed to the involved personnel. And this all should be presented in the format that has been used to model the business process.

As with any debugger, animation can be used in two different modes: the process debugging mode and the process regression test mode. In the debugging mode, the process modeler tests the process by stepping forward and backward through the process. In the regression test mode, a stored script is automatically executed.

Figure 11.5 shows the windows that are displayed when the process modeler invokes animation for a process model. The top window shows the control panel to navigate through the process model; the left window shows the animated process model; the right window, the worklists of the participants.

Figure 11.5 Animation Windows

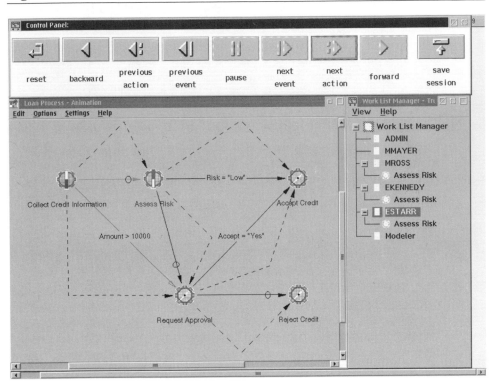

The control panel supports the navigation through the process model. It resembles the control panel of a video recorder and the buttons exhibit the well-known behavior. *Forward* moves forward following a stored script until the script ends or the modeler interrupts it by pressing the *pause* button. *Backward* moves backward through the original path of the process graph. This unique feature is not found in most program debuggers, but it is very useful. *Reset* moves to the beginning of the animation session or the script, respectively. *Next action* moves forward to the next action, which requires user input; *next event* provides a more granular level of navigation; the appropriate backward buttons cause the appropriate move to be performed in the reverse direction. *Save session* saves the session in a script for later reuse.

The status of activities and control connectors changes during the navigation. Status changes of activities are indicated by appropriately coloring icons and connectors, both control and data. A control connector, for example, is shown in green if the control connector has evaluated to true; and in red if the control connector has evaluated to false.

The worklist manager window simulates worklists for each participant in the workflow. When a user selects a workitem from a worklist, it is removed from the worklists of any user who was assigned this workitem too. The appropriate program implementing the activity is launched, and the appropriate input container data is made available to the program. The program reads the data from the input container and then writes the created data into the output container. This behavior is simulated. Whenever an activity is put into the ready state, staff resolution is performed and workitems are created for the selected users. For every selected user, an entry is placed into the user's simulated worklist. In Figure 11.5, for example, the user MROSS was assigned the work to perform activity Assess Risk. If the process modeler selects a workitem by double-clicking on an entry in the worklist, the workitem is removed from all other worklists, the status of the activity changes to running, and the animation object *Data Container* is displayed, as shown in Figure 11.6. The object shows all data, that is available to the activity implementation in the input container. It allows the process modeler to enter data into the output container.

Figure 11.6 shows the data container object for the activity Assess Risk. The upper part shows the input container with the fields filled with values that are copied from the output container of the Collect Credit Information activity. The appropriate data connector indicates which fields need to be moved. The lower part shows the output container into which the activity implementation writes by using the container API. During animation, entering container values is performed by the process modeler. Thus, the behavior of the program is specified by the values entered by the process modeler. In the example, the value Low is entered for Risk.

The values in the output container are now used to evaluate the exit condition of the activity and the transition conditions of the outgoing control connectors. If the exit condition evaluates to true, the flow of control follows those control connectors, which evaluate to true. In the case of the Assess Risk activity, the control connector leading to the Accept Credit is evaluated first. Because the transition condition field Risk is set to Low, this control connector evaluates to true and the control connector to Credit Check activity evaluates to false. The next activity will be the Accept Credit activity.

The regression test mode allows the process modeler to run regression tests for predefined scenarios. These scenarios are constructed by saving a running animation session. All information relevant to execution history, such as the state of the activities, the contents of the containers and all data entries is written to a file.

Figure 11.6 Container Object

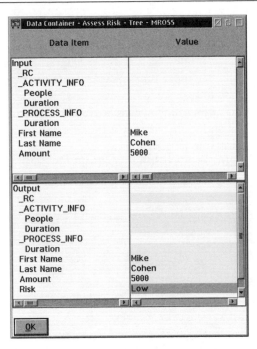

Animation, as described, allows the testing of the process logic before any code development is started. Implementation, testing, and debugging of the activity implementations is then done as a separate step in the development of workflow-based applications. We discuss this step in the next section. Animation, however, could optionally invoke the actual activity implementation if the program exists. Whether the animation can detect automatically the existence of the program depends on the invocation mechanism used for invoking the program. Upon user request, the animation could also call the debugger.

11.5 Debugging Activity Implementations

After the business processes have been verified for correctness, the appropriate programs must be implemented unless existing programs or business objects are used. These programs must then be tested to verify that they have implemented the logic correctly.

The difficulties with testing these programs are that they are invoked from the workflow management system and that the information between the program and the workflow management system is exchanged by the programming interface supplied by the workflow management system. Because testing of the interfaces to the programs, that implement the activities, has already been done, development and testing of the programs can be done in parallel, particularly true, when there is no major non-workflow related data flow, for example, by the applications reading and storing data in a common database.

It should be possible to test each program separately on its own. In addition, each of the programs must also be tested by invocation from the workflow management system.

Figure 11.7 shows the base architecture for stand-alone debugging of the programs.

Figure 11.7 Application Implementation Debugging

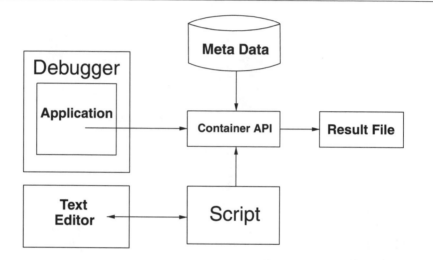

The program to test is linked with a modified container API. The original container API calls the workflow management system to obtain the container metadata, the actual values in the input container, and to write the data to the output container. The actual communication between the AP and the workflow management system is typically implemented as interprocess communication, where the workflow management system manages the data in shared memory. The modified container API obtains the container metadata either by retrieving the data structure information from the workflow management system's database, using the modeling API or by analyzing the appropriate FDL (which has been retrieved by the export function of the workflow management system). The input container data is retrieved from a file, which has a layout like the one shown in Code Example 11.1. The shown input container is the input container of the `Accept Credit` activity.

Any available text editor can create the input container value file. The API needs the process name and the activity name to access the data structure metadata. When the first API call is issued by the program to be debugged, the API opens the file, determines the name of the data structure, and uses this information to obtain

Code Example 11.1 Test File Contents

```
DATASTRUCTURE Credit Information
    CreditRequestor.FirstName 'Mike'
    CreditRequestor.LastName 'Cohen'
    Amount 5000
    Risk 'Low'
```

the data structure information for the input and the output containers. The API reads the input data and makes it available for the current and all subsequent API calls. It then opens the file for the output container. If the program requests storing a value in the output container, the value is written to the output file. After program completion, an output file, which contains the values of the output container in a form similar to the input container file, will have been created.

This architecture allows the application programmer to develop and debug the program in the individual development environment (IDE) provided by most compilers. Some compilers allow users to add new constructs to their IDE. This allows application programmers to add the capability to create and update input container values to such an environment, facilitating the construction of the test files.

Based on the outlined architecture, the workflow management system can provide a test tool that facilitates the debugging and testing of activity implementations. It delivers the functionality via an API. A GUI exploits this interface to make testing and debugging easier and less error prone. For ease of use, the information is stored in the workflow management system's database.

Data for the input container values is collected and updated through a screen similar to the screen used by the animation. The information is stored in the database on an activity-per-process basis. For each activity, multiple versions of the input container values may exist.

The tool also allows the process modeler to collect and update the expected output container values for a given input container value set. This information is then used during the testing of an activity implementation to compare the expected results with the actual results.

The program to be tested is either invoked directly or by the debugger. If a command line is to be passed to the program, it is constructed from the appropriate information and passed directly to the program. The tool takes care of calling the activity implementation in the proper way.

If desired, one can construct a script to support the execution of a series of programs. When the script is selected, all entries in the script are executed. Incidentally, these scripts can be generated from the scripts created by animation.

11.6   Application Database Design

An important factor in the overall performance of a workflow-based application is the performance of the databases that are accessed by the activity implementations. This means that a good physical database schema needs to be developed. To perform physical database schema, one needs two things: the transaction load and the data load. The transaction load is the number of operations made against the database: for relational databases, the number and type of SQL calls made against the different tables. Data load is the number of rows that each of the individual tables holds initially. Figure 11.8 shows the steps that need to be carried out to determine the transaction load and the data load.

Figure 11.8 Deriving Good Physical Database Scheme

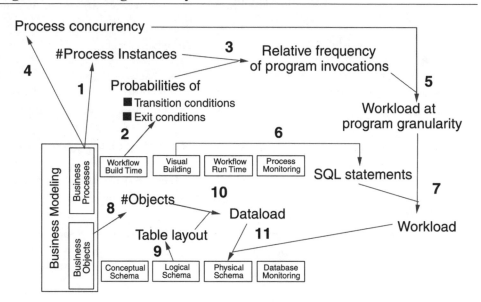

Calculation of the transaction load starts with determining the number of process instances that are created in a certain time frame (**1**). With the probabilities that exit and transition conditions are evaluated to true (**2**), the number of activities that are executed can be determined (**3**). This information is usually collected during business process modeling, where it is used to determine the number of people required to run the business process (see section 2.9.2 on page 51.

Of particular interest is the appropriate distribution over the day and the week rather than the average transaction load, this is the number of processes that are created within a given time frame (**4**). This information may have already been collected during business modeling, when there are significant peaks in the creation of processes and the overall process time is very short.

The process creation distribution multiplied by the activity probabilities gives the execution distribution of each of the activities (**5**). Here, the working-time distribution of the people carrying out the activities needs to be factored in. Typically, people work most from 9 a.m. to 11 a.m., and from 2 p.m. to 4 p.m. afternoon.

As part of creating the activity implementations, the appropriate database access calls are determined and usually documented in the associated development documentation. This documentation includes for each SQL call the type, such as insert, replace, or delete, the associated table, and the amount of data transported with the request or returned as the result of the request (**6**).

The information about the individual SQL calls combined with the activity execution distribution provides the transaction load that the database management system must sustain for each of the databases and tables (**7**). This information gives a first indication whether the database can handle the generated work load. In addition, it gives a first hint of whether the network can the network traffic generated by the database accesses.

The data load is determined as part of designing the database. Similarly to the processes, the number of objects is specified (**8**). Combining the derived logical schema (**9**) with the number of business objects gives the data load for each of the tables (**10**), and the number of rows within each of the tables, so the database designer can determine for each of the logical schemes the number of rows within each of the tables.

The calculated data load and transaction load together then allow the database designer to determine the best physical schema for the database management system (**11**).

11.7 Application Tuning

The workflow management system offers a plethora of options for tuning the workflow management system and the appropriate business processes. We show here some of the options (as provided, for example, by MQSeries Workflow), that are available to tune the individual workflow-based application. These options allow on to control how the workflow management system interprets the process. They can be specified on a process or activity level. Applied judiciously, they improve performance without impacting the intended use of the business process. We have already sketched some of the options when we discussed the appropriate functions; we just repeat them here for completeness.

As we pointed out in section 3.6 on page 105 a record is written to the audit trail for each action. This practice may cause the audit trail to grow rather rapidly. Options are provided to control the amount of data that is written to the audit trail by the AUDIT option. NONE causes no records to be written at all, an option that is perfect for inquiry processes. The opposite is FULL, where every action that has been carried out by the workflow management system is recorded. This option should be used when the information is needed for legal reasons or when a very thorough analysis is needed of how the processes are carried out. If this detail is not required, then CONDENSED provides the medium level of granularity. In essence it records the start and stop times of processes and activities. This is sufficient to determine throughput and elapsed time for processes and activities.

One of the major motivations for defining staff assignments and performing staff resolution is to get the job done as quickly as possible. One way to achieve this goal is to assign the task to many people so that it is picked up as soon as somebody finds the time to carry out the activity. The disadvantage associated with this approach is that (1) it could cost system resources that could be spent otherwise and (2) it could overwhelm users. Therefore several options are offered to fine tune staff resolution.

- The LEAST_WORKLOAD option checks which of the selected users has the least number of workitems on the worklist and just generates a workitem for this user.

- Workitems are sent to selected users irrespective of whether the user is at work or absent. For activities that need to be carried out fast, creating workitems for absent users can be considered superfluous. The PREFER_NOT_ABSENT option indicates that only users that are not absent should receive a workitem. If all users are absent, then workitems are generated for all users.

- If a workflow is carried out by multiple workflow management systems, workitems need to be shipped from the workflow management system that owns the workflow to other workflow management systems where users that qualify in the staff resolution exist. In this case, significant processing overhead is involved as we have discussed in section 10.7.3 on page 392. The PREFER_LOCAL_USERS option indicates that if local users are available, then workitems should be generated only for them. If there are no qualified users, then workitems are shipped to the remote users.

Workitems and processes are typically deleted from the appropriate worklists or process lists as soon as the activity or process has completed. There are, however, situations where it is necessary to keep workitems and process instances around for some time. How long is controlled by the parameters KEEP_FINISHED_PRO-CESSES_TIME or KEEP_FINISHED_WORKITEMS_TIME. For each of these parameters one can specify an appropriate option. FOREVER causes the workitems or processes to be kept until explicitly deleted by the user; IMMEDIATE causes them to be deleted immediately. Another option is to specify a time. When the time expires, the workitems or processes are deleted automatically by the workflow management system.

If the time that is allocated for an activity or process is exceeded, then appropriate notification messages are sent out. Several options allow the process modeler to fine-tune the notification mechanism. The NOTIFICATION_SUBSTITUTION option defines whether a substitute should receive the notification if the original addressee is absent. This option should only be used if processing of the notification is really urgent, because this option causes some overhead from determining the substitute. The DUPLICATE_NOTIFICATION option specifies whether a second notification should be sent even if the first notification has been sent to the same person. Receiving the same notification twice could become annoying, so sending the same notification twice to the same person should be reserved for important activities or processes.

When an activity implementation is invoked, the workflow management system makes the input and output containers available. The activity implementation uses the provided APIs for accessing the containers. If the activity implementation does not access the input container or the output container, it is overhead to ship the containers to a location where they are not needed. Two options are available to let the workflow management system know whether the activity needs the containers or not: INPUT_CONTAINER_ACCESS and OUTPUT_CONTAINER_ACCESS.

11.8   Optimization

The overall performance of workflow-based applications depends on how efficiently the two parts that make up the workflow-based application—the business process and the activity implementations—are carried out.

For the workflow management system performance it depends mainly on the following :

- Efficiency of the navigation through the process graphs

- The shipping of requests between servers and clients and different system groups

- Facility that launches the activity implementations

The only parameter that can be influenced by appropriate setup is the amount of traffic that flows between different system groups and the amount of work that is associated for managing this traffic as well as the underlying message and network systems. This traffic is caused by remote workitems, which can become substantial, as we showed in section 10.7.3 on page 392. Thus it is important that the number of remote work items is reduced. This reduction can be done by reassigning users to different system groups in such a way that the number of remote workitems or the costs associated with remote workitems are minimized.

This goal can be achieved by performing simulation similar to the ones we have shown, such as the distribution of software. For each business, process staff resolution obtains the set of users for each of the activities. This information and topology information allow the process modeler to determine the best setup of users.

Figure 11.9 illustrates how optimization works. Let us assume that we have a simple business process with two activities, A and B. Activity A is carried out by user 1 and user 4; activity B by user 2 and user 3. In the initial setup, the local system group would need to send, for both activities, a remote workitem to both remote system groups. In the optimized setup, it is sufficient to send for activity A a remote workitem request to remote SG 1 and for activity B a remote workitem request to remote SG 2. This approach halves the number of messages sent by half. In addition, it eliminates all messages that need to be exchanged to make sure that only one user carries out the activity.

Figure 11.9 Minimizing Network Traffic

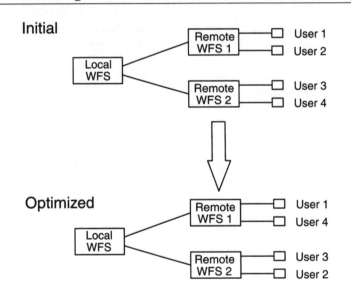

Appendix A

Travel Reservation Example

The travel reservation business process, shown in Figure A.1, is a process that the "Traveluck, Inc." company uses to offer trip reservation services to its customers.

Traveluck offers its services via the Internet. The appropriate home page asks its visitors for some information so that customized offers for interesting locations can be offered. This information includes hobbies of the visitor, as well as address and name. As a special service, Traveluck offers the reservation of itineraries com-

Figure A.1 Traveluck's Travel Reservation Process

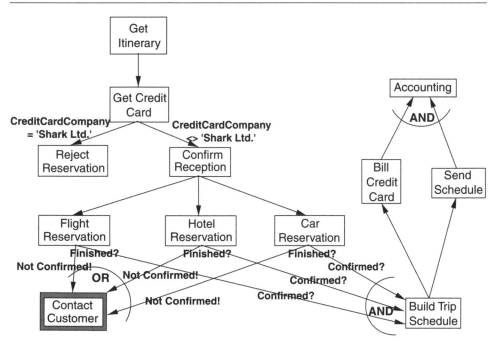

449

posed by a customer from the various Web offerings. This service is provided via
a business process that can be started from a browser. By clicking a corresponding
button, an instance of this process model is created by the customer; the customer
becomes the "process starter."

The model of the business process is called `Trip Reservation`. An instance of the `Person` data element is passed to the workflow as input. If a process
is started without all the needed `Person` data, the starter is prompted to complete
the data. This behavior is enforced by PROMPT_AT_START. As output, an instance
of `Trip` is produced. For legal reasons, an audit trail is maintained for each process. The full version of the audit trail is taken as indicated by the FULL parameter
of the AUDIT parameter. When the process does not terminate after four hours,
as indicated by NOTIFICATION AFTER 4 HOURS, the process administrator
is notified.

```
PROCESS 'TripReservation' ('Person', 'Trip')
  FULL AUDIT
  PROMPT_AT_PROCESS_START
  NOTIFICATION AFTER 4 HOURS
    TO PROCESS_ADMINISTRATOR

STRUCTURE 'Person'
  'Name':        STRING;
  'Salary':      FLOAT;
  'Address':     'Address';
  'Hobbies':     'Hobby'(15);
END 'Person'

STRUCTURE 'Trip'
  'Traveler':    'Customer';
  'Itinerary':   'Itinerary';
END 'Trip'

STRUCTURE 'Customer'
  'Name':        STRING;
  'Address':     'Address';
END 'Customer'

STRUCTURE 'Address'
  'City':        STRING;
  'Country':     STRING;
END 'Address'

STRUCTURE 'Itinerary'
  'Locations': 'Location'(20);
  'Flight Price Limit': STRING;
  'Hotel Price Limit': STRING;
END 'Itinerary'
```

```
STRUCTURE 'Location'
  'Arrival':    DATE;
  'Departure': DATE;
  'Visited Place': 'Address';
END 'Location'
```

The first activity that is scheduled is Get Itinerary. Its staff assignment specifies that the process starter has to perform the work. The activity lets the customer compose an itinerary, which is passed as output container to the workflow management system. The implementation associated with the activity is an applet that is started in the customer's browser.

```
PROGRAM_ACTIVITY 'Get Itinerary'
                ('Default Data Structure',
                 'Itinerary' )
  PROGRAM 'ItineraryApplet'
  START AUTOMATIC
  WHEN AT_LEAST_ONE CONNECTOR TRUE
  DONE_BY PROCESS_STARTER
END 'Get Itinerary'

PROGRAM 'ItineraryApplet'
        ('Default Data Structure',
         'Itinerary' )
  EVERYWHERE
    BROWSER
      TravlDat
END 'ItineraryApplet'
```

When the Get Itinerary activity has completed, the Get Credit Card activity is invoked in the customer's browser. It has Credit Card information as output. To make this activity happen, the activity is defined as an automatic activity and also has the process starter as staff assignment. START AUTOMATIC causes the automatic invocation of the activity implementation. DONE_BY PROCESS STARTER indicates that the process starter should carry out the activity. The preceding activity has also been defined this way. Thus, both activities are carried out without any workitem being displayed.

```
CONTROL FROM 'Get Itinerary'
        TO 'Get Credit Card'
```

```
PROGRAM_ACTIVITY 'Get Credit Card'
                ('Default Data Structure',
                 'Credit Card' )
  PROGRAM 'CCard Applet'
  START AUTOMATIC
    WHEN AT_LEAST_ONE CONNECTOR TRUE
  DONE_BY PROCESS_STARTER
END 'Get Credit Card'

STRUCTURE 'Credit Card'
  'Credit Card Company': STRING;
  'Number':              STRING;
  'Valid From':          DATE;
  'Valid To':            DATE;
END 'Credit Card'

PROGRAM 'CCard Applet'
        ('Default Data Structure',
         'Credit Card' )
  EVERYWHERE
    BROWSER
      CCDat
END 'CCard Applet'
```

One of Traveluck's policies is that it does not cooperate with the Shark Ltd. credit card company. Thus, if the name of the credit card provided in the Get Credit Card activity is 'Shark Ltd.', the reservation is rejected, otherwise, it is confirmed.

```
CONTROL FROM 'Get Credit Card'
        TO 'Reject Reservation'
        WHEN '''Credit Card Company'' = ''Shark Ltd.'''

CONTROL FROM 'Get Credit Card'
        TO 'Confirm Reception'
        WHEN '''Credit Card Company'' <> ''Shark Ltd.'''
```

As specified in its staff assignment, the Reject Reservation activity is performed on behalf of the administrator of the business process. Its input container provides the necessary Customer data which is mapped from the process's input container. Note that the process input container is represented via the SOURCE keyword in data map descriptions in flow definition language. The activity is started automatically. The implementation of this activity is a message queuing application defined by MESSAGE_QUEUING. Since it is immaterial where the activity implementation runs, EVERYWHERE is defined as the operating system. The queue from which the activity implementation reads is defined to the workflow management system by the INPUT_QUEUE keyword. The location is defined as EVERYWHERE.

As defined by the UNATTENDED keyword, no interaction with the user is required. This means, the staff assignment is only needed to define the person on whose behalf the activity should be carried out.

```
PROGRAM_ACTIVITY 'Reject Reservation'
                 ('Customer',
                  'Default Data Structure' )
   PROGRAM 'Reject Travel'
   START AUTOMATIC
   WHEN AT_LEAST_ONE CONNECTOR TRUE
   DONE_BY PROCESS_ADMINISTRATOR
END 'Reject Reservation'

DATA FROM SOURCE
   TO 'Reject Reservation'
   MAP 'Name' TO 'Name'
   MAP 'Address' TO 'Address'

PROGRAM 'Reject Travel'
        ('Customer',
         'Default Data Structure' )
   UNATTENDED
   EVERYWHERE
     MESSAGE_QUEUING
       INPUT_QUEUE 'RejectTravelInputQueue'

END 'Reject Travel'
```

The Confirm Reception activity runs similarly on a remote machine via a message-driven application. The activity gets as input the itinerary to be reserved, the credit card to be credited, and the customer's address.

```
PROGRAM_ACTIVITY 'Confirm Reception'
                 ('Confirmation Data',
                  'Default Data Structure')

   PROGRAM 'Confirm Travel Request'
   START AUTOMATIC
   WHEN AT_LEAST_ONE CONNECTOR TRUE
   DONE_BY SYSTEM
END 'Confirm Reception'

STRUCTURE 'Confirmation Data'
   'Itinerary':   'Itinerary';
   'Credit Card': 'Credit Card';
   'Customer':    'Customer';
END 'Confirmation Data'
```

```
PROGRAM 'Confirm Travel Request'
        ('Confirmation Data',
         'Default Data Structure')
  UNATTENDED
  EVERYWHERE
    MESSAGE_QUEUING
      INPUT_QUEUE 'ConfirmReceptionInputQueue'

END 'Confirm Travel Request'
```

Once the reception of the customer's order has been confirmed, the reservations for the flights, hotels, and rental cars corresponding to the itinerary are scheduled. These reservations are made in parallel to speed up the overall business process.

The reservation of the rental cars gets the itinerary as input and produces an instance of Cars as output. The latter container has a component that indicates whether the reservation is finished, i.e., all cars required for the itinerary are reserved or whether there is still more work to do. The exit condition of the activity checks this flag; if it is not set to "yes" when the activity implementation returns, the activity remains on the worklist of the responsible person. Another indicator signals when it was not possible to get confirmations for all cars needed for the itinerary, in which case a report about the failing reservations is put by the application into a special database. All confirmed reservations are listed in the remaining component of the container. The staff assignment of the activity prescribes that all car specialists get a workitem corresponding to the activity when its scheduling takes place. In case the workitem is not completed within two hours after creation, the manager of the owning agents is notified.

```
PROGRAM_ACTIVITY 'Car Reservation' ('Itinerary', 'Cars')
   PROGRAM 'Car Application'
   EXIT AUTOMATIC
     WHEN '''Finished'' = ''Yes'''
   DONE_BY MEMBER OF ROLE 'Car Specialists'
   DURATION 2 HOURS
     THEN NOTIFY MANAGER
END 'Car Reservation'

STRUCTURE 'Cars'
  'Finished':             STRING;
  'All Cars Confirmed':   STRING;
  'Error Report Number':  LONG;
  'Rental Cars':          'Rental Car'(20);
END 'Cars'
```

```
STRUCTURE 'Rental Car'
  'From':                'Date';
  'To':                  'Date';
  'Pickup':              'Address';
  'Drop':                'Address';
  'Price':               FLOAT;
END 'Rental Car'

PROGRAM 'Car Application' ('Itinerary', 'Cars')
  OS2
    EXEC
      PATH_AND_FILENAME 'CarApp.exe'
      START FOREGROUND
END 'Car Application'

ROLE 'Car Specialists'
END 'Car Specialists'
```

The activity Flight Reservation is similar.

```
PROGRAM_ACTIVITY 'Flight Reservation'
                 ('Itinerary',
                  'Flights')
  PROGRAM 'Flight Application'
  EXIT AUTOMATIC
    WHEN '''Finished'' = ''Yes'''
  DONE_BY MEMBER OF ROLE  'Flight Specialist'
  DURATION 2 HOURS
    THEN NOTIFY MANAGER
END 'Flight Reservation'

STRUCTURE 'Flights'
  'Finished':                STRING;
  'All Flights Confirmed':   STRING;
  'Error Report Number':     LONG;
  'Flight':                  'Flight'(35);
END 'Flights'

STRUCTURE 'Flight'
  'Departure':               'Flight Departure';
  'Arrival':                 'Flight Arrival';
  'Flight Number':           STRING;
  'Airline':                 STRING;
  'Fare':                    FLOAT;
END 'Flight'

STRUCTURE 'Flight Departure'
  'Departure Date':          DATE;
  'Departure Time':          TIME;
  'Airport':                 STRING;
END 'Flight Departure'
```

```
STRUCTURE 'Flight Arrival'
  'Arrival Date':          DATE;
  'Arrival Time':          TIME;
  'Airport':               STRING;
END 'Flight Arrival'

PROGRAM 'Flight Application' ('Itinerary', 'Flights')
  OS2
    EXE
       PATH_AND_FILENAME 'FlgtRsv.exe'
       START FOREGROUND
END 'Flight Application'

ROLE 'Flight Specialist'
END 'Flight Specialist'
```

And the Hotel Reservation is done similarly.

```
PROGRAM_ACTIVITY 'Hotel Reservation'
                ('Itinerary',
                 'Hotels')
  PROGRAM 'Hotel Application'
  EXIT AUTOMATIC
    WHEN '''Finished'' = ''Yes'''
  DONE_BY MEMBER OF ROLE 'Hotel Specialists'
  DURATION 2 HOURS
    THEN NOTIFY MANAGER
END 'Hotel Reservation'

STRUCTURE 'Hotels'
  'Finished':              STRING;
  'All Hotels Confirmed':  STRING;
  'Error Report Number':   LONG;
  'Hotels':                'Hotel'(20);
END 'Hotels'

STRUCTURE 'Hotel'
  'Arrival':               DATE;
  'Departure':             DATE;
  'Hotel Name':            STRING;
  'Hotel Address':         'Address';
  'Price Per Day':         FLOAT;
END 'Hotel'

PROGRAM 'Hotel Application' ('Itinerary', 'Hotels')
  OS2
    EXE
       PATH_AND_FILENAME 'HotelApp.exe'
       START FOREGROUND
END 'Hotel Application'
```

```
ROLE 'Hotel Specialists'
END 'Hotel Specialists'
```

If it was possible to get all required confirmations, control flows from the corresponding reservation activity to the `Build Trip Schedule` activity. Otherwise the control flows to the `Contact Customer` activity.

```
CONTROL FROM 'Car Reservation'
        TO 'Build Trip Schedule'
        WHEN '''All Cars Confirmed''
            = ''Yes'''
CONTROL FROM 'Car Reservation'
        TO 'Contact Customer'
        OTHERWISE

CONTROL FROM 'Hotel Reservation'
        TO 'Build Trip Schedule'
        WHEN '''All Hotels Confirmed''
         = ''Yes'''
CONTROL FROM 'Hotel Reservation'
        TO 'Contact Customer'
        OTHERWISE

CONTROL FROM 'Flight Reservation'
        TO 'Build Trip Schedule'
        WHEN '''All Flights Confirmed''
         = ''Yes'''
CONTROL FROM 'Flight Reservation'
        TO 'Contact Customer'
        OTHERWISE
```

The activity `Build Trip Schedule` creates a document describing the final schedule based on the incoming schedule data. The `Schedule Data` consists of all cars, hotels, and flights reserved. This information is mapped from the output containers of the corresponding reservation activities. The schedule document must only be created if all necessary reservations have been confirmed; that is all cars, flights, and hotels have been confirmed. For this purpose, `Build Trip Schedule` is a join activity. The join condition is an AND (ALL CONNECTORS TRUE), which ensures that all associated reservations have been confirmed. If only one of the transition conditions evaluates to false, the schedule document is not printed. The activity is implemented by the `Document Generation` program that runs unattended on behalf of the system, that is not for a specific user.

```
PROGRAM_ACTIVITY 'Build Trip Schedule'
                ('Schedule Data',
                 'Schedule')
```

```
     PROGRAM 'Document Generation'
     START AUTOMATIC
       WHEN ALL CONNECTORS TRUE
     DONE_BY SYSTEM
END 'Build Trip Schedule'

STRUCTURE 'Schedule'
  'Schedule Document': STRING;
END 'Schedule'

STRUCTURE 'Schedule Data'
  'Flights':              'Flights Reserved';
  'Hotels':               'Hotels Reserved';
  'Cars':                 'Cars Reserved';
END 'Schedule Data'

STRUCTURE 'Flights Reserved'
  'Flight':               'Flight'(15);
END 'Flights Reserved'

STRUCTURE 'Hotels Reserved'
  'Hotels': 'Hotel'(15);
END 'Hotels Reserved'

STRUCTURE 'Cars Reserved'
  'Rental Cars': 'Rental Car'(15);
END 'Cars Reserved'

DATA FROM 'Car Reservation'
  TO 'Build Trip Schedule'
  MAP 'Rental Cars' TO 'Cars.Rental Cars'

DATA FROM 'Hotel Reservation'
  TO 'Build Trip Schedule'
  MAP 'Hotels' TO 'Hotels.Hotels'

DATA FROM 'Flight Reservation'
  TO 'Build Trip Schedule'
  MAP 'Flight' TO 'Flights.Flight'

PROGRAM 'Document Generation'
        ('Schedule Data',
         'Schedule')
  UNATTENDED
  AIX
    EXE
      PATH_AND_FILENAME 'docgen.exe'
END 'Document Generation'
```

The Contact Customer activity is implemented by another process model.
Its join condition is an *or* (AT_LEAST ONE CONNECTOR TRUE) of the transition condition of the incoming control connectors, so it will be started if at least

one reservation of a necessary flight, hotel, or car failed, in which case the before mentioned schedule will not be printed. The members of the travel departments and all departments directly or indirectly reporting to it have the ability to start the corresponding instance. The contacting agents will discuss with the customer an alternative itinerary, which is the main output produced. The failed itinerary as well as references to the documents describing the associated failed reservations are input to this activity. When this path is taken, the Trip Reservation process terminates when Contact Customer finishes; the newly negotiated itinerary is passed as output and can be used for a new trip reservation.

```
PROCESS_ACTIVITY 'Contact Customer'
                ('Consultation Data',
                 'Trip')
  START AUTOMATIC
    WHEN AT_LEAST_ONE CONNECTOR TRUE
  DONE_BY ORGANIZATION 'Travel'
    INCLUDE_CHILD_ORGANIZATIONS
END 'Contact Customer'

STRUCTURE 'Consultation Data'
  'Errors':            'Failed Reservations';
  'Itinerary Failed': 'Itinerary';
END 'Consultation Data'

STRUCTURE 'Failed Reservations'
  'Flights':           LONG;
  'Hotels':            LONG;
  'Cars':              LONG;
END 'Failed Reservations'

STRUCTURE 'Trip'
  'Traveler':          'Customer';
  'Itinerary':         'Itinerary';
END 'Trip'

DATA FROM 'Car Reservation'
  TO 'Contact Customer'

DATA FROM 'Flight Reservation'
  TO 'Contact Customer'

DATA FROM 'Hotel Reservation'
  TO 'Contact Customer'

DATA FROM SOURCE
  TO 'Contact Customer'
```

```
DATA FROM 'Contact Customer'
  TO SINK
  MAP 'Traveler'     TO 'Traveler'
  MAP 'Itinerary'    TO 'Itinerary'

ORGANIZATION 'Travel'
END 'Travel'
```

Next, the `Send Schedule` and `Bill Credit Card` activities are scheduled.

```
CONTROL FROM 'Build Trip Schedule'
        TO 'Send Schedule'

CONTROL FROM 'Build Trip Schedule'
        TO 'Bill Credit Card'
```

`Bill Credit Card` gets an instance of the `Debit Data` data element as input; `Debit Data` contains all data necessary to receive money from the customer's credit card account. This container is materialized via mapping customer information from the process input container and credit card information from the output container of the `Get Credit Card` activity. The activity is carried out automatically.

```
PROGRAM_ACTIVITY 'Bill Credit Card'
                ('Debit Data',
                  'Default Data Structure')
    PROGRAM 'Debit Application'
    START AUTOMATIC
      WHEN AT_LEAST_ONE CONNECTOR TRUE
    DONE_BY SYSTEM
END 'Debit Credit Card'

STRUCTURE 'Debit Data'
  'Customer':    'Customer';
  'Credit Card': 'Credit Card';
END 'Debit Data'

PROGRAM 'Debit Application'
        ('Debit Data',
          'Default Data Structure')
    OS2
      EXE
        PATH_AND_FILENAME 'BCCARD.EXE'
        STYLE MINIMIZED
END 'Debit Application'
```

```
DATA FROM SOURCE
     TO 'Bill Credit Card'
     MAP 'Name' TO 'Customer.Name'
     MAP 'Address' TO 'Customer.Address'

DATA FROM 'Get Credit Card'
     TO 'Bill Credit Card'
     MAP '_STRUCT' TO 'Credit Card'
```

In parallel, the schedule is printed by a printer spooling program that gets its input from a queue.

```
PROGRAM_ACTIVITY 'Send Schedule'
                 ('Schedule',
                  'Default Data Structure')
     PROGRAM 'Printer Line'
     START AUTOMATIC
       WHEN AT_LEAST_ONE CONNECTOR TRUE
     DONE_BY SYSTEM
END 'Send Schedule'

PROGRAM 'Printer Line'
        ('Schedule',
         'Default Data Structure')
     EVERYWHERE
       MESSAGE_QUEUING
         INPUT_QUEUE 'PrinterInputQueue'
END 'Printer Line'
```

Once both activities have completed, control flows to the Accounting activity.

```
CONTROL FROM 'Bill Credit Card'
        TO 'Accounting'

CONTROL FROM 'Send Schedule'
        TO 'Accounting'
```

This activity is consequently a join node. The AND join condition ensures that the two preceding activities are performed. The implementation of Accounting is legacy system that has been implemented as a transaction runnning under the TP monitor CICS.

```
PROGRAM_ACTIVITY 'Accounting'
                ('Debit Data',
                 'Default Data Structure')
    PROGRAM 'Accounting System'
    START AUTOMATIC
      WHEN ALL CONNECTORS TRUE
    DONE_BY SYSTEM
END 'Accounting'

PROGRAM 'Accounting System'
        ('Debit Data',
         'Default Data Structure')
    EVERYWHERE
      SERVICE            CICS17
      SERVICE_TYPE       CICS
      INVOCATION_TYPE    TRPC
      EXECUTABLE         ATR
END 'Accounting System'
```

Appendix B

List of Symbols

$A_\bullet^\rightarrow$	Set of all regular sucessors of activity A
$A_*^\rightarrow$	Set of all join successors of activity A
$A^\rightarrow$	Set of all successors of activity A
$\mathcal{A}$	Set of all agents, that is people and computing devices
$\mathcal{C}^\leftarrow(A)$	Set of transition conditions of all control connectors pointing to activity A
$\mathcal{C}^\rightarrow(A)$	Set of transition conditions of all control connectors leaving activity A
$\mathcal{C}$	Set of all conditions (or business rules of Boolean functions or predicates or ...)
$\mathcal{D}^\rightarrow(A)$	Set of all dead successors of A
$\delta\mathcal{D}^\rightarrow(A)$	Dead successor boundary of activity A
$\mathcal{D}(P)$	Set of all dead nodes within process P
Δ	Data connector map
$\overrightarrow{\Delta}$	Process data connector map
E	Set of control connectors of a process model
$\mathcal{E}$	Set of all data connectors of a process model
E	Set of all data connectors of a process model
$\varepsilon(A)$	Exit condition of activity A
$\mathcal{G}$	Set of all atomic spheres
$\mathcal{H}$	Set of all activities and process models
$\iota(X)$	Input container of activity X
N	Set of all activities (sometimes, all activities of a particular process model; sometimes, all known activities)
$N_\bullet$	Set of all regular activities
N_*	Set of all join activities

$\wp(M)$	Power set of a given set M
$\mathcal{P}$	Set of all process models
π_j	Projection map onto the j-th component of Cartesian product
$\mathcal{Q}$	Set of all staff queries
$\mathcal{R}$	Set of all compensation spheres
$o(X)$	Output container of activity X
V	Set of all data elements
$\Phi(A)$	Join condition of activity A
$\Psi(A)$	Implementation of activity A
Ω	Staff assignment map
$\Omega(A)$	Staff assignment to activity A

Bibliography

[AGL98]   R. Agrawal, D. Gunopolus, and F. Leymann. Mining Process Models from Workflow Logs. In *Proc. Intl. Conf. on Extending Database Technology (EDBT), (Valencia, Spain)*, 1998.

[AKA⁺94]   G. Alonso, M. Kamath, D. Agrawal, A. El Abbadi, R. Günthör, and C. Mohan. Failure Handling in Large Scale Workflow Management Systems. In *Research Report RJ 9912*. IBM Almaden Research Center, 1994.

[BCN92]   C. Batini, S. Ceri, and S. B. Navathe. *Conceptual Database Design: An Entity–Relationship Approach*. Benjamin/Cummings Publishing Company, Redwood City, California, 1992.

[BHG87]   P. A. Bernstein, V. Hadzilacos, and N. Goodman. *Concurrency Control and Recovery in Database Systems*. Addison-Wesley Publishing Company, 1987.

[BHL95]   B. Blakely, H. Harris, and R. Lewis. *Messaging and Queuing using the MQI*. McGraw-Hill Inc., 1995.

[BN97]   P.A. Bernstein and E. Newcomer. *Principles of Transaction Processing*. Morgan Kaufmann Publishers, Inc., 1997.

[Boo91]   G. Booch. *Object Oriented Design With Applications*. Benjamin/Cummings Publishing Company, 1991.

[BS95a]   C. J. Bontempo and C. Maro Saracco. *Database Management: Principles and Products*. Prentice-Hall, 1995.

[BS95b]   M.L. Brodie and M. Stonebraker. *Migrating Legacy Systems*. Morgan Kaufmann Publishers, Inc., 1995.

[BSK94]   I. Z. Ben-Shaul and G. E. Kaiser. A Paradigm for Decentralized Process Modelling and its Realization in the Oz Environment. In *Proc. of the 16th International Conference on Software Engineering*, pages 179–188, 1994.

[Cha98]   D. Chamberlin. *A Complete Guide to DB2 Universal Database*. Morgan Kaufmann Publishers, Inc., San Mateo, California, 1998.

[Che76]   P. Chen. The Entity Relationship Mode—Toward a Unified View of Data. *ACM Transactions on Database Systems*, 1(1), 1976.

[Dat93]   C. Date. *Introduction in SQL*. Addison-Wesley Publishing Company, 1993.

[EL96]   J. Eder and W. Liebhart. Workflow Recovery. In *Proc. Intl. Conference on Cooperative Information Systems CoopIS '96 (Brussels, Belgium)*, 1996.

[Elm92]   Ahmed K. Elmagarmid, editor. *Database Transaction Models for Advanced Applications*. Morgan Kaufmann Publishers, Inc., 1992.

[EM85]   H. Ehrig and B. Mahr. *Fundamentals of Algebraic Specification 1: Equations and Initial Semantics*. Springer Verlag, 1985.

[EN94]   R. Elmasri and S. B. Navathe. *Fundamentals of Database Systems*. Benjamin/Cummings Publishing Company, Redwood City, California, 1994.

[Fai85]   R. Fairley. *Sofware Engineering Concepts*. McGraw-Hill Inc., 1985.

[FSW81]   E. B. Fernandez, R. C. Summers, and C. Wood. *Database Security and Integrity*. Addison-Wesley Publishing Company, 1981.

[Gmb]   IDS Prof. Scheer GmbH. http://www.ids-scheer.com.

[GMS87]   H. Garcia-Molina and K. Salem. Sagas. In *Proc. ACM Sigmod*, 1987.

[GR93]   J. Gray and A. Reuter. *Transaction Processing : Concepts and Techniques*. Morgan Kaufmann Publishers, Inc., 1993.

[Gro]   GIGA Information Group. http://www.gigaweb.com.

[HC94]   M. Hammer and J. Champy. *Reengineering the Corporation*. Addison-Wesley Publishing Company, 1994.

[HR83]   T. Härder and A. Reuter. Principles of Transaction-Oriented Database Recovery. *ACM Computing Survey*, 15:287–317, 1983.

[IBM94a]   IBM Corporation. *Customer Information Control System*, 1994. Available through IBM branch offices.

[IBM94b]   IBM Corporation. *Information Management System*, 1994. Available through IBM branch offices.

[IBM94c]   IBM Corporation. *MQSeries: Application Programming Reference*, 1994. Available through IBM branch offices.

[IBM95a]   IBM Corporation. *Building VisualAge C++ Parts for Fun and Profit*, 1995. Available through IBM branch offices.

[IBM95b]   IBM Corporation. *Visual Builder User's Guide*, 1995. Available through IBM branch offices.

[IBM96]   IBM Corporation. *IBM FlowMark Modeling Workflow Version 2 Release 3*, 1996. Available through IBM branch offices.

[IBM97]   IBM Corporation. *Component Broker Connector Overview*, 1997. Available through IBM branch offices.

[IBM98a]   IBM Corporation. *IBM MQSeries Workflow : Getting Started with Runtime*, 1998. Available thorugh IBM branch offices.

[IBM98b]   IBM Corporation. *IBM MQSeries Workflow: Concepts and Architecture*, 1998. Available through IBM branch offices.

[Inca]   Holosofx Inc. http://www.holosofx.com.

[Incb]   Tivoli Systems Inc. http://www.tivoli.com.

[ISO]   ISO. Step. Available thorugh ISO.

[JCJO92]   I. Jacobson, M. Christerson, P. Jonsson, and G. Overgaard. *Object-oriented Software Engineering*. Addison-Wesley Publishing Company, 1992.

[JEJ95]   I. Jacobson, M. Ericsson, and A. Jacobson. *The Object Advantage: Business Process Reengineering with Object Technology*. Addison-Wesley Publishing Company, Reading, Massachusetts, 1995.

[JH97]   S. Jajodia and K. Herschberg, editors. *Advanced Transaction Models and Architectures*. Kluwer, 1997.

[Kot89]   A. Kotz. *Triggermechanismen in Datenbanken*. Springer Verlag, 1989.

[LA94]   F. Leymann and W. Altenhuber. Managing Business Processes as an Information Resource. *IBM Systems Journal*, 33(2), 1994.

[Ley94]   F. Leymann. Towards the STEP Neutral Repository. *Computer Standards & Interfaces 16*, 1994.

[Ley95a]   F. Leymann. Supporting Business Transactions via Partial Backward Recovery in Workflow Management Systems. In *Proc. BTW '95*. Springer Verlag, Berlin, Germany, 1995.

[Ley95b]   F. Leymann.   Transaction Concepts for Workflow Management Systems (in German).   In G. Vossen and J. Becker, editors, *Geschäftsprozeßmodellierung und Workflow-Management*. International Thompson Publishing, 1995.

[Ley95c]   F. Leymann. Workflows Make Objects Really Useful. In *Proc. 6th Internal Workshop on High Performance Transaction Systems (Asilomar)*, 1995.

[Ley97]   F. Leymann. Transaction Support for Workflows (in German). *Informatik in Forschung & Entwicklung*, 12(1), 1997.

[LK82]   A. M. Law and D. W. Kelton. *Simulation, Modeling, and Analysis*. McGraw-Hill Inc., 1982.

[LR97]   F. Leymann and D. Roller. Workflow-based Applications. *IBM Systems Journal*, 36(1), 1997.

[Mos82]   J. E. B. Moss. Nested Transactions and Reliable Distributed Computing. In *Proc. IEEE Symposium on Reliability in Distributed Software and Database Systems*, 1982.

[Mul93]   S. Mullender, editor. *Distributed Systems*. ACM Press, 1993.

[Obj97]   Object Management Group. *Object Transaction Services V 1.1*, 1997. OMG Document TC 94.8.4.

[Obj98]   Object Management Group. *Workflow Management Facility*, 1998. OMG Document bom/98-06-07.

[OH97]   R. Orfali and D. Harkey. *Client/Server Programming with Java and CORBA*. John Wiley & Sons, Inc., 1997.

[OHE96]   R. Orfali, D. Harkey, and J. Edwards. *The Essential Distributed Objects Survival Guide*. John Wiley & Sons, Inc., 1996.

[Pat98]   Patricia Seybold Group (Boston,MA). *M.I.Kramer, Requirements for Successful Application Integration*, 1998.

[Pfi95]   G. Pfister. *In Search of Clusters*. Prentice-Hall, 1995.

[PTE89]   W. D. Potter, R. P. Trueblood, and C. M. Eastman. Hyper-Semantic Data Modeling. *Data & Knowledge Engineering*, 4:69–90, 1989.

[Rat97]   Rational Software Corporation. *Unified Modeling Language : Notation Guide*, 1997.

[RBP+91]   J. Rumbaugh, M. Blaha, W. Premerlani, F. Eddy, and W. Lorenzen. *Object Oriented Modelling and Design*. Prentice-Hall, 1991.

[Reu89]   A. Reuter. Managing Distributed Applications with ConTracts. In *Proc. 3th Internal Workshop on High Performance Transaction Systems (Asilomar)*, 1989.

[RSS97]   A. Reuter, K. Schneider, and F. Schwenkreis. ConTracts Revisited. In S. Jajodia and K. Herschberg, editors, *Advanced Transaction Models and Architectures*. Kluwer, 1997.

[SAP96]   SAP. *SAP Business Workflow*, 1996. Available from SAP Walldorf, Germany.

[Sch96]   R. Schulte. *Message Brokers: A Focused Approach to Application Integration*. Gartner Group, 1996. Strategic Analysis Report SSA R-401-102.

[Sch98]   M.-T. Schmidt. Building Workflow Business Objects. In *Proc. OOPSLA, 1998*, 1998.

[Ses98]   R. Sessions. *COM and DCOM : Microsoft's Vision for Distributed Objects*. New York, 1998.

[Sun99a]   Sun Microsystems Inc. *Java Transaction API (JTA) V 1.0*, 1999.

[Sun99b]   Sun Microsystems Inc. *Java Transaction Service (JTS) V 0.95*, 1999.

[Teo94]   T. J. Teorey. *Database Modeling & Design: The Fundamental Principles*. Morgan Kaufmann Publishers, Inc., 1994.

[Tra83]   I. L. Traiger. Trends in System Aspects of Database Management. In *Proc. 2nd Intl. Conf. on Databases (UCOD-2)*, 1983.

[TSMB95]   S. Teufel, C. Sauter, T. Müllherr, and K. Bauknecht. *Computerunterstützung für die Gruppenarbeit*. Addison-Wesley Publishing Company, Bonn, 1995.

[Ull88]   J. Ullman. *Principles of Database and Knowledge-Base Systems*. Computer Science Press, 1988.

[WBWW90]   R. Wirfs-Brock, B. Wilkensen, and L. Wiener. *Designing Object Oriented Software*. Prentice-Hall, 1990.

[Wor]   Workflow Management Coalition. http://www.wfmc.org.

[X/O93]   X/Open Company Ltd., U.K. *X/Open Guide, Distributed Transaction Processing Reference Model (Version 2)*, 1993.

[Yan97]   The Yankee Group - Internet Computing Strategies (Boston, MA). *Enterprise Application Integration and Information Flow*, 1997.

Index

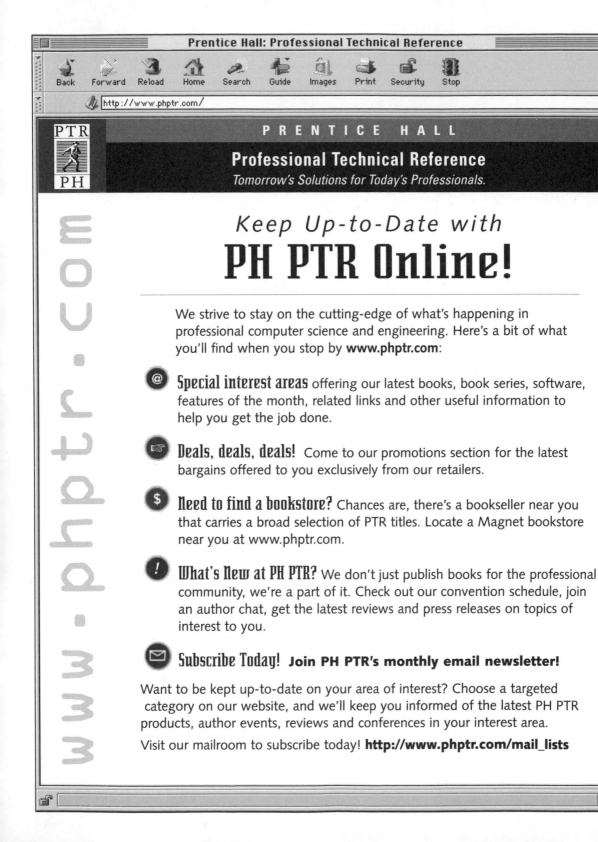